JZ6374 .C44 2004
Chesterman, Simon.
You, the people :
Northeast Lakeview Colleg
33784000123208

YOU, THE PEOPLE

A Project of the International Peace Academy

YOU, THE PEOPLE

The United Nations, Transitional Administration, and State-Building

SIMON CHESTERMAN

OXFORD UNIVERSITY PRESS

OXFORD
UNIVERSITY PRESS

Great Clarendon Street, Oxford OX2 6DP

Oxford University Press is a department of the University of Oxford. It furthers the University's objective of excellence in research, scholarship, and education by publishing worldwide in

Oxford New York

Auckland Cape Town Dar es Salaam Hong Kong Karachi Kuala Lumpur Madrid Melbourne Mexico City Nairobi New Delhi Taipei Toronto Shanghai

With offices in

Argentina Austria Brazil Chile Czech Republic France Greece Guatemala Hungary Italy Japan South Korea Poland Portugal Singapore Switzerland Thailand Turkey Ukraine Vietnam

Oxford is a registered trade mark of Oxford University Press in the UK and in certain other countries

Published in the United States by Oxford University Press Inc., New York

© International Peace Academy 2004

The moral rights of the author have been asserted
Database right Oxford University Press (maker)

First published 2004

All rights reserved. No part of this publication may be reproduced, stored in a retrieval system, or transmitted, in any form or by any means, without the prior permission in writing of Oxford University Press, or as expressly permitted by law, or under terms agreed with the appropriate reprographics rights organization. Enquiries concerning reproduction outside the scope of the above should be sent to the Rights Department, Oxford University Press, at the address above

You must not circulate this book in any other binding or cover and you must impose this same condition on any acquirer

British Library Cataloguing in Publication Data
Data available

Library of Congress Cataloging in Publication Data
(Data available)

ISBN 0-19-926348-5

3 5 7 9 10 8 6 4

Typeset by Newgen Imaging Systems (P) Ltd., Chennai, India
Printed in Great Britain by
Biddles Ltd., King's Lynn, Norfolk

Foreword

It is a privilege to commend this volume to readers. Simon Chesterman, whose fine book *Just War or Just Peace* proved highly influential on the contentious issue of humanitarian intervention, returns to the fray with an account of—and a profusion of ideas on—contemporary international administration of distressed countries and regions. This book represents the culmination of a research and policy development project directed by Dr Chesterman at the International Peace Academy during the period 2000–3. The project focused on the role of the United Nations in the transition of societies from war to peace through a period of international supervision.

With the successful conclusion of the decolonization process in the 1960s and 1970s, most of us believed that the notion of trusteeship was consigned to history. We could not foresee that a number of these newly independent countries and others would fall apart as the stabilities of the cold war—toxic and murderous as they often were—ended. *Faute de mieux*, and very much compelled by circumstances, the 1990s saw the UN Security Council experiment with UN administration as a temporary measure until power could be transferred to legitimate local authorities. A rapid graduation to international legitimacy after UN-organized elections was possible for Cambodia in 1993, though its democracy remains imperfect at best. Both Bosnia and Kosovo, by contrast, continue to be administered by distinct forms of international authority with no clear exit strategy in sight. East Timor's independence in 2002 was a uniquely clear exit, preceded by a period of international administration overseen by the late Sergio Vieira de Mello.

Dr Chesterman's project initially aimed to tease out the principal policy lessons from the UN operations in Kosovo and East Timor, drawing on earlier cases such as Cambodia, Namibia, and Western Sahara by way of comparison. More recent events in Afghanistan and Iraq added very different complications, however, when the United Nations had to finesse a role for itself alongside a minimalist government in Kabul and a foreign military occupation in Baghdad.

It has been a pleasure working alongside Dr Chesterman and charting his intellectual path in these challenging policy waters. He is a fine colleague in every respect and made many new friends in the process of his research, not least Sergio Vieira de Mello and Rick Hooper, a senior UN staffer of exceptional quality, killed with Sergio in Baghdad on

19 August 2003. Some of the memories associated with this project will, therefore, always be bittersweet. The bombing of the UN headquarters in Iraq reminds us that the business of nation-building is a risky as well as difficult one. (Our own insurance company essentially refused to cover Dr Chesterman during his visit to Afghanistan in 2002.)

I am very grateful for the consistent support Dr Chesterman received from various IPA Board members during his research. The funders of this project—Carnegie Corporation of New York, together with the Ford Foundation and the John D. and Catherine T. MacArthur Foundation—granted Dr Chesterman considerable latitude in developing his project and in encouraging wide-ranging conclusions. They are here richly rewarded, but their generosity and openness of mind deserve special recognition.

Historically, this account is fascinating. In policy terms, it is deeply instructive and relevant at a time when international actors grapple with a variety of unattractive options in Iraq. I trust the reader will enjoy the investment of time required to absorb and reflect on Dr Chesterman's material. I certainly have.

David M. Malone
President, International Peace Academy

Foreword

If history, as Napoleon asserted, is indeed 'a myth that men agree to believe', then one of the most enduring and influential historical myths at the core of the contemporary challenges addressed in this volume is the much invoked and misunderstood Peace of Westphalia. The vaunted 'nation-state' that became the pre-eminent political organizing principle in Europe and, ultimately, the rest of the world was, presumably, spawned by this set of peace treaties between the Holy Roman Empire and its continental rivals in 1648. However the reality surrounding this epochal event may have diverged from the rhetoric, the fact remains that for centuries to come, much blood and treasure would be expended in the pursuit and defence of this principle. When the yoke of colonialism was finally and, in some cases, tortuously lifted from subject peoples the world over, it was the idealized Westphalian nation-state that served as the template for popular and elite aspirations.

But as post-colonial history attests from the new nation-states that emerged from the demise of the sclerotic Spanish, Ottoman, and Russian empires to more recent examples from the imperial remnants of the Belgians, British, Dutch, French, and Soviets, the melding of the often diverse peoples comprising a 'nation' with the political and administrative functions of the classic Weberian 'state' is an exceedingly difficult and costly task. In almost every case, nascent 'nation-states' required assistance in attempting to achieve this end, whether from former colonial masters or representatives of the broader international community. The very nature of the relationship between external benefactor and internal beneficiary inevitably raised the spectres of paternalism and neo-colonialism that continue to colour perceptions of the challenge to this day. A 'benevolent autocracy'—the apt term used in this volume to describe the form in which this assistance has often been provided—is, after all, still an autocracy.

Complicating this challenge has been the recognized need, first given prominence during the 1990s but made even more salient after the events of 11 September 2001, to prevent a traumatized or newly emerging nation-state from failing, or to intervene when the state apparatus has ceased to function. This imperative has put into stark relief the long-standing tensions between the sovereign right of territorial states and the responsibility of the international community to both protect a collapsing state's beleaguered inhabitants, and restore its political and economic viability. Ongoing efforts in Afghanistan and Iraq are only the most dramatic recent examples of attempts to reconcile these contending notions. As this volume presciently explains, not only has the international community, led by the United Nations, had to install 'transitional administrations' to assume temporary sovereign powers in East Timor and Kosovo, but the list of candidates for similar treatment is likely to grow alarmingly long in the decades ahead.

Given the threat that failed or failing states pose to international peace and security, and the need for new thinking and approaches to this burgeoning challenge, Carnegie Corporation of New York has been interested in related questions concerning evolving notions of sovereignty and enduring expressions of national self-determination in the contemporary world. Through our grant-making on these themes we have sought to advance policy-relevant research and dialogue on a wide array of issues, including non-military forms of intervention and the design of stable political structures in multinational states at risk. As a Corporation grantee, the International Peace Academy (IPA) has been a leading exponent of the need for drawing upon both theory and practice in the search for solutions to pressing international problems. This volume represents IPA's most recent effort in this regard, and offers a rich source of highly relevant and informed analysis for both scholars and policymakers alike.

Vartan Gregorian
President, Carnegie Corporation of New York

Chapter Outline

Contents

Acknowledgements

Any research organization depends not only on its staff, but also on those who support it and those who are prepared to speak to it and listen to it. The International Peace Academy (IPA), where this volume was researched and written, is blessed in all three areas.

David M. Malone, President of IPA from 1998 to 2004, was both an inspiring leader and an inspired manager. After playing a central role in developing the research project on Transitional Administration, he encouraged me to find my own voice in this field, providing advice and introductions throughout my research. It has been an honour and a pleasure to work with him. Other colleagues contributed directly or indirectly, through constructive engagement with the subject and participation in the intellectual life of IPA more generally. I am particularly indebted to Sebastian von Einsiedel, who joined IPA in 2002 and rapidly made himself indispensable.

My research was funded by Carnegie Corporation of New York, with additional funding from the Ford Foundation and the John D. and Catherine T. MacArthur Foundation. I am especially pleased that Vartan Gregorian, President of the Corporation and an authority on Afghanistan in his own right, was able to contribute a foreword to the book. Stephen J. Del Rosso, Jr, also at Carnegie Corporation, was both instrumental in the original conception of the project and flexible in seeing it evolve to embrace Afghanistan and Iraq. To them and all their colleagues at Carnegie, Ford, and MacArthur, warmest thanks.

Most of the interviews conducted in the course of field research were confidential. I am unable to list everyone to whom I spoke, but wish to acknowledge some of those who shared their time and their wisdom with me in New York, Washington, London, Paris, Phnom Penh, Belgrade, Sarajevo, Pristina, Dili, and Kabul: General John Abizaid, Rafeeuddin Ahmed, Ali Alatas, Prime Minister Marí Alkatiri, Jean Arnault, Lloyd Axworthy, Eileen Babbitt, Arsenio Paixão Bano, M. Cherif Bassiouni, Alex Boraine, Lakhdar Brahimi, Ian Brownlie, Youk Chhang, Noam Chomsky, Jarat Chopra, Hans Corell, Vjosa Dobruna, Toby Dodge, Michael Doyle, Gareth Evans, Daan Everts, Nigel Fisher, Joaquim Fonseca, Thomas M. Franck, Peter Galbraith, Ashraf Ghani, Richard Goldstone, Jaque Grinberg, President Xanana Gusmão, Hans Haekkerup, Hurst Hannum,

Fazel-Rabi Haqbeen, Ramush Haradinaj, David Harland, Lao Mong Hay, Louis Henkin, Michael Ignatieff, Fr Filomeno Jacob, Khieu Kanharith, Jacques Paul Klein, Ciara Knudsen, Tom Königs, Bernard Kouchner, Laith Kubba, Oleg Levitin, Ian Martin, Dennis McNamara, Edward Mortimer, Amin Saikal, Mu Sochua, Fron Nazi, Milena Pires, Béatrice Pouligny, Jonathan Prentice, Sam Rainsy, José Ramos-Horta, Andrew Reynolds, Barnett Rubin, Lieutenant General John M. Sanderson, Philippe Sands, Kamalesh Sharma, Aderito de Jesus Soares, Ok Serei Sopheak, Alvaro de Soto, Mohammad Masoom Stanikzai, Colin Stewart, Hansjoerg Strohmeyer, Shibley Telhami, Hashim Thaçi, Momcilo Trajkovic, Stephen Tull, Danilo Türk, Sergio Vieira de Mello, and Susan Woodward.

I am also grateful to the following friends and colleagues who reviewed the text in whole or in part: Mats Berdal, Michael Byers, Robert Dann, Shepard Forman, Michael Fullilove, Sven Koopmans, Dino Kritsiotis, Kimberly Marten, Edward Newman, Heiko Nitzschke, Alexandra Novosseloff, Caitlin Reiger, Benjamin Reilly, Marina Skuric-Prodanovic, Chandra Lekha Sriram, Patricia Shuming Tan, and Neclâ Tschirgi. Samuel C. Brown and Fredrik Wesslau provided valuable research assistance towards the end of the project. Errors and omissions remain, of course, my own.

The text develops certain ideas first published elsewhere. The section on Nuremberg in Chapter One draws upon 'No Justice Without Peace? International Criminal Law and the Decision to Prosecute', in Simon Chesterman (ed.), *Civilians in War* (Lynne Rienner, 2001). Chapter Two appears in abbreviated form as 'Virtual Trusteeship: Security Council Authorizations of Transitional Administrations' in David M. Malone (ed.), *The United Nations Security Council* (Lynne Rienner, 2004). Parts of Chapter Three are drawn from 'Blue Helmet Blues' (2003), 34 *Security Dialogue*, 365; and parts of Chapter Five from 'Justice Under International Administration: Kosovo, East Timor, and Afghanistan' (2001), 12 *Finnish Yearbook of International Law*, 143. Some passages on East Timor appeared first in 'East Timor in Transition: Self-Determination, State-Building and the United Nations' (2002), 9(1) *International Peacekeeping*, 45; early work on Afghanistan was published as 'Walking Softly in Afghanistan: The Future of UN State-Building' (2002), 44(3) *Survival*, 37; and 'Humanitarian Intervention and Afghanistan', in Jennifer Welsh (ed.), *Humanitarian Intervention and International Relations: Theory and Practice* (Oxford University Press, 2004). Paragraphs here and there also rehearse arguments first made in the *International Herald Tribune*, many of them co-authored with David M. Malone.

Permission to reproduce all of the relevant sections is gratefully acknowledged.

The manuscript was finalized at the Rockefeller Foundation's Study and Conference Center in Bellagio, Italy, where Gianna Celli and her staff created a home for us and the other residents at the Villa Serbelloni. My final thanks go to Ming, for ensuring that that 'us' doesn't sit there like a stone but is made, like bread; remade all the time, made new.

Abbreviations

AACA	Afghan Assistance Coordination Authority
ASDT	Timorese Social Democratic Association
CAP	Consolidated inter-agency appeal process
CEO	Chief executive officer
CIA	Central Intelligence Agency
CNRT	National Council of Timorese Resistance
CPP	Cambodian People's Party
DDR	Disarmament, demobilization, and reintegration
DOMREP	Mission of the Special Representative of the Secretary-General in the Dominican Republic
DPKO	Department of Peacekeeping Operations
ECOMOG	ECOWAS Military Observer Group
ECOWAS	Economic Community of West African States
ETTA	East Timorese Transitional Administration
EU	European Union
EUAM	European Union Administration of Mostar
Falintil	Armed Forces for the National Liberation of East Timor
FDTL	Timorese Defence Force
Frente Polisario	Popular Front for the Liberation of Saguia el Hamra and Río de Oro
Fretilin	Revolutionary Front of Independent East Timor
FRY	Federal Republic of Yugoslavia
Funcinpec	United National Front for an Independent, Neutral, Peaceful, and Cooperative Cambodia
GAOR	General Assembly Official Records
GA Res	General Assembly resolution
GNP	Gross national product
ICJ	International Court of Justice
ICSC	International Civil Services Commission
ICTY	International Criminal Tribunal for the Former Yugoslavia
IFOR	Implementation Force
ILM	International Legal Materials
IMF	International Monetary Fund
INTERFET	International Force in East Timor
IPA	International Peace Academy

ISAF	International Security Assistance Force
IWPR	Institute for War and Peace Reporting
KFOR	Kosovo Force
KLA	Kosovo Liberation Army
LNTS	League of Nations Treaty Series
MINURSO	UN Mission for the Referendum in Western Sahara
MONUC	UN Organization Mission in the Democratic Republic of the Congo
NATO	North Atlantic Treaty Organization
NCC	National Consultative Council
NGO	Non-governmental organization
OAU	Organization of African Unity
ODA	Official development assistance
OECD	Organization for Economic Cooperation and Development
ONUC	UN Operation in the Congo
ORHA	Office for Reconstruction and Humanitarian Assistance
OSCE	Organization for Security and Cooperation in Europe
PRT	Provincial Reconstruction Team
ROE	Rules of Engagement
RUF	Revolutionary United Front
SCOR	Security Council Official Records
SC Res	Security Council resolution
SFOR	Stabilization Force
SHIRBRIG	Standby High-Readiness Brigade
SNC	Supreme National Council
SRSG	Special Representative of the Secretary-General
SWAPO	South-West African People's Organization
TNI	Indonesian Armed Forces
UDT	Timorese Democratic Union
UNAMA	UN Assistance Mission in Afghanistan
UNAMET	UN Mission in East Timor
UNAMI	UN Assistance Mission for Iraq
UNAMSIL	UN Mission in Sierra Leone
UNAVEM	UN Angola Verification Mission
UNCIO	UN Conference on International Organization
UNDOF	UN Disengagement Observer Force
UNDP	UN Development Programme
UNEF	UN Emergency Force

UNEF II	Second UN Emergency Force
UNFICYP	UN Peacekeeping Force in Cyprus
UNGOMAP	UN Good Offices Mission in Afghanistan and Pakistan
UNHCR	UN High Commissioner for Refugees
UNICEF	UN Children's Fund
UNIFEM	UN Development Fund for Women
UNIFIL	UN Interim Force in Lebanon
UNIIMOG	UN Iran–Iraq Military Observer Group
UNIPOM	UN India–Pakistan Observation Mission
UNITA	National Union for the Total Independence of Angola
UNITAF	Unified Task Force
UNMIBH	UN Mission in Bosnia and Herzegovina
UNMIK	UN Interim Administration Mission in Kosovo
UNMISET	UN Mission of Support in East Timor
UNMOGIP	UN Military Observer Group in India and Pakistan
UNOMSIL	UN Observer Mission in Sierra Leone
UNOSOM	UN Operation in Somalia
UNOSOM II	UN Operation in Somalia II
UNPREDEP	UN Preventive Deployment Force
UNPROFOR	UN Protection Force
UNRWA	UN Relief and Works Agency
UNSCOP	UN Special Committee on Palestine
UNSF	UN Security Force
UNTAC	UN Transitional Authority in Cambodia
UNTAES	UN Transitional Administration for Eastern Slavonia, Baranja, and Western Sirmium
UNTAET	UN Transitional Administration in East Timor
UNTAG	UN Transitional Assistance Group
UNTEA	UN Temporary Executive Authority
UNTS	United Nations Treaty Series
UNTSO	UN Truce Supervisory Organization
UNYOM	UN Yemen Observation Mission
WFP	World Food Programme

Introduction

> He who desires or attempts to reform the government of a state, and wishes to have it accepted and capable of maintaining itself to the satisfaction of everybody, must at least retain the semblance of the old forms; so that it may seem to the people that there has been no change in the institutions, even though in fact they are entirely different from the old ones.
>
> Niccolò Machiavelli[1]

> This war is not as in the past; whoever occupies a territory also imposes on it his own social system. Everyone imposes his own system as far as his army can reach. It cannot be otherwise.
>
> Josef Stalin[2]

Is it possible to establish the conditions for legitimate and sustainable national governance through a period of benevolent foreign autocracy? This contradiction between ends and means has plagued recent efforts to govern post-conflict territories in the Balkans, East Timor, Afghanistan, and Iraq—just as it plagued the colonies and occupied territories that are their political forebears. Such state-building operations combine an unusual mix of idealism and realism: the idealist project that a people can be saved from themselves through education, economic incentives, and the space to develop mature political institutions; the realist basis for that project in what is ultimately military occupation.

In early 1995, chastened by the failed operation in Somalia, the failing operation in Bosnia and Herzegovina, and inaction in the face of genocide in Rwanda, UN Secretary-General Boutros Boutros-Ghali issued a conservative supplement to his more optimistic 1992 *Agenda for*

[1] Niccolò Machiavelli, *The Prince and the Discourses* [1531], translated by Christian E. Detmold (New York: Modern Library, 1950), 182.

[2] Milovan Djilas, *Conversations with Stalin*, translated by Michael B. Petrovich (New York: Harcourt, Brace, and World, 1962), 114.

Peace.[3] The supplement noted that a new breed of intra-state conflicts presented the United Nations with challenges not encountered since the Congo operation of the early 1960s. A feature of these conflicts was the collapse of state institutions, especially the police and judiciary, meaning that international intervention had to extend beyond military and humanitarian tasks to include the 'promotion of national reconciliation and the re-establishment of effective government'. Nevertheless, he expressed caution against the United Nations assuming responsibility for law and order, or attempting to impose state institutions on unwilling combatants.[4] General Sir Michael Rose, then commander of the UN Protection Force in Bosnia (UNPROFOR), termed this form of mission creep 'crossing the Mogadishu line'.[5]

Despite such cautious words, by the end of 1995 the United Nations had assumed responsibility for policing in Bosnia under the Dayton Peace Agreement. The following January, a mission was established with temporary civil governance functions over the last Serb-held region of Croatia in Eastern Slavonia. In June 1999, the Security Council authorized an 'interim' administration in Kosovo to govern part of what remained technically Serbian territory for an indefinite period; four months later a transitional administration was created with effective sovereignty over East Timor until independence. These expanding mandates continued a trend that began with the operations in Namibia in 1989 and Cambodia in 1993, where the United Nations exercised varying degrees of civilian authority in addition to supervising elections.

The expansion was part of a larger growth in activism by the Security Council through the 1990s, which showed itself willing to interpret internal armed conflicts, humanitarian crises, and even disruption to democracy as 'threats to international peace and security' within the meaning of the UN Charter—and therefore warranting a military response under its auspices. The 'new interventionism' was, however, constrained by the inability of the United Nations to develop an independent military capacity; as a result, Council action was generally

[3] An Agenda for Peace: Preventive Diplomacy, Peacemaking, and Peacekeeping (Report of the Secretary-General pursuant to the statement adopted by the Summit Meeting of the Security Council on 31 January 1992), UN Doc A/47/277–S/24111 (17 June 1992).

[4] Supplement to An Agenda for Peace: Position Paper of the Secretary-General on the Occasion of the Fiftieth Anniversary of the United Nations, UN Doc A/50/60–S/1995/1 (3 January 1995), paras. 13–14.

[5] 'Patience and Bloody Noses', *Guardian* (London), 30 September 1994. See Michael Rose, *Fighting for Peace: Lessons from Bosnia* (London: Warner, 1999).

limited to circumstances that coincided with the national interests of a state or group of states that were prepared to lead.[6]

This highlights a second tension in transitional administration operations: the inadequacy of available means to achieve the stated ends. The United States and others assumed their obligations under the Dayton Agreement on the basis that troops deployed in Bosnia would be withdrawn in twelve months. Kosovo remains in political limbo because there is no political will to resolve the issue of its final status that underlies every aspect of its governance problem. Relative peace and security in Afghanistan remains largely confined to Kabul and its immediate environs, the only area where contributing countries were prepared to deploy troops. And the willingness to commit such resources to reconstruction has yet to reach Africa. There has, however, been great reluctance to equip the United Nations with a capacity to undertake this kind of mission independently. The Brahimi Report on UN Peace Operations, released in 2000, observed that missions such as those in Kosovo and East Timor 'face challenges and responsibilities that are unique among United Nations field operations'; nevertheless, the controversial nature of such operations—in particular, suggestions that they resemble colonialism or military occupation—meant that it was not possible to make significant recommendations on developing a UN capacity to fulfil the required functions.[7]

The 11 September 2001 terrorist attacks in New York and Washington, DC, transformed this debate. While the heightened focus on national security (especially, but not solely, on the part of the United States) appeared to diminish the likelihood of interventions for purely humanitarian reasons, the fact that Al Qaeda had used lawless Afghanistan as a base suggested the importance of strong state governments in combating the terrorist threat. This view found doctrinal expression in the National Security Strategy produced by the White House in September 2002, which observed that 'America is

[6] See Simon Chesterman, *Just War or Just Peace? Humanitarian Intervention and International Law* (Oxford: Oxford University Press, 2001), 112–218.

[7] Report of the Panel on United Nations Peace Operations (Brahimi Report), UN DocA/55/305–S/2000/809 (21 August 2000), available at www.un.org/peace/reports/peace_operations, paras. 77–8. See Chapter Two, Section 1.2. For earlier discussion of these questions, see Gerald B. Helman and Steven R. Ratner, 'Saving Failed States', *Foreign Policy* 89, Winter 1992, 3; Peter Lyon (1993) 'The Rise and Fall and Possible Revival of International Trusteeship', *Journal of Commonwealth and Comparative Politics*: 31(1) 96; Yossi Shain and Juan J. Linz, *Between States: Interim Governments and Democratic Transitions* (Cambridge: Cambridge University Press, 1995).

now threatened less by conquering states than we are by failing ones'.[8] 'Nation-building', repudiated by US President George W. Bush while a candidate, was reluctantly embraced in the course of war with Afghanistan. In 2002–3, it became central to the US policy of regime change in Iraq.

The term 'nation-building', sometimes used in this context, is a broad, vague, and often pejorative one. In the course of the 2000 US presidential campaign, Governor Bush used it as a dismissive reference to the application of US military resources beyond traditional mandates. The term was also used to conflate the circumstances in which US forces found themselves in conflict with the local population—most notably in Somalia—with complex and time-consuming operations such as those underway in Bosnia, Kosovo, and East Timor. Although it continues to be used in this context, 'nation-building' also has a more specific meaning in the post-colonial context, in which new leaders attempted to rally a population within sometimes arbitrary territorial frontiers. The focus here is on the *state* (that is, the highest institutions of governance in a territory) rather than the *nation* (a people who share common customs, origins, history, and frequently language) as such.[9]

Within the United Nations, 'peacebuilding' is generally preferred. This has been taken to mean, among other things, 'reforming or strengthening governmental institutions'[10] or 'the creation of structures for the institutionalization of peace'.[11] It tends, however, to

[8] *The National Security Strategy of the United States of America* (Washington, DC: President of the United States, September 2002), available at www.whitehouse.gov/nsc/nss.html, 1.

[9] Massimo D'Azeglio famously expressed the difference in the context of post-Risorgimento Italy: 'We have made Italy', he declared. 'Now we must make Italians.' On the creation of states generally, see James Crawford, *The Creation of States in International Law* (Oxford: Clarendon Press, 1979). On nation building see, e.g. Benedict Anderson, *Imagined Communities: Reflections on the Origin and Spread of Nationalism* (London: Verso, 1983); Ranajit Guha (ed.), *A Subaltern Studies Reader, 1986–1995* (Minneapolis: University of Minnesota Press, 1997); Jim MacLaughlin, *Reimagining the Nation-State: The Contested Terrains of Nation-Building* (London: Pluto Press, 2001).

[10] Agenda for Peace, para. 55.

[11] Supplement to An Agenda for Peace, para. 49. From a UN development perspective, peacebuilding aims 'to build and enable durable peace and sustainable development in post-conflict situations'. See, e.g. *Role of UNDP in Crisis and Post-Conflict Situations* (Policy Paper Distributed to the Executive Board of the United Nations Development Programme and of the United Nations Population Fund), DP/2001/4 (New York: UNDP, 27 November 2000), available at www.undp.org, para. 51. The Development Assistance Committee (DAC) of the OECD maintains that peacebuilding and reconciliation focuses 'on long-term support to, and establishment of, viable political and socio-economic and cultural

embrace a far broader range of activities than those particular operations under consideration here—at times being used to describe virtually all forms of international assistance to countries that have experienced or are at risk of armed conflict.[12]

In this book, the term *state-building* refers to extended international involvement (primarily, though not exclusively, through the United Nations) that goes beyond traditional peacekeeping and peacebuilding mandates, and is directed at constructing or reconstructing institutions of governance capable of providing citizens with physical and economic security. This includes quasi-governmental activities such as electoral assistance, human rights and rule of law technical assistance, security sector reform, and certain forms of development assistance.[13] Within this class of operations, *transitional administration* denotes the less common type of operation in which these ends have been pursued by assuming some or all of the powers of the state on a temporary basis.

Where such operations have been undertaken, a third set of tensions has emerged as international administrators balance demands for high international standards—in areas from health and education to the conduct of elections—against the need for locally sustainable institutions. In the mid-1990s, the widely held view appeared to be that any post-conflict environment should hold war crimes trials today and elections tomorrow. As the months of administration of Bosnia turned into years, these views changed, encouraging a reassessment of post-conflict institution-building. 'Ownership' is a much-abused term in this context. Local control of political power is appropriately seen as the end of a transitional administration, but if an international actor has assumed some or all governmental power then local ownership is surely not the means. Indeed, the rhetoric of ownership has frequently been accompanied by an assumption that a political vacuum exists prior to the arrival of international staff. This is rarely, if ever,

institutions capable of addressing the root causes of conflicts, as well as other initiatives aimed at creating the necessary conditions for sustained peace and stability': OECD, Helping Prevent Violent Conflict, Development Assistance Committee Guidelines (Paris: OECD, 2001), available at www.oecd.org, 86.

12 Elizabeth M. Cousens, 'Introduction', in Elizabeth M. Cousens and Chetan Kumar (eds.), *Peacebuilding as Politics* (Boulder, CO: Lynne Rienner, 2001), 1, 5–10.

13 It is distinct, however, from analogous activities such as the administration of large camps housing refugees or internally displaced persons, as sometimes undertaken by the UN High Commissioner for Refugees: Ralph Wilde (2001) 'From Danzig to East Timor and Beyond: The Role of International Territorial Administration', *American Journal of International Law*, 95: 583–4.

the case. One of the errors that is often repeated in these situations is the conscious or unconscious assumption that, when the institutions of the state collapse or are so divided as to be dysfunctional, politics ceases to happen. In fact, the control of power becomes more important than ever, for the very reason that it may be exerted through informal or incoherent means.

Each of the individual cases discussed here has been treated at length in other works; the book is, therefore, necessarily selective in its approach. Rather than present each as a discrete case study, the various operations are drawn upon to illustrate trends, themes, and concerns that have arisen repeatedly. Two of the most important lessons are that local politics matter and that the personalities of local and international staff can change the course of an operation. These insights are a warning against constructing templates or models for post-conflict reconstruction. Nevertheless, some generalizations are possible.

The first two chapters survey the brief history of transitional administration. There are, of course, precedents for the exercise of such powers that pre-date recent activism by the United Nations: colonialism and military occupation. These are the subject matter of Chapter One. Despite the conceit that transitional administration was invented in the 1990s, much can be learned concerning the development of an institutional capacity to administer territory from examining the manner in which the colonial empires were regulated and subsequently dismantled. An age less attuned to political sensitivities also provides a clearer-eyed assessment of the requirements of such administration, challenging the conventional wisdom that 'ownership' on the part of the local population is essential to the process.

Though colonialism is now condemned as an international crime, international humanitarian law—specifically the 1907 Hague Regulations and the Fourth Geneva Convention of 1949—provides the legal basis for an occupying power to exercise temporary authority over territory that comes under its control.[14] The occupying power is entitled to ensure the security of its forces, but is also required

[14] Military occupation is a question of fact rather than intent. The Hague Regulations, for example, provide that '[t]erritory is considered occupied when it is actually placed under the authority of the hostile army': Convention (IV) Respecting the Laws and Customs of War on Land and Its Annex: Regulations Concerning the Laws and Customs of War on Land (1907 Hague Regulations), done at The Hague, 18 October 1907, available at www.icrc.org/ihl, art. 42. The Fourth Geneva Convention confirms that the provisions on occupation apply 'even if the... occupation meets with no armed resistance': Convention Relative to the Protection of Civilian Persons in Time of War (Fourth Geneva Convention), done at Geneva, 12 August 1949, available at www.icrc.org/ihl, art. 2.

to 'take all the measures in his power to restore, and ensure, as far as possible, public order and safety, while respecting, unless absolutely prevented, the laws in force in the country'. In addition to other positive obligations, such as ensuring public health and sanitation, as well as the provision of food and medical supplies, the occupying power is prohibited from changing local laws except as necessary for its own security and is limited in its capacity to change state institutions.[15] As the purpose of transitional administration is precisely to change the laws and institutions, further legal authority is therefore required.

In most of the cases examined here, that authority has tended to come from the UN Security Council. Chapter Two, therefore, considers the evolution of Council practice in this area. As in much of the Council's work, practice has led theory in the area of transitional administration, with some members of the Council and the wider UN community apparently allergic to the development of doctrine. This chapter also provides a brief account of the various operations that have taken place under the auspices of the Council and of other bodies since the Second World War. Analysis of these operations tends to be chronological or organized by the scope of powers assumed by the international presence. In keeping with the call for political clarity in such operations, this book takes a thematic approach, addressing five distinct political purposes for which a transitional administration (or comparable mission) has been established.

Chapters Three to Seven examine five key issues that have posed the greatest political and practical challenges to these operations: peace and security, the role of the United Nations as government, judicial reconstruction, economic reconstruction, and exit strategies. Unless security is established on the ground, none of the political purposes of a transitional administration can be achieved. Nevertheless, as Chapter Three shows, the response of military authorities to the security vacuum that follows the collapse or defeat of state institutions has been varied. With respect to forces operating under UN command, this reflects an equivocation over the use of force that has run through the history of UN peace operations, persuading some that the organization is simply unsuited to military operations. At the same time, the armed forces of many countries (and their civilian commanders-in-chief) have resisted taking on 'policing' functions. The military is rightly reluctant to embrace law and order duties that are outside its expertise, but failure to do so may irreparably damage the credibility

[15] 1907 Hague Regulations, art. 43; Fourth Geneva Convention, arts. 54–6, 64.

of the international presence and thus undermine the political goals that justified the original military engagement.

Once control has been established, how should the territory be governed? What treaties and conventions bind the temporary administration? Chapter Four directly confronts the inconsistency between ends and means highlighted earlier. The UN Transitional Administration in East Timor (UNTAET) was granted a period of benevolent autocracy to prepare East Timor for local democratic rule. In Kosovo, ongoing security concerns and the absence of a clear future made the UN-administered province an oddity: the depository of human rights treaties itself detained persons without trial for over a year at a time and acted with impunity. Different attempts have been made to restrain the power of the United Nations, including ombudspersons in East Timor and Kosovo (with varying degrees of success) and a Timorese Office of the Inspector General to oversee the trust fund set up with the World Bank. In addition to concerns about abuse of power, questions also arise about the impact of such rule on the development of mature political actors within the population under international administration.

A related issue, examined in Chapter Five, is how faith in local institutions—most importantly the rule of law—can be supported. In many situations, the very laws to be enforced will themselves be controversial, as Serb laws were in post-conflict Kosovo. Similarly, appointment of judges gives rise to tensions between the need to involve local actors and the desire of international actors to maintain high standards of accountability (for the locals as well as themselves). These tensions may come to a head around the most political crimes, in turn raising the question of how to address a legacy of human rights abuse.

If a peace settlement mediated in part through a transitional administration is to work, it is necessary that disparate parties 'buy into' the peace process. This, like 'ownership', is generally meant metaphorically, but it should also be understood literally: unless the new regime is seen to encourage economic activity and provide basic public goods, any such settlement is likely to be short-lived. Chapter Six deals with the role of external actors in providing emergency humanitarian and medium-term development assistance to a population living under a transitional administration. Such assistance is notoriously supply- rather than demand-driven, with the result that it is more responsive to the politics of donors than that of recipients. Together with the perverse economic effects that a sudden influx of foreign capital and personnel may have, these factors can undermine the short-term political stability and the medium-term economic viability of the territory in question.

The transfer of power to a legitimate and sustainable local authority, typically mediated through an election, is the central purpose of any transitional administration. Elections and other 'exit strategies' are discussed in Chapter Seven. The preference for democratic forms of governance is sometimes linked to the 'democratic peace' thesis, which holds that authentic democracies do not fight each other, or that such conflicts are exceptional. First elections can, however, mark an extremely unstable period in the life of a country emerging from conflict—indeed, quantitative research has produced the embarrassing finding that autocracies in the process of democratization actually become *more* likely to go to war. In practice, a great deal more attention has been paid to the technical side of elections than to their political purpose and significance. Meaningful state-building depends on a deeper engagement with local stakeholders before and after voting takes place.

Underlying all these issues is the most basic question of whether the United Nations and other international actors should be undertaking this sort of function at all. Chapter Eight returns to the three sets of contradictions discussed in this Introduction—that the means are inconsistent with, inadequate for, and, at times, irrelevant to the ends—and recasts them in light of the changing role of the United Nations and its relationship to the United States. This relationship is important not merely because US political, economic, and military power may determine the success or failure of a transitional administration, but because US perceptions of its national security dictated the military operations in Afghanistan and Iraq in the first place. While the United Nations may be politically constrained from viewing transitional administrations through the lens of military occupation, the United States has sometimes appeared incapable of viewing them as anything else.

As the quotations from Machiavelli and Stalin suggest, the dilemmas of whether and how to rebuild and shape political structures in foreign lands are neither new nor solely the province of starry-eyed idealists. A central argument of this book is that resolving the contradictions highlighted here requires an acceptance that even where the ends of transitional administrations may be idealistic, the means cannot be. The challenge, then, is to manage the interests of the various international and local actors through a framework that provides a realistic opportunity for the population in a territory to take control of their political destiny, while managing expectations about the time frame within which this will take place and the difficulties that independence will bring.

1

Colonies and Occupied Territories: Transitional Administration Through the Twentieth Century

> Let it be admitted at the outset that European brains, capital, and energy have not been, and never will be, expended in developing the resources of Africa from motives of pure philanthropy; that Europe is in Africa for the mutual benefit of her own industrial classes, and of the native races in their progress to a higher plane; that the benefit can be made reciprocal, and that it is the aim and desire of civilised administration to fulfil this dual mandate.
>
> Lord Lugard[1]

One of the many ironies in the recent history of transitional administration of territory by international actors is that the practice is regarded as novel. Attempts to draw analogies either with trusteeships and decolonization on the one hand, or the post-war occupation of Germany and Japan on the other, are seen as invitations to charges that the United Nations or the United States are engaging in neocolonialism or imperialism respectively. Within the United Nations in particular, such comparisons are politically impossible.

Nevertheless, there are clear parallels between, say, the indeterminate status of Kosovo today and the fifteen year administration of the Saar Basin by the League of Nations. The origins of the dispute in East Timor lie in its long-delayed decolonization; the more recent role of the United Nations may be seen as a modern form of trusteeship leading to independence. Bosnia and Herzegovina—subject to an occupying

[1] F. D. Lugard, *The Dual Mandate in British Tropical Africa*, 3rd edn. (Edinburgh and London: W. Blackwood & Sons, 1926), 617.

military power, an international war crimes process, and summary dismissal of its politicians by an international administrator—bears more than a passing resemblance to occupied Germany of 1945–9.

The failure to appreciate such historical resonance has contributed to the ad hoc nature of practice in this area. It has also, on occasion, undermined operations that might have profited from past experience. This chapter surveys twentieth-century activity in this area before turning to the current legal and political framework within which state-building operations are conducted. The first section considers the League of Nations in the aftermath of the First World War, a period that saw the creation of the Mandates System and diverse roles for the League in territorial settlements within Europe. The second section examines the occupation of Germany after the Second World War, focusing on three aspects of ongoing interest: political reconstruction, war crimes trials, and the Marshall Plan. The final section turns to the Trusteeship System and the lasting significance of decolonization.

In the search for historical context, a striking element in the record surveyed here is the functional nature of international administration. Such operations have always been designed according to the challenges they are seen to confront, but both those challenges and the means of addressing them have been interpreted by reference to the interests of the powers providing the resources to do so. For all their reprehensible elements, colonial forms of administration were at least clear about this relationship. Contemporary transitional administration is sometimes criticized for being colonial in character. Despite the protestations of the United Nations and the various actors involved, such criticism is often accurate. Yet the problem, as we shall see, is not that transitional administration is colonial in character; rather, the problem is that sometimes it is not colonial enough.[2]

[2] It would be impossible to encompass the wealth of literature on the colonial experience more generally. See, e.g. Sydney Smith Bell, *Colonial Administration of Great Britain* [1859] (New York: Augustus M. Kelley, 1970); *The Cambridge History of the British Empire*, 2nd edn. (Cambridge: Cambridge University Press, 1963); David Kenneth Fieldhouse, *The Colonial Empires: A Comparative Survey from the Eighteenth Century* (London: Weidenfeld and Nicolson, 1966); Mark A. Burkholder (ed.), *Administrators of Empire* (Aldershot: Ashgate, 1998); A. J. R. Russell-Wood (ed.), *Government and Governance of European Empires: 1450–1800* (Aldershot: Ashgate, 2000). Similarly, there is not space here to consider the phenomenon of internationalized waterways—such as the Dardanelles, Suez, Panama, Danube, Rhine—which some have compared to international administration of territory. See, e.g. David G. LeMarquand, *International Rivers: The Politics of Cooperation* (Vancouver: Westwater Research Centre, University of British Columbia, 1977).

1. The League of Nations

Following the conclusion of the First World War, the Treaty of Versailles provided for a radical redrawing of the map of Europe and a reallocation of the colonial possessions of the defeated Powers. These territorial adjustments coincided with the emergence of the League of Nations as an institution and of self-determination as a principle, both championed by US President Woodrow Wilson.[3] Concerning lands outside Europe, self-determination found much favour insofar as it applied to the former colonies of Germany and the Ottoman Empire. Within Europe, attempts to redraw nation-states along ethnic and linguistic lines were also largely confined to the territories of those who lost the war—a substantial project after the simultaneous defeat and collapse of the Ottoman, Habsburg, and Russian empires.

The League of Nations played a significant part in both areas. In deference to the political sensibilities of the day, the German and Ottoman colonies were recast as 'mandates' to be administered by nominated states.[4] There had been some consideration of the League administering these territories directly, but this was rejected as impractical—though the driving motivation appears to have been the desire of Britain, its dominions, and France to annex certain of the territories themselves. The League was more active within Europe, exercising a supervisory role in the Saar Basin, Danzig, and Upper Silesia—three disputed areas previously occupied by Germany.

These early instances of international administration by the League are of interest for the light they shed on the changing conception of whether and how international actors can and should prepare a state for independence. They also provide an historical backdrop to a number of cases that matured only late in the twentieth century, such as the colonial possession of South-West Africa (now Namibia), which was originally passed to South Africa under the Covenant of the League

[3] See, e.g. Woodrow Wilson, 'Fourteen Points' (Address to a Joint Session of Congress, 8 January 1918), available at www.yale.edu/lawweb/avalon/wilson14.htm. On self-determination generally, see Alfred Cobban, *The Nation State and National Self-Determination*, rev. edn. (London: Collins, 1969); Derek Heater, *National Self-Determination: Woodrow Wilson and his Legacy* (London: St Martin's Press, 1994); Antonio Cassese, *Self-Determination of Peoples: A Legal Reappraisal* (Cambridge: Cambridge University Press, 1995). On Versailles itself, see Margaret MacMillan, *Paris 1919: Six Months That Changed the World* (New York: Random House, 2002).

[4] See generally Neta C. Crawford, *Argument and Change in World Politics: Ethics, Decolonization, and Humanitarian Intervention* (Cambridge: Cambridge University Press, 2002).

of Nations. Within Europe, the same process that gave the League of Nations the administration of disputed German territories also created the Kingdom of Serbs, Croats, and Slovenes; the eventual collapse of this manufactured state, known from 1929 as Yugoslavia ('land of the south Slavs'), gave rise to no less than three state-building missions in the 1990s.

1.1. The Mandates System

The Covenant of the League of Nations provided that the former German and Ottoman colonies should be the subject of a 'sacred trust'. As the people of these territories were 'not yet able to stand by themselves under the strenuous conditions of the modern world', the 'tutelage of such peoples should be entrusted to advanced nations who by reason of their resources, their experience or their geographical position can best undertake this responsibility, and who are willing to accept it'.[5]

The mandated territories fell into three categories. The first group were the former Ottoman possessions in the Middle East, which were sufficiently developed for their existence as independent nations to be recognized provisionally, 'subject to the rendering of administrative advice and assistance by a Mandatory until such time as they are able to stand alone'. The wishes of these communities were to be a 'principal consideration' in the selection of the Mandatory.[6] These Class A mandates applied to Iraq and Palestine (including Transjordan), both administered by Britain, and Syria and the Lebanon, initially administered as a single mandate by France. All these territories achieved independence by 1949, but the terms and application of the mandates were later blamed to various degrees for the hostilities that broke out periodically later in the twentieth century and into the twenty-first.[7]

Class B mandates comprised German colonies in Africa that were deemed to be at a stage in their development when an 'advanced nation' had to be responsible for their administration. This did not grant unfettered power, however. Rather, the Mandatory was required to

[5] Covenant of the League of Nations, available at www.yale.edu/lawweb/avalon/leagcov.htm, art. 22.

[6] Ibid.

[7] Quincy Wright, *Mandates Under the League of Nations* (Chicago: University of Chicago Press, 1930), 593–611. On Palestine, see Mark Tessler, *A History of the Israeli-Palestinian Conflict* (Bloomington, IN: Indiana University Press, 1994), 157–65. On Iraq's claims in relation to Kuwait, see Richard Schofield, *Kuwait and Iraq: Historical Claims and Territorial Disputes* (London: Royal Institute of International Affairs, 1991).

administer the territory under conditions that would, among other things, guarantee freedom of conscience and religion, subject only to the maintenance of public order and morals.[8] Further obligations required the Mandatory to secure 'equal opportunities for the trade and commerce of other Members of the League'—suggestive of the not-entirely-altruistic motives admitted by Lord Lugard, quoted at the beginning of this chapter. The territories administered in this way were Tanganyika and parts of Togoland and the Cameroons (Britain), Ruanda–Urundi (Belgium), and the greater part of Togoland and the Cameroons (France). All these territories remained under the Mandates System through the Second World War and were transformed into trusteeships under the United Nations.[9]

Finally, there were German territories such as South-West Africa and some Pacific islands that were determined to be best administered as 'integral portions' of the territory of the Mandatory, subject to the same safeguards with respect to the indigenous population as the Class B mandates. In addition to South-West Africa (South Africa), these Class C mandates were applied to former German Samoa (New Zealand), New Guinea (Australia), Nauru (Australia on behalf of the British Empire), and former German islands in the Pacific north of the equator (Japan).[10] German (later Western) Samoa, New Guinea, and Nauru all passed into the Trusteeship System; the islands administered by Japan became the UN Trust Territory of the Pacific Islands, administered by the United States. South Africa refused to transfer South-West Africa into the Trusteeship System, purporting to integrate the territory. This was rejected by the United Nations and subsequent legal proceedings determined that South Africa continued to be bound by the original mandate, with the United Nations assuming the supervisory function formerly exercised by the League.[11]

The Mandates System was a compromise between those who advocated outright annexation and those who wished to entrust the colonial territories to international administration. Other views, such

[8] This included 'the prohibition of abuses such as the slave trade, the arms traffic, and the liquor traffic, and the prevention of the establishment of fortifications or military and naval bases and of military training of the natives for other than police purposes and the defence of territory': Covenant of the League of Nations, art. 22.

[9] Wright, *Mandates*, 611–18. See Section 3 in this chapter.

[10] Ibid, 618–21. See Tadao Yanaihara, *Pacific Islands Under Japanese Mandate* (London: Oxford University Press, 1940).

[11] GA Res 65 (I) (1946); *International Status of South-West Africa (Advisory Opinion)* [1950] ICJ Rep 128. See also Chapter Two, Section 2.1.1.

as independence and even restoration to the defeated Powers, were suggested but never seriously considered. Annexation was barred by specific pledges, notably in President Wilson's 'Fourteen Points' speech, which had been formally accepted in the course of the First World War as the basis for peace.[12] Internationalization of Palestine had been proposed in the Sykes–Picot Agreement of 1916;[13] socialist circles in Britain and France had advocated similar treatment of the colonies of belligerents in tropical Africa.[14] The 'sentiment' in favour of vesting the government of these peoples in the League of Nations was, however, given pause by the inefficiencies of international institutions:

> The experiences in Egypt, Morocco, Samoa, the New Hebrides, and elsewhere have demonstrated conclusively that international government foments intrigues among the governors and faction and disorder among the governed. The general result of such experiences has been paralysis of action with inevitable retrogression.[15]

Nevertheless, concerns about efficiency appear to have been secondary to the desire of certain allied belligerents to administer enemy colonies themselves. This desire was supported by the occupation forces that had already assumed effective control of a number of such territories, either through conquest or the operation of secret treaties.[16]

The provisions in the Covenant as adopted can be traced to the publication of a pamphlet, *The League of Nations: A Practical Suggestion*,[17] by the South African General Jan Smuts, two months before the peace conference. The text changed significantly in this very brief

[12] Harold William Vazeille Temperley (ed.), *A History of the Peace Conference of Paris*, vol. 2 (London: Oxford University Press, 1920), 226. Wilson himself had gone further, stating that the United States 'was indifferent to the claims of both Great Britain and France over peoples unless those people wanted them': Ray Stannard Baker, *Woodrow Wilson and World Settlement*, vol. 3 (Garden City, NY: Doubleday, Page & Co, 1922), 12.

[13] This Agreement was concluded as part of a deal to ensure Arab support for Britain against the Ottoman Empire. It provided for the independence of the Arab peninsula with the exception that '[w]ith a view to securing the religious interests of the Entente Powers, Palestine with the "Holy Places" is to be separated from Turkish territory and subjected to a special *régime* to be determined by agreement between Russia, France and Great Britain': Temperley (ed.), *History of the Peace Conference*, vol. 6, 1–22.

[14] Wright, *Mandates*, 26; Temperley (ed.), *History of the Peace Conference*, vol. 1, 217.

[15] Temperley (ed.), *History of the Peace Conference*, vol. 2, 232.

[16] Wright, *Mandates*, 27.

[17] Jan Smuts, 'The League of Nations: A Practical Suggestion', in David Hunter Miller (ed.), *The Drafting of the Covenant*, vol. 2 (New York: G. P. Putnam's Sons, 1928), 23.

period from December 1918 to February 1919. Wilson's embrace of the Smuts proposal expanded the application of the system from the fallen empires of Austria–Hungary, Russia, and Turkey to include the German Colonial Empire, while Austria–Hungary and Russia were subsequently dropped at the request of Italy. In this way, a system originally intended to solve the nationality problem of Eastern Europe and the Near East was applied to solving the colonial problem in parts of Asia, Africa, and the Pacific.[18] As the geographical range expanded, the role accorded to the League diminished. The original proposals gave the League a reversionary right to the empires and empowered it to substitute a new Mandatory in the event of a breach of mandate. The Covenant and relevant treaties shifted the first right to the principal Allies and omitted the second. Another significant change concerned the nature of consultation with the indigenous inhabitants of the various territories. The original proposal had clearly contemplated approval of the Mandatory by the 'wishes of these communities'; the Covenant required this only for the Class A mandates.[19]

It is not possible to explore here in depth the political context of the Mandates System or the subsequent conduct of the various mandatories.[20] Of particular interest, however, are three aspects of the debates over the system that later became themes in debates on transitional administration. The first was the coincidence of interests that was central to the acceptance of the system, which applied only to the colonies of the defeated Powers and only to the extent that it would not interfere with the desire of the mandatories for unfettered control of the territories. The second was the reluctance to entrust significant responsibility to a multilateral forum—in part because of concerns about the organization, but largely because such multilateralism might constrain the pursuit of the interests that led to acceptance of the mandate in the first place. Third, it is clear that there was significant ambivalence as to the agency of the subject populations in such

[18] Wright, *Mandates*, 33. Smuts had written that 'The German colonies in the Pacific and Africa are inhabited by barbarians, who not only cannot possibly govern themselves, but to whom it would be impracticable to apply any ideas of political self-determination in the European sense': Smuts, 'Practical Suggestion'.

[19] Wright, *Mandates*, 33–4.

[20] See, e.g. Peter A. Dumbuya, *Tanganyika Under International Mandate, 1919–1946* (Lanham, MD: University Press of America, 1995); Michael D. Callahan, *Mandates and Empire: The League of Nations and Africa, 1914–1931* (Brighton: Sussex Academic Press, 1999).

matters, whose fate was determined by grand political strategies that were often of little relevance to the governed themselves.

1.2. Administration by the League Under the Treaty of Versailles

The League of Nations assumed a more active role in the European territorial adjustments provided for in the Versailles Treaty than it did with respect to the colonies. In three cases, the League was given varying degrees of supervisory power over territory in dispute: the Saar Basin, claimed by France from Germany, and Danzig and Upper Silesia, two areas of dispute between Germany and Poland. The variation was in part a response to the idiosyncrasies of each situation, but all three were referred to as 'experiments'.[21] Foreshadowing subsequent efforts in this area by the United Nations, clear tensions emerged among the different political interests at stake, demonstrating at the same time the difficulty of mediating those interests through a multilateral forum. Unifying all three 'experiments' was the rhetoric of self-determination, cast against the backdrop of an intermission to the war that soon resumed in Europe.

1.2.1. The Saar Basin, 1920–1935 The League's administration of the Saar Basin was heralded at the time as embodying the aspirations of the new organization. Describing the inauguration of the Saar government as the first characteristic act of the League, a Council rapporteur enthused that it constituted the incarnation of that body's high principles.[22]

The origins of the Saar as an autonomous region, however, had less to do with the new models of self-determination being developed at the time than with economic claims by France against a defeated Germany. Under the Versailles Treaty, Germany ceded to France

[21] See, e.g. Temperley (ed.), *History of the Peace Conference*, vol. 2, 183. Similar regimes were also proposed in relation to Fiume (now Rijeka, Croatia) and the Dalmatian coast but never implemented: Méir Ydit, *Internationalised Territories: From the 'Free City of Cracow' to the 'Free City of Berlin'* (Leyden: A. W. Sythoff, 1961), 51–9.

[22] Report on the Saar Basin presented by Monsieur Caclamanos (1920) *Official Journal of the League of Nations* 2: 45, 49. On the Saar Basin episode, see further W. R. Bisschop, *The Saar Controversy* (London: Sweet & Maxwell, 1924); Frank M. Russell, *The International Government of the Saar* (Berkeley: University of California Press, 1926); Sarah Wambaugh, *The Saar Plebiscite* (Westport, CT: Greenwood Press, 1971).

'in full and absolute possession... the coal mines situated in the Saar Basin'.[23] Given the apparent French ambitions to annex the territory completely, temporary administrative control was transferred to the League.[24] Germany thus renounced 'in favour of the League of Nations, in the capacity of trustee, the government of the territory'.[25] These arrangements were to last for fifteen years, after which a plebiscite would be held in which the population would choose from three options: 'union with France', 'union with Germany', or a continuation of the regime established by the treaty. Following the plebiscite, the League of Nations was to determine the sovereignty under which the territory was to be placed, 'taking into account' the wishes of the inhabitants. The intriguing third option, which would have required Germany to make 'such renunciation of her sovereignty in favour of the League of Nations as the latter shall deem necessary', remained hypothetical, as the plebiscite overwhelmingly supported union with Germany and the territory was duly transferred back to German control in 1935.[26]

The regime in the Saar Basin is worthy of historical note, partly because of the way in which it disaggregated sovereignty into three discrete elements: formal title, which remained with Germany; material interests, accorded in large part to France; and governing power, vested in the League of Nations and, ultimately, the population itself. This marked a striking departure from the traditional conception of sovereignty in international law both 'upward' to an intergovernmental organization and 'downward' to the people,[27] though its importance in the emergence of the principle of self-determination is limited if

[23] Treaty of Peace, done at Versailles, 28 June 1919, 2 Bevans 43, available at www.yale.edu/lawweb/avalon/imt/menu.htm, art. 45.

[24] See Temperley (ed.), *History of the Peace Conference*, vol. 2, 177–9.

[25] Versailles Treaty, art. 49.

[26] Ibid., Annex to Part III, §IV (after art. 50), paras. 34–5. See F. P. Walters, *A History of the League of Nations* (New York: Oxford University Press, 1952), 586–98. Following the Second World War, the Saar was placed under French military occupation. Following a further referendum, it became a state (Saarland) of the Federal Republic of Germany on 1 January 1957. Saarland, together with the Ruhr, became the focus of the European Coal and Steel Community, and thus the crucible of the modern European Union.

[27] Nathaniel Berman (1993) '"But the Alternative Is Despair": Nationalism and the Modernist Revival of International Law', *Harvard Law Review*, 106: 1792, 1879. Cf. Christopher Greenwood, 'The Administration of Occupied Territory in International Law', in Emma Playfair (ed.), *International Law and the Administration of Occupied Territories* (Oxford: Clarendon Press, 1992), 241.

contrasted with the position of colonial peoples that remained subject to the 'tutelage' of the European Powers.

1.2.2. Free City of Danzig, 1920–1939 The origins of the internationalized status of Danzig (now Gdansk) may be traced to Woodrow Wilson's 'Fourteen Points' speech. This speech, widely credited as an important milestone in the development of self-determination, called for the creation of an independent Polish state that would include 'indisputably Polish populations' and be assured 'free and secure access to the sea'.[28] How such access might be obtained was left an open question. Polish negotiators at the Paris Peace Conference made it clear that they felt it should be done through the annexation of Danzig; the Allied Powers were reluctant to grant this, however, due to its overwhelmingly German population. The eventual compromise was to ensure Poland access to the sea via Danzig, which would be severed from Germany, but with its German character protected through establishing it as a 'Free City' under the protection of the League of Nations.[29]

Under the provisions of the Versailles Treaty, a constitution for Danzig was drawn up by locally appointed representatives in agreement with a High Commissioner appointed by the League. Administrative powers were granted primarily to the Free City authorities, but Poland enjoyed significant domestic authority (e.g. in the area of transportation) and was responsible for the conduct of Danzig's foreign relations. The League itself had two basic functions accorded to it: settling differences between Danzig and Poland in the interpretation of their respective powers (of which there were many), and guaranteeing the city's 'free' status through approving or disapproving amendments to the constitution.[30]

The arrangement was unique in that it gave the League a significant and open-ended role in Danzig, but it was probably unsustainable even

[28] Wilson, 'Fourteen Points', point XIII.

[29] Versailles Treaty, art. 102. See Temperley (ed.), *History of the Peace Conference*, vol. 2, 292–3; Ydit, *Internationalised Territories*, 186–7; John Kuhn Bleimaier, 'The Legal Status of the Free City of Danzig 1920–1939: Lessons to Be Derived from the Experience of a Non-State Entity in the International Community' [1989] *Hague Yearbook of International Law* 69. For an examination of the status of Danzig and its population, see *Treatment of Polish Nationals in Danzig Case* (Advisory Opinion) [1932] PCIJ (ser A/B) No 44. The corridor that connected Warsaw and Danzig had a Polish majority; in addition to the new status of Danzig, the corridor separated the province of East Prussia from the rest of Germany.

[30] Versailles Treaty, arts. 103–4.

without the commencement of hostilities in Europe in 1939. Constant tensions between Danzig and Poland strained the League's capacity as an arbiter, which was finally proven wanting when a National Socialist government was elected in Germany in May 1933. Danzig in the period 1933–9 was a microcosm of the storm building more generally; the failure to protect Danzig from Nazi occupation on 1 September 1939 was part of a wider collapse of the League system as war returned to Europe.[31]

1.2.3. Upper Silesia Mixed Commission, 1922–1937 Among the many adjustments made to Germany's territory after the First World War, the Versailles Treaty provided for the appointment of International Commissions by the Allied and Associated Powers to conduct plebiscites for the purpose of resolving certain boundary disputes. This applied, for example, to the Danish border at Schleswig (Slesvig) and to parts of the Polish border in Eastern Prussia and Upper Silesia. In Schleswig and Eastern Prussia the results of the plebiscites were clear, with 75 per cent or more of the different constituencies voting to be incorporated into one or the other country.[32]

The Industrial Triangle of Upper Silesia was more complicated. A plebiscite held in March 1921 was in favour of Germany by the proportion of six to four, taken by individual votes; by communes the margin was five to four. After an armed uprising of the Polish inhabitants, the League of Nations Council established a rapporteurs' committee, which recommended dividing the territory in accordance with the results of the plebiscite and conferring ultimate authority to determine the frontier line upon the Conference of Ambassadors of the Allied Powers. The result was an entangled boundary that gave most of the region's coal mines to Poland and the predominantly industrialized districts to Germany. In order to guarantee some measure of economic continuity of the region during the period of readjustment, the Council recommended establishing a special regime for an interim period.[33] Germany and Poland thus concluded a Convention to allow for free traffic of the population across the new frontier and free exportation of coal from the region into either country. Other provisions dealt with protection of the cultural and linguistic rights of the respective minorities. To supervise implementation of the agreement,

[31] Ydit, *Internationalised Territories*, 218–29; Walters, *History of the League*, 793–7.

[32] Ydit, *Internationalised Territories*, 46.

[33] Walters, *History of the League*, 152–6.

a Mixed Commission was established, consisting of two German and two Polish nationals, and a president from a neutral country appointed by the League Council. This situation was to lapse after fifteen years.[34]

Though the League was less active in Upper Silesia than in either the Saar Basin or Danzig, it retained a right of veto over laws issued by Germany or Poland as they applied to Upper Silesia and remained the final arbiter in disputes concerning the Convention.[35] The mandate of the Mixed Commission duly terminated in 1937, and the peaceful settlement of a potentially violent ethnic conflict was commonly regarded at the time as one of the League's few successes.

If it was a success, it was brief. With the Nazi government in power in Germany, renewal of any part of the Convention was out of the question.[36] On 31 August 1939, German troops wearing civilian clothes attacked a radio station in Gleiwitz (now Gliwice), on the German side of the Upper Silesian partition border. They broadcast a message that the station was in Polish hands and left behind a dead German concentration camp inmate in a Polish army uniform. This was one of the pretexts used by Adolf Hitler to justify the invasion of Poland that commenced the next day.[37] The very region in which attempts to mediate nationalist conflict through law found their most elaborate expression later became the site of one of Nazi Germany's most notorious extermination camps at Auschwitz (now Oswiecim).

1.3. Other Quasi-Administrative Activity by the League

The League exercised some measure of administrative power in two further cases, the Memel Harbour Board in Lithuania and Leticia in Colombia. In each case, the League's powers were exercised as part of an attempt at conflict resolution.[38] This marked something of a departure from its earlier role in fulfilling the tasks accorded to it under the Versailles agreement and more closely approximates the type of

[34] Convention Concerning Upper Silesia, Germany–Poland, done at Geneva, 15 May 1922, 9 LNTS 466, arts. 562–606.

[35] Ibid., arts. 3, 147–9, 157.

[36] Walters, *History of the League*, 157.

[37] Trial of the Major War Criminals Before the International Military Tribunal (1948), vol. 22, 16–17, available at www.yale.edu/lawweb/avalon/imt/proc/08-28-46.htm.

[38] Other attempts at dispute resolution also provided for lesser oversight by the League, such as the Åland Islands dispute, but will not be considered in depth here. See generally George Scott, *The Rise and Fall of the League of Nations* (London: Hutchinson, 1973); F. S. Northedge, *The League of Nations: Its Life and Times, 1920–1946* (Leicester: Leicester University Press, 1986).

function given to the United Nations in the 1990s. A key factor in the success or failure of such operations was and remains the sustainability of the peace agreement.

1.3.1. Memel Harbour Board, 1924–1939 Under the Versailles Treaty, Germany renounced its sovereignty over the Memel Territory (now Klaipeda, Lithuania) in favour of the Allied and Associated Powers, and undertook to accept a settlement on status as decided by these Powers.[39] Held as a temporary condominium of Britain, France, Italy, and Japan, and occupied by French troops, the Memel was initially administered by a French High Commissioner. Various proposals were made as to the future status of the territory—all opposed by Lithuania, which remained at war with Poland and for which the Port of Memel was the sole entry to the Baltic Sea. In January 1923, Lithuania presented the Powers with a fait accompli by seizing the territory in a surprise attack and forcing the French garrison of 200 men to surrender.[40]

The Conference of the Ambassadors, representing the condominium, was surprisingly receptive to this unorthodox solution of the Memel problem and declared its willingness to transfer sovereignty over the territory to Lithuania—provided that the local German population was granted full cultural autonomy, that the Port of Memel was administered by an 'International Harbour Board', and that Poland was granted the right of free transit to and from the Port.[41] Lithuania eventually adopted the Memel Statute in a convention signed in May 1924 with the Principal Allied Powers. The Statute recognized Lithuania's sovereignty over the Memel Territory with some provision for a local autonomous government. The Port of Memel was declared to be 'of international concern' and a Harbour Board was constituted including one Lithuanian, one person from the Memel itself, and one appointed by the League of Nations. This board was to report annually to the Government of Lithuania, the new Directorate of Memel, and the League.[42]

39 Versailles Treaty, art. 99.

40 Ydit, *Internationalised Territories*, 48. See generally Ian F. D. Morrow, *The Peace Settlement in the German-Polish Borderlands: A Study of Conditions To-Day in the Pre-War Prussian Provinces of East and West Prussia* (London: Oxford University Press, 1936); C. A. Whomersley (1993) 'The International Legal Status of Gdansk, Klaipeda and the Former East Prussia', *International and Comparative Law Quarterly*, 42: 919.

41 Ydit, *Internationalised Territories*, 48.

42 Convention Concerning the Territory of Memel, France–Italy–Japan–Lithuania–United Kingdom, done at Paris, 8 May 1924, 29 LNTS 87, arts. 2, 5.

As with Danzig and Upper Silesia, the League's responsibilities in the Memel Territory were overtaken by events. After it left the League in 1933, Germany ended the series of appeals that it had made to the League Council and made clear its intention to recover the Memel by other methods. This was eventually achieved in March 1939 without significant resistance on the part of the Lithuanians or of the Western Powers, at the same time that Bohemia was occupied.[43]

1.3.2. Leticia, 1933–1934 The attempt by a League of Nations Commission to resolve a territorial dispute between Colombia and Peru was a marginal case of international administration. Nevertheless, it was the first incident in which the League was the primary actor in a dispute resolution process, rather than acting through, or at the behest of, a consortium of Powers.

In September 1932, Peruvian irregular forces invaded and occupied the Colombian town and district of Leticia. This territory, which provided Colombia with access to the Amazon, had been ceded by Peru in a treaty signed in 1922 but ratified only in 1928.[44] Though the action was disavowed by Lima, a Colombian police expedition that approached Leticia was warned that reoccupation by force would be resisted by the Peruvian military. After a brief attempt at mediation by Brazil, the matter was referred to the League Council in early 1933.[45]

As a matter of international law, the situation was uncomplicated: Peru would have to withdraw. In order to achieve this without further violence, however, it was proposed that Peru should hand the territory to a Commission of the League, which would administer the area for the period of one year. This was initially resisted by Peru and agreement was reached only after the (apparently unrelated) assassination of President Sanchez Cerro. A convention was signed on 25 May 1933; thirty days later the Commission arrived and Peruvian forces withdrew. The League administered Leticia 'in the name of the Government of Colombia', which was responsible for the costs of

43 Walters, *History of the League*, 305.

44 Treaty Between Colombia and Peru Regarding Frontiers and Free Inland Navigation, done at Lima, 24 March 1922, 74 LNTS 13.

45 L. H. Woolsey (1933) 'The Leticia Dispute Between Colombia and Peru', *American Journal of International Law*, 27: 317; Idem (1935) 'The Leticia Dispute Between Colombia and Peru', *American Journal of International Law*, 29: 94; Walters, *History of the League*, 525–6, 536–8; Ydit, *Internationalised Territories*, 59–60.

administration; Colombia provided troops for the Commission and its flag flew alongside that of the League.[46]

The League's involvement was, formally, to ensure the smooth transfer of territory back to Colombia—comparable to the task given to the UN Transitional Administration for Eastern Slavonia (UNTAES) six decades later. As in that case, key elements of the relative success of the operation were the clarity of the political outcome, the adequacy of resources, and the strong support of the United States. In due course, the League handed over Leticia to Colombia. One measure of success noted by the Commission after completion of its mandate was that the population had increased fourfold during the year of League supervision.[47]

2. *Allied Occupation of Germany, 1945–1949*

The territorial settlements after the Second World War were in some respects similar to those that followed the First. Once again, the colonies were largely confirmed in their status with minimal oversight from an embryonic international organization; once again, necessary adjustments within Europe received greater scrutiny and greater resources. These similarities were superficial, however. The Trusteeship System, considered in the third section below, was the Trojan Horse that led to the dismantling of empires that had spanned the globe. Within Europe, the decision to dismember and then to reconstruct Germany represented state-building—and, importantly, nation-building[48]—on a scale previously unimagined.

This section briefly examines three aspects of the Allied occupation that are of continuing relevance to contemporary transitional administration: political reconstruction, the administration of justice, and economic reconstruction. The focus is on the occupation of Germany, though one could equally focus on post-war Italy, Austria, or Japan—or, indeed, the many countries in which civilian administration

[46] Agreement Relating to the Procedure for Putting into Effect the Recommendations Proposed by the Council of the League of Nations, Peru–Colombia, done at Geneva, 25 May 1933, 138 LNTS 253; Ydit, *Internationalised Territories*, 59–62; Walters, *History of the League*, 536–40.

[47] Protocol of Friendship and Co-operation, Colombia–Peru, done at Rio de Janeiro, 24 May 1934, 164 LNTS 21; Walters, *History of the League*, 540. On UNTAES see Chapter Two, Section 2.2.3.

[48] On the distinction between the two, see the Introduction, text accompanying n. 8–9.

had to be reconstructed as Axis forces withdrew.[49] Nevertheless, in so far as lessons can be drawn from this period, the German experience is of more lasting significance because of the multilateral nature of the occupation and the important legacy of the Nuremberg Trials. The Marshall Plan, which is now celebrated as a paradigm of post-conflict economic reconstruction, was both multilateral in implementation and regional in its scope.

The privileging of multilateral approaches reflects this book's primary interest in transitional administration by international organizations. The possibility of future unilateral military occupations remains, of course, as the US-led occupation of Iraq demonstrated in 2003.[50] Nevertheless, the modern rejection of colonization and the difficulties of post-conflict administration suggest an ongoing preference to some form of multilateral approach. This, at least, appeared to be the significance of the vague role accorded to the United Nations in Iraq under Security Council resolution 1483 (2003).[51]

2.1. *Political Reconstruction*

In August 1941—four months before the Pearl Harbour attack brought the United States into the Second World War—US President Franklin D. Roosevelt and British Prime Minister Winston Churchill issued the Atlantic Charter, which elaborated the principles according to which the war and a subsequent peace were to be conducted. Stating that they sought no territorial aggrandizement, the Powers (later joined by the Soviet Union) declared their respect for 'the right of all peoples to choose the form of government under which they will live' and their wish 'to see sovereign rights and self-government restored to those who have been forcibly deprived of them'. While they affirmed their determination to destroy the 'Nazi tyranny', it was clear that they understood these principles as applying not merely to countries then under German occupation but to the German people themselves.

[49] See generally Hajo Holborn, *American Military Government: Its Organization and Policies* (Washington, DC: Infantry Journal Press, 1947); Michael Schaller, *The American Occupation of Japan* (Oxford: Oxford University Press, 1985); Theodore Cohen, *Remaking Japan: The American Occupation as New Deal* (New York: Free Press, 1987); Robert E. Ward and Sakamoto Toshikuzu, *Democratizing Japan: The Allied Occupation* (Honolulu: University of Hawaii Press, 1987); John W. Dower, *Embracing Defeat: Japan in the Wake of World War II* (New York: W. W. Norton, 1999).

[50] David E. Sanger and Eric Schmitt, 'US Has a Plan to Occupy Iraq, Officials Report', *New York Times*, 11 October 2002.

[51] See further, Chapter Two, Section 3.2; Chapter Eight, Section 2.

Plans for post-war Germany thus proceeded on the assumption that a German government would eventually be restored.[52]

The Atlantic Charter was invoked at the Crimea Conference in February 1945, but plans for post-war Germany had shifted, reflecting in part the influence of US Secretary of the Treasury Henry J. Morgenthau, Jr on Roosevelt.[53] The Communiqué from Yalta was explicit:

It is our inflexible purpose to destroy German militarism and Nazism and to ensure that Germany will never again be able to disturb the peace of the world. We are determined to disarm and disband all German armed forces; break up for all time the German General Staff. . .; remove or destroy all German military equipment; eliminate or control all German industry that could be used for military production; bring all war criminals to just and swift punishment. . .; wipe out the Nazi party, Nazi laws, organizations and institutions, remove all Nazi and militarist influences from public office and from the cultural and economic life of the German people; and take in harmony such other measures in Germany as may be necessary to the future peace and safety of the world. It is not our purpose to destroy the people of Germany, but only when Nazism and Militarism have been extirpated will there be hope for a decent life for Germans, and a place for them in the comity of nations.[54]

Terms for the German surrender were amended to state that Britain, the United States, and the Soviet Union would possess 'supreme authority' with respect to Germany. 'In the exercise of such authority they will take such steps, including the complete dismemberment of Germany as they deem requisite for future peace and security.'[55]

At the same time, the three Powers issued a Declaration of Liberated Europe, envisioning a continent transformed in accordance with democratic ideals: 'The establishment of order in Europe and the rebuilding of national economic life must be achieved by processes

[52] Atlantic Charter, United Kingdom–United States, 14 August 1941, available at www.yale.edu/lawweb/avalon/wwii/atlantic.htm. These principles were approved by the Soviet Union (together with twenty-five other states) in a declaration on 1 January 1942: Declaration by United Nations, done at Washington, DC, 1 January 1942, available at www.yale.edu/lawweb/avalon/decade/decade03.htm. See also Harold Zink, *The United States in Germany, 1944–1955*, 2nd edn. (Westport, CT: Greenwood Press, 1974), 19.

[53] Marshall Knappen, *And Call It Peace* (Chicago: University of Chicago Press, 1947), 53–5; Holborn, *American Military Government*, 40–1.

[54] Report of the Crimea Conference, §II, in Diane Shaver Clemens, *Yalta* (New York: Oxford University Press, 1970), 296.

[55] Protocol of Proceedings of the Crimea Conference (Declaration of Liberated Europe), Soviet Union–United Kingdom–United States, done at Yalta, 11 February 1945, available at www.yale.edu/lawweb/avalon/wwii/yalta.htm, §III.

which will enable the liberated peoples to destroy the last vestiges of Nazism and fascism and to create democratic institutions of their own choice.' To foster these conditions, the three governments would jointly assist the population of any liberated European state or former Axis state to 'form interim governmental authorities broadly representative of all democratic elements in the population and pledged to the earliest possible establishment through free elections of Governments responsive to the will of the people'.[56] These principles were affirmed at the Potsdam Conference, convened two months after the unconditional surrender of all German forces on 7 May 1945. Germany was also to be reconstituted as a democratic state, but not on so swift a schedule. The Potsdam Declaration stated that the political purposes of the impending Allied occupation would be to ensure the complete disarmament and demilitarization of Germany, to eliminate all remaining traces of the Nazi state, and to prepare for 'eventual reconstruction of German political life on a democratic basis'.[57]

Early allied plans had not provided for the establishment of a central government, as the military had intended that supreme authority temporarily vested in the Supreme Commander would be transferred to lawful indigenous governments at the earliest date compatible with military interests. From 1944, however, plans to divide Germany into zones of occupation also provided for the establishment of a Control Council that would exercise supreme authority in matters affecting Germany as a whole, consisting of the Commanders-in-Chief acting together as a body.[58] Even as late as the Spring of 1945, however, the Allies had assumed that *some* form of central government would survive in Germany and be competent at least to effect the necessary transfer of authority in Germany to the Allies. It soon became evident that this would not be the case and that a new legal basis for occupation and control had to be devised. This took the form of a declaration that Germany had been completely defeated and lacked a government competent to maintain order. In these circumstances, the Allied

[56] Protocol of Proceedings of the Crimea Conference (Declaration of Liberated Europe), Soviet Union–United Kingdom–United States, done at Yalta, 11 February 1945, available at www.yale.edu/lawweb/avalon/wwii/yalta.htm, §II.

[57] Potsdam Declaration, Soviet Union–United Kingdom–United States, done at Berlin, 2 August 1945, available at www.yale.edu/lawweb/avalon/decade/decade17.htm, §II.A(3).

[58] Protocol on Zones of Occupation in Germany and the Administration of 'Greater Berlin', Soviet Union–United Kingdom–United States, done at London, 12 September 1944; Agreement on Control Machinery in Germany, Soviet Union–United Kingdom–United States, done at London, 14 November 1944.

Representatives, 'acting by authority of their respective Governments and in the interests of the United Nations' (then referring to the states that had signed the 1942 'Declaration by United Nations'), assumed supreme authority over the territory of Germany.[59]

Implementation of the occupation plans began fitfully. Final advances by the various armies had overshot their allocated zones of occupation, leaving British and US troops in some places over a hundred miles into the Russian zone, and Russian forces in control of the whole of Berlin. Britain and the United States did not assume full control over their respective zones until two months after victory in Europe on 8 May 1945. Even then, many of the policies that had been formulated for occupation did not survive deployment. Basic economic policy had been left uncertain until the Potsdam Conference and the translation of those broad outlines into specific policies provoked bitter and prolonged debate in the Control Council. Political reconstruction also remained uncertain: though the possibility of dismembering Germany had been agreed to in principle at Yalta and was never formally renounced, by Potsdam opinion had hardened against it—if only because it might limit the funds available to pay reparations.[60]

The question of whether and when to revive German political institutions prefigured subsequent debates over the timing of elections in post-conflict territories administered by the United Nations. In occupied Germany, different approaches were adopted in the three Western zones.[61] France and the United States made early moves towards democratization, drawing upon forms of elected local government that had pre-existed the Nazi regime. Under this system (which had not been uniform throughout Germany), chief officials were professional civil servants with a long and secure tenure who could be dismissed by a local legislature. In the British Zone, a December 1945 instruction to transform the administration from direct to indirect led to attempts to replace the German system with one modelled on local

[59] Declaration Regarding the Defeat of Germany and the Assumption of Supreme Authority by Allied Powers, Soviet Union–United Kingdom–United States–Provisional Government of the French Republic, done at Berlin, 5 June 1945, available at www.yale.edu/lawweb/avalon/wwii/ger01.htm. See F. S. V. Donnison, *Civil Affairs and Military Government North-West Europe, 1944–1946* (London: H. M. Stationery Office, 1961), 247–9.

[60] Donnison, *Civil Affairs*, 260–8.

[61] The Soviet Union installed a Socialist Unity Party (SED) government in the German Democratic Republic, though elections of a kind were periodically staged.

government in Britain, where policies were determined by an elected council and mayor, and implemented by professionals employed by the council. This appears to have been unpopular with the Germans and was, in the view of at least some of the British officials concerned, misconceived.[62]

The United States, in turn, was criticized for what its allies called an 'unholy zeal to arrange for early elections in the occupied countries'. This was considered symptomatic of an American willingness to accept 'a semblance of democratic activity as the realization of democracy in order to be excused from further tedious duties overseas'.[63] Close examination of the various approaches taken over time by the United States, however, suggests that just as Nazism was frequently regarded as a 'disease' that might be excised from the German body politic, so democracy was seen as a subject in which they might be educated. Similar arguments about the appropriate timing and the pedagogical value of elections continue to be heard in the Balkans and elsewhere.[64]

The political reconstruction of Germany was swiftly eclipsed by the beginning of the cold war. Britain, France, and the United States increasingly coordinated their policies, and in 1948 the Soviet Union withdrew from the Control Council. The ongoing occupation by the Western Allies soon became explicitly linked to opposing the Soviet presence in the east of Germany. On 12 May 1949—the day a year-long Soviet blockade on Berlin was lifted and a little more than a month after the North Atlantic Treaty was signed, creating NATO[65]—the three Western Military Governors passed an Occupation Statute, which stated that the occupying powers desired that the German people should 'enjoy self-government to the maximum possible degree consistent with such occupation'.[66] The Federal Republic of Germany was proclaimed eleven days later, with its 'temporary' capital in Bonn. Allied troops remained and West Germany gained effective sovereignty only in 1955 with the entry into force of the

[62] Wolfgang Gaston Friedmann, *The Allied Military Government of Germany* (London: Stevens, 1947), 101–4.

[63] Holborn, *American Military Government*, 109.

[64] Patricia Shu Ming Tan, 'Idea Factories: American Policies for German Higher Education and Reorientation, 1944–1949' (D.Phil thesis, Modern History, University of Oxford, 2000), 242. See Chapter Seven, Section 3.2.

[65] North Atlantic Treaty, done at Washington, DC, 4 April 1949, 34 UNTS 243, available at www.yale.edu/lawweb/avalon/nato.htm.

[66] Occupation Statute Promulgated by Military Governors and Commanders-in-Chief of the Western Zones of Germany, 12 May 1949.

Paris Agreements.[67] The Soviet Union dissolved its occupation of what became the German Democratic Republic in October 1949, although Soviet troops remained and the Allies refused to recognize East Germany until the early 1970s.[68] Following the reunification of West and East Germany on 3 October 1990, the four occupying powers formally relinquished all remaining rights from the occupation in a treaty that came into effect on 15 March 1991.[69]

High politics thus dominated the project of rebuilding a German polity. This provided a foretaste of the political context of state-building projects later in the twentieth century—most notably in Kosovo, where the ambiguous UN mandate also reflected policy differences between Britain, France, Russia, and the United States. A more lasting legacy from the occupation of Germany than political reconstruction is generally seen in the Nuremberg Trials of the major Nazi war criminals, though the potential for subsequent development of international criminal law was undermined by the cold war. The decision as to whether prosecution should take place at all provides an illuminating backdrop to ongoing contemporary debates about the relative importance of peace and justice.

2.2. *War Crimes Trials*

In his opening statement before the Nuremberg Tribunal, US Chief of Counsel Justice Robert H. Jackson argued that the trials represented an historic victory for the rule of law: 'That four great nations, flushed with victory and stung with injury, stay the hand of vengeance and voluntarily submit their captive enemies to the judgment of the law is one of the most significant tributes that Power has ever paid to Reason.'[70] Even in the closing moments of the war, however, it was far from clear that the Allies would pursue legal avenues to punish the Nazi leadership. Churchill, for example, had favoured the summary execution of fifty or so leading members of the Nazi apparatus. Soviet

[67] Convention on the Rights and Obligations of Foreign Forces and Their Members in the Federal Republic of Germany, France–United Kingdom–United States–Federal Republic of Germany, done at Bonn, 26 May 1952, 332 UNTS 3, as amended by Protocol on the Termination of the Occupation Regime in the Federal Republic of Germany, France–United Kingdom–United States–Federal Republic of Germany, done at Paris, 23 October 1954.

[68] Both the Federal Republic of Germany and the German Democratic Republic joined the United Nations in 1973.

[69] Treaty on the Final Settlement with Respect to Germany, done at Moscow, 12 September 1990, 1992 UNTS 124.

[70] *Trial of the Major War Criminals*, vol. 2, 99.

Premier Josef Stalin approved: in a 'semi-jocular' recommendation he suggested that 50,000 German general staff officers be shot.[71]

This exchange is commonly dismissed as an aberration, but executing the Nazi leadership was a serious proposition at the time. Such an approach enjoyed the virtues of simplicity and candour. It would spare the Allies the tedious process of organizing the mechanisms and material necessary to present a watertight case, precluding legal rationalizations and dilatory tactics that the guilty might employ to delay their judgment. And, crucially, the victors would not be required to 'disguise a punishment exacted by one sovereign upon another by appeal to the neutral instrument of the law'.[72] The creation of an international tribunal was due largely to US involvement. Henry L. Stimson, the US Secretary of War, believed that a duly constituted international tribunal would have a greater effect on posterity: the Germans would not be able to claim (as they had of the Treaty of Versailles) that admissions of war guilt had been exacted under duress.[73] Roosevelt wavered, but his successor, Harry S Truman, had utter contempt for the British solution of summary executions. In the event, the final decision to cede 'Power... to Reason' was formalized on a particularly inauspicious date. In one of history's more brutal ironies, the treaty that established the Nuremberg Trials was signed by the Allies on the same day that the United States dropped its second atomic bomb on Japan.

These debates highlight competing objectives in the Allies' decision to prosecute the Nazi leadership for war crimes: retribution and deterrence. The retributive element was clear from the earliest preparations for war crimes trials. In October 1941, Churchill articulated his horror at the 'Nazi butcheries', stating that '[r]etribution for these crimes must henceforward take its place among the major purposes of the war'.[74] By 1942, the United States and the Soviet Union had publicly affirmed their commitment to punishing the 'barbaric crimes of the invaders'.[75] The Moscow Declaration of 1 November 1943,

[71] Telford Taylor, *The Anatomy of the Nuremberg Trials: A Personal Memoir* (New York: Knopf, 1992), 29–30.

[72] Lawrence Douglas (1995) 'Film as Witness: Screening Nazi Concentration Camps Before the Nuremberg Tribunal', *Yale Law Journal*, 105: 449, 457–8.

[73] Geoffrey Robertson, *Crimes Against Humanity: The Struggle for Global Justice* (London: Allen Lane, 1999), 199.

[74] Quoted in UN War Crimes Commission, *History of the United Nations War Crime Commission and the Development of the Laws of War* (London: H. M. Stationery Office, 1948), 88. The declaration, issued on 25 October 1941, was part of a joint declaration with the United States—then neutral in the war.

[75] President Roosevelt, Declaration of 21 August 1942, quoted in ibid., 93.

however, captured the Allies' ambivalence as to the relative worth of a juridical or purely military resolution: 'Most assuredly the three Allied Powers will pursue them to the uttermost ends of the earth and will deliver them to their accusers in order that justice may be done.'[76]

The second desired outcome of the Nuremberg Trials was that they should serve a deterrent function. This stemmed in part from the view that the Second World War might have been prevented if the initiators of the First had been justly punished. Similarly, the Tokyo Trials and other war crimes tribunals allocating individual responsibility were justified on the basis of their capacity to reach individual actors and, presumably, to deter other individuals from performing such acts in future. The applicability of international law to individuals came to constitute the first of the 'Nuremberg Principles' adopted by the UN General Assembly in 1950.[77] Over the course of the trials, this was variously justified by reference to the precedent established by piracy as an international crime, to international duties that 'transcend the national obligations of obedience imposed by the individual state',[78] and to the results that would flow from allowing individuals to hide behind the veil of sovereignty:

> The principle of personal liability is a necessary as well as logical one if International Law is to render real help to the maintenance of peace. An International Law which operates only on states can be enforced only by war because the most practicable method of coercing a state is warfare. . .Only sanctions which reach individuals can peacefully and effectively be enforced.[79]

The Nuremberg Trials marked a significant development in the law, but the political and historical circumstances that made them possible came to be seen as unique to the Second World War. The trials presaged legal instruments codifying the crime of genocide in

[76] Moscow Declaration, Republic of China–Soviet Union–United Kingdom–United States, done at Moscow, October 1943, available at www.yale.edu/lawweb/avalon/wwii/moscow.htm, reprinted in *The Times* (London), 3 November 1943.

[77] Principles of International Law Recognized in the Charter of the Nuremberg Tribunal and in the Judgment of the Tribunal, 5 GAOR (Supp No 12), UN Doc A/1316 (29 July 1950).

[78] *Trial of the Major War Criminals*, vol. 22, 466. The analogy with piracy is questionable at the least; the prosecution of pirates falls within international criminal law as their crimes do not fall within the jurisdiction of any one state. See, e.g. A. Carnegie (1963) 'Jurisdiction over Violations of the Laws and Customs of War', *British Yearbook of International Law*, 39: 421.

[79] Robert H. Jackson, *The Nürnberg Case* (New York: Knopf, 1947), 88.

1948[80] and the laws of armed conflict in the 1949 Geneva Conventions, but attempts to create a comprehensive regime of individual criminality soon foundered. The International Law Commission adopted a draft Code of Offences against the Peace and Security of Mankind in 1954,[81] but then suspended work until 1983. With the notable exception of episodic national prosecutions of Nazi war crimes, the field of international criminal law remained essentially dormant for half a century.[82]

The failure to realize the promise of Nuremberg is commonly attributed to the geopolitics of the cold war. Attempts to codify the law—let alone create institutions to enforce it—were hamstrung by political differences and widespread doubts as to the use of international law in resolving issues of power. These concerns found voice in the reification of sovereignty as the brittle shell around individual polities: impermeable, but occasionally shattered by violence.[83] A second factor was that few conflicts concluded with the clarity of the Second World War. Initially, at least, post-war Germany was regarded as a clean slate upon which the Allies could inscribe a new legal and political culture. There was, therefore, no serious consideration of amnesties being granted to the Nazi leadership as part of a peace deal; as indicated earlier, the dilemma was whether or not to dignify their punishment with the trappings of legal procedure. Similarly, the ad hoc legal institutions that were created in Germany were limited in their jurisdiction and could not be used against the victorious Allies that were enforcing the law. Half a century later, the South African Constitutional Court observed that the trial of war criminals of a defeated nation is 'simplicity itself as compared to the subtle and dangerous issues that can divide a country when it undertakes to punish its own violators.'[84]

[80] Convention on the Prevention and Punishment of the Crime of Genocide, 9 December 1948, 78 UNTS 277.

[81] [1954] 2 *Yearbook of the International Law Commission* 140.

[82] See generally Timothy L. H. McCormack and Gerry J. Simpson (eds.), *The Law of War Crimes: National and International Approaches* (The Hague: Kluwer, 1997).

[83] The main sticking point in debates on the criminal code was, in the end, the precise definition of the term 'aggression': see M. Cherif Bassiouni, *The Statute of the International Criminal Court: A Documentary History* (Ardsley-on-Hudson, NY: Transnational, 1998), 12–14. The term remains undefined in the Statute of the International Criminal Court (Rome Statute), UN Doc A/Conf.183/9 (17 July 1998), art. 5(2).

[84] *Azanian Peoples Organization (*AZAPO*)* v *President of the Republic of South Africa* (1996) 4 SA 671, para. 31, quoting Marvin E. Frankel, *Out of the*

In any event, Allied enthusiasm for prosecutions waned quickly. Many senior officers were considered too valuable to prosecute; others either escaped or were not pursued. An implicit principle of both Nuremberg and Tokyo was to hold a few highly publicized trials of certain leaders for a process of criminality in which hundreds of thousands had actually been culpable in one way or another.[85] In terms of retribution, the Nuremberg Trials were highly selective; in terms of deterrence, their effect appears to have been negligible.

2.3. The Marshall Plan

A third element of post-war reconstruction that is frequently cited in modern circumstances is the European Recovery Program, known more commonly as the Marshall Plan. The Plan was regarded in its time as a success and history has been kinder to it than to most other foreign policy endeavours. Between 1948 and 1951, Europe's aggregate gross national product (GNP) jumped by a third, agricultural production increased 11 per cent, and industrial output increased 40 per cent over pre-war levels. The Plan is variously attributed with laying the foundations of a prosperous European Union and launching the opening salvoes of the cold war; today it is invoked like a mantra in the response to social and economic problems across the globe.[86]

In a speech at Harvard University on 5 June 1947, US Secretary of State George C. Marshall urged that Western Europe's faltering economic recovery had to be addressed at a systemic rather than piecemeal level, and that Europe itself should take the lead in drawing up programmes for implementation. Within ten months, this fairly vague proposal was developed into a detailed programme and made into law, providing $11.8 billion in grants (plus a further $1.5 billion in loans that were repaid) distributed across sixteen countries. In 2003 dollars, this would be the equivalent of about $100 billion.[87]

Shadows of Night: The Struggle for International Human Rights (New York: Delacorte Press, 1989).

[85] Adam Roberts (1995) 'The Laws of War: Problems of Implementation', *Duke Journal of Comparative and International Law*, 6: 11, 26–7.

[86] See Michael J. Hogan, *The Marshall Plan: America, Britain, and the Reconstruction of Western Europe, 1947–1952* (Cambridge: Cambridge University Press, 1987), 431; Walt W. Rostow (1997) 'Lessons of the Plan: Looking Forward to the Next Century', *Foreign Affairs*, 76(3): 205; Peter Grose (1997) 'The Marshall Plan—Then and Now', *Foreign Affairs*, 76(3): 159.

[87] George C. Marshall, 'Speech Delivered by General George Marshall at Harvard University on 5 June 1947' (1947) XVI(415) *Department of State Bulletin*

Churchill called it 'the most unsordid act in history', but the motivation behind the Marshall Plan was not unvarnished altruism. Marshall himself stressed the impact that Europe's continuing weakness could have on the US economy: an injection of US funds would remedy the 'dollar gap' and enable Europe to purchase US raw materials and parts necessary for the continent's reconstruction.[88] And, though Marshall had emphasized that the policy was 'directed not against any country or doctrine but against hunger, poverty, desperation and chaos', US officials were deeply concerned about the leftward turn in European politics. Writing in 1947, George Kennan argued that the Marshall Plan would be an effective tool in the strategy of containment.[89] The Soviet blockade of Berlin from 1948–9 actually saved the Plan for West Germany, as it undermined British and French efforts to use US contributions to their respective zones of occupation as a source of funds for war reparations.[90]

Speaking in April 2002, US President George W. Bush likened reconstruction efforts in Afghanistan to Marshall's programme for Europe, though the analogy was criticized for being stronger on rhetoric than cash.[91] The experience of Bosnia suggests that the success of reconstruction is not dependent on funds alone: far more has been spent per capita there than under the Marshall Plan, yet the economy remains feeble.[92] The scale of the funding was certainly important—Senator

1159. See Imanuel Wexler, *The Marshall Plan Revisited* (Westport, CT: Greenwood Press, 1983), 249. The participating countries established the Organization for European Economic Cooperation to supervise the distribution of aid, which in 1961 became the Organization for Economic Cooperation and Development (OECD).

[88] See also Scott Jackson (1979) 'Prologue to the Marshall Plan: The Origins of the American Commitment for a European Recovery Program', *Journal of American History*, 65: 1043, 1055.

[89] Policy Planning Staff Paper on Aid to Western Europe, 23 May 1947, PPS/1. Kennan, who directed the State Department's Policy Planning Staff, anonymously published the article that was the intellectual basis for US containment policy through the cold war: X [George Kennan] (1947) 'The Sources of Soviet Conduct', *Foreign Affairs*, 25(4): 566.

[90] Diane B. Kunz (1997) 'The Marshall Plan Reconsidered: A Complex of Motives', *Foreign Affairs*, 76(3): 162, 168.

[91] Mike Allen, 'Bush Resumes Case Against Iraq; Democratic Nations Must Confront "Axis of Evil", President Tells VMI Cadets', *Washington Post*, 18 April 2002; 'If Afghanistan Goes Down', *Washington Post*, 9 July 2002.

[92] Jacques Paul Klein, 'What Does It Take to Make UN Peacekeeping Operations Succeed? Reflections from the Field' (New York: Paper presented at 10th Anniversary of the Department of Peacekeeping Operations, 29 October 2002).

Arthur Vandenberg responded to an early report of the proposed figures for Marshall's initiative by suggesting that a mistake must have been made, as Congress would never appropriate that amount of money to save anybody.[93] Equally significant, however, was the multilateral nature of the assistance and the fact that it was channelled through local institutions. It is easy to overstate the level of European ownership; in private, US intervention was said to be 'frequent, often insistent'. But appearances had to be and were preserved. These appearances were bolstered by a public relations campaign that may represent the largest international propaganda operation in peacetime.[94] This use of local institutions combined with a due regard for propaganda was repeated in the reconstruction component in Afghanistan in 2002. Such genuine and tactical forms of ownership—at least in the area of economic reconstruction—have generally been more effective than mere reliance on its rhetoric.[95]

3. *The United Nations and Decolonization*

When the United Nations was established in 1945, 750 million people—approximately one-third of the world's population—lived in territories classed as non-self-governing. By the twenty-first century, fewer than one million people lived in such territories. Such a transformation was far from inevitable at the conclusion of the Second World War. Though the Atlantic Charter had proclaimed the Allies' intention to 'respect the right of all peoples to choose the form of government under which they will live',[96] Roosevelt and Churchill differed strongly on the future of the colonies. Aboard the ship on which the Atlantic Charter was signed, Roosevelt provoked Churchill on the question of Britain's colonial possessions.[97] In 1942, Churchill declared in a speech to Parliament, later affirmed at Yalta, that 'I have not become the King's First Minister in order to preside over the liquidation of the British Empire.'[98]

[93] Charles P. Kindleberger (1997) 'In the Halls of the Capitol', *Foreign Affairs*, 76(3): 185, 186.

[94] David Reynolds (1997) 'The European Response: Primacy of Politics', *Foreign Affairs*, 76(3): 171, 182–3.

[95] See Chapter Two, Section 3.1; Chapter Six, Section 2.2.

[96] Atlantic Charter, para. 3.

[97] Elliott Roosevelt, *As He Saw It* (New York: Duell, Sloan, and Pearce, 1946), 35–8.

[98] Martin Gilbert, *Winston S. Churchill, Volume 7: Road to Victory, 1941–1945* (Boston: Houghton Mifflin, 1986), 254.

The provisions in the UN Charter concerning the Trusteeship System and non-self-governing territories show that these differences were not resolved. The question of trusteeship had been omitted from the Dumbarton Oaks Proposals drafted in October 1944. When it was raised at the Yalta Conference of February 1945, Churchill suspected that the proposed UN trusteeships were a device whereby the United States would dismantle the British Empire.[99] US negotiators sought to assure him that trusteeships were not intended to apply to the Empire, but Churchill's objections led to a 'clarification' in the Conference protocol that survives largely intact as Article 77 of the Charter: trusteeships would apply only to existing League Mandates, former enemy territories, and territories voluntarily submitted to the system.[100] Other non-self-governing territories would be subject to a vaguer system of obligations for their administering powers as provided for in Article 73.

The key difference between the trust territories and the other non-self-governing territories was that the former were explicitly destined for independence. All but a handful of the island territories had achieved it by the late 1960s; the last trust territory, Palau, became independent in 1994. Non-self-governing territories, by contrast, were to remain subject to the presumably benevolent control of a colonial power. This did not stop the tide of decolonization that saw the membership of the United Nations double between 1945 and 1960. Sixteen non-self-governing territories remain, with a total population of about 700,000.

3.1. The International Trusteeship System

The United Nations Trusteeship System differed from the League of Nations Mandates System in both scope and objective. The Mandates System had confined itself solely to the colonial possessions of former enemy states; chapter XII of the UN Charter potentially applied to all colonies and dependencies. In practice, however, the Trusteeship System primarily affected territories previously held under League mandates. All Class B and C mandates, except South-West Africa, were transferred to the Trusteeship System, with Japanese mandated territories being transferred to the United States as trust territories. Although it was envisaged that additional territories might

[99] Clemens, *Yalta*, 240–3. Churchill had carefully excluded such considerations from the Atlantic Charter: ibid., 45.

[100] Declaration of Liberated Europe. Cf. UN Charter, art. 77.

be added by agreement, this only happened once, with the inclusion of Italian Somaliland in 1949.[101] (Italy's other African colonies, Libya and Eritrea, were dealt with differently: Libya achieved independence in 1952, after a brief period of assistance headed by a UN Commissioner;[102] within the same period, Eritrea was constituted as an autonomous unit federated with Ethiopia under the sovereignty of the Ethiopian Crown.[103]) A proposal to establish Jerusalem as a trust territory of the United Nations itself was never implemented.[104]

The differing objectives of the two systems were more significant. Whereas the Covenant of the League of Nations had envisaged the independence only of Class A mandates, the UN Charter abandoned such distinctions in favour of a general obligation to promote 'progressive development' towards self-government or independence, depending on the particular circumstances of each territory and 'the freely expressed wishes of the peoples concerned'. Trusteeship agreements were also more sensitive to local circumstances, and were to be agreed upon 'by the states directly concerned'—subject to approval by the General Assembly or, in the case of 'strategic areas', the Security Council.[105]

In pursuit of these objectives, the Charter created a Trusteeship Council whose general powers and occasional willingness to go against the wishes of the administering authorities distinguished its work from that of the Permanent Mandates Commission.[106] The Council's basic responsibilities were to consider reports from the administering power, to accept petitions from inhabitants, and to provide for periodic visits. The power to consider reports was augmented by a further provision enabling the Council to formulate a questionnaire on the political, economic, social, and educational advancement of the inhabitants of the trust territories, which was

[101] GA Res 289A (IV) (1949). The Trusteeship Agreement was notable for its explicit inclusion of a time limit of ten years, after which Italian Somaliland was to become independent: James N. Murray, Jr, *The United Nations Trusteeship System* (Urbana, IL: University of Illinois Press, 1957), 79–116; James Crawford, *The Creation of States in International Law* (Oxford: Clarendon Press, 1979), 428.

[102] An earlier effort to divide the territory up into three separate trust territories administered by Britain, France, and Italy was defeated in the General Assembly. See further Adrian Pelt, *Libyan Independence and the United Nations: A Case of Planned Decolonization* (New Haven, CT: Yale University Press for the Carnegie Endowment for International Peace, 1970).

[103] GA Res 390A (V) (1950).

[104] See Chapter Two, Section 1.1.2.

[105] UN Charter, arts. 76(b), 79, 83, 85.

[106] Ian Brownlie, *Principles of Public International Law*, 5th edn. (Oxford: Clarendon Press, 1998), 571.

to form the basis of an annual report to the UN General Assembly. This essentially mirrored the practice that had developed over time in the Mandates Commission, though there was a slow move towards a greater emphasis on supervision of, rather than cooperation with, the administering power.[107] The ability to receive and consider petitions from the inhabitants of trust territories also reflected earlier practice; compared with the halting and largely ineffective procedure grudgingly allowed by the Mandates Commission, however, the Trusteeship Council was relatively active.[108]

Perhaps the most important power exercised by the Trusteeship Council was through its missions to the trust territories themselves. Administering powers had rejected such a function for the Mandates System: Lord Lugard, for example, stated that it would be 'impossible for the Commission to adopt the policy of challenging the whole administration of any mandatory Power by visiting the territory in order to listen to all who criticized it. Such a course would be a signal for trouble.'[109] In the first decade of the Trusteeship Council, only one mission was sent,[110] but from 1956 the Council began sending missions more frequently, including eight to observe plebiscites or elections.[111]

The eleven territories that were administered under the Trusteeship System all achieved independence. British Togoland united with the Gold Coast, a non-self-governing territory also administered by Britain, becoming Ghana in 1957; French Togoland became Togo in 1960. Italian Somaliland joined the protectorate of British Somaliland to become independent Somalia in 1960. French Cameroons became Cameroon in 1960; it was joined the following year by the southern part of British Cameroons, the northern part of which united with Nigeria. Tanganyika became independent in 1961, uniting in 1964 with the former protectorate of Zanzibar to form Tanzania. Western Samoa (known from 1997 simply as Samoa) gained its independence in 1962, the same year that Ruanda–Urundi divided into the two

[107] UN Charter, arts. 87–8. Murray, *UN Trusteeship System*, 128–49.

[108] Wright, *Mandates*, 169–78; Murray, *UN Trusteeship System*, 150–74.

[109] Minutes of the Permanent Mandates Commission, Seventh Session (1925), 128.

[110] This was to Western Samoa in response to a petition: Murray, *UN Trusteeship System*, 175–97.

[111] These were Togoland (1956, 1958), Cameroons (1959), Western Samoa (1961), Ruanda–Urundi (1961), Northern Mariana Islands (1976), Federated States of Micronesia (1984), and Palau (1986). See Gregory H. Fox, 'The Right to Political Participation in International Law', in Gregory H. Fox and Brad R. Roth (eds.), *Democratic Governance and International Law* (Cambridge: Cambridge University Press, 2000), 48, 72 n. 126.

sovereign states of Rwanda and Burundi. Nauru became independent in 1968; New Guinea united with the non-self-governing territory of Papua to become independent Papua New Guinea in 1975. The Trust Territory of the Pacific Islands (with the exception of Palau) was dissolved in 1986, with Northern Mariana Islands becoming a commonwealth under US sovereignty and the Marshall Islands and the Federated States of Micronesia entering compacts of free association with the United States as independent countries. Palau also concluded a compact of free association with the United States in 1986, but it was not approved until 1993, entering into force the following year. The last trusteeship agreement was, therefore, terminated on 10 November 1994.[112]

By a resolution on 25 May 1994, the Trusteeship Council amended its rules of procedure to remove the obligation to meet annually, agreeing instead to meet as required.[113] Secretary-General Boutros Boutros-Ghali recommended that the Council be eliminated through a Charter amendment,[114] but Malta, among others, urged that the Trusteeship Council be recast as a forum through which member states could exercise their collective trusteeship over areas of common concern, such as the environment and the high seas.[115] There was little evidence of enthusiasm for such a move, but since the Council no longer meets, has almost no staff, and uses no UN resources there has been little impetus to shut it down.[116]

3.2. Non-Self-Governing Territories

The second category of territories considered in the UN Charter concerned territories administered by members of the United Nations

[112] SC Res 956 (1994).

[113] Trusteeship Council resolution 2200 (LXI) (1994). The Council now meets by its decision or the decision of its President, or at the request of a majority of its members or the General Assembly or the Security Council.

[114] Report of the Secretary-General on the Work of the Organization, UN Doc A/49/1 (2 September 1994), para. 46. This was reiterated in subsequent annual reports by Boutros Boutros-Ghali.

[115] See GA Res 50/55 (1995).

[116] Membership of the Council originally included the five permanent members of the Security Council, those states administering trust territories, and enough other members elected by the General Assembly for three-year terms to make an equal division between administering and non-administering countries: UN Charter, art. 86. As there are no remaining trust territories, membership currently consists only of the permanent five. The Council last met on 22 October 2002—its first meeting since 1998—to elect a president and vice-president from its five members.

and 'whose peoples have not yet attained a full measure of self-government'. Chapter XI of the Charter is entitled 'Declaration Regarding Non-Self-Governing Territories' and provides that members 'recognize the principle that the interests of the inhabitants of these territories are paramount, and accept as a sacred trust the obligation to promote to the utmost... the well-being of the inhabitants of these territories, and, to this end... to develop self-government'. In contrast to the trusteeship provisions, the Charter makes no express provision for supervision by UN organs of non-self-governing territories beyond requiring the regular submission of reports 'for information purposes'. Nevertheless, and despite the vagueness of the obligations, the General Assembly has been vigorous in pressing for implementation of the declaration.[117]

Non-self-governing territories were initially identified by a voluntary listing process by the states responsible for their administration—Australia, Belgium, France, Netherlands, New Zealand, Britain, and the United States. When Portugal and Spain joined the United Nations in 1955, however, they refused to bring any of their colonial territories within the reporting system of chapter XI. In response, the General Assembly elaborated criteria for non-self-governing territories and quickly applied them to Portuguese and Spanish colonies. The same provisions were later applied to Southern Rhodesia and certain French territories, most recently New Caledonia in 1986.[118]

The criteria were adopted in the same session that the General Assembly adopted the 1960 Declaration on the Granting of Independence to Colonial Countries and Peoples, notable for being the first major reference to self-determination as a right, rather than as a principle. Reflecting the moral and political imperatives of decolonization, the Declaration 'solemnly proclaims the necessity of bringing to a speedy and unconditional end colonialism in all its forms and manifestations'; rejecting the language of both the Mandates and Trusteeship Systems, it stated that 'inadequacy of political, economic, social or educational preparedness should never serve as a pretext for delaying independence'.[119]

[117] UN Charter, art. 73. See Brownlie, *Principles*, 572.

[118] GA Res 1541 (XV) (1960) (criteria); GA Res 1542 (XV) (1960), para. 1 (Portuguese territories), para. 5 (Spanish territories); GA Res 1747 (XVI) (1962) (Southern Rhodesia); GA Res 2069 (XX) (1965) (Condominium of New Hebrides); GA Res 2228 (XXI) (1966) (French Somaliland); GA Res 3161 (XXVIII) (1973) (Comoros); GA Res 41/41A (1986) (New Caledonia).

[119] GA Res 1514 (XV) (1960), preamble, paras. 2–3. See Hurst Hannum (1993) 'Rethinking Self-Determination', *Virginia Journal of International Law*, 34: 1.

In the following year, the General Assembly established a special committee to 'make suggestions and recommendations' on implementing the Declaration. Commonly referred to as the Special Committee of 24 on Decolonization, the Committee meets annually to discuss developments in non-self-governing territories, hears statements from appointed and elected representatives from the territories and petitioners, sends visiting missions, and organizes seminars. It is also able to disseminate information in support of decolonization. The persistence of the Committee and disputes over the extent of its competence led a number of administering powers to leave it in the early 1970s.[120]

The formal status of East Timor and Western Sahara as non-self-governing territories was important in their respective independence struggles. In East Timor's case, Portugal went so far as to bring an action against Australia in the International Court of Justice to challenge an agreement Australia had concluded with Indonesia concerning the delimitation and exploitation of East Timor's continental shelf. By concluding the 1989 agreement, Portugal alleged that Australia had infringed the right of the people of East Timor to self-determination.[121] Portugal was later a signatory to the 1999 agreement for a popular consultation on the territory's future.[122] Spain, by contrast, asserted as of 1976 that it considered itself exempt from any responsibility of an international nature in connection with Western Sahara. Nevertheless, the General Assembly asserted in 1990 that the territory's status remained a question of decolonization to be completed by the people of Western Sahara.[123] Both cases are considered further in the next chapter.

Almost all of the non-self-governing territories have now attained independence. Only sixteen territories, including Western Sahara, continue to be recognized as non-self-governing by the United Nations. Ten of these are administered by Britain: Anguilla, Bermuda, the British Virgin Islands, the Cayman Islands, the Falkland Islands (Malvinas), Gibraltar, Montserrat, Pitcairn, St Helena, and the Turks and Caicos Islands. The United States administers American Samoa,

[120] GA Res 1654 (XVI) (1961). The committee originally had seventeen members but was expanded to twenty-four in 1962.

[121] *Case Concerning East Timor (Portugal* v *Australia)* [1995] ICJ Rep 90. The Court held that it could not decide on the merits of the case without first ruling on the lawfulness of Indonesia's entry into and continuing presence in East Timor; since Indonesia was not a party to the proceedings and did not recognize the Court's jurisdiction, the Court refused to make a ruling on the matters of substance.

[122] See Chapter Two, Section 2.1.2.

[123] GA Res 45/21 (1990). See Chapter Two, Section 2.2.2.

Guam, and the US Virgin Islands; France administers New Caledonia; and New Zealand administers Tokelau. All have a population of fewer than 300,000 and, with the exception of Western Sahara and Gibraltar, all are islands.

The conflation of the categories of trusteeship and non-self-governing territories in the first decades of the United Nations reflected the simultaneous rise of the principle of self-determination and the decline of the British and other empires. By 1970, the distinction forcefully demanded by Churchill at Yalta had all but lost its relevance. The Declaration on Friendly Relations, passed by the General Assembly in 1970, affirmed the 'separate and distinct' status of a non-self-governing territory from the state administering it, which status exists 'until the people of the colony or Non-Self-Governing Territory have exercised their right of self-determination'.[124] It is arguable that non-self-governing territories should now be considered constructive trusteeships.[125]

4. Conclusion

The end of colonialism was one of the most significant transformations in the international order since the emergence of sovereign states. Though explanations of the cause of this transformation tend to focus on economic or political explanations—that the costs of colonial occupation began to outweigh the benefits for the colonial powers (and more efficient methods were found to obtain desired resources from the subject territories), or that imperial powers became overstretched—the consequences have been normative. 'Military occupation of another country against the wishes of the people of that country is internationally condemned', Julius Nyerere has written. 'This means that colonialism in the traditional and political sense is now almost a thing of the past.'[126] As Nyerere suggests, this applied not merely to colonialism but to territorial expansion through military conquest more generally. Any lessons to be drawn from the twentieth-century experience of colonialism and military occupation are, therefore, of necessarily limited application. Nevertheless, in

[124] GA Res 2625 (XXV) (1970) (Declaration on Principles of International Law concerning Friendly Relations and Co-operation among States in accordance with the Charter of the United Nations).

[125] Brad R. Roth, *Governmental Illegitimacy in International Law* (Oxford: Clarendon Press, 1999), 211–12.

[126] Julius Nyerere, 'Foreword', in Chakravarthi Raghavan, *Recolonization: GATT, the Uruguay Round, and the Third World* (London: Zed Books, 1990), 19.

addition to the historical background they provide to contemporary efforts in transitional administration, two broad themes that emerged in this period are of ongoing relevance.

First, the dismantling of the colonial system through the twentieth century was accompanied by the halting development of institutions to supervise this process. The more significant institutional changes were driven less by the European colonial powers themselves than by pressure from the United States and newly independent former colonies. Acceptance of the Mandates and Trusteeship Systems depended on clear acknowledgement of the interests at stake—hence the limitation of both systems to the colonies of defeated states, while the separate category of non-self-governing territories was created in large part for the benefit of the British Empire. This pragmatic assessment of interests was also reflected in the hesitation with which power was granted to multilateral institutions: concerns about the competence of such institutions were typically outweighed by concerns that the multilateral approach might constrain pursuit of the interests at stake.

Second, throughout this process there remained significant ambivalence as to the recognition that should be accorded to the subject populations. The Mandates System provided minimal opportunity for local voices to reach the supervisory institutions; it appears that the UN Trusteeship System was intended to be no more powerful. Even so, the limited powers to formulate questionnaires and consider reports, to accept petitions from inhabitants, and to undertake periodic visits represented a greater level of accountability (at least in principle) than was available to the populations of Bosnia, Kosovo, or East Timor in the 1990s. Against this, the project to rebuild Germany serves as a useful contrast to the conventional wisdom that 'ownership' on the part of the local population is a necessary element for success in post-conflict reconstruction. In the early years of the occupation, German political participation was a low priority,[127] there was no question of active involvement in the administration of justice,[128] and direct engagement in the Marshall Plan did not begin until opposition to

[127] This was a point of contention between the US Departments of War and State, with the latter advocating greater involvement of the local population. See Tan, 'Idea Factories'.

[128] German officials did play a significant role in sector-level tribunals (*Spruchkammern*) under the supervision of the respective occupying powers. See Earl F. Ziemke, *The US Army in the Occupation of Germany, 1944–1946* (Washington, DC: Center of Military History, 1975), 445–6; Edward N. Peterson, *The American Occupation of Germany: Retreat to Victory* (Detroit: Wayne State University Press, 1977), 340–1.

the Soviet Union overtook denazification as the political focus of the occupation. Germany nevertheless emerged, eventually, as a robust member of the international community.

As a lesson for future application, however, the Allied occupation is of limited value. The circumstances in which Nazi Germany fell under Allied control—unconditional surrender, with the ideology of the former elite utterly discredited—were exceptional. Germany also provided a more technologically advanced basis for reconstruction than most comparable situations of transitional administration. In development terms, there was a great deal of 'capacity' whereas a central problem of such operations is often capacity-building.[129] Most importantly, however, military occupation by the forces of a state or group of states is today generally deemed unacceptable, without at least a mandate from the Security Council and a civilian presence legitimated through some form of multilateral arrangement. Though plans for a US-led military government in Iraq modelled on the US occupation of Japan were leaked in October 2002, the Bush administration quickly distanced itself from the reports. In particular, Bush offered assurances that the United States would 'never seek to impose our culture or our form of government' on another nation.[130] Less than a month before the commencement of hostilities, Bush made a more direct comparison with the reconstruction of Germany, arguing that the United States 'has made and kept this kind of commitment before—in the peace that followed a world war. After defeating enemies, we did not leave behind occupying armies, we left constitutions and parliaments. We established an atmosphere of safety, in which responsible, reform-minded local leaders could build lasting institutions of freedom.'[131] The implications of this return to the language of occupation are considered in Chapter Eight.

Similarly, comparisons between modern transitional administrations and former colonies are generally frowned upon. International representatives regularly dismiss local political leaders in the Balkans as 'immature'—an adjective that would never have been used in East Timor as it would almost certainly be interpreted as racist. There are, occasionally, calls to revive the Trusteeship Council in order to provide an institutional or normative basis for the United Nations to exercise quasi-governmental authority over territory.

[129] See Chapter Eight, Section 1.3.

[130] David E. Sanger, 'Bush Says US Won't Force Its Ways on a Beaten Iraq', *New York Times*, 12 October 2002.

[131] George W. Bush, 'President Discusses the Future of Iraq' (Washington, DC, 26 February 2003), available at www.whitehouse.gov.

As the Charter specifically prohibits the Trusteeship System from applying to members of the United Nations, it would require a Charter amendment.[132] This seems unlikely.

The political constraints on these historical analogies are, of course, closely connected to the normative developments that led to the abolition of colonialism. But the failure to learn from these past experiences—and, on occasion, to accept that being 'colonial' may be a necessary evil in the temporary exercise of power over territory—leads to a measure of doublethink on the part of administering authorities. In particular, not acknowledging the interests at stake in the creation of recent transitional administrations sometimes gives rise to dubious claims of altruism on the part of international actors. Meanwhile, disingenuous assertions that local 'ownership' is central to the success of an operation ignore the political circumstances that required international administration of the territory at the outset.[133]

It is in this sense that contemporary transitional administrations might benefit from being more, not less, colonial—even as that relationship is regarded as a temporary if necessary evil. Lord Lugard's suspicions of 'pure philanthropy' remain salient today: the recognition and accommodation of interests on the part of local and international actors continue to be central to the project of transformation, which justifies this modern colonial enterprise in post-conflict territories.

132 UN Charter, art. 78. See further Chapter Two, Section 1.2.
133 See further Chapter Eight, Section 1.1.

2

Power and Change: The Evolution of United Nations Complex Peace Operations

> The United Nations is, for good reasons, reluctant to assume responsibility for maintaining law and order, nor can it impose a new political structure or new state institutions.
>
> Boutros Boutros-Ghali, 3 January 1995[1]

The power of the United Nations Security Council to administer territory is not mentioned in the UN Charter. Nor, however, is peace-keeping, the formula that came to define UN military activities. Here, as in many other areas of the Council's activities, practice has led theory and the Charter has been shown to be a flexible—some would say malleable—instrument.[2]

This chapter considers the different political contexts within which transitional administrations have been authorized by the Council. First, it will review the nature of this evolution in Council practice. The term 'evolution' is used advisedly, suggesting a process of natural selection inspired by essentially unpredictable events. Second, the chapter will briefly sketch out the context for each of the major operations in this area. Analysis of these operations tends to be chronological, reflecting the transformations over time of policy in this area. It is

[1] *Supplement to An Agenda for Peace: Position Paper of the Secretary-General on the Occasion of the Fiftieth Anniversary of the United Nations*, UN Doc A/50/60–S/1995/1 (3 January 1995), para. 14.

[2] Cf. James Crawford, 'The Charter of the United Nations as a Constitution', in Hazel Fox (ed.), *The Changing Constitution of the United Nations* (London: British Institute of International and Comparative Law, 1997), 1.

instructive, however, to look instead at the discrete reasons for which the Council has authorized different forms of transitional administration. Third, the very different responsibilities of the United Nations in Afghanistan and Iraq will be considered as a possible correction to the trend towards ever-expanding mandates identified here.

An underlying tension to be examined is that between the increased *civilian* responsibilities of UN operations and the reluctance to entrust the United Nations with *military* command outside of traditional peacekeeping.[3] It is frequently argued that unified command of both civilian and military components increases the chances for success of such missions and that the lack of unified command has compromised them. In the Balkans, for example, divided responsibilities led to inconsistent policies on law and order, including the reluctance to pursue war crimes suspects; in Afghanistan the military objectives of US forces occasionally put them directly at odds with the political objectives of the UN civilian mission. These increased civilian responsibilities continue to be handled largely by the UN Department of Peacekeeping Operations (DPKO)—suggesting the extent to which the organizational structure of the United Nations has been forced to adapt to its new role. More broadly, these developments may herald a transformation in the politics of peacebuilding: just as the Council now provides legal authorization only for those enforcement actions that coincide with the willingness of certain key states to lead a military operation, it is possible that transitional administrations will be used to consolidate the peace as those key states move on to other battles.

1. Security Council Administration of Territory in Theory and in Practice

Council action in the area of transitional administration has been characterized by reaction and improvisation. This, together with the highly sensitive nature of the Kosovo conflict in particular, has hampered efforts to develop best practices for such operations or plan for future contingencies. In the same year that the Kosovo mission was established, for example, the United Nations conducted the referendum on East Timor's independence from Indonesia. Though many outsiders predicted a landslide vote in favour of independence and the probable outbreak of violence, the staff within the Secretariat were unable (or believed themselves unable) to prepare for post-referendum

[3] See Chapter Three, Section 1.

contingencies that presumed the bad faith of the Indonesian security forces. An additional barrier to the development of best practices is that the success of certain past operations—notably the Transitional Administration for Eastern Slavonia (UNTAES)—is often closely connected to ultimately political questions, notably of formulating the mandate and exercising command and control over the military component of a mission. This section considers the legal basis for the Council's authority in this area before moving on to the political context of the recent spate of operations.

1.1. The Power of the Council to Administer Territory

That the Security Council might be required to administer a state or territory was, in fact, contemplated in the drafting of the UN Charter. At the San Francisco Conference that led to the adoption of the Charter in 1945, Norway proposed to amend the chapter VII enforcement powers of the Council to provide that it should, in special cases, temporarily assume the administration of a territory if administration by the occupant state itself represented a threat to the peace.[4] This was withdrawn out of a concern that including such specific powers might be interpreted as suggesting that other powers not listed were implicitly excluded.[5]

In 1947, the possibility of Council administration swiftly assumed practical significance in two cases: the Free Territory of Trieste and Jerusalem. In the event, neither proposal was implemented. As with most of the Council's powers, transitional administration remained largely an intriguing prospect until after the conclusion of the cold war. And, as with the Council's activities in other areas, the manner in which this power has subsequently been exercised departed substantially from what was envisaged when the Charter was drafted.

1.1.1. Free Territory of Trieste, 1947 (Never Implemented) Trieste, like Danzig, is an ancient port city that has enjoyed many masters. Long under Austrian rule, Trieste preserved cultural and linguistic ties with Italy and was included in the secret 1915 Treaty of London by which Italy joined with the Allies against the Central Powers in the First World War. The Italian claim to the territory was explicitly acknowledged in President Woodrow Wilson's 'Fourteen Points' speech, which stated that a 'readjustment of the frontiers of Italy

4 (1945) 3 UNCIO 365, 371–2, Doc 2G/7 (n)(1).
5 (1945) 12 UNCIO 353–5, Doc 539 III/3/24.

should be effected along clearly recognizable lines of nationality'.[6] Italy duly annexed Trieste along with the rest of the Istrian Peninsula (including the western territories of what is now Slovenia), with its claim recognized by the Kingdom of the Serbs, Croats, and Slovenes (later Yugoslavia) in the 1920 Treaty of Rapallo.[7] Here the border remained until Italy joined Germany in invading Yugoslavia in 1941. After the conclusion of the Second World War, Trieste was once more on the negotiating table. Yugoslavia, which had succeeded in occupying Trieste, was persuaded to accept an agreement for an Allied Military Government to administer 'Zone A' (comprising the city, the port, and a few small villages) on a provisional basis.[8] A Yugoslav Military Government was given control of 'Zone B' (comprising a larger rural area east of Trieste proper inhabited mainly by Slovenes).[9] The border between the two occupation zones, named the 'Morgan Line' after General Sir Frederick Morgan, lay at the heart of what came to be called the Trieste Problem.

The failure of various conferences to reach a satisfactory resolution led to the suggestion that, as in the case of Danzig, Trieste be constituted as a 'free territory'.[10] Though the initial proposal by the French Foreign Minister Georges Bidault had been to limit the period of administration to ten years, the 1947 Treaty of Peace with Italy included as an annex the 'Permanent Statute of the Free Territory of Trieste'. In a provision that distinguished it from Danzig, the Statute provided that the Free Territory's 'integrity and independence shall be assured by the Security Council of the United Nations', which was required to: *(a)* ensure the observance of the present Statute and in particular the protection of the basic human rights of the inhabitants; and *(b)* ensure the maintenance of public order and security in the Free Territory. The Statute also provided that the Council would appoint a Governor, who should not be a citizen of Italy, Yugoslavia, or the Free Territory, and would be paid by the United Nations. The Governor was given a right of review over all legislation and wide

6 Woodrow Wilson, 'Fourteen Points' (Address to a Joint Session of Congress, 8 January 1918), available at www.yale.edu/lawweb/avalon/wilson14.htm. See Chapter One, Section 1.1.

7 Treaty of Rapallo, Kingdom of the Serbs, Croats, and Slovenes–Italy, done at Rapallo, 12 November 1920, 18 LNTS 388.

8 Agreement for the Provisional Administration of Venezia Giulia, Yugoslavia–United Kingdom–United States, done at Belgrade, 9 June 1945, 59 Stat 1855, available at www.yale.edu/lawweb/avalon/wwii/venezia.htm.

9 Méir Ydit, *Internationalised Territories: From the 'Free City of Cracow' to the 'Free City of Berlin'* (Leyden: A. W. Sythoff, 1961), 238.

10 Ibid., 240.

'Special Powers', including the right to assume control of the security services. The Statute—effectively an interim constitution—balanced this by granting the popularly elected Assembly the right to petition the Security Council directly on the exercise of these powers.[11]

The powers of the Governor of the Free Territory went far beyond those granted to the League of Nations High Commissioner in Danzig,[12] but are comparable to those later conferred on special representatives of the Secretary-General in Eastern Slavonia, Kosovo, and East Timor. What remains unusual, however, are the human rights obligations that were imposed directly upon the Council with respect to Trieste and the effective right of appeal to the Council made available to the inhabitants through their elected representatives. These obligations had been explicitly accepted by the Council,[13] but Trieste was soon caught up in the geopolitics of the cold war and the failure to agree upon appointment of a governor prevented the operation of the Statute. The proposed solution to the Trieste Problem thus remained hypothetical. Its temporary situation became permanent under the 1954 London Agreement, which provided that Zones A and B—still administered by Allied and Yugoslav Military Governments—should, with minor rectifications, be apportioned to Italy and Yugoslavia, respectively.[14]

1.1.2. The Statute of Jerusalem, 1947 (Never Implemented) The internationalization of some or all of Israel and Palestine was considered at various points in the twentieth century and continues to be discussed in some plans for the creation of a viable Palestinian state.[15] The most concerted early effort began in 1947 but was swiftly overtaken by events.[16]

The proposal came in the form of a report of the UN Special Committee on Palestine (UNSCOP), which recommended the termination of the British Mandate over Palestine in favour of a two-state solution—an Arab state and a Jewish state—with Jerusalem established

[11] Treaty of Peace with Italy, done at Paris, 10 February 1947, 49 UNTS 126, Annex VI, arts. 2, 11, 17, 19, 21, 22.

[12] See Chapter One, Section 1.2.2.

[13] SC Res 16 (1947).

[14] Memorandum of Understanding Regarding the Free Territory of Trieste, Italy–United Kingdom–United States–Yugoslavia, done at London, 5 October 1954. See Ydit, *Internationalised Territories*, 256–69. This was formalized in the Treaty Between the Socialist Federal Republic of Yugoslavia and Italy, done at Osimo, 10 November 1975.

[15] For a brief discussion of the Sykes–Picot Agreement of 1916, see Chapter One, Section 1.1.

[16] See generally Ydit, *Internationalised Territories*, 273–315.

as a *corpus separatum* [separate entity] under an international regime and administered by the United Nations.[17] This was subsequently endorsed by the General Assembly, which envisaged termination of the British Mandate by 1 August 1948 and called on the Trusteeship Council to prepare a Statute for the City of Jerusalem.[18] The Trusteeship Council duly completed a draft on 21 April 1948, but the outbreak of hostilities in May 1948 prevented further action to implement the plan.

The Statute was unusual in that the internationalization of Jerusalem was not merely intended to prevent conflict between its residents. The preamble to the Statute explained its purpose as being to 'foster and preserve the unique spiritual and religious interests located in the City of the three great monotheistic faiths throughout the world, the Christian, the Jewish, and Moslem, to this end to ensure that order and peace, and especially religious peace reign in Jerusalem'. The more worldly operative articles provided that the Trusteeship Council would discharge the obligations of the United Nations in administering the city by appointing a Governor, who would have control of internal security and external affairs. The Statute contained extensive provision for the protection of the 'Holy Places', as well as provisions on human rights, appointment of a local judiciary, citizenship, and the creation of an 'Economic Union of Palestine'. It was to come into force two months after the evacuation of British troops from the former Mandate and to remain in force for ten years, after which it would be re-examined by the Trusteeship Council. At that point, the Trusteeship Council would lay down the procedure for a referendum by which the residents of the city could express their wishes as to possible modifications of the international regime.[19]

Given the apparent enmity between the Jewish and Arab peoples in the area, the powers of the Governor were even greater than those accorded to the proposed Governor of Trieste.[20] Where the latter exercised a powerful review over the local exercise of power and could assert executive powers if the situation required it, the Governor of Jerusalem was to exercise executive power on a day-to-day basis, from conducting external affairs down to proposing the budget. Though Jerusalem was to be administered under the Trusteeship Council instead of the Security Council, the city's local representative bodies

17 UN Special Committee on Palestine Report to the General Assembly, UN Doc A/364 (31 August 1947).

18 GA Res 181 (II) (1947).

19 Trusteeship Council resolution 34 (II) (1948); [Draft] Statute of Jerusalem, UN Doc T/118 Rev. 2 (21 April 1948).

20 See Section 1.1.1 in this chapter.

would have enjoyed a right of petition to the supervising organ of the United Nations. This was comparable to the petitioning processes available to peoples in trust territories—a formal mechanism to examine the exercise of power in the name of the United Nations that has been lacking in more recent operations.[21]

War on the ground and opposition from both sides did not remove the question from the UN agenda. In December 1949 the General Assembly reiterated its intention to place Jerusalem under an international regime, referring the 'Statute' problem back to the Trusteeship Council.[22] The impossibility of progress without cooperation from either Israel or Jordan (which had formally incorporated those parts of Palestine under its occupation) led the Trusteeship Council in turn to refer it back to the Assembly in 1950. By this time, however, the Soviet Bloc had removed its support for internationalization and the resolution failed to get the necessary two-thirds support. The matter subsequently disappeared from the agenda, though variations on internationalization are still proposed from time to time.[23]

1.2. *Reaction and Improvisation*

There is now little doubt that the Security Council possesses the power to administer territory on a temporary basis and that it may delegate that power to the Secretary-General (or his or her representative).[24] Early objections had been voiced when the Council initially undertook its obligations in Trieste—notably by the representative of Australia, who abstained on the relevant resolution on the grounds that the Council lacked the authority to exercise such governmental functions.[25] Secretary-General Trygve Lie argued then that the Council enjoyed a broad power to maintain peace and security under Article 24 of the Charter, a position that was accepted at the time by the other Council members and subsequently endorsed by the

[21] See Chapter Four.

[22] GA Res 303 (IV) (1949).

[23] Ydit, *Internationalised Territories*, 306–8. See, e.g. Herb Keinon, 'Germany's New Ambassador Missteps on Jerusalem', *Jerusalem Post*, 10 August 2000.

[24] Danesh Sarooshi, *The United Nations and the Development of Collective Security: The Delegation by the UN Security Council of its Chapter VII Powers* (Oxford: Clarendon Press, 1999), 59–63.

[25] SC Res 16 (1947). See further Hans Kelsen, *The Law of the United Nations* (London: Stevens & Sons, 1950), 825–36.

International Court of Justice.[26] Recent practice in Eastern Slavonia, Kosovo, and East Timor suggests that this power is now an accepted arrow in the very limited quiver with which the Council may respond to threats to international peace and security.

Acceptance in practice, however, has not meant acceptance in theory. The lack of an institutional capacity to respond to the demands of transitional administration has left the United Nations relying on a variety of structures built around a core of peacekeeping personnel. The different operations have, thus, adopted idiosyncratic mission structures that reflect the varying capacities of the regional organizations and UN agencies involved in each situation. It is occasionally argued that some form of structural change in the UN system would enable it to respond more effectively to such challenges in the future. Reviving the Trusteeship Council, which suspended operations in 1994,[27] is sometimes mentioned in this regard—most prominently by the International Commission on Intervention and State Sovereignty. Its report, *The Responsibility to Protect*, suggests that a 'constructive adaptation' of chapter XII of the Charter might provide useful guidelines for the behaviour of administering authorities.[28] For the Trusteeship Council to provide more than guidance, however, would require a Charter amendment, as Article 78 explicitly prevents the Trusteeship System from applying to territories that are members of the United Nations.[29] In any case, the direct associations with colonialism would be politically prohibitive for the reasons discussed earlier.[30]

More general political barriers to any such institutional changes were implicit in the Brahimi Report on UN Peace Operations. Despite the 'evident ambivalence' among member states and within the UN Secretariat, the Report noted that the circumstances that demand such operations were likely to recur:

> Thus, the Secretariat faces an unpleasant dilemma: to assume that transitional administration is a transitory responsibility, not prepare for additional

[26] (1947) 2 SCOR, No 3, 44; *Legal Consequences for States of the Continued Presence of South Africa in Namibia (South West Africa) Notwithstanding Security Council Resolution 276 (1970) (Advisory Opinion)*[1971] ICJ Rep 16.

[27] See Chapter One, Section 3.1.

[28] International Commission on Intervention and State Sovereignty, The Responsibility to Protect (Ottawa: International Development Research Centre, December 2001), available at www.iciss.gc.ca, paras. 5.22–5.24. The Commission was established by the Government of Canada in 2000 to seek consensus on the question of humanitarian intervention. Its co-chairs were Gareth Evans and Mohamed Sahnoun.

[29] UN Charter, art. 78.

[30] See Chapter One.

missions and do badly if it is once again flung into the breach, or to prepare well and be asked to undertake them more often because it is well prepared. Certainly, if the Secretariat anticipates future transitional administrations as the rule rather than the exception, then a dedicated and distinct responsibility centre for those tasks must be created somewhere within the United Nations system. In the interim, [the Department of Peacekeeping Operations] has to continue to support this function.[31]

This was not the subject of any recommendation and was not addressed in the Secretary-General's response to the Report.[32]

It seems probable, then, that any institutional reforms within the United Nations will be incremental, driven by the exigencies of circumstance rather than institutional or doctrinal development. The next section turns, therefore, to an examination of the conditions that have led to the creation of transitional administrations in practice.

2. *Forms of Transition*

In the growing literature on transitional administration, categorization and subdivision of the powers exercised tend to predominate. Michael Doyle, for example, divides the various forms of what he terms 'ad hoc semisovereign mechanisms' into four categories according to the power exercised: *supervisory authority* (East Timor, Kosovo, and Brcko in Bosnia and Herzegovina), *executive authority* (Eastern Slavonia, Bosnia after the assertion of the Bonn Powers from 1997, and Liberia under ECOMOG), *administrative authority* (Mozambique, Cambodia, Bosnia from 1995–7, Western Sahara, and Somalia under UNOSOM II—one might add the UN Relief and Works Agency (UNRWA) in the Occupied Territories), and a range of *monitoring* operations (this would include the formal powers given to the United Nations in Afghanistan).[33] Other categorizations, such as the different 'generations' of peacekeeping—the second and third

[31] Report of the Panel on United Nations Peace Operations (Brahimi Report), UN Doc A/55/305–S/2000/809 (21 August 2000), available at www.un.org/peace/reports/peace_operations, para. 78.

[32] Report of the Secretary-General on the Implementation of the Report of the Panel on United Nations Peace Operations, UN Doc A/55/502 (20 October 2000).

[33] Michael W. Doyle, 'War-Making and Peace-Making: The United Nations' Post-Cold War Record', in Chester A. Crocker, Fen Osler Hampson, and Pamela Aall (eds.), *Turbulent Peace: The Challenges of Managing International Conflict* (Washington, DC: United States Institute of Peace Press, 2001), 529. Jarat Chopra also adopts four categories of 'transitional authority' operations, but they are subtly different: *governorship*, where the United Nations

of which were, confusingly, born within a matter of months—are possible.[34]

More important than the amount of power exercised, however, is its purpose and trajectory. Categorizing operations according to the amount of civilian power given to the special representative is a useful taxonomical exercise for analysing the capacities of the United Nations, but in terms of understanding the missions themselves it is comparable to categorizing peacekeeping operations by the number of troops deployed. Such an approach may help develop best practices for the logistical difficulties of large deployments, but it does not help in determining the appropriateness of such deployments for the different types of circumstances that may arise in the future. Within the limited experience of transitional administrations, this leads to an overemphasis on the administration rather than its transitional nature. Indeed, though Kosovo and East Timor are comparable in terms of the powers transferred to the special representative in each case, the assumption of their similarity as operations was one of the major mistakes made on the ground when the United Nations deployed in East Timor.

In this section, the various operations will be considered by reference to the local political context within which they operated. Five categories will be used, though it would be possible to consider the missions through different lenses:

(1) the final act of decolonization leading to independence;
(2) temporary administration of territory pending peaceful transfer of control to an existing government;
(3) temporary administration of a state pending the holding of elections;
(4) interim administration as part of an ongoing peace process without an end state;
(5) de facto administration or responsibility for basic law and order in the absence of governing authority.

assumes direct governmental authority; *control*, involving deployment of UN personnel throughout existing state institutions to exercise direct control; *partnership*, where the UN mission acts as an equal partner in administering still coherent institutions; and *assistance*, where a state administration continues to function: Jarat Chopra, 'Introducing Peace-Maintenance', in Jarat Chopra (ed.), *The Politics of Peace-Maintenance* (Boulder, CO: Lynne Rienner, 1998), 1, 13–14.

34 See Chapter Eight, Section 1.

2.1. Decolonization

Decolonization is, perhaps, the simplest context within which a transitional administration may operate. This is not to suggest that the transformation of a former colony into a functioning state is a simple task, but the clarity of the endpoint and the universal acceptance of the desirability of this outcome avoid many of the problems that have plagued other missions.

Though such comparisons are politically fraught, the task of the United Nations in such a situation may be compared to that of an administering authority under the Trusteeship System. The basic goals of that system, as articulated in the Charter, were to further international peace and security; to promote the political, economic, social, and educational advancement of the inhabitants with a view to achieving self-government or independence; and to encourage respect for human rights.[35] One of the first occasions in which the United Nations was called upon to exercise quasi-governmental powers was in the course of facilitating the independence of Namibia in 1989–90—a former mandate known until 1968 as South-West Africa.

Relative simplicity at the level of global norms has, on occasion, led to false assumptions of simplicity at the local level. In East Timor, for example, it was taken for granted by the expatriate expert community that the territory in late 1999 was a political and economic vacuum. Economically, this might have been true; politically, however, the situation was more complex. Though the basic aim of transferring power to a broadly representative government was clear, consultation with local actors proceeded fitfully and the lack of local capacity undermined efforts to 'Timorize' the institutions of government.

The operations in West New Guinea (Papua) and Western Sahara also took place in the context of the withdrawal of European colonial powers. Despite commitments to respect the right of self-determination of the respective inhabitants, however, these operations are more properly considered as facilitating the transfer of territory from one power to another.

2.1.1. Namibia, 1989–1990 The UN Transitional Assistance Group (UNTAG) began operations in 1989, but was created by the United Nations over a decade earlier. Security Council resolution 385 (1976), '*Reaffirming* the legal responsibility of the United Nations over Namibia', declared that 'in order that the people of Namibia may be

[35] UN Charter, art. 76. See further Chapter One, Section 3.1.

enabled freely to determine their own future, it is imperative that free elections under the supervision and control of the United Nations be held for the whole of Namibia'.[36] The 'legal responsibility' of the United Nations referred to UN Council for Namibia, created by the General Assembly in 1967 as the legal administrator of the territory.[37] Following the conclusion of the Second World War, South Africa had refused to transfer the mandate to the new UN Trusteeship System and purported to integrate the territory into its own. This was rejected by the General Assembly and led to the anomalous situation of a League mandate continuing past the demise of the League itself.[38]

In 1978, a 'Western Contact Group' (Britain, Canada, France, Germany, and the United States) issued a proposal to implement resolution 385 (1976), calling for a large United Nations presence.[39] Secretary-General Kurt Waldheim drew upon these recommendations in a report to the Security Council, endorsed in resolution 435 (1978), in which the Council established UNTAG for a period of up to twelve months in order to bring about the early independence of Namibia through free elections under the supervision and control of the United Nations.[40]

South Africa's refusal to accept UNTAG prevented its deployment for over a decade. This long delay enabled more time for preparation than is generally possible for such missions. For example, Special Representative Martti Ahtisaari was able to visit Namibia a number of times to determine the logistical requirements of UNTAG and began recruiting and training officials for the job long before UNTAG deployed.

[36] SC Res 385 (1976), para. 7. See generally David Lush, *Last Steps to Uhuru: An Eye-Witness Account of Namibia's Transition to Independence* (Windhoek: New Namibia Books, 1993); Lionel Cliffe, *The Transition to Independence in Namibia* (Boulder, CO: Lynne Rienner, 1994); Laurent C. W. Kaela, *The Question of Namibia* (London: Macmillan, 1996); Roger Hearn, *UN Peacekeeping in Action: The Namibian Experience* (Commack, NY: Nova Science, 1999).

[37] GA Res 2248 (S-V) (1967). Among other things, the Council for Namibia in 1982 ratified the International Convention on the Elimination of All Forms of Racial Discrimination as the Administering Authority of Namibia. See GA Res 38/21 (1983).

[38] See Chapter One, Section 1.1.

[39] Letter dated 10 April 1978 from the representatives of Canada, Germany, France, the United Kingdom, and the United States to the President of the Security Council, 33 SCOR (Supp. for April, May, and June), UN Doc S/12636 (10 April 1978).

[40] Report of the Secretary-General submitted pursuant to para. 2 of Security Council resolution 431 (1978) concerning the situation in Namibia (UNTAG Plan), 33 SCOR (Supp. for July, August, and September), UN Doc S/12827 (29 August 1978); SC Res 435 (1978), para. 3.

One reason for the delay was the linkage that South Africa established between the withdrawal of its troops from Namibia and the removal of Cuban troops from Angola. In late 1988, South Africa, Angola, and Cuba agreed that UNTAG would deploy in Namibia on 1 April 1989, with the UN Angola Verification Mission (UNAVEM) moving into Angola at the same time to monitor Cuba's withdrawal.[41]

Elections were held on 7–11 November 1989, with a high turnout, no violence, and ballot secrecy preserved. The South-West African People's Organization (SWAPO) gained 57 per cent of the vote and forty-one of the seventy-two seats in the new constituent assembly. SWAPO's main rival, the South African-sponsored Democratic Turnhalle Alliance, received twenty-one seats, with the remainder going to five small parties. The members of the Constituent Assembly met for the first time on 21 November to begin drafting a constitution; under the UN plan this required a two-thirds majority. Eighty days later, the assembly adopted the new constitution by consensus. Namibia became independent on 21 March 1990.

As Western Sahara shows, a long lead-time is in itself insufficient to guarantee success.[42] A second important element was the certainty as to the political outcome—independence—at the conclusion of the mission. This was also key to the political success of the far more ambitious state-building exercise in East Timor.

2.1.2. East Timor (Timor-Leste), 1999–2002 Some years after East Timor (now Timor-Leste) voted overwhelmingly for independence from Indonesia, it is still difficult to understand the violence that consumed the island in September 1999. What is confusing is that unrest before the vote was both sporadic and, it seemed, controllable. When pressure was placed on the Indonesian Armed Forces (TNI), the limited instances of intimidation stopped. Moreover, there was little trouble on the day of the vote itself. If the intention had been to prevent East Timor's independence, this could have been achieved easily by killing a few UN Volunteers, or burning down some of the buildings used by expatriates.

With the benefit of hindsight, two key factors were at work. The first was that most of the Indonesian cabinet, relying on remarkably

41 Agreement Among the People's Republic of Angola, the Republic of Cuba, and the Republic of South Africa, 22 December 1988, 28 ILM 957. See Steven R. Ratner, *The New UN Peacekeeping: Building Peace in Lands of Conflict After the Cold War* (New York: St Martin's Press, 1996), 118.

42 See Section 2.2.2 in this chapter.

bad intelligence, genuinely believed that in a free vote the Timorese would choose to remain within Indonesia (or, perhaps, that the result would be close enough to dispute). Officials at the United Nations and in concerned governments anticipated precisely the opposite result, but were constrained from planning openly for independence by the delicate political balance that had made a vote possible in the first place. This set the stage for a very swift transition, with little planning for either the logistics of independence or management of the inevitable political crisis it would cause within Indonesia. The second factor was the erroneous assumption on the part of most international actors that the Indonesian government and military could be assumed to work in concert. Quite apart from the dubious reliance placed on Indonesia's occupying forces to maintain 'peace and security' during the vote, there appears to have been great reluctance within the TNI to leave the battleground—sometimes described as Indonesia's Vietnam—as anything other than scorched earth.

Many of the Timorese, by contrast, appear to have known precisely what was going to happen. Across the island there were reports of entire towns packing their belongings and leaving in anticipation of the violence to come. One UN observer in Maliana reported a day before the vote that his entire town had disappeared, only to find people streaming back from the hillsides from 4 a.m. to queue up, vote, and depart once more.[43]

The origins of the complex role played by the United Nations in East Timor lie in Indonesia's 1975 invasion of the former Portuguese colony. Since the purported annexation of East Timor by Indonesia was never explicitly recognized by the vast majority of governments (Australia's recognition in 1978 was a notable exception), it is questionable what legitimate interest Indonesia had in the territory's transition to independence.[44] In practice, however, East Timor's independence only became possible following the replacement of Indonesian President Suharto by B. J. Habibie, who offered to hold a plebiscite on the territory's future. An agreement dated 5 May 1999, between Indonesia and Portugal (as the administering power of a

[43] See generally Paul Hainsworth and Stephen McCloskey (eds.), *The East Timor Question: The Struggle for Independence from Indonesia* (London: I. B. Tauris, 2000); Damien Kingsbury (ed.), *Guns and Ballot Boxes: East Timor's Vote for Independence* (Clayton: Monash Asia Institute, 2000); United Nations, *The United Nations and East Timor: Self-Determination Through Popular Consultation* (New York: UN Department of Public Information, 2000).

[44] See Antonio Cassese, *Self-Determination of Peoples: A Legal Reappraisal* (Cambridge: Cambridge University Press, 1995), 223–30.

non-self-governing territory), provided for a 'popular consultation' to be held on East Timor's future on 8 August of the same year.[45]

The date of the consultation fell squarely in the middle of Indonesia's first presidential elections in forty-four years. Crucially, the agreement left security arrangements in the hands of Indonesia's military—the very forces that had actively suppressed the East Timorese population for twenty-four years. On 11 June 1999, the Security Council established the UN Mission in East Timor (UNAMET) to organize and conduct the consultation.[46] A month later, with the consultation postponed until the end of August, the Secretary-General reported to the Council that 'the situation in East Timor will be rather delicate as the Territory prepares for the implementation of the result of the popular consultation, whichever it may be'.[47] Despite threats of violence, 98 per cent of registered East Timorese voted in the referendum, with 78.5 per cent choosing independence.[48]

The violence that followed took place under the direction of the Indonesian military, if not the government itself.[49] At the time there was great reluctance within the international community to intervene, despite the apparent double standard given the international response to the situation in Kosovo. There seems to have been no legal basis for requiring Indonesia's consent to such an operation. Nevertheless, as a practical matter, it was clear that no form of enforcement action would have been possible without it. A fortuitously timed

[45] Agreement on the Question of East Timor, Indonesia–Portugal, done at New York, 5 May 1999, UN Doc S/1999/513, Annex I; Agreement Regarding the Modalities for the Popular Consultation of the East Timorese Through a Direct Ballot, Indonesia–Portugal–Secretary-General of the United Nations, done at New York, 5 May 1999, UN Doc S/1999/513, Annex II; East Timor Popular Consultation (Security Provisions), Indonesia–Portugal–Secretary-General of the United Nations, done at New York, 5 May 1999, UN Doc S/1999/513, Annex III.

[46] SC Res 1246 (1999).

[47] Question of East Timor: Report of the Secretary-General, UN Doc S/1999/862 (9 August 1999), para. 5.

[48] The East Timorese were asked to vote on the following question: 'Do you accept the proposed special autonomy for East Timor within the unitary state of the Republic of Indonesia? or, Do you reject the proposed special autonomy for East Timor, leading to East Timor's separation from Indonesia?' See generally Ian Martin, *Self-Determination in East Timor: The United Nations, the Ballot, and International Intervention* (Boulder, CO: Lynne Rienner, 2001).

[49] The Security Council mission to Dili and Jakarta included analysis by UNAMET that the violence was 'nothing less than a systematic implementation of a "scorched earth" policy in East Timor, under the direction of the Indonesian military', UN Doc S/1999/976, Annex, para. 1.

meeting of the Asia Pacific Economic Cooperation Forum (APEC) in Auckland, New Zealand, enabled political and economic pressure to be brought to bear on Indonesia, and resolution 1264 (1999) welcomed a 12 September statement by the Indonesian President that expressed the readiness of Indonesia to accept an international peacekeeping force through the United Nations in East Timor.[50] Australia—driven by domestic political pressure, concern about a refugee crisis, and some measure of contrition for its previous policies on East Timor—offered to lead the force and on 15 September the Security Council authorized the International Force in East Timor (INTERFET) to restore peace and security to the territory.[51]

This was followed on 25 October by resolution 1272 (1999), establishing the UN Transitional Administration in East Timor (UNTAET). A persistent, if slightly unfair, criticism of UNTAET is that it relied too greatly on the experiences of the immediately preceding operation in Kosovo. The Department of Peacekeeping Operations assumed control over UNTAET following an internal turf battle with the Department of Political Affairs, which had overseen the 5 May agreement and had been the lead agency throughout the UNAMET referendum. Much as the International Criminal Tribunal for Rwanda was substantially modelled on the Hague Tribunal for the Former Yugoslavia, UNTAET drew directly upon the institutional and personal knowledge of the UN Interim Administration Mission in Kosovo (UNMIK). The planning staff were, it seems, told to 're-jig' the Kosovo plan for East Timor; the Special Representative and Transitional Administrator, Sergio Vieira de Mello, came from a position as head of UNMIK, bringing many core personnel with UNMIK backgrounds.[52]

The criticism is unfair because when the United Nations entered East Timor it was reasonable to assume that it was entering an area of potential conflict. Kosovo represented the most relevant experience in pacifying territory that had come under UN control, where a deeply polarized society faced the continued threat of violence. In Kosovo, the failure to contain and demobilize the Kosovo Liberation Army (KLA)

[50] SC Res 1264 (1999), preamble. See Martin, *Self-Determination*, 106–7.

[51] SC Res 1264 (1999).

[52] Joel C. Beauvais (2001) 'Benevolent Despotism: A Critique of UN State-Building in East Timor', *New York University Journal of International Law and Politics*, 33 : 1101. See also Jarat Chopra (2000) 'The UN's Kingdom of East Timor', *Survival*, 42(3): 27; [Australian] Department of Foreign Affairs and Trade, *East Timor in Transition 1998–2000: An Australian Policy Challenge* (Canberra: Brown and Wilton, 2000).

had caused problems that continued to plague the mission. Building upon previous experiences in the former Yugoslavia, the result was that centralized control and neutrality dominated the mandate and initial activities of UNTAET personnel.

The problem, rather, was that the mandate and mindset, once established, was slow to change with the reality on the ground. It was quickly established that the violence in East Timor had been caused by militia, supported and organized by the Indonesian military. When INTERFET arrived, many of the militia had left East Timor. By 26 January 2000, the Secretary-General was able to report that internal security had greatly improved: 'For most people, there is now no threat of violence and they can circulate freely.'[53] UNTAET was, therefore, established first and foremost as a peacekeeping operation. But with the evacuation of most of the militia and the arrival of over 8,000 troops, the demands of security were supplanted by demands for political and economic development in preparation for independence. Both were hindered by the initial choices made in New York in 1999. A further difference worth noting is that the United Nations played a more muted role in Kosovo, thanks to the burden assumed by European institutional actors. The absence of such actors in East Timor both increased the demands on UNTAET and reduced the opportunity for engagement by interested states with senior UN staff over differing interpretations of the situation on the ground.

On 20 May 2002, UN Secretary-General Kofi Annan joined East Timorese President Xanana Gusmão and the heads of state from over a dozen countries to lower the UN flag and raise the Timorese one. Timor-Leste became the 191st member state of the United Nations on 27 September 2002.[54]

2.2. *Transfer of Territory*

The transfer of territory has not generally been an explicit purpose of transitional administration. Nevertheless, this was the outcome of the first operation in which the United Nations formally undertook such powers in the field. Nominally intended to facilitate the decolonization of Dutch West New Guinea and the realization of the population's

[53] Report of the Secretary-General on the United Nations Transitional Administration in East Timor, UN Doc S/2000/53 (26 January 2000), para. 2.

[54] Particular aspects of the East Timor operation are discussed in greater detail elsewhere in the book. On the changing forms of consultation, see Chapter Four, Section 1.2. On justice and the rule of law, see Chapter Five, Section 3. On elections and exit strategies, see Chapter Seven, Section 3.3.

right to self-determination, the United Nations effectively facilitated its handover to Indonesia. The operation, lasting from 1962 to 1963, was authorized by the UN General Assembly rather than the Security Council. As in the later operation in Western Sahara, it was originally intended that the people of West New Guinea exercise their right to self-determination through a popular consultation. In both cases, however, this relatively simple proposition became far more complicated as the withdrawal of a European colonial power was followed by the entry of a neighbouring one—a move tacitly accepted in each case by the United Nations. West New Guinea's 'act of free choice' resulted, remarkably, in a unanimous vote in favour of joining with Indonesia. In Western Sahara, frustration with the failure to hold a referendum called for in the decade since 1991 led to a May 2001 proposal by the Secretary-General's Personal Envoy that would see Morocco's claims to the territory effectively recognized for a period of up to five years, prior to a vote on Western Sahara's future.

A key element in the success of a transitional administration is the existence of political clarity. An agreement to transfer control of territory to an existing state embodies such clarity, but is only generally possible following either acceptance of this arrangement by the international community or the defeat of the alternative regime on the battlefield. The former situation applied to West New Guinea and, as seems probable, Western Sahara. The latter applied to UNTAES, which is frequently touted as the one of the most successful transitional administrations to date. Croatian offensives against Serb forces had established the inevitable political outcome in the Danube region of Croatia; the UN presence was to ensure that this outcome was attained peacefully—and on these terms the mission was indeed a success.

2.2.1. West New Guinea (Papua), 1962–1963 Prior to decolonization, the territory of West New Guinea (now the Indonesian province of Papua) had been in the possession of the Netherlands from 1828. When the Netherlands recognized the independence of Indonesia in 1949, which it had held since seventeenth century, the status of West New Guinea was unclear. Mediation efforts led to an agreement between Indonesia and the Netherlands on 15 August 1962.[55] On 21 September the General Assembly passed resolution 1752 (XVII) (1962), taking note of the agreement and authorizing the

[55] Agreement Concerning West New Guinea (West Irian), Indonesia–Netherlands, 15 August 1962, 437 UNTS 274.

Secretary-General 'to carry out the tasks entrusted to him'. Although this occurred at the height of the controversy over the expanding operations then underway in the Congo, the resolution was passed without objection—perhaps due to the operation's short duration and clear mandate, the consent of the relevant states, and the fact that Indonesia and the Netherlands agreed to pay for the operation themselves.[56]

Under the terms of the agreement, administration of West New Guinea was to be transferred by the Netherlands to a UN Temporary Executive Authority (UNTEA), headed by a UN Administrator who was to be appointed by the Secretary-General. Under the Secretary-General's jurisdiction, UNTEA would have full authority to administer the territory, to maintain law and order, to protect the rights of the inhabitants, and to ensure uninterrupted normal services from 1 October 1962 until 1 May 1963, when administration would be provisionally transferred to Indonesia. The agreement also provided for a UN Security Force to assist UNTEA with 'such security forces as the United Nations Administrator deems necessary'.[57] (An advance team of the Security Force had already commenced monitoring a ceasefire that had been agreed prior to the formal establishment of a mandate.)

By 1 October 1962, the day on which power was transferred to the United Nations, three-quarters of the lower-ranking Dutch civil servants had left the territory, creating a space that UNTEA had to fill. Due to a shortage of adequately trained Papuans, the Secretary-General's Representative and Temporary Administrator, José Rolz-Bennett (later replaced by Djalal Abdoh), began recruiting international personnel. In effect, however, Indonesians soon replaced the Dutch civil servants, with UN staff holding senior positions for the six-month transitional period. Ultimate authority was duly passed to Indonesia as scheduled on 1 May 1963, leading to early assessments that the operation had been a success.

The agreement required Indonesia to make arrangements, with the assistance and participation of the UN Representative and his staff, to give the people of the territory the opportunity to exercise freedom of choice in determining their future. The inhabitants were to make

[56] GA Res 1752 (XVII) (1962) (adopted 89–0–14; 5 not participating). See Henry Wiseman, 'United Nations Peacekeeping: An Historical Overview', in Henry Wiseman (ed.), *Peacekeeping: Appraisals and Proposals* (New York: Pergamon Press, 1983), 19, 37; Ratner, *New UN Peacekeeping*, 110.

[57] Agreement Concerning West New Guinea (West Irian), art. VIII.

the decision to 'remain with Indonesia' or to 'sever their ties with Indonesia', through a plebiscite to be held no later than 1969. Whether half a decade of Indonesian rule in the intervening period would affect the freedom with which the population might make this decision was not explained.

Whatever one thinks of the first phase of the operation, the second phase showed the United Nations to be, at best, ineffective. At worst, it was complicit in fraud. Six years later, Indonesia organized the 'act of free choice' for what was then called West Irian between 14 July and 2 August 1969. Having rejected calls by the UN Representative, Fernando Ortiz-Sanz, for a one-man one-vote method supplemented by consultations in remote areas, Indonesia announced that it would consult only with representative councils chosen by Indonesian authorities. Enlarged representative councils (consultative assemblies), comprising a total of 1,026 members, were asked to state, on behalf of the people of the territory, whether they wished to remain with Indonesia or sever their ties with it. The vote was unanimously in favour of remaining with Indonesia.[58]

In his final report to the Secretary-General in November 1969, Ortiz-Sanz expressed 'regret' that Indonesia had not fulfilled its obligations to guarantee the rights of the Papuan inhabitants, having 'exercised at all times a tight political control over the population'. He could only observe that within

> the limitations imposed by the geographical characteristics of the territory and the general political situation in the area, an act of free choice has taken place in West Irian in accordance with Indonesian practice, in which the representatives of the population have expressed their wish to remain within Indonesia.[59]

UNTEA provided a dubious model for future operations and is seen most properly in the particular context of decolonization. Its closest parallel is Western Sahara, where a process of local consultation also seems likely to be overridden by great power interests.

[58] Report of the Secretary-General Regarding the Act of Self-Determination in West Irian, UN Doc A/7723, Annex II (6 November 1969). See generally Paul W. van der Veur (1964) 'The United Nations in West New Guinea: a Critique', *International Organization*, 18: 53; Rosalyn Higgins, *United Nations Peace-keeping 1946–1967: Documents and Commentary: Vol 2, Asia* (London: Oxford University Press, 1970), 109; United Nations, *The Blue Helmets: A Review of United Nations Peace-keeping*, 1st edn. (New York: UN Department of Public Information, 1985), 303–16; John Saltford, *The United Nations and the Indonesian Takeover of West Papua, 1962–1969: The Anatomy of Betrayal* (London: RoutledgeCurzon, 2002).

[59] UN Doc A/7723.

2.2.2. Western Sahara, 1991– Western Sahara, like East Timor, was a self-determination problem born of failed Iberian decolonization.[60] When Spain withdrew, both Morocco and Mauritania claimed the territory, a claim opposed by the Polisario movement, a rebel group composed largely of indigenous Sahrawis. Mauritania renounced its claim in 1979, but conflict continued between Morocco and Polisario, the latter receiving inconstant support from Algeria.

The Secretary-General's good offices, offered in conjunction with those of the Organization of African Unity in 1985, led to 'settlement proposals' that were put to the parties in August 1988. Taking note of what Secretary-General Javier Pérez de Cuéllar had called an 'agreement in principle', the Security Council authorized the appointment of a special representative and a report on the proposed referendum on the territory's future.[61] In 1990, the Security Council approved a report from the Secretary-General containing the full text of the proposals and the outline of a plan to implement them.[62] Security Council resolution 690 (1991) of 29 April 1991 established the UN Mission for the Referendum in Western Sahara (MINURSO). The plan provided for a transitional period in which the Special Representative was to have sole and exclusive responsibility over all matters relating to a referendum in which the people of Western Sahara would choose between independence and integration with Morocco. The transitional period was to begin on 6 September 1991, with the referendum to be held in January 1992.

It soon became apparent that there had, in fact, been no genuine agreement by the parties and that Pérez de Cuéllar had been less than forthcoming about the reservations they had expressed since 1988.[63] By September 1991 it was clear that the transitional period could not begin at this time; MINURSO's initial deployment was limited to 100 military observers to verify the ceasefire. The ceasefire generally held, but differences over the substance of the settlement proposals—most importantly concerning the eligibility to vote—continued to prevent completion of the mandate. The eligibility question arose in significant part because of Morocco's mischievous interpretation of a 1975 advisory opinion of the International Court of Justice concerning

[60] Adekeye Adebajo, 'Sheikhs, Soldiers and Sand', *World Today*, January 2000, 19.

[61] SC Res 621 (1988).

[62] SC Res 658 (1990), approving the Report of the Secretary-General, UN Doc S/21360 (18 June 1990), further elaborated in a subsequent report, UN Doc S/22464 (19 April 1991).

[63] Marrack Goulding, *Peacemonger* (London: John Murray, 2002), 201–8.

Western Sahara, after which a state-sponsored 'Green March' saw 350,000 Moroccans walk across the border.[64] MINURSO established an Identification Commission in May 1993, and in August 1994 began the process of identifying voters. This was suspended in May 1996, until agreements between the Secretary-General's new Personal Envoy, James Baker, and the parties enabled the process to restart in December 1997, with applicants from all tribes other than three contested groupings being completed by September 1998. These groups were processed from 15 June 1999 until the end of December 1999. The parties continued to disagree over the process that would deal with some 131,038 appeals.[65]

In May 2001, Baker proposed a radical departure from MINURSO's original mandate. Rather than attempting to hold a referendum immediately, Morocco would effectively be recognized as administering power of a non-self-governing territory. Under the draft Framework Agreement, Morocco would be given exclusive competence over foreign relations, national security, and external defence, while a Western Saharan executive body would be elected to carry out other functions. On the central question of the final status of Western Sahara, the draft Framework provided that a referendum should be held within five years, and abandoned the eligibility process of the preceding decade in favour of a simple requirement of full-time residency in Western Sahara for the year preceding the referendum.[66] Given the 'facts on the ground' established by Morocco's population transfers since 1975, this would, presumably, lead to an eventual integration of Western Sahara into Morocco.

The draft Framework amounted to an abandonment of previous efforts to determine the status of Western Sahara without recognizing the validity of Morocco's actions after 1975. With the benefit of hindsight, it should have been clear that the substantive agreement to hold a referendum would be held hostage to the procedures put in place to determine who was eligible to vote. This was more than a procedural question, as the energy put into contesting the eligibility and appeals processes demonstrated. In addition, however, Western Sahara suffered from a lack of interest of key states that might have exerted greater diplomatic pressure on the parties to come to an agreement.

64 *Western Sahara Case (Advisory Opinion)* [1975] ICJ Rep 12.

65 Report of the Secretary-General on the Situation Concerning Western Sahara, UN Doc S/2001/613 (20 June 2001), para. 28.

66 Draft Framework Agreement on the Status of Western Sahara, UN Doc S/2001/613, Annex I (20 June 2001).

This was exacerbated by the apparent decision by the United States and France that integration into Morocco would facilitate access to nearby oil reserves. In his memoir, Marrack Goulding (then head of the Department of Political Affairs) suggests that Baker's appointment in February 1997 was on the basis that he should 'negotiate a deal based on enhanced autonomy for Western Sahara within the Kingdom of Morocco'.[67] In later discussions, Baker is said to have been asked by Polisario representatives why the United Nations was treating Western Sahara differently from East Timor. He replied to the effect that if the Sahrawis wanted to be treated like the Timorese they had best go find themselves an Australia to lead a military action on their behalf.

2.2.3. Eastern Slavonia (Danube Region of Croatia), 1996–1998

Though frequently cited as a paradigm of successful transitional administration, the UN administration in Eastern Slavonia is more properly seen as facilitating the peaceful transfer of territory from one state to another.

Following Croatia's declaration of independence from the Socialist Federal Republic of Yugoslavia (SFRY) in 1991, three areas with significant Serbian populations within Croatia in turn declared themselves independent of the new entity: the area surrounding the Krajina, Western Slavonia, and Eastern Slavonia. Heavy fighting in late 1991 saw the areas fall under the control of local Serbs assisted by Serb paramilitaries and the Yugoslav National Army; almost all the Croatian inhabitants fled the area, in some cases replaced by Serbs displaced from elsewhere in Croatia. The Krajina and Western Slavonia were brought under Croatian control in May and July 1995 (Operations 'Flash' and 'Storm'), but the government, in response to international pressure, abandoned plans to move into Eastern Slavonia—the last Croatian region with a sizeable Serbian community.

On 12 November 1995, a month before the Dayton Peace Agreement was concluded, Croatia and the Serbian authorities in Eastern Slavonia signed the Basic Agreement on the Region of Eastern Slavonia, Baranja, and Western Sirmium (the Erdut Agreement),[68] which called

[67] Goulding, *Peacemonger*, 214. In January 2003, Baker presented a draft peace plan to the parties, which incorporated elements of the draft framework agreement. See Report of the Secretary-General on the Situation Concerning Western Sahara, UN Doc S/2003/565 (23 May 2003); Toby Shelley and Mark Turner, 'Security Council Backs Peace Plan for Western Sahara', *Financial Times* (London), 1 August 2003.

[68] Basic Agreement on the Region of Eastern Slavonia, Baranja, and Western Sirmium (Erdut Agreement), Government of the Republic of Croatia–local

upon the Security Council to establish a transitional administration. On 15 January 1996, the Security Council unanimously adopted resolution 1037 (1996), establishing UNTAES (the UN Transitional Administration for Eastern Slavonia, Baranja, and Western Sirmium) for an initial twelve-month period (later extended for two six-month periods).

UNTAES comprised a military and a civilian component. The military component was to supervise and facilitate the demilitarization of the region; monitor the voluntary and safe return of refugees and displaced persons in cooperation with the UN High Commissioner for Refugees (UNHCR); contribute, through its presence, to the maintenance of peace and security; and otherwise assist in implementing the Erdut Agreement. The civilian component was to establish a temporary police force; undertake tasks relating to civil administration and the functioning of public services; facilitate the return of refugees; organize elections; and assist in the coordination of plans for the development and economic reconstruction of the region. The Council also requested that the Secretary-General appoint a transitional administrator to have overall authority with regard to both components.

On 20 May 1996, UNTAES was fully deployed, with Jacques Paul Klein (a General in the US Air Force Reserve) as Special Representative (succeeded on 1 August 1997 by William Walker, also from the United States). Demilitarization of the Army of the Republika Srpska Krajina was formally declared complete on 21 June 1996, leading to the withdrawal of the Croatian Army from its forward positions. Various development programmes were undertaken in the following year, though few refugees returned. Incident-free elections were held on 13–14 April 1997, with the newly formed Independent Democratic Serb Party (SDSS) winning an absolute majority in eleven of twenty-eight municipalities. Following a military drawdown, UNTAES concluded its mandate on 15 January 1998 and was succeeded by a support group of 180 civilian police monitors.

Writing in 2001, former force commander Johan Schoups observed that the relative success of the UNTAES operation could be partly explained by the very limited nature of its mandate. In particular, it was based on a treaty that represented an unequivocal political resolution—peaceful reintegration into Croatia—to be achieved in a limited time. In addition, the military component was credible and under unified command and control, with broad rules of engagement (including the

Croatian Serb authorities, done at Erdut, 12 November 1995, UN Doc S/19995/951, Annex, reprinted in 35 ILM 189.

threat of NATO air power) to enforce the agreement if necessary. UNTAES also enjoyed relatively solid diplomatic support throughout the preparation and implementation of its mandate, and broad support on the ground.[69]

If success is measured by the failure of Serbs and Croats to return to conflict and the region being duly handed over to Croatian sovereign control, demilitarized and secure, then success was total. If measured by the preservation of multi-ethnicity, the answer is mixed. Though reliable figures are unavailable, the official UN estimate that only 10 per cent of an estimated Serbian population of 130,000 chose to emigrate from Croatia by the end of the UNTAES period seems low.[70] The Office of the High Commissioner for Refugees put the figure at between 15,000 and 20,000, with a further 30,000 having moved their property to Serbia.[71] The Organization for Security and Cooperation in Europe (OSCE) estimated that the number of Serbs leaving was closer to 40,000, characterizing it as a 'silent exodus'.[72] If success were to be measured by the extent of reconciliation, it remains too early to tell. In 2002, the Croat Mayor and the Serb Deputy Mayor in Vukovar were said not to be on speaking terms.

2.3. *Elections*

A third form of transition ties the purpose of international administration directly to the staging of elections, with the powers granted to the administration limited to the fulfilment of that end. Elections have been held in almost all of the situations in which the United Nations has exercised quasi-governmental authority, but for present purposes this category is limited to those situations where a transitional administration has been empowered primarily to hold an election and

[69] Johan Schoups, 'Peacekeeping and Transitional Administration in Eastern Slavonia', in Luc Reychler and Thania Paffenholz (eds.), *Peacebuilding: A Field Guide* (Boulder, CO: Lynne Rienner, 2001), 389.

[70] Report of the Secretary-General on the United Nations Transitional Administration for Eastern Slavonia, Baranja, and Western Sirmium, UN Doc S/1997/953 (4 December 1997), para. 6.

[71] 'Eastern Slavonia: The Croatians Are Coming', *Economist*, 8 January 1998.

[72] '"Silent Exodus" Evident in Danube Region', *OSCE Newsletter* 5(3), March 1998: 6. Following the reintegration of UNTAES-administered territory into Croatia, a further large-scale population flow into the Federal Republic of Yugoslavia was observed: Update on Regional Developments in the Former Yugoslavia, UN High Commissioner for Refugees, 48th Session, EC/48/SC/CRP.10 (2 April 1998), para. 8.

then withdraw. The category is, therefore, distinct from situations in which a referendum on the future of a territory is held (as in West New Guinea and Western Sahara) and where elections are part of a broader state-building project (as in Namibia and East Timor) or an ongoing peace process (as in the Balkans and Afghanistan). It is also different from missions with an electoral assistance function that have not exercised executive authority (as in El Salvador and Mozambique). This leaves Cambodia, where the UN Transitional Authority in Cambodia (UNTAC)—unprecedented at the time in both scale and mandate—was given a clearly defined role under the peace agreement signed in Paris in 1991, with the Security Council being invited to establish the mission in accordance with the wishes of the parties.

The importance of elections in this context is connected with the expansion of electoral observation missions by the United Nations and other actors, as well as the emerging norm of democratic governance as a 'right'. Nevertheless, there is now growing recognition that an election—especially a first election—can mark a highly unstable point at which to end a mission.[73]

2.3.1. Cambodia, 1992–1993 Though there are occasional claims that instability and violence is somehow genetically encoded in the people of Cambodia,[74] its political life has been dominated by foreign intervention of one kind or another since its independence from France in 1954. The United States supported the Lon Nol coup of 1970, China was the primary ally of the Khmer Rouge during its reign of terror from 1975, and Vietnam installed the Hun Sen regime in 1979 and maintained a military presence until 1989. The Vietnamese were soon followed by an international presence of a different kind when UNTAC entered Cambodia in 1992. At its peak, UNTAC involved some 22,000 military and civilian personnel at a cost of around $1.6 billion over its eighteen-month duration. The administrative powers exercised by the international actors were explicitly limited to ensuring a neutral political environment for the elections—nevertheless, they exceeded

[73] Thomas M. Franck (1992) 'The Emerging Right to Democratic Governance', *American Journal of International Law*, 86: 46; Gregory H. Fox and Brad R. Roth (eds.), *Democratic Governance and International Law* (Cambridge: Cambridge University Press, 2000). See Chapter Seven, Section 1.

[74] See Peter Sainsbury, 'UN Human Rights Center Gets New Chief', *Phnom Penh Post*, 17–30 March 2000, cited in International Crisis Group, Cambodia: The Elusive Peace Dividend (Phnom Penh/Brussels: ICG Asia Report No 8, 11 August 2000), available at www.crisisweb.org, 16.

anything seen since the colonial era and the Allied occupations of Germany and Japan following the Second World War.[75]

The Agreements on the Comprehensive Political Settlement of the Cambodia Conflict were signed in Paris on 23 October 1991. The Agreements created a Supreme National Council (SNC), defined as the 'unique legitimate body and source of authority in which, throughout the transitional period, the sovereignty, independence and unity of Cambodia are enshrined'.[76] This mechanism was designed to avoid the thorny question of how to obtain consent for an international presence from two parties, both of which claimed to be the legitimate government of Cambodia.[77] The SNC in turn delegated to the United Nations 'all powers necessary to ensure the implementation of this Agreement':

> In order to ensure a neutral political environment conducive to free and fair general elections, administrative agencies, bodies and offices which could directly influence the outcome of elections will be placed under direct United Nations supervision or control. In that context, special attention will be given to foreign affairs, national defence, finance, public security and information. To reflect the importance of these subjects, UNTAC needs to exercise such control as is necessary to ensure the strict neutrality of the bodies responsible for them. The United Nations, in consultation with the SNC, will identify which agencies, bodies and offices could continue to operate in order to ensure normal day-to-day life in the country.[78]

The Security Council was then invited to create UNTAC 'with civilian and military components under the direct responsibility of the Secretary-General of the United Nations', 'to provide UNTAC with the mandate set forth in this Agreement', and 'to keep its implementation under continuing review'.[79]

The Security Council duly passed resolution 745 (1992), establishing UNTAC for a period not to exceed eighteen months, with elections to be held by May 1993. Elections were held and declared to be free and fair by Special Representative Yasushi Akashi on 29 May 1993.

[75] Michael W. Doyle, *UN Peacekeeping in Cambodia: UNTAC's Civil Mandate* (Boulder, CO: Lynne Rienner, 1995), 13. See also James Mayall (ed.), *The New Interventionism 1991–1994: United Nations Experience in Cambodia, Former Yugoslavia and Somalia* (Cambridge: Cambridge University Press, 1996); Sorpong Peou, *Intervention and Change in Cambodia: Towards Democracy?* (New York: St Martin's Press, 2000).

[76] Agreements on a Comprehensive Political Settlement of the Cambodia Conflict, done at Paris, 23 October 1991, 31 ILM 183, art. 3.

[77] Ratner, *New UN Peacekeeping*, 147.

[78] Paris Agreements, art. 6.

[79] Ibid., art. 2.

From a field of twenty political parties, the royalist Funcinpec party won a plurality (45 per cent) of the vote. As required by the constitution, Funcinpec shared power with the Cambodian People's Party (CPP) (38 per cent), with Prince Norodom Ranariddh (Funcinpec) and Hun Sen (CPP) being appointed as joint Prime Ministers.[80] What followed—a coup led by Second Prime Minister Hun Sen in 1997 and flawed elections the following year—suggested that early assessments of the success of elections as an exit strategy from Cambodia were overly positive. What was learned from this, and the problematic experience of elections in the Balkans, will be considered in Chapter Seven.[81]

2.4. Peace Process

The fourth class of transitional administrations has a rationale quite different from the previous three. Whereas the preceding categories each embody some form of political certainty in their outcome, the implicit object of the missions discussed below was to take on some or all government functions without a clear exit point—or in the hope that one would appear at a later date. The clearest examples of this are in Bosnia and Kosovo. Due to frustrations with the UN system throughout the Bosnian war, primary civilian responsibility in Sarajevo was granted to a High Representative and military security was guaranteed by the NATO-led Stabilization Force (SFOR), operating as a multinational force under a Council mandate renewed every six months. In Kosovo, the dystopia of Bosnia under the High Representative and the political controversy surrounding NATO's 'humanitarian intervention' led to civilian administration there being placed under a UN umbrella.

It is in such operations that the contradiction between the means and the ends of transitional administration become most apparent, as international actors endeavour to establish the conditions for democracy through benevolent autocracy.[82] If the circumstances in which these conditions may be met—or the process for achieving them—are unclear, it may lock both international and local actors into a cycle of dependence. The Dayton Agreement, for example, has become a

[80] See further Sorpong Peou, *Conflict Neutralization in the Cambodian War: From Battlefield to Ballot-Box* (Oxford: Oxford University Press, 1997); International Crisis Group, Back from the Brink: Cambodian Democracy Gets a Second Chance (Phnom Penh/Brussels: ICG Cambodia Report No 4, 26 January 1999), available at www.crisisweb.org.

[81] See Chapter Seven, Section 3.1.

[82] See further Chapter Four, Section 1.1.

de facto constitution for Bosnia.[83] This served its purpose as a peace agreement but it proved utterly unworkable as a constitution; any attempt to change it, however, is seen as a threat to reignite the conflict. Kosovo, by contrast, remains paralysed by the requirement that international staff profess to have no view on the most fundamental aspect of its political development: whether it will eventually become independent.

The UN mission in Afghanistan, considered in Section 3, presents an alternative model for involving the United Nations in an ongoing peace process on a more limited scale. Almost certainly, however, such a confined role would have been inadequate to the task of enforcing the peace in Bosnia after Dayton, or preventing further revenge killings and attempts at secession after NATO completed its air operations in defence of the Kosovar Albanians.

2.4.1. Bosnia and Herzegovina, 1995– Under the Dayton Agreement, Bosnia, Croatia, and the Federal Republic of Yugoslavia requested designation of a High Representative to facilitate its implementation.[84] The High Representative, who was to exercise sweeping powers, would be appointed 'consistent with relevant United Nations Security Council resolutions', although the operation was not going to be run by the United Nations. Key states saw the United Nations as so discredited by its peacekeeping performance in the Balkans that the drafters never seriously contemplated appointing a UN special representative instead of an independently constituted High Representative.[85]

In accordance with Dayton, the Security Council did establish a civilian police contingent known as the International Police Task Force. Its mandate was to assist parties in meeting their obligations to provide a safe and secure environment for all persons in their respective jurisdictions.[86] In practice, the UN Mission in Bosnia and Herzegovina (UNMIBH) later asserted far greater control through a combination of mission creep and sometimes combative relations with

[83] The Agreement does, in fact, include a constitution in Annex 4; the reference here is to the peace agreement as a whole—especially the military aspects in Annex 1A: General Framework Agreement for Peace in Bosnia and Herzegovina (Dayton Agreement), Bosnia and Herzegovina–Croatia–Federal Republic of Yugoslavia, done at Dayton, 14 December 1995, UN Doc S/1995/999, available at www.yale.edu/lawweb/avalon/intdip/bosnia/daymenu.htm.

[84] Ibid., Annex 10, art. 1(2).

[85] Elizabeth M. Cousens and Charles K. Cater, *Toward Peace in Bosnia: Implementing the Dayton Accords* (Boulder, CO: Lynne Rienner, 2001), 46.

[86] SC Res 1035 (1995), para. 2; Dayton Agreement, Annex 11, art. 1.

the High Representative. UNMIBH ultimately exercised a wide range of functions related to law enforcement in Bosnia; it also coordinated other UN activities in the country relating to humanitarian relief and refugees, de-mining, human rights, elections, and rehabilitation of infrastructure and economic reconstruction.[87]

The military presence was generally regarded to be effective, but SFOR's narrow interpretation of what constituted security and a lack of coordination between the civilian and military pillars caused problems—most obviously in the failure to apprehend war crimes suspects. On the civilian front, it soon became apparent that the amount of authority delegated to the High Representative was inadequate. Civilian authority was unclear and divided: the Office of the High Representative coordinated many organizations, but its powers with respect to the parties and other implementing organizations were sometimes unclear. The High Representative, the OSCE, and others were able to make determinations of compliance and lack of compliance with the Dayton Agreement, but they lacked the 'quasi-sovereign authority' to make determinations of policy when the parties disagreed. The mandate thus assumed a degree of cooperation and commitment to reconciliation between the parties that simply did not exist. This changed at the Bonn Summit of the Peace Implementation Council of December 1997, after which the High Representative began to take decisions against the will of the parties.[88]

The expansion of powers built, on a country-wide level, on the experiences of international administration in two of the most divided towns in Bosnia. Mostar, an historic town in Herzegovina, had been the scene of fierce fighting between Bosnian Serbs, Croats, and Muslims. By the time a ceasefire was established in the summer of 1994, the Croats and Bosnian Muslims (later referred to as Bosniaks) occupied opposing sides of the Neretva River; the sixteenth-century bridge that had connected the once cosmopolitan town was destroyed in the fighting. Under the terms of a Memorandum of Understanding, the European Union Administration of Mostar (EUAM) was established to administer the city until local agreement was reached on unification, supported by a police contingent supplied by the Western European

[87] Report of the Secretary-General on the United Nations Mission in Bosnia and Herzegovina, UN Doc S/2001/1132 (29 November 2001). See generally Michael Rose, *Fighting for Peace: Lessons from Bosnia* (London: Warner, 1999); David Chandler, *Bosnia: Faking Democracy After Dayton* (London: Pluto Press, 1999).

[88] Doyle, 'War-Making and Peace-Making'. The Bonn Powers are discussed further in Chapter Four, Section 1.1.1.

Union.[89] The EUAM was a vehicle for reconstruction activities in and around Mostar, as well as civic activities culminating in the first post-war elections in 1996. The office was then transformed into the Office of the Special Envoy for Mostar until January 1997, when a regional office of the High Representative was opened. Despite years of attention and the expenditure of hundreds of millions of dollars, Mostar remains a divided city.[90]

A second divided city was Brcko, a stumbling block at Dayton, whose future had been deferred to international arbitration under a specially constituted tribunal.[91] Once a multi-ethnic city, its 87,000 people lay at the crossroads of Bosnia's two constitutive entities, where the narrowest portion of Republika Srpska (the 5 km-wide Posavina Corridor) met the Bosniak–Croat Federation. In February 1997, the tribunal determined that the Republika Srpska had failed to implement its return and free movement obligations and called for the appointment of a 'Supervisor' by the High Representative. This person was to be granted administrative powers, including the power to issue binding regulations that would override any conflicting laws, in order to promote the objectives of return and democratization.[92] These potentially limitless powers were intended as a temporary measure in order to push the parties towards a sustainable solution, an effort that was deemed to have failed in the Final Award issued in March 1999. The tribunal's Solomonic decision established Brcko as a new district to be held in condominium by the two entities, within the territory of both but controlled by neither.[93] This was formalized in the adoption of a statute that established that the district would be self-governing with its own multi-ethnic police force—effectively making Brcko a third entity.[94] The Supervisor nominated and oversaw Brcko's executive;

[89] Memorandum of Understanding on Mostar, Member States of the European Union–Member States of the Western European Union–Republic of Bosnia and Herzegovina–Federation of Bosnia and Herzegovina–Local Administration of Mostar East–Local Administration of Mostar West–Bosnian Croats, 5 July 1994.

[90] International Crisis Group, Reunifying Mostar: Opportunities for Progress (Sarajevo/Washington/Brussels: ICG Balkans Report No 90, 19 April 2000), available at www.crisisweb.org.

[91] Dayton Agreement, Annex 2, art. V.

[92] Dispute over Inter-Entity Boundary in Brcko Area (*Republika Srpska* vs. *Federation of Bosnia and Herzegovina*) (Arbitration 14 February 1997), UN Doc S/1997/126, reprinted in 36 ILM 396 (1997), para. 104.

[93] Dispute over Inter-Entity Boundary in Brcko Area (*Republika Srpska v Federation of Bosnia and Herzegovina*) (5 March 1999). Cf. the status of the Memel Territory: See Chapter One, Section 1.3.1.

[94] Statute of the Brcko District of Bosnia and Herzegovina, 7 December 1999, 39 ILM 879 (2000).

in the absence of local elections, the Supervisor also appointed the twenty-nine-member legislative assembly. The autonomy of the Supervisor was, reportedly, the subject of some envy on the part of other international agencies, including the Office of the High Representative. By 2003, Brcko was the only Bosnian municipality with significant minority returns and the beginnings of a functioning multi-ethnic police, judiciary, and town council.[95]

The approach taken in Bosnia was comparable to that taken in Cambodia—in both cases, wartime regimes were left intact after the war, with the international community generally empowered to 'monitor' implementation and 'promote' compliance.[96] The territory remains stable, in large part due to the 13,000 SFOR troops who remain in the country. On 31 December 2002, UNMIBH transferred its international police monitoring duties to the European Union Police Mission. Bosnia was, in the end, to become a European problem.[97]

2.4.2. Kosovo, 1999– In one of his final speeches as head of UNMIK, Bernard Kouchner likened leading the operation to being in Alice's Wonderland. It takes all the running you can do to keep in the same place, he observed—if you want to get somewhere else, you have to run at least twice as fast as that. Many things about Kosovo suggest a through-the-looking-glass quality to the UN protectorate. Where else does one find human rights activists arguing in favour of the imposition of martial law and reminiscing about the reign of a communist dictator? Where else would one find the United Nations imprisoning suspected terrorists for over a year without trial? As Kosovo's majority Albanian population began to exercise uncertain powers

[95] See, e.g. International Crisis Group, Courting Disaster: The Misrule of Law in Bosnia and Herzegovina (Sarajevo/Brussels: ICG Balkans Report No 127, 25 March 2002), available at www.crisisweb.org, 49; International Crisis Group, Bosnia's Brcko: Getting In, Getting On, and Getting Out (Sarajevo/Brussels: ICG Balkans Report No 144, 2 June 2003), available at www.crisisweb.org; Mark Landler, 'Rare Bosnia Success Story, Thanks to US Viceroy', *New York Times*, 17 June 2003.

[96] Richard Caplan, *A New Trusteeship? The International Administration of War-Torn Territories* (Oxford: Oxford University Press, 2002), 16.

[97] See International Crisis Group, Bosnia's Nationalist Governments: Paddy Ashdown and the Paradoxes of State-Building (Sarajevo/Brussels: ICG Balkans Report No 146, 22 July 2003), available at www.crisisweb.org. Note that the High Representative continues to be appointed by the Peace Implementation Council and the United States continues to command SFOR, as well as accounting for approximately one-third of the force's strength.

through the 'Provisional Institutions of Self-Government' established in 2001—and Serbia was gradually welcomed back into the international community—the paper-thin compromise that saw the United Nations follow NATO into Kosovo began to appear more like a permanent substitute for a solution.[98]

Security Council resolution 1244 (1999) was adopted just hours after the last bomb was dropped in the course of NATO's Operation Allied Force. The resolution built upon principles adopted by the G-8 Foreign Ministers a month earlier, which in turn had been 'elaborated' in a document finally agreed to by Belgrade. The military aspects authorized the deployment of the Kosovo Force (KFOR)—an international security presence with 'substantial' NATO participation. But the central contradiction of UNMIK's mandate was that it avoided taking a position on the key political question of Kosovo's relationship to Serbia. With Milosevic in power, it was long an open secret within UNMIK that Kosovo would eventually be granted independence. Nevertheless, the authorizing resolutions and official statements continued to emphasize respect for the territorial integrity and political independence of the Federal Republic of Yugoslavia. Timothy Garton Ash referred to this at the time as 'virginity and motherhood combined'.[99] Every aspect of UNMIK's work in Kosovo depends on the answer to this question, but the answer will be decided according to political considerations that have only partial relevance to what is actually happening in Kosovo.[100]

Whatever Kosovo's final status, the involvement of Serbs in the political process will remain an important measure of international action in Kosovo. Apart from the formal recognition of Serbian sovereignty over Kosovo, some international staff felt betrayed by the Kosovar Albanians who, when given the chance, turned on

[98] See generally Michael Ignatieff, *Virtual War: Kosovo and Beyond* (New York: Metropolitan, 2000); Independent International Commission on Kosovo, *The Kosovo Report* (Oxford: Oxford University Press, 2000); Tim Judah, *Kosovo: War and Revenge* (New Haven, CT: Yale University Press, 2000); William G. O'Neill, *Kosovo: An Unfinished Peace* (Boulder, CO: Lynne Rienner, 2002).

[99] Timothy Garton Ash, 'Anarchy and Madness', *New York Review*, 10 February 2000, 48.

[100] Aspects of the Kosovo operation are discussed in greater detail elsewhere in the book. On consultation, see Chapter Four, Section 1.1.3. On the rule of law, see Chapter Five, Section 2. On elections and exit strategies, see Chapter Seven, Section 3.2.

their Serbian neighbours in a manner comparable to their own persecution.[101]

The transfer of Slobodan Milosevic to The Hague on 28 June 2001 provoked complicated reactions among the various communities in Kosovo. Among the Serbs in Kosovo, many were angry at what was seen as a craven deal made under US pressure and the inducements of a $1.3 billion package of aid and grants. Some Serbs, however, saw it as a necessary step in closing an unfortunate chapter in their history, although the date on which he was extradited—St Vitus's Day—left a bitter taste in many mouths. Appropriately, perhaps, this was exactly twelve years after an inflammatory speech in Kosovo first raised Milosevic to national prominence. But that speech was made on the 600th anniversary of the Battle of Kosovo Polje, when Serb forces were slaughtered by their Turkish foe. It also marked the date in 1914 on which a Bosnian Serb, Gavrilo Princip, assassinated Archduke Franz Ferdinand, sparking the First World War, and the date in 1948 that Stalin expelled Yugoslavia from the Communist Bloc. Such coincidences play into the conspiracy theories that are a daily staple in Serbia.

Complex emotions were at work within the Kosovar Albanian community also. On the one hand, many were pleased that Milosevic was going to be forced to answer for his actions in Kosovo. At the same time, however, some Kosovar Albanians recognized that the new regime in Belgrade was attempting to draw a line between itself and the Milosevic era. And the more Belgrade shook off its pariah status, the less likely it was that the Kosovar Albanians would soon achieve their goal of formal independence.

One immediate consequence of Milosevic's extradition was the collapse of the Yugoslav federal government. This, in turn, led to what remained of Yugoslavia being re-christened 'Serbia and Montenegro' in February 2003—an entity barely held together by that fairly weak conjunction. As resolution 1244 (1999) refers to the 'sovereignty and territorial integrity of the Federal Republic of Yugoslavia' rather than Serbia, it is arguable that the final demise of the 'land of the south Slavs' would remove the formal hurdles to Kosovo's independence. Most stakeholders in Kosovo would prefer to avoid that argument.

101 See, e.g. Hans Haekkerup, 'UNMIK at Two Years' (Pristina, 13 June 2001): 'I think the worst thing that happened after NATO and UNMIK arrived were the atrocities committed against Kosovo Serbs in that period. This is behind much of the situation that has been an obstacle to having a true multi-ethnic society in Kosovo.'

Veton Surroi, editor of the Kosovo daily *Koha Ditore*, writes of the 'Taiwan scenario', in which Kosovo, Montenegro, and Serbia concentrate on developing the functioning of their respective states rather than on international recognition.[102] Others prefer to use the example of Scotland—less for its limited devolution than for its location within the European Union.

In fact, a better analogy is found much closer to Kosovo: Cyprus. UN peacekeepers were deployed in Cyprus in 1964, and since 1974 they have policed a line of partition brought about by Turkey's occupation of the north of the island. A Turkish Republic of Northern Cyprus was declared in 1983, but only Turkey recognized this republic—the administration in the south, run by Greek Cypriots, remains recognized internationally as the legitimate Government of Cyprus. Security Council resolutions continue to call on all states to respect the sovereignty, independence, and territorial integrity of Cyprus, and reaffirm the Council's position that a settlement must be based on a state of Cyprus with 'single sovereignty'. In June 1999, however, the Council requested that the Secretary-General invite the leaders of the two sides of the divided island to talks and spoke of a negotiation with 'all issues on the table' and 'full consideration of relevant United Nations resolutions and treaties'—language more acceptable to the Turkish Cypriots.[103] In December 1999, the European Council stated that a political settlement to the Cyprus problem would facilitate accession to the European Union, but that it was not a 'precondition' for entry. This was the framework for negotiations to combine membership with the creation of a loose federation reunifying the island.[104]

Entry to the European Union is unlikely to come soon to Kosovo, but the possibility is frequently used as a carrot to encourage a 'European' approach to political life: 'The way to Europe is not through ethnic separation but only, and I say *only*, through mutual tolerance', Hans Haekkerup once warned Kosovars.[105] In the short-term, however, Kosovo will stay as it is: an international protectorate with limited administrative powers devolved to the local population,

[102] Dana H. Allin, 'Unintended Consequences: Managing Kosovo Independence', in Dimitrios Triantaphyllou (ed.), *What Status for Kosovo?* (Paris: Institute for Security Studies, Western European Union, 2001), 12.

[103] SC Res 1250 (1999), para. 7. Cf. SC Res 1251 (1999), para. 11.

[104] Helsinki European Council, Presidency Conclusions (10–11 December 1999), available at http://ue.eu.int/en/info/eurocouncil, para. 9. These negotiations came to an end in March 2003: Alex Efty, 'Attempt to Unify Cyprus Before Entry into EU Fails', *Washington Post*, 12 March 2003.

[105] Haekkerup, 'UNMIK at Two Years'.

and with an international military and civilian presence. In this respect, Bosnia remains the best analogy. Both Kosovo and Bosnia suffer from being governed by peace agreements that were aimed at stopping fighting rather than consolidating peace, though Kosovo has the advantage of being a single political entity.[106]

2.5. State Failure

Perhaps the most complex political environment in which the United Nations has been called upon to exercise transitional administration-like powers is where it was not explicitly authorized by the Security Council to do so. In Congo, Somalia, and Sierra Leone the United Nations and other actors found themselves in situations where a dearth of state power demanded that some form of basic law and order functions be exercised by the only actors capable of it. Similar situations have arisen in the early stages of other operations, such as the first phase of the Kosovo and East Timor interventions. In those cases, law and order functions fell to the intervening forces—with very different results.[107] But there is a difference between the temporary activities undertaken in Kosovo and East Timor until the deployment of a civilian administration and the activities that were thrust upon the United Nations by stealth or by default in the three operations discussed below. It is no coincidence that all three took place in Africa. Somalia, in particular, highlighted the dangers of a mission's mandate going beyond the political will of troop contributors—even as it led to the implicit policy of some developed states (notably the United States) not to contribute troops to resolving African conflicts.[108]

2.5.1. Congo, 1960–1964 The UN Operation in the Congo (ONUC) was a watershed in the history of UN peacekeeping in terms of both the scale of the operation and the responsibilities it had to assume. In addition to a peacekeeping force with a peak strength of nearly 20,000, its civilian component went far beyond previous operations. It was originally mandated to provide the Congolese Government with 'such military and technical assistance as may be necessary' until national security forces were able to keep order on their own. This assistance was required after Congo's independence in 1960 led to widespread unrest, the collapse of essential services, attempted secession by the

[106] See also Chapter Seven, Section 3.2.

[107] See Chapter Three, Section 2.

[108] See Chapter Three, Section 1.2.

copper-rich Katanga province, and a military intervention by former colonial power Belgium.[109]

Given the length of time it now takes to deploy a peacekeeping operation, it is astonishing that UN contingents began to arrive in the Congo within forty-eight hours of the passage of Security Council resolution 143 (1960). After the assassination of former Prime Minister Patrice Lumumba in January 1961, the rules of engagement were strengthened to include 'all appropriate measures to prevent the occurrence of civil war in the Congo, including... the use of force, if necessary, in the last resort'.[110] A comparable expansion was evident in the civilian activities undertaken by ONUC. Administrative functions were initially assumed on the basis that Belgium had failed to develop local capacity prior to its departure; as formal government collapsed because of the ongoing conflict, these powers were sometimes exercised against the wishes of such local governing structures as actually existed.[111]

ONUC was a traumatic operation for the United Nations, which suffered 250 fatalities, including the loss of Secretary-General Dag Hammarskjöld—more than in any operation before or since.[112] There was some measure of success in implementing the limited mandate, but positive evaluations of the Congo mission tend to ignore what came afterwards, the idiosyncratic kleptocracy of Mobutu Sese Seko and the instability that laid the foundations for war in the 1990s and beyond.[113]

2.5.2. Somalia, 1993–1995 An arms embargo and humanitarian relief supported by peacekeepers were insufficient to deal with the problems

[109] SC Res 143 (1960), para. 2. See generally Georges Abi-Saab, *The United Nations Operation in the Congo 1960–1964* (Oxford: Oxford University Press, 1978); Rosalyn Higgins, *United Nations Peacekeeping 1946–1967: Documents and Commentary: Vol 3, Africa* (London: Oxford University Press, 1980), 364–78; William J. Durch, 'The UN Operation in the Congo: 1960–1964', in William J. Durch (ed.), *The Evolution of UN Peacekeeping: Case Studies and Comparative Analysis* (New York: St Martin's Press, 1993), 315.

[110] SC Res 161 (1961). This was further strengthened in November 1961, when the Council authorized 'vigorous action, including the use of the requisite measure of force' to detain or expel foreign mercenaries: SC Res 169 (1961).

[111] Ratner, *New UN Peacekeeping*, 105–9. In February 1963, after Katanga province had been reintegrated, the UN force was progressively phased out and completely withdrawn by the end of June 1964. Civilian aid continued in the largest single programme of assistance undertaken until that time by the United Nations and its agencies, with some 2000 experts in Congo at the peak of the programme in 1963–4.

[112] DPKO statistics, available at www.un.org/depts/dpko/fatalities.

[113] See also Chapter Seven, Section 3.

caused by the power vacuum that followed the January 1991 ousting of Somalia's President Mohammed Siad Barre. The Unified Task Force (UNITAF), led by the United States, was authorized in December 1992 to use 'all necessary means' to create a secure environment for the delivery of humanitarian aid. Partially successful, UNITAF was succeeded by the UN Operation in Somalia II (UNOSOM II) in May 1993. Crisis conditions of widespread famine, inter-clan fighting, and general lawlessness continued to prevail as organized government collapsed in Somalia.[114]

Security Council resolution 814 (1993) requested that the Secretary-General, through his Special Representative, 'direct the Force Commander of UNOSOM II to assume responsibility for the consolidation, expansion, and maintenance of a secure environment throughout Somalia'.[115] In exercising this function, the Special Representative declared that the former Somali Penal Code of 1962 was the criminal law in force in Somalia. It is unlikely that the Council mandate gave him this sort of legislative power.[116] Indeed, the report of the Commission of Inquiry established by Security Council to investigate subsequent armed attacks against UNOSOM II stated that 'the promulgation of the Somali Penal Code of 1962... was capable of being interpreted by [General Mohamed Farah Aideed's faction] as an overstepping of the UNOSOM II mandate'.[117] Nevertheless, in the absence of any functioning government authority this was clearly an exceptional case.[118]

Somalia presented the United Nations with a situation in which it was the de facto government when it lacked the mandate, the resources, and, ultimately, the inclination to fulfil that role. The withdrawal from

114 See John Drysdale, *Whatever Happened to Somalia?* (London: Haan Associates, 1994), 27–38.

115 SC Res 814 (1993), para. 14.

116 Sarooshi, *Development of Collective Security*, 63.

117 Report of the Commission of Inquiry Established Pursuant to Security Council Resolution 885 (1993) to Investigate Armed Attacks on UNOSOM II Personnel Which Led to Casualties Among Them, UN Doc S/1994/653 (1 June 1994).

118 Martin R. Ganzglass, 'The Restoration of the Somali Justice System', in Walter Clarke and Jeffrey Herbst (eds.), *Learning from Somalia: The Lessons of Armed Humanitarian Intervention* (Boulder, CO: Westview, 1997). This was replicated on a smaller scale in the town of Baidoa, where Australian peacekeepers assumed an aggressive stance in protecting humanitarian workers and the commander assumed the mantle of military governor: see Robert G. Patnam (1997) 'Disarming Somalia: The Contrasting Fortunes of US and Australian Peacekeepers During UN Intervention, 1992–93', *African Affairs*, 96: 509.

Somalia prejudiced future operations, most notably in relation to the international community's reluctance to involve itself in the Rwandan genocide in 1994. The Commission of Inquiry produced its report just as preparations were being made to strengthen the UN peacekeeping presence in the wake of the genocide. In particular, the Commission concluded that 'the UN should refrain from undertaking further peace enforcement actions within the internal conflicts of States'.[119]

2.5.3. Sierra Leone, 1999– Another, more far-reaching report on UN peace operations—the Brahimi Report—was being drafted in 2000 even as the UN Mission in Sierra Leone (UNAMSIL) nearly collapsed as a result of poor planning, under-equipped and badly trained personnel, inadequate communication, weak to the point of mutinous command and control, and determined local spoilers.[120] Though never granted the authority of transitional administrations in Kosovo and East Timor, UNAMSIL briefly attempted to fulfil basic law and order and some governance functions as a measure of peace and security was restored to Sierra Leone.

From the eruption of civil war in 1991, the dominant external actor in Sierra Leone had been the Military Observer Group (ECOMOG) of the Economic Community of West African States (ECOWAS), whose actions received some measure of legitimacy from the Security Council. Fighting between government and rebel forces continued, however, and in 1998 the Council established an Observer Mission (UNOMSIL) to monitor the security situation, disarmament, and observance of international humanitarian law.[121] A peace agreement of sorts was subsequently signed in Lomé in July 1999 and the Observer Mission's mandate was taken over that October by UNAMSIL, which was granted a broader mandate to 'afford protection to civilians under imminent threat of physical violence'.[122] This mandate was sorely tested when the peace agreement broke down the following year. When Nigeria decided to withdraw its troops from ECOMOG, UNAMSIL's mandate was expanded in February 2000—almost doubling the number of military personnel to over 11,000 (later increased again to

[119] S/1994/653. On the implications that this had for Rwanda, see Report of the Independent Inquiry into the Actions of the United Nations During the 1994 Genocide in Rwanda, UN Doc S/1999/1257 (15 December 1999). See further, Chapter Three.

[120] David M. Malone and Ramesh Thakur (2001) 'UN Peacekeeping: Lessons Learned?', *Global Governance*, 7(1): 11. The crisis occurred just after the Panel on UN Peace Operations convened in May 2000.

[121] SC Res 1181 (1998).

[122] SC Res 1270 (1999), para. 14.

17,500) and adding further civilian and administrative responsibilities. These included providing security at key locations, such as government buildings, important intersections, and major airports, as well as coordinating with and assisting the Sierra Leonean law enforcement authorities in their responsibilities.[123]

The language of coordination was somewhat misleading. As noted in the Secretary-General's report that recommended the expansion, a robust UNAMSIL was 'indispensable' to maintaining the necessary security conditions for extending state administration throughout the country and, in due course, for the holding of elections.[124] This blend of assistance with and assumption of governmental tasks was repeated in the establishment of the Special Court for Sierra Leone, which eventually issued its first indictments in March 2003.[125]

As in Somalia, UNAMSIL lacked the clear mandate, resources, and political will to let it complete its mission successfully. For the duration of the mission, UNAMSIL claimed to operate in support of Sierra Leonean authorities rather than in their stead. As various functions were assumed by default, this proved to be operationally disingenuous. In subsequent operations, however, such assertions were embraced as being at least politically virtuous.[126] This became clearest in the 'Assistance Mission' in Afghanistan.

3. *State-Building and the War on Terror*

The 1990s was a period of high—perhaps excessively high—optimism for the United Nations. The end of the cold war, a period of relative concord between the major powers, and the rhetoric of a 'New World Order' combined to raise hopes that the United Nations could not merely manage conflict but play a larger part in preventing it. The limitations of this concordat were displayed in African conflicts such as Somalia and Rwanda, suggesting that the New World Order depended more upon a coincidence of national interests than a genuinely novel approach to international affairs. In the Balkans, the

[123] SC Res 1289 (2000); SC Res 1346 (2001).

[124] Second Report of the Secretary-General Pursuant to Security Council Resolution 1270 (1999) on the United Nations Mission in Sierra Leone, UN Doc S/2000/13 (11 January 2000), para. 44.

[125] SC Res 1315 (2000); Report of the Secretary-General on the Establishment of a Special Court for Sierra Leone, UN Doc S/2000/915 (4 October 2000); Rory Carroll, 'Seven Put on Trial for Atrocities in Sierra Leone', *Guardian* (London), 11 March 2003.

[126] See also Operation Palliser discussed in Chapter Three, Section 1.2.

capacity of industrialized countries to wage either war or peace even when their interests were involved was called into question. In January 2001, US President George W. Bush entered office sceptical about the usefulness of the United Nations as an institution and allergic to the prospect of the United States being involved in future 'nation-building' missions.[127]

The 11 September 2001 attacks against the United States changed this strategic environment. Nineteen persons of non-US nationality hijacked four US commercial passenger jets and crashed them into the World Trade Centre in New York, the Pentagon in Washington, DC, and the Pennsylvania countryside. Approximately 3,000 people died in the incidents—the largest number of casualties experienced in the United States in a single day since the Civil War.[128] Following the terrorist attacks, there was an immediate call within the United States for a military response. Bush stated that the United States would 'hunt down and punish those responsible for these cowardly acts',[129] a goal later amplified in the President's response to a question as to whether he wanted Osama bin Laden dead: 'I want justice. There's an old poster out west, as I recall, that said, "Wanted: Dead or Alive." '[130]

The broader implications of the new role being carved out by the United States and its relationship with the United Nations will be considered in Chapter Eight.[131] This section will discuss the two major state-building operations that were conducted within the context of the so-called 'war on terror': Afghanistan and Iraq.

3.1. Afghanistan and the 'Light Footprint'

Just under a month after the 11 September 2001 attacks, a US-led coalition commenced military action in Afghanistan aimed at eliminating the Al Qaeda terrorist network and toppling the Taliban regime that had harboured them in Afghanistan. By mid-November, the Taliban

[127] See Chapter Eight, Section 2.1.

[128] Sean D. Murphy (2002) 'Contemporary Practice of the United States Relating to International Law', *American Journal of International Law*, 96: 237.

[129] George W. Bush, 'Remarks by the President Upon Arrival at Barksdale Air Force Base' (Barksdale Air Force Base, Louisiana, 11 September 2001), available at www.whitehouse.gov.

[130] George W. Bush, 'Remarks by the President to Employees at the Pentagon' (Washington, DC, 17 September 2001), available at www.whitehouse.gov.

[131] See Chapter Eight, Section 2.

had been effectively removed from power and on 5 December 2001 a UN-sponsored Afghan peace conference in Bonn, Germany, agreed to establish an Interim Authority pending an Emergency Loya Jirga (National Assembly) to be held in June 2002.[132] This body would, in turn, decide upon a Transitional Authority to lead Afghanistan until elections were held within two years from the convening of the Emergency Loya Jirga.[133]

During the initial stages of the military action, there was considerable discussion about the part that the United Nations would play in post-conflict Afghanistan. Some feared that the United Nations would be handed a poisoned chalice once the United States had completed its military objectives; others eagerly looked forward to the 'next big mission' and a dominant position for the United Nations in rebuilding Afghanistan on the model of Kosovo and East Timor.[134] These expectations were tempered by the hostile security environment and the decision by major states contributing forces to the International Security Assistance Force (ISAF) to limit their presence to the capital city of Kabul and its immediate vicinity.[135] (Ongoing coalition actions in the east of the country continued to provide additional coercive power—referred to as the 'B-52 factor'—but this was outside the control, and frequently beyond the knowledge, of the United Nations.) Expectations were also limited by the political context within which the United Nations was to operate: however dysfunctional, Afghanistan had been and remained a state with undisputed sovereignty. This was quite different from the ambiguous status of Kosovo and the embryonic sovereignty of East Timor.

Under the leadership of Lakhdar Brahimi, architect of the Bonn process, the UN mission adopted the guiding principle that it should first and foremost bolster Afghan capacity—both official and non-governmental—and rely on as limited an international presence and as many Afghan staff as possible. This came to be referred to as the

[132] Agreement on Provisional Arrangements in Afghanistan Pending the Re-Establishment of Permanent Government Institutions (Bonn Agreement), done at Bonn, 5 December 2001, UN Doc S/2001/1154. See also SC Res 1383 (2001).

[133] Bonn Agreement, art. I(4).

[134] This was encouraged by the impending staff reductions in East Timor, as well as staff cuts in UNHCR.

[135] See SC Res 1386 (2001), para. 1. The United States and France were particularly adamant that the force would not be expanded outside Kabul and its immediate surrounds.

'light footprint' approach.[136] Such a departure from the expansive mandates in Kosovo and East Timor substantially reduced the formal political functions of the UN Assistance Mission in Afghanistan (UNAMA). This was in keeping with the limited status accorded to the United Nations in the Bonn Agreement, negotiated in December 2001. But it also represented a philosophical challenge to the increasing aggregation of sovereign powers exercised in UN peace operations since the mid-1990s.[137]

On paper, UNAMA resembled earlier assistance missions that provided governance and development support to post-conflict societies. In practice, however, UNAMA remained intimately involved with the Afghan Transitional Authority and therefore with the peace process that had put it in place. This disjunction between formal authority and practical influence posed challenges not only for the specific operation in Afghanistan but also to accepted models of UN peace operations more generally.

Senior UN staff in the mission were blunt about the reasons for the light footprint approach. A mission on the scale of East Timor's transitional administration was 'not necessary and not possible', according to Brahimi.[138] Bolstering Afghanistan's capacity to govern itself required Afghans taking charge of their situation wherever possible, an end that would have been compromised by throwing international staff at a problem. A larger international presence would also have exacerbated the perverse effects on both politics and the economy. As another senior UN official put it, 'we are protecting a peace process from the hubris of the international liberal agenda as promoted by donors'. Such an agenda might include setting policy (on, for example, human rights, democracy, gender, the rule of law) in accordance with donor requirements and time-lines rather than on the basis of what was locally feasible.

In any case, armchair generals' enthusiasm for the benevolent takeover of Afghanistan was cooled by its history of resistance to foreign rule. For this reason, the Security Council-mandated ISAF was reluctant to deploy outside its original sphere of operations in and around Kabul. UN senior staff argued that expansion beyond Kabul was essential to the stability of the Interim Authority put in place by

[136] See *The Situation in Afghanistan and Its Implications for International Peace and Security* (Report of the Secretary-General), UN Doc A/56/875–S/2002/278 (18 March 2002), para. 98.

[137] See, e.g. Caplan, *New Trusteeship*.

[138] Lakhdar Brahimi, interview with the author, Kabul, 9 May 2002.

the Emergency Loya Jirga, but were careful to limit themselves to 'endorsing' Chairman Hamid Karzai's call for a wider deployment. The United States was customarily reluctant to submit itself to a UN mandate and actively opposed any expansion of ISAF. This opposition diminished as mopping up operations in search of Osama bin Laden and Al Qaeda operatives scaled down, leaving only the reluctance of those countries that would actually supply the troops.

Most importantly, however, a limited role for the United Nations was what was politically feasible at the time of the Bonn Agreement. One should be careful about taking formal passivity at face value, of course—the 'procedural' decision to invite Karzai to speak at the Bonn meeting was not unconnected with his eventual appointment as Chairman of the Interim (and later Transitional) Authority. But a central element of the peace was encouraging Afghan leaders of various stripes to see their interests as being served by buying into a political process. Asserting a lead position for the United Nations, it was argued, would have fatally undermined this aim.

This hands-off approach became central to the political strategy pursued by the United Nations in Afghanistan—a high-risk strategy that required two conceptual leaps from the normal mould of peace operations. The first was that it would be possible to blur the distinction that is generally assumed between negotiating a peace agreement ('peace-making' in the UN argot) and implementing it. Thus the Bonn Agreement was seen not as a final status agreement but as a framework for further negotiations, mediated through the institutions that it provided for over the subsequent two-and-a-half year period (the Interim Authority, the Emergency Loya Jirga, the Transitional Authority, the Constitutional Loya Jirga, and so on). The flexibility inherent in this approach may be contrasted with the peace agreements that locked the United Nations and other international actors into their roles in Bosnia and Kosovo. The Bonn Agreement avoided these pitfalls, but presumed that the United Nations could continue to have a meaningful part in the ongoing negotiations. Again, on paper, there was little formal authority for the United Nations to do so, but through high-level diplomacy and subtle interventions in its capacity as an assistance mission, it endeavoured to 'cook' the political process into a sustainable outcome.

This assumed the success of the second conceptual leap, which was that the United Nations could make up for its small mandate and limited resources through exercising greater than normal political influence. Brahimi goes one step further, arguing that it is *precisely* through recognizing Afghan leadership that one obtains credit and influence.[139] Such an approach places extraordinary importance on the personalities involved. It is generally recognized that Brahimi was instrumental to the success of Bonn, but his continuing involvement and his personal relationship with Karzai and the three Panjshiri 'musketeers' that largely wield power (Defence Minister and Vice-President Muhammad Qassem Fahim, Foreign Affairs Minister Abdullah Abdullah, and Education Minister and Special Adviser Mohammed Yunus Qanooni) were essential to the process remaining on track.

And, until the Emergency Loya Jirga, things were always likely to remain on track. Indeed, the greatest achievement of the operation was that no major group opted out of the Bonn process entirely. There were cases of intimidation and pressure on the part of local commanders to have themselves or their men 'elected', but these were sanguinely interpreted as a compliment to the perceived importance of the political process. Few people deluded themselves into thinking that the Loya Jirga was a meaningful popular consultation—the aim was to encourage those who wielded power in Afghanistan to exercise it through politics rather than through the barrel of a gun. Mao Zedong's aphorism is apposite here because the most dangerous period for the United Nations comes as Afghanistan prepares for elections. At this point, if politics is not seen to deliver at least some of the benefits that were promised, those commanders may revert to more traditional methods of promoting their interests.[140]

3.2. Operation Iraqi Freedom

The relationship between the war on terror and the US-led invasion of Iraq in 2003 was controversial. In addition to genuine security concerns, both the United States and Britain manipulated or falsified evidence in order to augment the imminence of the threat posed by Iraq and to establish links between Saddam Hussein and the terrorist organization Al Qaeda. Agreement on the part of the Security Council for the return of weapons inspectors to Iraq in November 2002 merely delayed the outbreak of hostilities.[141]

By the time operation 'Iraqi Freedom' commenced on 20 March 2003, two discrete post-conflict scenarios for Iraq were in the public

[139] Brahimi, interview.

[140] See Chapter Seven, Section 2.2.3.

[141] See, e.g. Seymour M. Hersh, 'Selective Intelligence', *New Yorker*, 12 May 2003, 44; Joseph C. Wilson, 'What I Didn't Find in Africa', *New York Times*, 6 July 2003; 'The War Isn't over for Tony: Blair Under Attack', *Economist*, 12 July 2003.

domain. The first was broadly consistent with the plans leaked by the Pentagon in October 2002 for an American-led military government in Iraq modelled on the US occupation of Japan, with the United Nations providing humanitarian assistance.[142] The second scenario, advanced by Britain and, to a lesser extent, by the US State Department, included a larger—if essentially undefined—role for the United Nations. The latter position was implicit in the Azores Declaration issued by the leaders of Britain, Spain, and the United States days before the outbreak of hostilities,[143] but was subsequently downplayed by the Bush administration.

Testifying before the Senate Foreign Relations Committee in February 2003, the Departments of State and Defence affirmed that the United States—rather than the United Nations or some provisional government of Iraqi exiles—would take charge in Baghdad. Civilian tasks would be carried out under the authority of the Pentagon's new Office for Reconstruction and Humanitarian Assistance (ORHA), established by Bush on 20 January 2003. ORHA's director, retired Army Lieutenant General Jay M. Garner, would report to the President through General Tommy Franks of Central Command and Secretary of Defence Donald Rumsfeld. Garner's tenure in Iraq was a debacle, plagued by inexperience, bureaucratic infighting, and inertia. In less than a month he was replaced by L. Paul Bremer III.[144]

Discussion within the United States tended to focus on a political function for the United Nations only when considering the question of how the occupation might be paid for. As the war began, US, British, and UN officials were exploring the possibility of transforming Iraq's Oil-for-Food programme, established by the Security Council in April 1995, into a more flexible arrangement to allow the United Nations to control goods purchased under its auspices throughout the country.[145] (Suggestions that oil revenues might actually cover military expenses incurred by the United States in defeating and administering

142 See, e.g. David E. Sanger and Eric Schmitt, 'US Has a Plan to Occupy Iraq, Officials Report', *New York Times*, 11 October 2002.

143 'Statement of the Azores Summit', *Washington Post*, 17 March 2003.

144 See, e.g. Joshua Hammer and Colin Soloway, 'Who's in Charge Here?', *Newsweek*, 26 May 2003.

145 Until the suspension of the programme during the conflict, the Iraqi government had prepared distribution plans and contracts for the entire country, distributing goods itself in the centre and south; the UN distributed goods in the north. The expansion was approved unanimously during the second week of the war: SC Res 1472 (2003).

Iraq were confined to the most radical US think tanks.[146]) Bringing the post-conflict phase of operations under UN auspices had other financial attractions. Most prominently, Chris Patten, the EU Commissioner for External Relations, stated before the war that if the United States attacked Iraq without Security Council approval the European Union might withhold money for reconstruction. This received vocal support from French President Jacques Chirac after military operations commenced, who argued that France would not support any Security Council resolution that gave retrospective legitimacy to the conflict. Companies invited to tender for reconstruction projects also expressed concern about the legal implications of ongoing Council economic sanctions.[147]

Though the outcome of the conflict was never in serious doubt, the manner in which the war was fought served as a proxy for debates within the United States on the size and posture of its armed forces. The swift victory demonstrated a paradox of the 'revolution in military affairs': a smaller, faster, more lethal US military might be able to achieve quick victories over anyone that might stand against it, but, as Rumsfeld understated it, the aftermath of such wars can be most 'untidy'.[148] It soon became apparent that little serious planning had been done on stabilizing the post-conflict situation, perhaps because of reliance upon best-case scenarios in which a minimal US presence could draw heavily upon the pre-existing Iraqi bureaucracy and security sector. Work had commenced in April 2002 within the State Department's Future of Iraq Project, including the development of extensive plans for post-conflict justice mechanisms, but was shelved when responsibility was transferred to the Department of Defence in January 2003.[149]

146 See, e.g. Nile Gardiner and David B. Rivkin, *Blueprint for Freedom: Limiting the Role of the United Nations in Post-War Iraq* (Washington, DC: Heritage Foundation, Backgrounder No 1646, 2003). The Hague Regulations support this interpretation, allowing an occupying power to administer public assets as a trustee and levy funds for the administration of the territory: see Convention (IV) Respecting the Laws and Customs of War on Land and Its Annex: Regulations Concerning the Laws and Customs of War on Land (1907 Hague Regulations), done at The Hague, 18 October 1907, available at www.icrc.org/ihl, arts. 48, 49, 55.

147 Jackie Spinner, 'Firms Cite Concerns With Iraqi Sanctions', *Washington Post*, 3 May 2003.

148 Peter J. Boyer, 'The New War Machine', *New Yorker*, 55, 30 June 2003, 70–1.

149 Peter Slevin and Dana Priest, 'Wolfowitz Concedes Iraq Errors', *Washington Post*, 24 July 2003. For one of the earliest reports on the Future of Iraq Project, see Julian Borger, 'Future of Iraq: Rebel Groups Reject CIA Overtures

For its part, the United Nations engaged in only halting planning for post-conflict scenarios. An early planning cell was shut down in December 2002 due to concerns that its very existence might be interpreted as undermining the position of UN weapons inspectors then in Iraq. A confidential internal 'pre-planning' report was requested in February 2003, which was promptly leaked to the press. The report stressed that the United Nations lacked the capacity to take on the responsibility of administering Iraq, preferring a political process similar to that followed in Afghanistan. The favoured option—in the context of what was, as the Secretary-General later emphasized, only preliminary thinking—called for an assistance mission that would provide political facilitation, consensus-building, national reconciliation, and the promotion of democratic governance and the rule of law. The people of Iraq, rather than the international community, should determine national government structures, a legal framework, and governance arrangements.[150]

There is, of course, a certain irony to this controversy about planning. The United Nations is pilloried when, as in East Timor in 1999, it fails to plan for a scenario that many regarded as likely. In Iraq it was criticized for engaging in preliminary thinking on an eventuality that most regarded as inevitable. But the tension within the planning process also reflected concerns about a role that might be thrust upon the United Nations in order to provide political cover for what was essentially a US military occupation. This suggested an additional incentive for the United States and Britain to bring the operation under some form of UN umbrella. The Fourth Geneva Convention limits the capacity of an occupying power to change the status of public officials and to impose new laws.[151] As the stated war aims in Iraq included regime change and the transformation of Iraq into a 'liberal democracy', Security Council authorization provided a sounder basis for such activities.

Resolution 1483 (2003), adopted by the Council on 22 May 2003, was an uncomfortable compromise that straddled this divide. The resolution explicitly recognized that the United States and Britain—the

down on the Farm', *Guardian* (London), 10 July 2002. Similar tensions between the US Departments of State and War undermined planning for the occupation of Germany during the Second World War.

150 James Bone, 'UN Leaders Draw up Secret Blueprint for Postwar Iraq', *The Times* (London), 5 March 2003. Humanitarian contingency planning—some of which was leaked in December 2002—was less controversial and more advanced.

151 See the Introduction, text accompanying n. 14–15.

'Coalition Provisional Authority'—were occupying powers in Iraq and called on them to comply with their obligations under the Geneva Conventions and the 1907 Hague Regulations. Nevertheless, the resolution called upon the Authority 'to promote the welfare of the Iraqi people through the effective administration of the territory, including in particular working towards the restoration of conditions of security and stability and the creation of conditions in which the Iraqi people can freely determine their own political future'.[152]

The responsibilities of the United Nations in Iraq were ambiguous. Though its role was repeatedly said to be 'vital', the powers given to the Special Representative were intentionally vague: these included 'coordinating', 'reporting', 'assisting', 'promoting', 'facilitating', and 'encouraging' various aspects of humanitarian relief and reconstruction. On the fundamental question of political structures, the Special Representative was empowered to work 'intensively with the Authority, the people of Iraq, and others concerned to advance efforts to restore and establish national and local institutions for representative governance, including by working together to facilitate a process leading to an internationally recognized, representative government of Iraq'. In the meantime, the Council supported the formation 'by the people of Iraq with the help of the Authority and working with the Special Representative' of an interim administration 'run by Iraqis'.[153] Senior Defence Department officials described their relationship with the United Nations as 'input but no veto'. Sergio Vieira de Mello, previously Special Representative in both Kosovo and East Timor, was appointed Special Representative for Iraq and head of the UN Assistance Mission for Iraq (UNAMI).[154] Vieira de Mello and twenty-one UN colleagues and visitors were killed by a truck bomb in Baghdad on 19 August 2003 in the worst attack on civilian staff in the organization's history.[155]

Iraq was unique as a transitional administration. Previous operations where international administrative structures were required can be divided into two broad classes: where state institutions were divided and where they had failed. The first class encompasses situations where governance structures were the subject of dispute

[152] SC Res 1483 (2003), preamble, paras. 4, 5. This was later confirmed in SC Res 1500 (2003), which also welcomed the establishment of the Governing Council of Iraq.

[153] SC Res 1483 (2003), preamble, paras. 8, 9.

[154] Report of the Secretary-General Pursuant to Paragraph 24 of Security Council Resolution 1483 (2003), UN Doc S/2003/715 (17 July 2003), paras. 2, 100.

[155] See, e.g. Robert F. Worth, 'Last Respects Are Paid to Head of UN Mission in Iraq', *New York Times*, 22 August 2003.

with different groups claiming power (as in Cambodia or Bosnia), or ethnic tensions within the structures themselves (such as Kosovo). The second class comprises circumstances where such structures simply did not exist (as in Namibia or East Timor). Neither applied to Iraq. In particular, Iraq had far greater resources (human, institutional, and economic) than any comparable situation in which the United Nations or other actor had exercised civilian administration functions since the Second World War. Nevertheless, comparisons with occupied Japan and Germany were stretched.[156]

In the medium-term, the invasion of Iraq certainly weakened the Security Council as the body with primary responsibility for peace and security, including the power to authorize the use of force.[157] Nevertheless, the United Nations remains an indispensable framework for the multilateral cooperation necessary to rebuild a country of the size of Iraq. This was brought home when India decided against sending a full division of 17,000 peacekeepers to assist in post-conflict security in Iraq in the absence of a Council resolution authorizing the presence.[158] The United States determined that it did not need the United Nations going into Iraq, but later acknowledged that it might need the United Nations to get out.

4. *Conclusion*

It is ironic that UNAMA reached its toughest test—the June 2002 Loya Jirga—within weeks of East Timor's independence celebrations on 20 May 2002. UNTAET may come to represent the high-water mark of UN transitional administrations, where the United Nations exercised effective sovereignty over a territory for more than two years. The UN mission in Afghanistan has a fraction of UNTAET's staff and budget and operates in a country perhaps forty times the size and thirty times the population of East Timor. Brahimi hoped that people would look back at East Timor and question whether it was necessary to assert such powers.[159] Any such evaluation may well be coloured by the fate of the UN operation in Afghanistan.

Afghanistan, therefore, suggests a different, 'lighter' approach to post-conflict reconstruction to the East Timor model, but East Timor is likely to be exceptional for other reasons. In particular, its small size

156 See Chapter One, Section 4.

157 See Chapter Three, Section 1.2.

158 Christopher Marquis, 'US May Be Forced to Go back to UN for Iraq Mandate', *New York Times*, 19 July 2003.

159 Brahimi, interview with the author.

and the uncontroversial nature of its future status made it a relatively simple case—certainly compared with the complexity of the security situation in Afghanistan, the political uncertainty of Kosovo, and the controversy surrounding Iraq. More generally, however, the 11 September 2001 attacks against the United States began to animate states with the idea that such reconstruction projects may involve greater national interest than had previously been recognized.[160] Future experimentation with the models of East Timor and Afghanistan is therefore likely to be dominated by the national interests at stake. At the same time, avoiding the appearance of imperialism or colonialism may demand a formal UN umbrella for any such operation if widespread participation is needed. The post-conflict operation in Iraq exhibited both these trends.

The accepted wisdom within the UN community, articulated most recently in the report that bears Brahimi's name, is that a successful UN peace operation should ideally consist of three sequential stages. First, the political basis for peace must be determined. Then a suitable mandate for a UN mission should be formulated. Finally, that mission should be given all the resources necessary to complete the mandate.[161] The accepted reality is that this usually happens in the reverse order: member states determine what resources they are prepared to commit to a problem and a mandate is cobbled together around those resources—often in the hope that a political solution will be forthcoming at some later date.

This reality means that the Council learns, if it learns at all, largely by doing. And, though political resistance may prevent development of a policy or institutional framework for future transitional administrations in theory, it is unlikely to prevent the demand for such operations in practice.

[160] See Chapter Eight, Section 2.1.

[161] Brahimi Report, paras. 9–83.

3

Peace and Security: The Use of Force to Maintain Law and Order

Peacekeeping is not a job for soldiers, but only a soldier can do it.

Dag Hammarskjöld,
as quoted in US Army Field Manual on Peace Operations[1]

Carrying out civil administration and police functions is simply going to degrade the American capability to do the things America has to do. We don't need to have the 82nd Airborne escorting kids to kindergarten.

Condoleezza Rice[2]

German sociologist Max Weber held that an essential quality of a modern state was its claim to the monopoly of the legitimate use of force within its borders.[3] In situations where the United Nations or another international actor has assumed some or all governmental authority, this has commonly included a monopoly of the use of force. When properly deployed, such a monopoly should include a division between a military presence, to deal with external threats and armed groups within the territory, and a civilian police presence, to provide for general law and order. Until police arrive or are established locally,

1 US Army, Field Manual 100–23 Peace Operations (Headquarters, Department of the Army, December 1994), available at www.dtic.mil/doctrine/jel/service_pubs/fm100_23.pdf, 1.

2 Quoted in William Drozdiak, 'Bush Plan Worries Europeans; Removing US Troops from Balkans Is Seen as Divisive', *Washington Post*, 24 October 2000.

3 See, e.g. Max Weber, *The Theory of Social and Economic Organization* [1922], translated by A. M. Henderson and Talcott Parsons (Oxford: Oxford University Press, 1947), 156.

however, responsibility for law and order falls either on the military or on no one at all.

This chapter reviews the changing approach to the use of force in UN peace operations generally,[4] before considering responses to the security vacuum that has confronted virtually every transitional administration-type operation. How should an international presence address the lawlessness that follows a breakdown in state security institutions? The diverse experience of how the military has responded to such situations—demonstrated by the contrasting approaches in Kosovo and East Timor—suggests the need to plan for at least a temporary assumption of this burden. It should include preparation for the transfer of law and order responsibilities to local or international civilian police at the earliest possible moment. Nevertheless, the impressions formed during the first months of an operation affect both the character of the mission and the internal security of the territory for the immediate future. Since it is unlikely that civilian police will ever be in a position to deploy within that time frame, military personnel will be dealing with these situations in practice whether they plan for it or not.

It will not be possible to encompass the entirety of this topic in the present work. The focus here is on the initial military phase of a complex peace operation, responses to a security vacuum, and the establishment of the conditions for civilian rule under international administration. The deployment of troops and their command structures, for example, raise more general issues about UN peace operations that will not be discussed here.[5] Similarly, disarmament, demobilization, and reintegration (DDR) programmes are an integral part of the medium-term success of a return to civilian rule, but apply to a far wider range of peace operations than those considered in this chapter;[6] the activities of civilian police will also be addressed only

[4] The term 'peace operations' is understood to include both peacekeeping operations and enforcement actions, as well as the contested category of 'peace enforcement'. See Section 1 in this chapter.

[5] See Ian Brownlie, *International Law and the Use of Force by States* (Oxford: Clarendon Press, 1963); John Hillen, *Blue Helmets: The Strategy of UN Military Operations*, 2nd edn. (Washington, DC: Brassey's, 2000); Trevor Findlay, *The Use of Force in UN Peace Operations* (Oxford: SIPRI & Oxford University Press, 2002).

[6] See UN Department of Peacekeeping Operations, Disarmament, Demobilization and Reintegration of Ex-Combatants in a Peacekeeping Environment: Principles and Guidelines (New York: Lessons Learned Unit, December 1999), available at www.un.org/Depts/dpko/lessons; Natalie Pauwels (ed.), *War*

briefly.[7] Some related activities intended to promote the rule of law under transitional administration are considered in Chapter Five.

The failure to prepare for a security vacuum remains a very real problem. After the defeat of Iraqi forces in 2003, widespread looting and civil unrest ensued as the state security apparatus collapsed. The most surprising element of these events was the suggestion that they were unexpected: the *Washington Post* reported that military officers, administration officials, and defence experts with peacekeeping experience from the 1990s were mystified by the failure of senior military and civilian leaders at the Pentagon to plan for a quick transition from war-fighting to stability operations.[8] Without security, none of the more complex political tasks that are intended to justify the use of force in the first place can be achieved.

1. *The Use of Force in Peace Operations*

The United Nations has generally been reluctant to allow military units under its command to use force. The three peace operations in which troops under UN command engaged in the use of force on a significant scale—Congo from 1960 to 1963, Somalia in 1993, and Bosnia and Herzegovina from 1994 to 1995—were traumatic experiences for the organization; the controversies to which they gave rise were surpassed only by two occasions on which force was not used at all, in Rwanda and Srebrenica. Such reluctance is consistent with the traditional conception of peacekeeping as an impartial activity undertaken with the consent of all parties, in which force is used only in self-defence. Over the years, however, all three characteristics of traditional peacekeeping (impartiality, consent, minimum use of force) have been brought into question.

Peacekeeping was a creative effort to marry the limited means at the disposal of the United Nations to the lofty ends of maintaining international peace and security. Secretary-General Dag Hammarskjöld

Force to Work Force: Global Perspectives on Demobilization and Reintegration (Baden-Baden: Nomos, 2000).

[7] See William Hubert Lewis and Edward Marks, *Strengthening International Civilian Police Operations* (Washington, DC: Center for Strategic and International Studies, 2000); Annika S. Hansen, *From Congo to Kosovo: Civilian Police in Peace Operations* (Oxford: Oxford University Press for the International Institute for Strategic Studies, 2002).

[8] Peter Slevin and Vernon Loeb, 'Plan to Secure Postwar Iraq Faulted; Pentagon Ignored Lessons from Decade of Peacekeeping, Critics Say', *Washington Post*, 19 May 2003.

located peacekeeping in the interstices between the peaceful and coercive measures available to the Security Council—'Chapter VI½' as he famously called it—a blurring of the distinction between the two that suggests the early origins of a doctrinal problem now believed to have arisen on the streets of Mogadishu.[9]

By the 1990s, peace operations had come to be seen as falling into two discrete camps: peacekeeping and enforcement actions. The former were the 'Blue Helmet' operations that took place under the formal command of the UN Secretary-General; the latter were war-fighting operations typically conducted by multinational forces or 'coalitions of the willing' under the aegis, but not the command, of the Security Council. The first enforcement action was undertaken in Korea in 1950, when the Council 'recommended' action under the unified command of the United States. The next major enforcement action was Operation Desert Storm in 1991, when the Council authorized 'Member States co-operating with the Government of Kuwait' (i.e. states other than Israel) to drive Iraq from occupied Kuwait.[10] Resolution 678 (1990) provided the template for enforcement actions that took place through the 1990s: it depended on the willingness of certain states to undertake (and fund) a military operation; it conferred broad discretion on those states to determine when and how the goals of that operation might be achieved; it limited Council involvement to a vague request to keep its members 'regularly informed'; and it failed to provide an endpoint for the mandate.

Despite ongoing deference to this dichotomy, peacekeeping operations are now routinely given the more robust chapter VII authorization denied to their cold war predecessors. This has happened in three sets of circumstances. First, chapter VII has been invoked out of an apparent desire to emphasize that peacekeepers retain the right to use force in self-defence. Second, when peacekeeping missions have experienced difficulties (notably the UN Protection Force (UNPROFOR) in the former Yugoslavia) mandates have been revised to include chapter VII authorization—again, in theory, merely to emphasize the right of self-defence. In both cases, recourse to chapter VII has tended to represent a rhetorical escalation in lieu of greater material or political support. Third, peacekeeping operations have received chapter VII

[9] For a discussion of the role of the Council in authorizing the use of force, see Simon Chesterman, *Just War or Just Peace? Humanitarian Intervention and International Law* (Oxford: Oxford University Press, 2001), 163–218.

[10] In 1966, the Security Council also 'called upon' the United Kingdom to use force to prevent the violation of sanctions against Southern Rhodesia: SC Res 221 (1966).

mandates to conduct what are effectively enforcement actions (most infamously UNOSOM II in Somalia).[11]

This conflation of categories is of more than academic importance. As the United Nations has been drawn into an increasing number of internal armed conflicts, the political assumptions that go with 'traditional' peacekeeping have become largely artificial. Peacekeepers have had to respond to complex situations that bear little resemblance to a ceasefire between standing armies of states. These problems have been exacerbated when the United Nations itself has assumed some or all governmental control over territory, either by design or default. In the security gap left by departing Indonesian forces in East Timor in 1999, the peacekeeping force that followed the Australian-led International Force in East Timor (INTERFET) operation became, in essence, the army of East Timor while the territory was under UN control.[12] Similar roles were played by the peacekeeping force in Eastern Slavonia, by the multinational Implementation and Stabilization Forces (IFOR and SFOR) in Bosnia after 1995, and by KFOR in Kosovo. Where the United Nations has exercised less than complete control over territory, international military contingents have still played an extremely important role in providing internal security, as in Sierra Leone, Afghanistan, and Iraq. Within the United Nations, however, there has been a great deal of reluctance to accept this as an established class of UN peace operations and plan accordingly.

1.1. From Self-Defence to Defence of the Mission

The first peacekeeping operation that used armed military personnel was the UN Emergency Force (UNEF), established by the General Assembly in 1956 to supervise the ceasefire in the Middle East after the Suez invasion.[13] Soon after the crisis broke out, Canadian Foreign Minister Lester B. Pearson suggested the need for 'a truly international peace and police force... large enough to keep these borders at peace while a political settlement is being worked out'.[14] The proposal that Hammarskjöld later submitted to the General Assembly did not specifically mention the use of force, but did state that 'there was no intent in the establishment of the Force to influence the military balance

[11] Findlay, *Use of Force*, 9.

[12] SC Res 1272 (1999).

[13] UNEF was preceded by the unarmed military observers of the UN Truce Supervisory Organization (UNTSO) (1948–) and the UN Military Observer Group in India and Pakistan (UNMOGIP) (1949–).

[14] Brian Urquhart, *Ralph Bunche: An American Life* (New York: W. W. Norton, 1993), 265.

in the current conflict, and thereby the political balance affecting efforts to settle the conflict'.[15] UNEF was later described as a 'plate-glass window'—not capable of withstanding assault, but nonetheless 'a lightly armed barrier that all see and tend to respect'.[16] Tensions between the use of force in self-defence and in defence of the broader purposes of the mission were present even in this first armed peacekeeping operation. At various points after its deployment, the Force Commander, Canadian Major-General E. L. Burns, attempted to reinterpret UNEF's mandate in order to deter violations of the ceasefire. He appears to have been genuinely surprised when his requests for a force robust enough to pose a deterrent threat to the parties was refused by New York.[17]

Contradictions between the political basis for peacekeeping and military imperatives on the ground were laid bare in the UN Operation in the Congo (ONUC) in 1960. ONUC began as a conventional peacekeeping mission modelled on UNEF; like UNEF, it was mandated to use force only in self-defence and only as a last resort. Such a model was of little use in the reality of civil war and collapsed state institutions, however. Self-defence was, therefore, interpreted more broadly as new requirements arose, including preventing peacekeepers from being disarmed and attacked, their posts and installations from being besieged, and their mandated activities disrupted. The mandate was later extended in practice to allow peacekeepers to protect civilians at risk of death, injury, or gross violations of human rights. ONUC was ultimately authorized to use force beyond self-defence, if necessary, to prevent civil war and to expel foreign mercenaries. Though UN staff maintained throughout the operation that force was being used only in self-defence, this became, in strategy and tactics, indistinguishable from a standard military campaign.[18]

Compounded by controversies about ONUC's mandate and the interference this posed in the internal affairs of a sovereign state, the operation split the Security Council, almost bankrupted the United Nations, and ensured that force was not used on a comparable scale for decades.[19] For the next quarter of a century, peacekeeping was limited

[15] Report of the Secretary-General on Basic Points for the Presence and Functioning in Egypt of the United Nations Emergency Force, UN Doc A/3302 (6 November 1956).

[16] Finn Seyersted, *United Nations Forces in the Law of Peace and War* (Leyden: A. W. Sijthoff, 1966), 48.

[17] Findlay, *Use of Force*, 50.

[18] See further Chapter Two, Section 2.5.1. For a discussion of ONUC's civilian responsibilities, see Section 2.1 in this chapter.

[19] Findlay, *Use of Force*, 51–86.

to small observation or goodwill missions, most of them monitoring post-conflict situations.[20] Only two missions were deployed in civil wars—Cyprus in 1964 and Lebanon in 1978—and in both cases the mandates were crafted to avoid any escalation of the use of force. Far from being regarded as a new type of operation, Congo was regarded as an aberration: the UN Secretariat and the member states were 'more interested in forgetting than in learning, more interested in avoiding future ONUCs than in doing them better'.[21]

The main doctrinal advance on the question of the use of force occurred with the creation of the second UN Emergency Force in the Middle East (UNEF II), though in practice this was a 'traditional' peacekeeping operation. Established after the October 1973 war between Israel and Egypt, UNEF II was tasked with supervising the ceasefire and the staged disengagement of Israeli forces from the Sinai. Although it could have drawn solely upon existing precedents, Secretary-General Kurt Waldheim issued new guidelines for the use of force that formed the basis for all subsequent UN peacekeeping operations. The guidelines stated that '[s]elf-defence would include resistance to attempts by forceful means to prevent [UNEF II] from discharging its duties under the mandate of the Security Council'.[22]

It is not immediately clear why this expansive definition of self-defence was used in respect of what was otherwise a fairly standard peacekeeping operation. The stronger words were certainly not backed up with additional hardware; nor were there expectations that force was likely to be used in theatre. In fact, it appears that UNEF II forces never actually fired more than warning shots.[23] Nevertheless, with hindsight this came to be regarded as a sea change in UN doctrine on the use of force. The 1995 *General Guidelines for Peacekeeping Operations* noted that such a conception of self-defence 'might be interpreted as entitling United Nations personnel to open fire in a wide variety of

[20] These were UNSF (1962–3); UNYOM (1963–4); UNFICYP (1964–); DOMREP (1965–6); UNIPOM (1965–6); UNEF II (1973–9); UNDOF (1974–); UNIFIL (1978–); UNGOMAP (1988–90); UNIIMOG (1988–91).

[21] William J. Durch, 'The UN Operation in the Congo: 1960–1964', in William J. Durch (ed.), *The Evolution of UN Peacekeeping: Case Studies and Comparative Analysis* (New York: St Martin's Press, 1993), 315, 349. Cf. International Peace Academy, *Peacekeeper's Handbook* (New York: Pergamon Press, 1984), 38.

[22] Report of the Secretary General on the Implementation of Security Council Resolution 340 (1973), UN Doc S/11052/Rev. 1 (27 October 1973). See Marrack Goulding (1993) 'The Evolution of United Nations Peacekeeping', *International Affairs*, 69: 451, 455.

[23] Findlay, *Use of Force*, 100–3.

situations'.[24] Or, as one commentator put it more bluntly: 'Allowing a force to take positive action in defence of its purpose is no different from allowing them to enforce it.'[25] Until the missions in Somalia and Bosnia, these possibilities remained hypothetical.

1.2. Peacekeeping After the End of the Cold War

The end of the cold war and Operation Desert Storm (1991) radically changed the context within which force was used under the auspices of the United Nations. Amid euphoric talk of a 'New World Order', the Security Council asserted that an increasingly broad range of circumstances could constitute threats falling within its purview.[26] Importantly, this was seen as including internal armed conflicts. With a small measure of revisionist historiography, the 1960s operation in the Congo was seen to be a precedent for operations in Liberia and Somalia.

The failure to implement the collective security system envisaged in the Charter, however, (which presumed that troops would be made available to the Council 'on its call'[27]) led to a reliance on delegation of the Council's powers. Enforcement actions were thus limited to situations where acting states had the political will to bear the financial and human costs. The Unified Task Force (UNITAF) operation in Somalia illustrated this in graphic terms: Security Council resolution 794 (1992) was not merely contingent on a US offer of troops—the first draft was written in the Pentagon. A similar approach was adopted in Rwanda (led by France), Haiti (led by the United States), Albania (led by Italy), and East Timor (led by Australia). Regional arrangements have also been authorized to intervene or keep the peace in the former Yugoslavia (NATO), Liberia and Sierra Leone (ECOMOG), the Democratic Republic of the Congo (European Union), and Afghanistan (NATO).[28] In many cases, different classes

[24] UN Department of Peacekeeping Operations, General Guidelines for Peacekeeping Operations, UN Doc UN/210/TC/GG95 (October 1995), available at www.un.org/Depts/dpko/training, 20.

[25] N. D. White, *The United Nations and the Maintenance of International Peace and Security* (Manchester: Manchester University Press, 1990), 201.

[26] Security Council Summit Statement Concerning the Council's Responsibility in the Maintenance of International Peace and Security, UN Doc S/23500 (31 January 1992).

[27] UN Charter, art. 43(1).

[28] ECOMOG is the Economic Community of West African States (ECOWAS) Military Observer Group. Operation Artemis (2003) in the Democratic Republic of the Congo was technically an EU operation though it was dominated by France. NATO assumed control of ISAF in Afghanistan in August 2003.

of operations have been closely related to one another and sometimes overlapped. Peacekeeping operations authorized in Somalia, Haiti, Rwanda, Bosnia, and Sierra Leone were followed by enforcement actions when they proved incapable of discharging their mandates; enforcement actions were, in turn, followed by peacekeepers in Somalia, Haiti, Sierra Leone, Kosovo, and East Timor.[29]

Somalia (1993) and Bosnia (1994–5) confirmed the emerging view that forces under UN command were unsuited to war-fighting. The inability of the UN Operation in Somalia (UNOSOM) to protect the delivery and distribution of humanitarian aid in Somalia led to the creation of UNITAF, a US-led operation that massively reinforced the peacekeeping presence and was briefly regarded as a success. Unfortunately, early signals that one of UNITAF's primary goals was to leave Somalia as quickly as possible were interpreted by the Somali factions as meaning that any temporary inconvenience caused by the US presence could probably be waited out.[30] The peacekeeping operation that followed, UNOSOM II, was remarkable for being the first mission organized and commanded by the United Nations to be explicitly mandated under chapter VII of the Charter, and the first since the Congo to receive a specific mandate to use force beyond self-defence.[31] As with UNOSOM and UNITAF, the lack of a Somali government had removed the question of its consent to the operation. But it was the departure from the other two characteristics of traditional peacekeeping (impartiality and the minimum use of force) that became the *bête noire* of the mission. After an ambush in June 1993 resulted in the deaths of twenty-four Pakistani peacekeepers and another fifty-seven wounded—the highest number of casualties in a single day in UN peacekeeping history—the Security Council authorized the Secretary-General as Commander-in-Chief of UNOSOM II to take 'all necessary measures against all those responsible', including 'their arrest and detention for prosecution, trial and punishment'.[32] There appears to have been little understanding at the time of how significant a departure this was from UNOSOM's original mission, as it amounted to a declaration of war against General

[29] The enforcement actions in Kosovo and Sierra Leone were not authorized by the UN Security Council.

[30] William J. Durch, 'Introduction to Anarchy: Humanitarian Intervention and "State-Building" in Somalia', in William J. Durch (ed.), *UN Peacekeeping, American Policy, and the Uncivil Wars of the 1990s* (New York: St Martin's Press, 1996), 311, 321.

[31] Findlay, *Use of Force*, 184.

[32] SC Res 837 (1993), para. 5.

Mohamed Aideed's militia.[33] This culminated in the 3 October 1993 raid on the Olympia Hotel in Mogadishu—undertaken independently by the United States—in which three US helicopters were shot down and eighteen US Rangers and one Malaysian soldier were killed.[34] Four days later, President Bill Clinton announced that US troops would withdraw by 31 March 1994, regardless of the situation on the ground.[35] Troop contributors to UNOSOM II soon announced their withdrawal also. By February 1994, it was clear that a sustained presence was impossible and the Council adopted a scaled-down mandate prior to a gun-cocked retreat in March 1995.[36]

Meanwhile, in Bosnia, lightly armed UN forces were given a nominally impartial role when there was, in reality, no peace to keep. As the situation deteriorated, the Security Council proclaimed the existence of 'safe areas' around five Bosnian towns and the city of Sarajevo, while UNPROFOR was given an ambiguous mandate to protect them while 'acting in self-defence'.[37] At the same time, an apparently general authorization was given to member states (meaning NATO) to take 'all necessary measures, through the use of air power' to support UNPROFOR in and around the safe areas.[38] This served to deter attacks in the short-term, but when it was overrun by the Bosnian Serbs in 1995, the name of one of the safe areas—Srebrenica—became synonymous with the disjunction between Council rhetoric and resolve.[39]

Conventional wisdom concerning the fall of the Bosnian safe areas was that the United Nations had failed to learn the two lessons of Somalia: that absolute impartiality was the keystone to a peacekeeping operation—in other words, the 'Mogadishu line' had been crossed—and that UN command provided an unworkable structure for the

[33] John L. Hirsch and Robert Oakley, *Somalia and Operation Restore Hope: Reflections on Peacemaking and Peacekeeping* (Washington, DC: United States Institute of Peace Press, 1995), 118, n. 118; Findlay, *Use of Force*, 196.

[34] See Mark Bowden, *Black Hawk Down: A Story of Modern War* (New York: Atlantic Monthly Press, 1999).

[35] Paul F. Horvitz, 'Fending Off Congress, Clinton Links Pullout to Safety for Somalis', *International Herald Tribune*, 7 October 1993.

[36] SC Res 897 (1994). See also Chapter Two, Section 2.5.2.

[37] SC Res 819 (1993); SC Res 824 (1993); SC Res 836 (1993).

[38] SC Res 836 (1993), para. 10. Though unclear in the resolution, the decision to initiate the use of air power was to be taken by the Secretary-General in consultation with the members of the Security Council: Report of the Secretary-General Pursuant to Security Council Resolution 836 (1993), UN Doc S/25939 (14 June 1993).

[39] Jan Willem Honig and Norbert Both, *Srebrenica: Record of a War Crime* (London: Penguin, 1996). See also Chapter Two, Section 2.4.1.

alternative to peacekeeping: an enforcement action.[40] The success of NATO air strikes later that year in coercing the parties to the negotiating table in Dayton, Ohio, reinforced this view, and the Dayton Peace Agreement was implemented and maintained by IFOR and SFOR—NATO-run operations authorized by but independent of the Security Council. Such wisdom gave rise to three policy changes. First, the strict dichotomy between peacekeeping and enforcement actions was reasserted, most notably by the Secretary-General in his *Supplement to An Agenda for Peace* .[41] Second, subsequent enforcement actions (when they were actually undertaken) were kept under national command, with the obligation only to report to the Council on the action taken in its name. Third, Bosnia was taken as proof that superior air power could provide a 'clean' resolution to a messy conflict on the ground by coercing belligerents to negotiate. (This view overlooked the importance of Croatia's ground offensive in reversing Bosnian Serb gains and the effect that the prolonged ground war had had on the parties.[42])

The effects of this last point concerning air power were seen most clearly in Kosovo, when NATO commenced a seventy-eight-day air campaign without Council authorization in 1999. While some NATO governments interpreted Kosovo at the time as heralding a new era of NATO activism without the constraints of Council politics, the United States appears to have drawn different conclusions: specifically, that the operational constraints of acting in concert with its NATO allies were even more frustrating than the political constraints of seeking Council authorization. The result has been that the apartheid sometimes identified in UN peace operations—where industrialized countries fight the wars they choose and developing countries provide peacekeepers to do dangerous peacekeeping in less strategic areas[43]—is now more properly understood as a three-tier class structure. Developing countries continue to make up over three-quarters of the troop contributors for peacekeeping operations under

40 See, e.g. Mats R. Berdal, *Whither UN Peacekeeping?* (London: International Institute for Strategic Studies, 1993), 39–41; Dick A. Leurdijk, *The United Nations and NATO in Former Yugoslavia: Partners in International Cooperation* (The Hague: Netherlands Atlantic Commission, 1994), 81.

41 Supplement to An Agenda for Peace: Position Paper of the Secretary-General on the Occasion of the Fiftieth Anniversary of the United Nations, UN Doc A/50/60–S/1995/1 (3 January 1995). This was disseminated in January 1995. See also Shashi Tharoor (1995) 'The Changing Face of Peace-Keeping and Peace-Enforcement', *Fordham International Law Journal*, 19: 408.

42 See, e.g. Richard Holbrooke, *To End a War* (New York: Random House, 1998), 72–3.

43 David M. Malone and Ramesh Thakur, 'Racism in Peacekeeping', *Globe and Mail* (Toronto), 30 October 2000.

the command of the United Nations, notably in Africa. A number of industrialized countries (especially those in NATO) provide troops that operate under national command but with UN authorization, in operations such as SFOR, KFOR, and ISAF. And the United States, in addition to participating selectively in NATO activities, effectively operates as a free agent.[44]

Sierra Leone provides an example of how this works in practice. The disastrously planned, trained, and commanded UNAMSIL operation nearly collapsed in early 2000, while 500 peacekeepers were taken hostage by Foday Sankoh's Revolutionary United Front (RUF). Britain soon dispatched six warships to its former colony. The ostensible purpose of Operation Palliser was the safe evacuation of British and other foreign nationals, action undertaken with the consent of the government in Freetown. In reality, however, the force was soon organizing and training UN troops, establishing fortified positions, manning roadblocks, securing Freetown and its airports, conducting joint patrols with UNAMSIL, and coming under fire—which it returned in 'robust' self-defence.[45] After securing the airport and the release of most of the UN forces, Operation Palliser was scaled down in mid-June 2000 to leave only British military advisers to work with UNAMSIL forces and the Sierra Leonean Army.[46] British forces operated at all times outside the UN command and control, though they attended UN planning meetings. The Secretary-General later observed that the presence was 'a pivotal factor in restoring stability'.[47] This is widely regarded as the turning point in UNAMSIL's operations, after which it became more aggressive in addressing—and, on occasion, pre-empting—the ongoing challenges posed by the RUF. By January 2002, some 45,000

44 Cf. Report of the Panel on United Nations Peace Operations (Brahimi Report), UN Doc A/55/305–S/2000/809 (21 August 2000), available at www.un.org/peace/reports/peace_operations, para. 103. Over three-quarters of the troops participating in peacekeeping operations are now typically from developing countries. The five permanent members of the Security Council in total contribute less than 3 per cent of all peacekeepers, with the United States and China supplying a grand total of two peacekeepers each: DPKO, Monthly Summary of Contributions (March 2003), available at www.un.org/Depts/dpko/dpko/contributors.

45 Findlay, *Use of Force*, 301.

46 See generally John L. Hirsch, *Sierra Leone: Diamonds and the Struggle for Democracy* (Boulder, CO: Lynne Rienner, 2001).

47 Fourth Report of the Secretary-General Pursuant to Security Council Resolution 1270 (1999) on the United Nations Mission in Sierra Leone, UN Doc S/2000/455 (19 May 2000), para. 14.

rebels had been disarmed and demobilized; two months later President Ahmad Tejan Kabbah announced the end of a four-year state of emergency.[48]

The position of the United States on the use of force under Security Council auspices is, of course, best demonstrated by the war in Iraq in 2003. Iraq may come to represent both the high-water mark and the lowest ebb of Security Council authority on the use of force. When the United States and Britain, together with Australia and Poland, commenced military operations against Saddam Hussein's regime in March 2003 without explicit Council authorization, many commentators heard the death knell of the Council as the body with primary responsibility for international peace and security. Ironically, the seeds of this marginalization were sewn in the enforcement action authorized by the Council in November 1990. This was true in relation to the (tenuous) legal argument that resolution 678 (1990) provided ultimate legal authority for the action, but also more generally in that Operation Desert Storm established the model of contracting out UN enforcement actions to coalitions of the willing. As noted earlier, military action under the auspices of the Council through the 1990s took place only when circumstances on the ground coincided with the national interests of a state that was prepared to act, with the result that one analyst described the Council as becoming the equivalent of a 'law-laundering service'.[49] Indeed, it is misleading to suggest that the Council ever worked effectively as an objective arbiter in the area of peace and security—or that it was ever realistically expected to do so. The Council was and remains an inherently political body; the fact that the United States, which spends as much on its own military as the next fifteen countries combined, is unwilling to submit itself to regulation or commit its troops to operations commanded by others should come as little surprise. The more important question is how to ensure that the United States remains engaged with the United Nations, without making the United Nations merely a tool of US foreign policy.[50]

The aftermath of military success in Iraq—widespread looting, sporadic revenge killings, and resistance to military occupation—demonstrated the importance of linking military and political strategies

48 'Sierra Leone Lifts Emergency Ahead of Polls', *Agence France Presse*, 2 March 2002. See also Chapter Two, Section 2.5.3.

49 Richard A. Falk (1994) 'The United Nations and the Rule of Law', *Transnational Law and Contemporary Problems*, 4: 611, 628.

50 See further Chapter Eight, Section 2.

to rebuild the institutions of a defeated state, comparable to the imperatives in rebuilding an internally riven or collapsed state. The swift creation and replacement of the Pentagon's Office of Reconstruction and Humanitarian Assistance (ORHA), which was operational in Iraq for less than a month under retired General Jay Garner, together with the withdrawal and then reinforcement of US troops in the weeks following the defeat of Iraq's military, suggested that the United States and its coalition partners had spent far more time planning to win the war than they had to win the peace.[51] This repeated a failure of many peace operations, combined with a general unwillingness to task the military with 'policing' functions. As the next section argues, however, allowing a security vacuum to develop may irreparably undermine the larger project of consolidating a lasting peace.

2. *Emergency Law and Order*

The single most important aim of any peace operation is to establish the conditions for sustainable security for the civilian population. Traditional peacekeeping seeks to achieve this through monitoring a ceasefire between states that have been at war; this normalization of relations is intended to allow state institutions to maintain order within their respective territories. When a peace operation attempts to bring order to territory in which the institutions of the state have ceased to function, however, the United Nations and other international actors confront the dilemma of whether and how to use the military to provide for internal security. A related dilemma frequently arises: whether to regard 'spoilers' that challenge the new regime as political opponents, criminal elements, or military enemies.[52]

The stability of a peace accord and the credibility of peacekeepers depend greatly on first impressions. The first six- to twelve-week period is critical for establishing the basis for an effective international presence; credibility and political momentum lost during this period can be difficult to regain.[53] The missions in Bosnia and Kosovo continue to suffer from the failure to assert military and policing

[51] For a discussion of early indicators of the lack of planning, see Simon Chesterman and David M. Malone, 'Postwar Challenge: Who Plans for Rebuilding Iraq?' *International Herald Tribune*, 5 December 2002. The Iraq operation is considered further in Chapter Two, Section 3.2.

[52] See Stephen John Stedman (1997) 'Spoiler Problems in Peace Processes' *International Security*, 22(2): 5.

[53] Brahimi Report, para. 87.

authority in the early stages of the operations. In Bosnia, slow deployment of civilian police gave Bosnian Serb authorities time to prepare a forced evacuation of Sarajevo's Serb suburbs, ransacking and burning homes as they left.[54] In Kosovo, reluctance to exert authority in the remaining Serb-controlled areas led to the entrenchment of informal systems of law enforcement, such as the 'bridge-watchers' in northern Mitrovica.[55] East Timor presents a more promising example: the Australian-led force that first entered East Timor arguably had a narrower mandate to restore law and order than KFOR in Kosovo. Nevertheless, it interpreted its mandate to restore peace and security as encompassing arrests of individuals accused of committing serious offences.

This section surveys the emergency phase of a series of operations and the various strategies that have been adopted to deal with short-term law and order problems. It then considers attempts to systematize the lessons learned in this period at the level of doctrine.

2.1. *Law and Order in UN Peace Operations*

Congo was the first occasion on which basic responsibility for law and order fell ultimately to personnel under UN command. In the absence of an effective government, ONUC assumed many of the law and order functions of a civilian police force, including the apprehension and detention of criminals, as well as establishing and enforcing curfews, and conducting short- and long-range patrols.[56] These functions were carried out despite the absence of a clear power of arrest, jails, or functioning courts—it was also unclear what law ONUC was to uphold, as the newly independent state had not had time to codify a Congolese version of the old Belgian law. Such problems were compounded by the inadequacy of troops for such tasks: it became increasingly clear that highly trained riot police would have been more suited to such tasks than military regiments; where civilian police from Ghana and

[54] Richard Caplan, *A New Trusteeship? The International Administration of War-Torn Territories* (Oxford: Oxford University Press, 2002), 31.

[55] The bridge-watchers are Serbs in northern Mitrovica who seek to prevent ethnic Albanians from crossing the river from the south of the divided city. See, e.g. Nicholas Wood, 'Division and Disorder Still Tearing at Kosovo', *Washington Post*, 22 June 2002.

[56] Second Progress Report to the Secretary General from his Special Representative in the Congo, Mr Rajeshwar Dayal, UN Doc S/4557 (2 November 1960).

Nigeria operated, they were regarded as worth 'twenty times their number of the best fighting infantry'.[57]

As indicated earlier, Congo was generally regarded as an aberration rather than as a precursor of the missions that would occupy the United Nations in later years. The next operation with a comparable mandate was the UN Transitional Authority in Cambodia (UNTAC) (1992–3), whose rules of engagement for the first time specifically identified the prevention of crimes against humanity as warranting the use of 'all available means', including armed force. The Force Commander, Lieutenant General John Sanderson of Australia, assumed that these rules permitted defence of 'anyone going about their legitimate business under the Paris Agreement', including non-uniformed UN personnel and Cambodians.[58] Yet this approach was applied inconsistently. Special Representative of the Secretary-General Yasushi Akashi interpreted self-defence strictly, with the result that UNTAC failed to resist harassment from Khmer Rouge elements. In May 1992, a confrontation took place between the Khmer Rouge and the Special Representative and Force Commander at a Khmer Rouge roadblock in north-west Cambodia. In what was seen as a humiliation for UNTAC, they were turned away at a bamboo pole across the road. Criticism for failing to challenge the Khmer Rouge did not only come from outside the mission. The Deputy Force Commander, French Brigadier-General Jean-Michel Loridon, was dismissed after advocating the use of force against the Khmer Rouge.[59]

This position changed somewhat after the Khmer Rouge decided to boycott the electoral process. Concerned that a military attack might be launched to disrupt the elections scheduled for May 1993, General Sanderson redeployed UNTAC's military component to 'defend' the elections. More controversially, UNTAC also allowed the other

[57] Arthur Lee Burns and Nina Heathcote, *Peacekeeping by UN Forces: From Suez to the Congo* (New York: Praeger for the Center for International Studies, Princeton, 1963), 185; Catherine Hoskyns, *The Congo Since Independence: January 1960 to December 1961* (Oxford: Oxford University Press, 1965), 295. See Chapter Two, Section 2.5.1.

[58] John M. Sanderson, 'A Review of Recent Peacekeeping Operations' (Dacca: Paper presented at Pacific Armies Management Seminar, January 1994), quoted in Findlay, *Use of Force*, 125–6; James A. Schear, 'Riding the Tiger: The UN and Cambodia', in Durch (ed.), *UN Peacekeeping, American Policy*, 135, 143. See Chapter Two, Section 2.3.1.

[59] Trevor Findlay, *Cambodia: The Legacy and Lessons of UNTAC* (Oxford: Oxford University Press, 1995), 37; Second Progress Report of the Secretary-General on the United Nations Transitional Authority in Cambodia, UN Doc S/24578 (21 September 1992).

parties that had agreed to take part in the elections to use their own forces to repulse the Khmer Rouge and secure the safety of polling stations.[60] In a revolutionary step in January 1993, UNTAC appointed its own special prosecutor to issue warrants against suspected violators of human rights. Problems arose almost immediately: UNTAC had no jail, requiring the establishment of the first UN 'detention facility'. In addition, civilian police were not armed, and UNTAC's interpretation of its mandate was that it had no authority to exercise force for such a purpose. More importantly, Hun Sen's party was not prepared to prosecute its own members and could not guarantee the fair treatment of those from the other factions. The first two prisoners of the United Nations were thus held without habeas corpus and without trial.[61]

In Somalia, different interpretations of the law and order responsibilities of foreign troops turned on whether UNITAF was regarded as an occupation force. This varied between the different troop contributors. Australia, for example, argued that the presence of foreign troops was governed by the Fourth Geneva Convention, giving rise to an obligation to restore and maintain public order. As part of a civil affairs programme, the Australian UNITAF contingent in Baidoa re-established the local police force and legal system, including jails and courts.[62] UNITAF command rejected this interpretation: since this was a humanitarian rather than military operation, it argued that the military presence could not be regarded as an army of occupation; virtually no action was taken at the national level to re-establish a Somali police force or judiciary.[63] UNOSOM II later sought to address the lack of a legal regime by promulgating the former Somali Penal Code of 1962, an act that went beyond its mandate but was justified at the time by the absence of any functioning government authority whatsoever.[64]

[60] This was comparable to the situation in Namibia in April 1989, when restrictions on the South African Defence Forces were lifted in response to violations of the peace agreement by the South West Africa People's Organization (SWAPO): Marrack Goulding, *Peacemonger* (London: John Murray, 2002), 153–4.

[61] Michael W. Doyle, *UN Peacekeeping in Cambodia: UNTAC's Civil Mandate* (Boulder, CO: Lynne Rienner, 1995), 47.

[62] Findlay, *Use of Force*, 177. International humanitarian law and occupation is discussed in the Introduction.

[63] F. M. Lorenz (1993) 'Law and Anarchy in Somalia', *Parameters: US Army War College Quarterly*, 23(4): 27, 35. The United States directed some funds to rebuilding the Somali police after the 'Black Hawk Down' incident in October 1993, but by then it was too late: Walter Clarke and Jeffrey Herbst (1996) 'Somalia and the Future of Humanitarian Intervention', *Foreign Affairs*, 75(2): 70, 77.

[64] See Chapter Two, Section 2.5.2.

In Haiti, rules of engagement for the 21,000 strong multinational force that peacefully occupied the country in September 1994 were interpreted as leaving law enforcement to the Haitian Armed Forces. This was the same force that had terrorized the population for decades, however, and a public outcry followed television pictures of US troops standing by while Haitian soldiers beat pro-Aristide protesters, one of whom died. The interpretation of the rules of engagement (but not the rules themselves) was quickly changed to permit troops to use force to prevent the loss of human life and 1,000 additional US military police were dispatched to assist in maintaining public order.[65]

Bosnia after 1995 suffered from fewer procedural difficulties concerning law and order, many of which could be deferred to the International Criminal Tribunal for the Former Yugoslavia (ICTY). But the availability of institutions is always secondary to the willingness to act. While negotiating the Dayton Agreement, US Assistant Secretary of State Richard Holbrooke was under strict instructions to ensure that the NATO-supported IFOR was given only a narrow role that excluded any police functions.[66] IFOR subsequently resisted pressure from the High Representative and from the ICTY to arrest indicted war criminals. Given the dissatisfaction expressed concerning the United Nations in the Balkans, it is noteworthy that the first war criminals were actually captured not by NATO troops in Bosnia, but by UN peacekeepers in Eastern Slavonia. The two most wanted men in Bosnia, Radovan Karadzic and Ratko Mladic, remain at large despite the continuing presence of 13,000 SFOR troops.

The most immediate rule of law problem confronting the international presence in Kosovo in 1999 was the anarchy that followed the withdrawal of Serb authorities. Most had fled before NATO troops arrived, frequently taking whatever they could carry and destroying that which remained. 'Court buildings looked like a plague of heavily armed locusts had swept through', one commentator writes, 'scouring the grounds for anything valuable and leaving broken windows and ripped out electric sockets in their wake'.[67] Many international staff

[65] David M. Malone, *Decision-Making in the UN Security Council: The Case of Haiti, 1990–1997* (Oxford: Clarendon Press, 1998), 113; Findlay, *Use of Force*, 274.

[66] Holbrooke, *To End a War*, 218–23.

[67] William G. O'Neill, *Kosovo: An Unfinished Peace* (Boulder, CO: Lynne Rienner, 2002), 75. See also Matthew Kaminski, 'UN Struggles with a Legal Vacuum in Kosovo; Team Improvises in Effort to Build a Civil Structure', *Wall Street Journal*, 4 August 1999; Hansjoerg Strohmeyer (2001) 'Collapse and Reconstruction of a Judicial System: The United Nations Missions in Kosovo and East Timor', *American Journal of International Law*, 95: 46, 48.

later attributed the ongoing difficulties in establishing the UN Interim Administration Mission in Kosovo (UNMIK) as a credible force for law and order to failures in the first weeks and months of the operation. Two days before KFOR entered Kosovo, one of the 'measures of merit' General Wesley Clark established for the ground intervention was to avoid anarchy: 'get all Serb forces out, stop any crimes of revenge or Serb ethnic cleansing'.[68] Such orders, if made, were ineffective. Reporters came across Albanians, including members of the Kosovo Liberation Army (KLA), looting and driving Serbs and Roma from their homes. When one approached KFOR soldiers who were watching this take place he was informed that '[t]he orders are to let them plunder'.[69]

In the wake of the post-referendum violence in East Timor in September 1999, the Australian-led INTERFET had to decide how to respond to denunciations of alleged former militia. Such matters formally remained in the hands of the Indonesian police and judiciary, though this was on paper only. It was clear that this would soon become the responsibility of the UN Transitional Administration in East Timor (UNTAET) and an East Timorese judiciary, but these had yet to be established on the ground. INTERFET's Security Council mandate was silent on its responsibility or authority to carry out arrests. The Council resolution did, however, stress the responsibility of individuals committing violations of international humanitarian law and demand that they be brought to justice.[70] INTERFET ultimately decided that its broad mandate to restore peace and security could encompass arrests of individuals accused of committing serious offences—failure to do so might encourage Timorese people to take the law into their own hands.[71] INTERFET's commander, therefore, issued a Detainee Ordinance, creating various categories of prisoners. INTERFET troops were authorized to detain persons suspected of committing a serious offence prior to 20 September, and were required to deliver them to the Force Detention Centre in Dili within twenty-four hours. If a detainee was held for more than ninety-six hours, he or she was provided the grounds for being held,

[68] Wesley K. Clark, *Waging Modern War: Bosnia, Kosovo, and the Future of Combat* (New York: Public Affairs, 2001), 371.

[69] Tim Judah, *Kosovo: War and Revenge* (New Haven, CT: Yale University Press, 2000), p. x.

[70] SC Res 1264 (1999), para. 1.

[71] See, e.g. First Periodic Report on the Operations of the Multinational Force in East Timor, UN Doc S/1999/1025, Annex (4 October 1999), para. 23; Michael Ware, 'Murder Charge Bolsters Interfet Get-Tough Policy', *The Australian*, 17 December 1999.

together with material considered by the commander of INTERFET as the basis for continuing detention. Defending Officers were available to assist the detainee to show why he or she should not be so held, and a number of detainees were released because of insufficient evidence. The INTERFET Detention Centre handed over twenty-five detainees to UNTAET Civilian Police and the East Timorese judiciary on 14 January 2000.[72]

As the preceding review makes clear, the dominant variable in the different responses to internal security vacuums has been the preparedness of particular contingents and individuals to act. Comparable mandates were interpreted very differently in Kosovo and East Timor—as they were in different parts of Somalia. One reason for this inconsistency was the lack of clear direction from the Security Council. Clearer doctrine on when and how force is to be used in peace operations would remove some of the latitude that has commonly been given to field commanders in the interpretation of their mandate, though it may not be enough to generate the will to do so.

2.2. *The Need for Doctrine*

As Brigadier-General Anthony Zinni, Deputy for Operations of UNITAF in Somalia, once dryly observed, UNOSOM II's various contingents came to the battlefield with many different rules of engagement, 'which makes life interesting when the shooting begins'.[73] The obvious solution would be for the United Nations to develop standard rules of engagement, which might follow the production of standard operating procedures and standard form mandates from the Security Council. Member states of the United Nations have, however, been reluctant to allow it to develop doctrine in the area of peace operations. Members of the Non-Aligned Movement are said to have rejected the very idea of creating a unit in the Department of Peacekeeping Operations with the word 'doctrine' in the unit's title.[74]

Resistance on the part of certain member states is bolstered by those who adhere to the strict divide between peacekeeping and enforcement actions. UN Under-Secretary-General Shashi Tharoor is

[72] Report of the Secretary-General on the United Nations Transitional Administration in East Timor, UN Doc S/2000/53 (26 January 2000), para. 45.

[73] Anthony Zinni (1995) 'It's Not Nice and Neat', *Proceedings, US Naval Institute*, 121(8): 26, 30. Mogadishu airport in Somalia was defended by the forces of no less than eight nations: 'Was that because the airfield was so big or so threatened? No. It was because the forces of those eight nations could go no farther than the airfield when they got off the airplane', ibid.

[74] Findlay, *Use of Force*, 343.

representative when he argues that 'it is extremely difficult to make war and peace with the same people on the same territory at the same time.'[75] This position was reflected in the *General Guidelines for Peacekeeping*, which stated: 'Peacekeeping and the use of force (other than in self-defence) should be seen as alternative techniques and not adjacent points on a continuum. There is no easy transition from one to the other.'[76] Brian Urquhart, who joined the United Nations at its founding, put it best when he stressed that a true peacekeeper has no enemies—just a series of difficult and sometimes homicidal clients.[77]

Trevor Findlay is blunt about the reasons why a new doctrine is needed, though he tends to conflate the problem of use of force in peacekeeping operations with enforcement actions more generally: 'No one should have expected that the Bosnian Serbs, determined to seize as much of Bosnia and expel as many Muslims as they could in the cause of a Greater Serbia, would have been deterred by the sweet reason of the "Blue Helmets".'[78] He suggests that in Somalia the United Nations used too little force in the early days, when a show of force might have persuaded the factions to respect UN authority on issues such as disarmament, and too much indiscriminate force later on when pursuing General Aideed. In Bosnia, a broader interpretation of the rules of engagement might have enabled UNPROFOR to push through some of the low-level harassment directed at them without actually drawing fire. Nevertheless, the resources on hand and the vulnerability of forces on the ground tended to ensure that 'threats by commanders, usually soon after their arrival, to act more aggressively fell away as the realization of the implications of doing so for vulnerable humanitarian convoys and peacekeepers sank in'.[79]

Findlay's suggestion for avoiding such confusion in the future is to replace the line between peacekeeping and enforcement with a clearer line between chapter VI and chapter VII operations: all missions involving armed military personnel would receive a chapter VII mandate, with chapter VI restricted to unarmed observer missions and peacebuilding missions with no uniformed personnel. Moreover, all chapter VII mandates should 'make it explicit that the United Nations is obliged to protect civilians at risk of human rights abuses or other forms of attack'. These new chapter VII operations would be termed

[75] See ibid., 263.

[76] UN Department of Peacekeeping Operations, 1995 Guidelines, 21–2.

[77] Brian Urquhart, *A Life in Peace and War* (New York: W. W. Norton, 1987), 293.

[78] Findlay, *Use of Force*, 271.

[79] Ibid., 223–4.

peace enforcement.[80] This would clarify the questions of impartiality and use of force. But clarity would come with the loss of those operations where parties would be unwilling to allow well-armed troops with such a mandate into theatre.[81]

Marrack Goulding, who directed UN peacekeeping during what may come to be regarded as its heyday—the period 1986–93—is less revolutionary in his views, but these have undergone a notable shift in the period since he left the United Nations. In 1996, while head of the Department of Political Affairs, he argued that the United Nations needed to be strictly clear about whether it intervened as 'an impartial peacekeeper or as an avenging angel to punish the wicked and protect the righteous'. If a mission changed from peacekeeping to enforcement, 'the change must be clearly signalled to all parties concerned, there must be convincing evidence of a real political will to use force to achieve a strategic objective'.[82] The possibility of an intermediate type of operation was treated with great scepticism. By the publication of his 2002 memoir, *Peacemonger*, Goulding's position had changed somewhat: 'I now realize that we in the Secretariat adjusted too slowly to the demands of the new type of conflict which proliferated after the end of the Cold War', he writes.

> By the second half of the 1990s it had become clear that there was a need to revise peacekeeping doctrine. It had to provide for situations in which a party's consent had been given in general terms but the peacekeepers could nevertheless expect to encounter armed resistance from some of that party's adherents or, in states without effective government, from armed bandits with no political agenda... The essence of the new doctrine is that force is, if necessary, used against armed persons because of what they do, not because of the side they belong to.[83]

This echoes key passages in the Brahimi Report on UN Peace Operations, which noted that the peacekeeping shibboleth of consent is often manipulated in intra-state conflicts. If a party to a peace agreement is

[80] Findlay, *Use of Force*, 360–1. Peace enforcement is defined as an operation that aims to 'ensure the implementation of a peace agreement or arrangement (such as a ceasefire), including compliance by all parties with their undertakings, through the judicious application of incentives and disincentives, among them the robust use of force.' While this is partly a military strategy, it must ultimately be political, with the military playing 'a supporting role involving deterrence and compellence as necessary': Findlay, *Use of Force*, 376.

[81] The 1999 vote on East Timor's independence from Indonesia, for example, would not have happened if international negotiators had insisted on an international security presence. See further Chapter Two, Section 2.1.2.

[82] Marrack Goulding (1996) 'The Use of Force by the United Nations', *International Peacekeeping*, 3(1): 1, 15–16.

[83] Goulding, *Peacemonger*, 17.

clearly violating its terms, continued equal treatment of all parties by the United Nations leads to ineffectiveness at best and complicity with evil at worst: 'No failure did more to damage the standing and credibility of United Nations peacekeeping in the 1990s than its reluctance to distinguish victim from aggressor.'[84]

Findlay sees in Brahimi's advocacy of more robust, rapidly deployable forces with deterrent capabilities a call for a UN peace enforcement capability by stealth.[85] This does not appear to have been the Secretary-General's view, however. In his first report on implementation of the Report's recommendations, the Secretary-General noted that he did not interpret the Report as a recommendation to turn the United Nations into a war-fighting machine or to 'fundamentally change the principles according to which peacekeepers use force'.[86] Given ongoing wariness among the Non-Aligned Movement concerning the Standby High-Readiness Brigade (SHIRBRIG) concept, such caveats about the development of new doctrine are likely to continue, even as history forces the United Nations to violate them in practice.

2.3. *Model Rules of Engagement*

A working group was established in 1998 to produce a draft of model rules of engagement for future missions and for training purposes. Due in part to the concerns of developing states, the first draft considered only the use of force in self-defence and defence of the mission.[87] Further consultation in 2001—after the Rwanda and Srebrenica reports, and the Brahimi Report had been published—saw an evolution in thinking, but little consensus. In December 2001, the Secretary-General simply announced that the document, now known as the Guidelines for the Development of Rules of Engagement (ROE) for United Nations Peacekeeping Operations,[88] would remain a 'work in progress', but in the meantime was being used by military planning staff to prepare mission-specific rules of engagement and would soon be used for training purposes in troop-contributing countries.[89]

[84] Brahimi Report, p. ix.

[85] Findlay, *Use of Force*, 337.

[86] Report of the Secretary-General on the Implementation of the Report of the Panel on United Nations Peace Operations, UN Doc A/55/502 (20 October 2000), para. 7(e).

[87] Findlay, *Use of Force*, 347.

[88] UN Department of Peacekeeping Operations, Guidelines for the Development of Rules of Engagement for UN Peacekeeping Operations (Provisional), UN Doc MD/FHS/0220.0001 (May 2002).

[89] Implementation of the Recommendations of the Special Committee on Peacekeeping Operations and the Panel on United Nations Peace Operations (Report of the Secretary-General), UN Doc A/56/732 (21 December 2001), available at www.un.org/peace/reports/peace_operations, para. 70.

Of particular interest here is rule 5, concerning 'Reaction to civil action/unrest'. In two parts, the rule states the general principle that '[a]ction to counter civil unrest is not authorized.' This is then qualified by the following important provision that appears to reflect the experience of INTERFET in East Timor: 'When competent local authorities are not in a position to render immediate assistance, detention of any person who creates or threatens to create civil unrest with likely serious consequences for life and property is authorized.' This should be read together with rule 1.8, which authorizes the use of force 'up to, and including deadly force, to defend any civilian person who is in need of protection against a hostile act or hostile intent, when competent local authorities are not in a position to render immediate assistance'.[90] Despite the Secretary-General's caveats, this suggests a significant change in the use of force in peace operations. In 1999 and 2000, both UNAMSIL and the UN Organization Mission in the Democratic Republic of the Congo (MONUC) were given chapter VII mandates to protect 'civilians under imminent threat of physical violence', though no actual use of force appears to have been taken on this basis.[91]

3. Conclusion

Debates over the use of force within the United Nations frequently serve as a proxy for other issues. Opposition to SHIRBRIG, for example, places North–South rivalry ahead of the generally accepted need for a UN rapid-response capacity; in Bosnia, the reluctance to use military force was a cover for disagreements among the major powers about their objectives and the continuing absence of a coherent policy towards the conflict itself.[92]

As a result, Findlay concludes, 'the use of force by UN peacekeepers has been marked by political controversy, doctrinal vacuousness, conceptual confusion and failure in the field'. Few come out of his conclusions untainted. The Security Council has 'abdicated its responsibility, with mandates from the plainly undeliverable—in the Congo and Bosnia—to the outright irresponsible'—in the case of Somalia. The various Secretaries-General, 'with the notable exceptions

[90] UN Department of Peacekeeping Operations, ROE Guidelines, extracted in Findlay, *Use of Force*, 425–7.

[91] SC Res 1270 (1999), para. 14 (UNAMSIL); SC Res 1291 (2000), para. 8 (MONUC).

[92] Susan L. Woodward, *Balkan Tragedy: Chaos and Dissolution After the Cold War* (Washington, DC: Brookings Institution, 1995), 378.

of Dag Hammarskjöld and possibly Kofi Annan, have been essentially militarily illiterate'. The Secretariat, which survived the cold war with 'gifted amateurism', is regularly stretched beyond its capacity. Force commanders, on whom much has depended (if only out of a desire for deniability on the part of those higher in the chain of command), have sometimes been chosen with higher regard for nationality than for military competence, a criticism that may equally be levelled at special representatives of the Secretary-General. Peacekeepers themselves have been inconsistent in their actual use of force, though by and large they have been extremely reticent about using any force at all.[93]

The military is rightly reluctant to embrace law and order duties that are outside its expertise, but in many situations only the military is in a position to exercise comparable functions in the first weeks and months of an operation. Though desirable, it is unlikely that the United Nations will soon be able to deploy law and order 'packages' comprising civilian police and mobile courts with a skeleton staff of lawyers and judges. In the meantime, future situations like Kosovo and East Timor will present a choice between increasing the initial responsibilities of the military or accepting a temporary gap in law and order.[94] As Kosovo showed, such a gap will quickly be filled by informal local arrangements that may undermine the credibility of the international presence when eventually deployed.[95] By contrast, where KFOR adopted an aggressive but measured posture, violence tended to diminish.[96]

Differences between troop contributors suggest the possibilities for change even without radical reform of UN peace operations doctrine. The manner in which soldiers present themselves, for example, clearly has an impact on their effectiveness. The perceived obsession of US troops with force protection is frequently criticized as unhelpful. In Somalia, US troops always appeared in flak jackets and helmets, heavily armed and guarded by helicopters or other protection forces. This prompted Somalis to refer to them as 'human tanks' and is believed to have been a factor in promoting Somali aggression towards them in

93 Findlay, *Use of Force*, 351–5.

94 Aspen Institute, *Honoring Human Rights Under International Mandates: Lessons from Bosnia, Kosovo, and East Timor* (Washington, DC: Aspen Institute, 2003), 18.

95 Report of the Secretary-General on the United Nations Interim Administration Mission in Kosovo, UN Doc S/1999/779 (12 July 1999), para. 6.

96 O'Neill, *Kosovo*, 76.

the summer of 1993.[97] Similar stories are told of the US presence in Kosovo: reports of ethnic bullying in a school in the US sector would receive no response for a month—until a platoon in full body-armour would arrive, parade through the school grounds, and return to base. This may be contrasted with the British approach to urban peacekeeping, learned on the streets of Northern Ireland and characterized by soft berets and foot patrols. These considerations need to be balanced against necessary measures in self-defence, but gaining the respect and confidence of the local population tends to reduce the threats posed by local insurgents.[98]

Further advances, if any, are likely to be in the form of evolution rather than revolution, as forces on the ground respond to the competing military and political exigencies of their mission. The speed with which the United States came to be criticized for the civil disorder in Iraq in 2003 suggests some recognition of the responsibilities of an occupying force, but this criticism was probably enhanced by the controversial grounds on which the decision to go to war had been made. The refusal even to begin this task in Afghanistan undermined—perhaps fatally—efforts at reconstruction there, but has been the subject of minimal international interest.[99] These political dynamics primarily concern the troop-contributing countries themselves, but of course the most important dynamic is that which develops on the ground as informal political structures are swept away and new ones begin to emerge. As the Independent Inquiry into the Actions of the

[97] Gérard Prunier, 'The Experience of European Armies in Operation Restore Hope', in Walter Clarke and Jeffrey Herbst (eds.), *Learning from Somalia: The Lessons of Armed Humanitarian Intervention* (Boulder, CO: Westview, 1997), 135, 146–7 n. 118.

[98] Danna Harman, 'As Occupiers, Brits Bring Experience', *Christian Science Monitor*, 20 May 2003.

[99] Security remains the major concern in Afghanistan, with many analysts pointing to a 'security gap' between what is currently provided by the ISAF presence in Kabul, the coalition forces in pockets of the country—from early 2003 including mixed civil–military 'Provincial Reconstruction Teams' (PRTs)—and the embryonic Afghan national army. Many senior UN staff continue to see expansion of ISAF beyond Kabul as vital to the success of the larger mission, but significant expansion is now highly unlikely. Force command was transferred from Britain to Turkey on 20 June 2002, to Germany and the Netherlands on 10 February 2003, and to NATO on 11 August 2003. The number of troops remained at approximately 5,500, centred in and around Kabul. Examples of insecurity have been conspicuous: two ministers in the Afghan government have been assassinated and President Karzai himself narrowly escaped an assassination attempt on 5 September 2002, his life saved by US Special Forces acting as his bodyguards. See further Chapter Two, Section 3.1; Chapter Five, Section 4.

United Nations During the 1994 Genocide in Rwanda concluded, whether or not an obligation to protect civilians is explicit in the mandate of such a force, the United Nations and other actors must be prepared to respond to the expectation of protection created by their very presence.[100] A key finding from surveying past operations is that, very often, the more willing and able an operation is to use force, the less likely it is to have to do so.[101]

Weber's conception of the state as defined through violence is, of course, an incomplete one. Though the destruction or collapse of state institutions may lead to anarchy, the restoration of order in the person of the Leviathan is a necessary but insufficient end of intervention. It is necessary because consolidated state power is the condition for any regime with the capacity to protect the rights of its population.[102] But it is insufficient because contemporary understandings of state sovereignty go far beyond the assertion of a monopoly on the use of force. States are not merely expected to protect their populations from 'a war of every man against every man'.[103] The next three chapters, therefore, consider different aspects of how the provisional legitimacy of a transitional administration may be pursued through governance, promotion of the rule of law, and the provision of basic economic goods.

[100] Report of the Independent Inquiry into the Actions of the United Nations During the 1994 Genocide in Rwanda, UN Doc S/1999/1257 (15 December 1999), 51; Brahimi Report, para. 62.

[101] Findlay, *Use of Force*, 3.

[102] Michael Ignatieff, 'Intervention and State Failure', *Dissent*, Winter 2002, 114, 119.

[103] Thomas Hobbes, *Leviathan* [1651] (London: Dent, 1914), part 1, chapter XIII.

4

Consultation and Accountability: Building Democracy Through Benevolent Autocracy

> UNMIK is not structured according to democratic principles, does not function in accordance with the rule of law, and does not respect important international human rights norms. The people of Kosovo are therefore deprived of protection of their basic rights and freedoms three years after the end of the conflict by the very entity set up to guarantee them.
>
> Ombudsperson Institution in Kosovo, 2002[1]

The Security Council resolution that established the UN Interim Administration Mission in Kosovo (UNMIK) authorized the Secretary-General to establish an international civilian presence to govern the territory.[2] In its first regulation, UNMIK asserted plenary powers: 'All legislative and executive authority with respect to Kosovo, including the administration of the judiciary, is vested in UNMIK and is exercised by the Special Representative of the Secretary-General.' The Special Representative was further empowered to appoint or remove any person, including judges, to positions within the civil administration. Beneath its brief text, UNMIK Regulation No 1999/1 bore the signature 'Dr Bernard Kouchner, Special Representative of the Secretary-General'.[3]

[1] Ombudsperson Institution in Kosovo, Second Annual Report 2001–2002 (10 July 2002), available at www.ombudspersonkosovo.org.

[2] SC Res 1244 (1999), para. 10.

[3] UNMIK Regulation 1999/1 (25 July 1999), On the Authority of the Interim Administration in Kosovo, §1.

The governance of post-conflict territories by the United Nations embodies a central policy dilemma: how does one help a population prepare for democratic governance and the rule of law by imposing a form of benevolent autocracy? And to what extent should the transitional administration itself be bound by the principles that it seeks to encourage in the local population? The Ombudsperson established by the Organization for Security and Cooperation in Europe (OSCE) to monitor, protect, and promote human rights in Kosovo published a damning report on UNMIK's record on both fronts three years into the mission. As quoted at the start of this chapter, it argued that the very entity set up to protect the people of Kosovo was, in fact, depriving them of basic rights and freedoms.

This tension between the means and the ends of transitional administration highlights key differences between recent UN operations and the colonial and military occupations considered in Chapter One. The UN Trusteeship System (and the League Mandates System before it) imposed minimal constraints on colonial powers to consult with or respect the human rights of subject peoples.[4] Similarly, military occupation of the form seen in the aftermath of the Second World War put the rights of the local population a considerable distance below the military and political objectives of the occupation.[5] By contrast, territories administered by the United Nations have typically enjoyed the entire corpus of human rights law, which would, in theory, include the emerging right to democratic governance.

As the Ombudsperson's report quoted above makes clear, however, practice does not always follow theory. This chapter will explore that tension by considering the related questions of consultation and accountability. The first section looks at the different forms of consultation with local populations that have evolved in the various operations—a necessary precursor to the transfer of some or all power to local actors that has generally taken place through the staging of elections. (Elections themselves will not be considered here; they are the subject of Chapter Seven.) The second section then examines whether a transitional administration itself can or should be held accountable for its actions in either a legal or a political sense. The chapter will not consider the *personal* immunity of international staff, though this has been a troubling issue in these and other operations.[6]

[4] See Chapter One, Sections 1 and 3.

[5] See Chapter One, Section 2.

[6] See Convention on the Privileges and Immunities of the United Nations, 13 February 1946, 1 UNTS 15; Frederick Rawski (2002) 'To Waive or Not to Waive: Immunity and Accountability in UN Peacekeeping Operations', *Connecticut*

1. Consultation with Local Actors

It is commonly assumed that the collapse of state structures, whether through defeat by an external power or as a result of internal chaos, leads to a vacuum of political power. This is rarely the case. The mechanisms through which political power are exercised may become less formalized or consistent, but basic questions of how best to ensure the physical and economic security of oneself and one's dependants do not simply disappear when the institutions of the state break down. Non-state actors in such situations may exercise varying degrees of political power over local populations, at times providing basic social services from education to medical care. Even where non-state actors exist as parasites on local populations, political life goes on.[7]

The questions of whether and how to engage such non-state actors in a peace process has long occupied both writers on and practitioners of conflict resolution. Recognition of groups that have been accused of war crimes—such as the Khmer Rouge in Cambodia and the Revolutionary United Front (RUF) in Sierra Leone—as legitimate political actors is especially controversial. At the same time, however, the United Nations has been curiously reluctant to engage with religious organizations, such as the Catholic Church in East Timor. In this section, the focus will be limited to the question of consultation with local actors in circumstances where the United Nations or another international actor (such as the Office of the High Representative in Bosnia and Herzegovina) has assumed some or all governmental powers for a sustained period in Bosnia, Eastern Slavonia, Kosovo, and East Timor. The three cases from the Balkans (where elections have dominated the political landscape) will be discussed briefly before turning to a more detailed consideration of the evolution of appointed consultative mechanisms in East Timor.

1.1. Consultation in the Balkans

When authorizing the UN Transitional Administration for Eastern Slavonia, the Security Council requested the Secretary-General to appoint a transitional administrator, 'in consultation with the parties

Journal of International Law, 18: 103; Karel Wellens, *Remedies Against International Organisations* (Cambridge: Cambridge University Press, 2002).

7 See, e.g. Marie-Joëlle Zahar, 'Protégés, Clients, Cannon Fodder: Civil-Militia Relations in Internal Conflicts', in Simon Chesterman (ed.), *Civilians in War* (Boulder, CO: Lynne Rienner, 2001), 43; Robert I. Rotberg (ed.), *When States Fail: Causes and Consequences* (Princeton, NJ: Princeton University Press, 2004).

and with the Security Council'.[8] This must be read in the context of the demand by Croatian President Franjo Tudjman that a US General be appointed head of the UN operation, and the importance of ensuring Tudjman's and Yugoslav President Slobodan Milosevic's commitment to the peaceful transfer of Eastern Slavonia from Serb to Croat control.[9] In Kosovo, consultation in the appointment of the Special Representative was only required with the Council itself.[10] In Bosnia, which was not placed under UN control, other political constraints were at work. In particular, there was an implicit agreement among the guarantors at Dayton that the High Representative would always be European, that one chief deputy was likely to be German and the other a US national, and that the OSCE Head of Mission would always be from the United States.[11]

Appointment of senior international staff is, of course, only one of a great many decisions that are made in the course of such an operation. Neither the mission in Eastern Slavonia nor that in Kosovo included in its mandate an obligation to consult more generally with local actors. This may be contrasted with the mandate for East Timor, which stressed the need for the UN Transitional Administration (UNTAET) to 'consult and cooperate closely with the East Timorese people'.[12] Here it is noteworthy that senior UN staff in New York had a more restrictive view of the role of the early transitional administrations than they ultimately assumed. In particular, the UN Legal Counsel later lamented the fact that these bodies had become 'legislative factories', assuming for themselves governing powers beyond the temporary caretaker function initially envisaged.[13]

1.1.1. Bosnia and Herzegovina The problems attendant to rule by decree were most evident in Bosnia, where disputes between the local and international political elites occasionally degenerated into farce. As part of the efforts to undermine the leadership of Serb nationalist Radovan Karadzic, the High Representative in July 1997 supported Republika Srpska President Biljana Plavsic's dissolution of the

8 SC Res 1037 (1996), para. 2.

9 Cf. Richard Holbrooke, *To End a War* (New York: Random House, 1998), 236–9, 264–5.

10 SC Res 1244 (1999), para. 6. In East Timor the Council merely welcomed the intention of the Secretary-General to appoint a Special Representative: SC Res 1272 (1999), para. 6.

11 Elizabeth M. Cousens and Charles K. Cater, *Toward Peace in Bosnia: Implementing the Dayton Accords* (Boulder, CO: Lynne Rienner, 2001), 46.

12 SC Res 1272 (1999), para. 8.

13 Hans Corell, interview with the author, New York, 3 December 2002.

entity's National Assembly, then controlled by Karadzic's Serbian Democratic Party (SDS) party. The High Representative went so far as to overrule a decision by the Constitutional Court that the President's actions were unconstitutional, on the basis that the Court's decision was a consequence of political pressures. Such faith in Plavsic may have been overstated—she was later indicted herself by the Hague Tribunal for genocide and pleaded guilty to one count of crimes against humanity.[14]

Under the Dayton Peace Agreement, the High Representative was established to 'facilitate' efforts by the parties and to mobilize and coordinate the activities of the many organizations and agencies involved in the civilian aspects of the peace settlement. The High Representative was also granted 'final authority in theatre' to interpret the Agreement as it applied to the civilian implementation of the peace settlement.[15] After two years of ineffectual cohabitation, the Peace Implementation Council[16] at a summit in Bonn welcomed Carlos Westendorp's intention to use these powers 'to facilitate the resolution of any difficulties' in implementing the mandate—in particular, his power to make 'binding decisions' and to take 'actions against persons holding public office or officials... who are found by the High Representative to be in violation of legal commitments made at Dayton or the terms for its implementation'.[17] From March 1998 until mid-2003, the different High Representatives dismissed, suspended, or banned from public office over 100 elected officials at all levels of government—including a former Prime Minister of the

[14] International Criminal Tribunal for the Former Yugoslavia, Case No IT–00–40–I, Indictment, 3 April 2000. In a plea agreement filed on 30 September 2002, Plavsic agreed to plead guilty to a violation of Article 5(h) of the Statute of the International Tribunal (persecutions on political, racial, and religious grounds), in exchange for which the Prosecutor agreed to dismiss the remaining counts in the indictment.

[15] General Framework Agreement for Peace in Bosnia and Herzegovina (Dayton Agreement), Bosnia and Herzegovina–Croatia–Federal Republic of Yugoslavia, done at Dayton, 14 December 1995, UN Doc S/1995/999, available at www.yale.edu/lawweb/avalon/intdip/bosnia/daymenu.htm, Annex 10, arts. 1(2), 5.

[16] After the successful negotiations in Dayton in November 1995, a Peace Implementation Conference was held in London on 8–9 December 1995 to mobilize international support for the Agreement. The meeting resulted in the establishment of the Peace Implementation Council (PIC), comprising fifty-five countries and agencies that support the peace process.

[17] Conclusions of the Peace Implementation Conference (Bonn: Peace Implementation Council, 9–10 December 1997), available at www.oscebih.org, para. XI(2).

Bosnian Federation (Edhem Bicakcic), a President of Republika Srpska (Nikola Poplasen), and a member of the Bosnian Presidency (Ante Jelavic).[18]

The exercise of these 'Bonn Powers' has been criticized both for particular incidents and the broader message that it sends to local parties. The justification for Poplasen's dismissal, for example, was his refusal to accept as Prime Minister a moderate candidate who had majority support from the Republika Srpska National Assembly and was favoured by Western powers.[19] More generally, the accretion of these powers marked a reversal of moves towards self-governance. This was driven by Western frustration at the slow pace of implementation on the political side and the fact that nationalist parties by late 1996 had consolidated their control both politically and demographically.[20] That this was only twelve months after an ethnic war that had lasted more than three years led some to argue that these deadlines had less to do with Bosnia than with the domestic concerns of the intervening powers.[21] By 2000, the situation was characterized by the International Crisis Group as a paradoxical combination of a flawed democracy and a semi-international protectorate, in which international actors often appeared reluctant to use their powers effectively.[22]

1.1.2. Eastern Slavonia The UN Transitional Administration for Eastern Slavonia (UNTAES) enjoyed, by contrast, a relatively simple mandate: the peaceful reintegration into Croatia of its last Serb-held territory after a period of UN administration. Once Tudjman and Milosevic had accepted that political framework—albeit grudgingly and for different reasons—this guaranteed much of the local support necessary for implementation. Nevertheless, UNTAES stressed the need to enlist the 'cooperation' of local Serbs and Croats. Joint Implementation Committees were established on various issues as

18 Office of the High Representative, High Representative's Decisions by Topic, Removals and Suspensions, available at www.ohr.int/decisions/removalssdec. By year, the number of persons removed or suspended were as follows: 1998—7; 1999—32; 2000—28; 2001—14; 2002—21.

19 Office of the High Representative, Decision removing Mr. Nikola Poplasen from the Office of President of Republika Srpska (Sarajevo, 5 March 1999), available at www.ohr.int/decisions/removalssdec.

20 Cousens and Cater, *Toward Peace in Bosnia*, 129–30.

21 See, e.g. David Chandler, *Bosnia: Faking Democracy After Dayton* (London: Pluto Press, 1999).

22 International Crisis Group, Bosnia's November Elections: Dayton Stumbles (Sarajevo/Brussels: ICG Balkans Report No 104, 18 December 2000), available at www.crisisweb.org, 17.

a means of providing a forum for the two parties, though Special Representative Jacques Paul Klein retained the power to remove obstructive individuals from office—a power that was threatened and, on occasion, used against 'intransigent' local actors.[23]

UNTAES is now generally regarded as a success, though this had less to do with the consent of local parties than the prior agreement of the relevant external actors. In addition to the clarity (and relative simplicity) of the mandate, other key factors were the unity of command over civilian and military components, the threat of credible military force through NATO, and the strength of Klein's personal leadership. Rather than local ownership, then, UNTAES stands as an example of the importance of a strong and unified international presence.[24]

1.1.3. Kosovo Kosovo avoided Bosnia's hydra-headed structure, but the territory was politically stillborn. Security Council resolution 1244 (1999) authorized an international civil presence in Kosovo, but it was laced with compromise language necessary to achieve consensus in New York. In the end, the resolution stated that UNMIK was to provide

> an *interim administration* for Kosovo under which the people of Kosovo can enjoy *substantial autonomy within the Federal Republic of Yugoslavia*, and which will provide *transitional administration* while establishing and overseeing the development of *provisional democratic self-governing institutions* to ensure conditions for a peaceful and normal life for all inhabitants of Kosovo.[25]

This created a near impossible mandate on the ground. Some UN officials reported that Kouchner, head of the mission from July 1999 until January 2001, claimed to read the text of resolution 1244 (1999) twice every morning and still have no idea what 'substantial autonomy' meant.

A second lesson from Bosnia was avoiding a commitment to early elections. Instead, Kosovo was governed by UNMIK while structures were established through which Kosovar representatives could

[23] Report of the Secretary-General on the United Nations Transitional Administration for Eastern Slavonia, Baranja, and Western Sirmium, UN Doc S/1996/705 (28 August 1996), para. 5; UN Department of Peacekeeping Operations, Comprehensive Report on Lessons Learned from the United Nations Transitional Administration for Eastern Slavonia (New York: Lessons Learned Unit, June 1998), available at www.un.org/Depts/dpko/lessons, paras. 29–31.

[24] See Chapter Two, Section 2.2.3.

[25] SC Res 1244 (1999), para. 10 (italics added).

'advise' it. The only quasi-governmental body that included Kosovars was, for some time, the Kosovo Transitional Council. Intended to represent the main ethnic and political groups, it was designed to 'provide [the Special Representative] with advice, be a sounding board for proposed decisions and help to elicit support for those decisions among all major political groups'.[26] From February 2000, the Joint Interim Administrative Structure began to replace the parallel governance structures established by Kosovar Albanians that had, for some years, collected revenue and provided basic public services. The executive board of the new body was called the Interim Administrative Council, comprising the three Kosovar Albanian political leaders who were parties to the Rambouillet Accords of June 1999 (Rexhep Qosja, Ibrahim Rugova, and Hashim Thaçi), a Kosovar Serb observer (Rada Trajkovic), and four representatives of UNMIK. The Council was empowered to make recommendations to the Special Representative, who could either accept these or advise in writing within seven days of 'the reasons for his differing decision'.[27]

No one was under the illusion that these bodies wielded any actual power. In the wake of the October 2000 regime change in Belgrade, Serbia increased cooperation with UNMIK, suggesting that some sort of autonomy arrangement might be possible within a reconstituted Federal Republic of Yugoslavia. This caused anxiety within the Albanian population, but it seemed highly unlikely that Kosovo would ever be placed under the direct jurisdiction of Belgrade. Most Kosovar Albanians look eagerly towards the possibility of one day joining the European Union—and have been encouraged to do so, not least through the adoption of the euro in January 2002 to replace the German mark as the currency used in Kosovo. Full membership of the European Union is unlikely anytime soon. The most likely scenario is that Kosovo will remain an international protectorate of ambiguous status for some years to come.[28]

In the course of drafting the Constitutional Framework for Provisional Self-Government, adopted in May 2001, these tensions in the governance structures put UNMIK officials in the odd position of having to resist Albanian attempts to include reference to the 'will of the people'. Such a concept remained controversial in

[26] Report of the Secretary-General on the United Nations Interim Administration Mission in Kosovo, UN Doc S/1999/779 (12 July 1999), para. 20.

[27] UNMIK Regulation 2000/1 (14 January 2000), On the Kosovo Joint Administrative Structure.

[28] See Chapter Two, Section 2.4.2; Chapter Seven, Section 3.2.

Kosovo precisely because the one thing that excited all parties—the final status of Kosovo—was the issue on which senior UN staff officially had to profess not to have an opinion. It was, nevertheless, clear that Kouchner favoured independence, while his successor Hans Haekkerup held a more conservative interpretation of his mandate. Speaking in June 2001, Haekkerup said that a decision on the future status of Kosovo required a level of 'political maturity' and readiness to compromise that the parties had not yet attained.[29] The Constitutional Framework was specifically designed to force such compromises. A seven-member presidency of the Assembly was given control over procedure; it included two members from each of the two parties with the highest number of votes, one from the party that came third, as well as one representative from the Kosovar Serb community and one from a non-Serb minority group (including the Roma, Ashkali, Egyptian, Bosniak, Turkish, and Gorani communities). The government had to include at least one Serb and one non-Serb minority representative in ministerial positions. The framework also provided for the appointment of a President of the Assembly, a Prime Minister, and, more controversially, a President of Kosovo.[30]

These structures reflected the fact that politics in Kosovo continued to be fought strictly along ethnic lines. With the exception of the conflation of the Roma, Ashkali, and Egyptian communities (making up a total of, perhaps, 3 per cent of Kosovo's population), every active political party in Kosovo remained ethnically 'pure'. No one talks of reconciliation in Kosovo—on the second anniversary of UNMIK's arrival in Kosovo, Haekkerup observed that the hatred that fuels interethnic violence 'does not seem much diminished'.[31] 'A time will come for reconciliation between Albanians and Serbs', observed Fatmir Sejdiu, former General Secretary of the Democratic League of Kosovo (LDK). 'But not yet.'[32]

Quite apart from the implicit acceptance of ethnic politics, however, UNMIK's stated hopes of inter- and intra-community compromise were not supported by the process that led to adoption of the framework. None of the local participants agreed to the text as finally adopted—a 'compromise' that had to be forced on them by Haekkerup.

[29] Hans Haekkerup, 'UNMIK at Two Years' (Pristina, 13 June 2001). See also Chapter One, Section 4.

[30] A Constitutional Framework for Provisional Self-Government in Kosovo, UNMIK Regulation 2001/9 (15 May 2001), available at www.unmikonline.org/constframework.htm.

[31] Haekkerup, 'UNMIK at Two Years'.

[32] Fatmir Sejdiu, interview with the author, Pristina, 26 June 2001.

1.2. Consultation in East Timor

In contrast to the missions in Bosnia and Kosovo, East Timor had a uniquely clear political endpoint. The outcome of independence was never really questioned after the UN Transitional Administration was established, but the timing and the manner in which power was to be exercised in the meantime soon became controversial. This manifested both in the different forms of consultation attempted in the first two years of the mission and the process through which a constitution was ultimately adopted prior to independence.

1.2.1. Experimentation and Resignation The widespread assumption that East Timor in late 1999 was a political and economic vacuum was, perhaps, half-true. Even before the vote to separate from Indonesia, East Timor was one of the poorest parts of the archipelago; in the violence that followed, the formal economy simply ceased to function. Unemployment during the period of transitional administration remained at around 80 per cent, with much economic activity being parasitic on the temporary market for expatriate food and entertainment. The political situation was far more complex.

Certainly, East Timor exhibited an atypical form of political life. As the territory prepared for its first elections in August 2001, many ordinary Timorese expressed doubts about the need for political parties. This stemmed from the view that divisions between the Revolutionary Front of Independent East Timor (Fretilin) and Timorese Democratic Union (UDT) parties in 1974–5 had been exploited by Indonesia and facilitated its invasion and subsequent annexation.[33] Significantly, Xanana Gusmão, who later became East Timor's first president, was not formally associated with any political party. He was President of the National Council of Timorese Resistance (CNRT), an umbrella organization of groups that opposed Indonesia's occupation, but repeatedly stated that this was not a political party and that it would not run in the elections. (It was eventually dissolved in June 2001.) CNRT's status was important because it was the vehicle through which UNTAET haltingly attempted to carry out its mandate to consult with the Timorese population. From soon after UNTAET's deployment, CNRT was regarded as representing the Timorese people, giving enormous political sway to its leadership—arguably at the expense

[33] See, e.g. National Democratic Institute and the Faculty of Social and Political Science of the University of East Timor, Carrying the People's Aspirations: A Report on Focus Group Discussions in East Timor (Dili: NDI, February 2002), 9.

of other sections of the population. The questionably representative nature of CNRT was reflected in its August 2000 decision to adopt Portuguese as the official language of East Timor, a language understood by fewer than 10 per cent of the population and by virtually no one under 30.[34] This was compounded when Fretilin broke from CNRT in the same month, leading to a proliferation of smaller parties.

The flip side of the perceived lack of political sophistication among the Timorese was that many of the expatriates working for UNTAET and the seventy-odd international non-governmental organizations (NGOs) tended to treat the Timorese political system as a tabula rasa. This attitude led to the first significant civic education initiative proposed by the United Nations being rejected by the Timorese. A letter from Timorese NGOs to UNTAET's Director of Political Affairs, Peter Galbraith, complained of inadequate consultation in the development of the project, and the fact that the vast majority of the $8 million budget was earmarked for the salaries of international staff. This greatly underestimated the interest and capacity of Timorese actors to play an active role in civic education. Following changes of personnel and the formation of a steering committee with substantial local representation, Timorese civil society returned to the table in January 2001.

Many of these problems were referable to a contradiction within Security Council resolution 1272 (1999). It established UNTAET in order to give the East Timorese eventual control over their country, stressing the need for UNTAET to 'consult and cooperate closely with the East Timorese people'. At the same time, however, UNTAET followed the Kosovo model of concentrating all political power in UNTAET and the Special Representative,[35] while endowing the administration with all the institutional and bureaucratic baggage that the United Nations carries. The failure to elaborate on the meaning of

[34] Outcomes of the CNRT National Congress, 21–30 August 2000 (English Version), Commission III, Recommendation B(4)(c), adopted by the National Congress 362-0-3. Senior Timorese leaders have been the strongest advocates of Portuguese. The key reason that is generally presented concerns the identity of East Timor, a geographical anomaly bound together only by its history of Portuguese (as opposed to Dutch) colonialism. Other reasons advanced concern the importance of good relations with Lusophone countries (notably Portugal and Brazil), as well as the connection that Portugal grants into the European Union (and away from dependence on Asia—particularly Indonesia). In addition, Portuguese is said to support the development of Tetum, whereas Bahasa Indonesia would 'kill' it. Finally, there is resentment on the part of many (mostly older) Timorese to the imposition of Bahasa Indonesia during Indonesian occupation.

[35] SC Res 1272 (1999), paras. 1, 8.

'consult and cooperate closely' gave UNTAET considerable latitude in its interpretation of the mandate. The initial approach was to establish a non-elected council, comprising representatives of UNTAET and local political factions. Created in December 1999, the fifteen-member National Consultative Council (NCC) was a purely advisory body, though it reviewed (and endorsed) all UNTAET regulations.[36] Nevertheless, as the situation in East Timor became more stable, there were calls for wider and more direct participation in political life.

On 5 April 2000, Sergio Vieira de Mello, the Special Representative and Transitional Administrator, announced the appointment of Timorese deputy district administrators to operate under the thirteen international district administrators. New district advisory councils would also be established. These were to have 'broad participation of representatives of political parties, the Church, women and youth groups'. In particular, Vieira de Mello noted, 'We wish to establish advisory councils in the districts that are representative of the East Timorese civil society more than was possible in the NCC.' In addition, he announced that proceedings of the NCC, which had been criticized by some as overly secretive, would be opened to representatives of NGOs and of Falintil, the Timorese guerrilla force that had long resisted Indonesian rule.[37]

The criticisms of UNTAET in Dili were echoed and amplified in the districts, where district administrators complained of their exclusion from policy decisions. In a letter to Deputy Special Representative and head of UN administration Jean-Christian Cady, they warned that the appointment of deputy district administrators might exacerbate the problem if it was not accompanied by meaningful reform in the decision-making process: 'These high-level posts might satisfy the international community's demand for involvement but will not increase our authority at a local level if the process is not handled correctly. Unless it is part of a broader integration strategy it is likely to be perceived as tokenism.'[38] Weeks earlier, the head of district administration, Jarat Chopra, had resigned in a very public disagreement with senior UNTAET staff.[39]

36 UNTAET Regulation 1999/2 (2 December 1999). See Report of the Secretary-General on the United Nations Transitional Administration in East Timor, UN Doc S/2000/53 (26 January 2000), para. 4.

37 Sergio Vieira de Mello, 'Press Briefing' (Dili, East Timor, 5 April 2000).

38 Mark Dodd, 'UN Peace Mission at War with Itself', *Sydney Morning Herald*, 13 May 2000.

39 Idem, 'UN Staff Battle over Independence Policy', *Sydney Morning Herald*, 13 March 2000.

As Vieira de Mello later acknowledged at the National Congress of CNRT, more radical reform was needed:

UNTAET consulted on major policy issues, but in the end it retained all the responsibility for the design and execution of policy. What is more, the NCC came under increasing scrutiny for not being representative enough of East Timorese society, and not transparent enough in its deliberations. Faced as we were with our own difficulties in the establishment of this mission, we did not, we could not involve the Timorese at large as much as they were entitled to.[40]

In May 2000, the Special Representative presented two options to Timorese leaders. The first model was a 'technocratic model', by which the administration would be fully staffed with East Timorese, so a fully national civil service would be in place at independence. The second was a 'political model', whereby East Timorese people would also share responsibility for government in coalition with UNTAET and hold several portfolios in the interim government. He explained that the latter option was a mixed blessing, as those East Timorese would also share UNTAET's role as a 'punching bag'.[41]

The latter model was chosen, and a National Council (NC) was established by a regulation passed on 14 July 2000. Importantly, Vieira de Mello did not chair the NC and its members were exclusively East Timorese (though all appointed by the Special Representative). Its thirty-three (later thirty-six) members comprised representatives of CNRT and other parties, together with representatives from the Church, women's and youth organizations, NGOs, professional and labour organizations, the farming and business community, and Timor's thirteen districts.[42] On the same day, a 'Cabinet of the Transitional Government in East Timor' was established.[43] Of the eight posts initially created, four were assigned to East Timorese (Internal Administration, Infrastructure, Economic Affairs, and Social Affairs) and four to international staff (Police and Emergency Services, Political Affairs, Justice, and Finance). In October 2000, the NC was expanded

[40] Sergio Vieira de Mello, 'Address of SRSG Sergio Vieira de Mello to the National Congress of CNRT' (Dili, East Timor, 21 August 2000).

[41] Security Council Briefed by Sergio Vieira de Mello, Special Representative for East Timor, UN Doc SC/6882 (27 June 2000).

[42] UNTAET Regulation 2000/24, On the Establishment of a National Council (14 July 2000), para. 3.2.

[43] UNTAET Regulation 2000/23, On the Establishment of the Cabinet of the Transitional Government in East Timor (14 July 2000).

to thirty-six members and José Ramos-Horta was sworn in as Cabinet member for Foreign Affairs.[44]

Soon after establishing the National Council, UNTAET announced at a daily press briefing that the East Timorese Transitional Administration (ETTA) had replaced the Governance and Public Administration pillar, and that ETTA should now be referred to as a 'government'.[45] (UNTAET had originally been established with three components or pillars: governance and public administration, humanitarian assistance and emergency rehabilitation, and military.[46]) The idea, as senior UNTAET officials later explained, was that UNTAET should eventually be regarded as a UN assistance mission to ETTA. This was sometimes described as a 'co-government' approach, in contrast to the earlier 'two-track' approach.[47] Such an arrangement could only ever be theoretical, as the Special Representative retained ultimate power, but it represented a decisive shift in thinking less than one year into the mission.

With the benefit of hindsight, UNTAET officials later described the early attempts at consultation as 'confused at best', and as leading to justified criticism on the part of the East Timorese. Capacity-building and preparation for government were originally seen as requiring a 'bottom-up' creation of an East Timorese civil service, with minor consultation at senior levels. The inadequacy of that consultation, combined with the failure to achieve significant headway in 'Timorizing' the civil service, led to pressure to reform UNTAET's structure. Unlike the NCC, which was generally presented with draft regulations for approval, the National Council had power to initiate, modify, and recommend draft regulations; to amend regulations; and to call Cabinet members before it to answer questions regarding their respective functions.[48]

Nevertheless, these powers did not reflect the reality of governance in East Timor—at least, not to the satisfaction of the Timorese.

[44] Report of the Secretary-General on the United Nations Transitional Administration in East Timor (for the period 27 July 2000 to 16 January 2001), UN Doc S/2001/42 (16 January 2001), para. 9.

[45] UNTAET Daily Briefing, 8 August 2000.

[46] SC Res 1272 (1999), para. 3.

[47] See generally Joel C. Beauvais (2000) 'Benevolent Despotism: A Critique of UN State-Building in East Timor', *New York University Journal of International Law and Politics*, 33: 1101.

[48] UNTAET Regulation 2000/24, On the Establishment of a National Council (14 July 2000), para. 2.1.

Gusmão expressed the collective frustration in October 2000, arguing that the Timorese experience of the UN presence was limited to watching hundreds of white four-wheel-drive vehicles driving around Dili and receiving a succession of regulations passed by the UN administration.[49] The Timorese Cabinet members shared these sentiments; in December 2000 they threatened to resign. In a letter to Vieira de Mello, the Timorese Cabinet members (excluding José Ramos-Horta, who was out of East Timor at the time) complained of being 'used as a justification for the delays and the confusion in a process which is outside our control. The East Timorese Cabinet members are caricatures of ministers in a government of a banana republic. They have no power, no duties, no resources to function adequately.'[50]

The threat of resignation was used frequently as a political tool in East Timor. The Cabinet members' threat came soon after Gusmão himself threatened to resign from his position as speaker of the NC. Earlier that year, in the August 2000 CNRT Congress, both Gusmão and Ramos-Horta resigned, twice, only to be reinstated. Gusmão resigned once again from the NC in March 2001. In the absence of real political power, resignation—essentially an attempt to challenge UNTAET's legitimacy by undermining its claims to be consulting effectively—was the most effective means of expressing frustration and trying to bring about change.

1.2.2. A Constitution for Timor-Leste The most concrete political legacy that UNTAET left East Timor was its constitution. UNTAET officials stated repeatedly that they had no intention of involving themselves directly in the drafting process. UNTAET did, however, organize the vote for the Constituent Assembly and remained committed to a 'perfect election'. These positions reflected competing and potentially inconsistent obligations. On the one hand, the United Nations was committed to disseminating the values enshrined in the UN Charter and other treaties: the promotion of self-determination, democracy, freedom of association, and the rule of law. On the other, the choice of the political system to be adopted had to lie with the Timorese themselves. In discussions on a draft regulation on political parties, for example, UNTAET resisted a push to exclude parties that had opposed Timor's independence.

[49] Mark Dodd, 'Give Us a Say, Urges Gusmao', *The Age* (Melbourne), 10 October 2000.

[50] Idem, 'Give Us a Free Hand or We Quit, Leaders Say', *Sydney Morning Herald*, 5 December 2000.

A related problem was the possibility that East Timor would become a one-party state. Fretilin was always certain to win an overwhelming majority of the vote in the August 2001 elections—some estimates were as high as 90 per cent—and there were fears that it would then impose whatever constitution and legislative programme it wanted. Senior UNTAET staff confessed that they regarded such an outcome as undesirable, but were reserved as to what they should (or could) do to avoid it. As a start, they encouraged the Timorese to adopt a mixed voting system with proportional representation in the hope that smaller parties would be represented in the process. Fretilin eventually won fifty-five of the eighty-eight seats.[51]

Procedural difficulties also arose. The elected Constituent Assembly was tasked with drafting and adopting a constitution, which it did on 22 March 2002. The Assembly then transformed itself into the first legislature prior to presidential elections, held in April. But two of the most contentious questions for a constitution are (*a*) how the legislature is elected and (*b*) what powers it holds vis-à-vis the other organs of government. The process followed in East Timor presumed the existence of a consensus on at least the voting method before the assembly could be elected, and mandated that legislature-in-waiting to define the scope of its own powers.[52]

At the same time, some UNTAET staff warned of 'worrying authoritarian tendencies' within the Timorese leadership. Locally organized civic education programs were sometimes likened to propaganda campaigns. 'I have grave doubts that anything democratic will come out of this', observed one senior international official. 'Look at Cambodia: everyone regards it as a success but it was an utter disaster—look who we put in power!' The *Jakarta Post* ran a story along these lines bearing a title of fulsome irony for an Indonesian paper: 'The New Timor: A Xanana Republic?'[53] Gusmão railed against such criticisms in his 2001 New Year's speech, deriding those who 'spout forth points of view... in a remote-control-style'. He went on to draw what he saw as broader lessons from East Timor's engagement with international actors:

> We are witnessing another phenomenon in East Timor; that of an obsessive acculturation to standards that hundreds of international experts try to convey

51 See Chapter Seven, Section 3.3.

52 The new legislative assembly, not surprisingly, endorsed the method by which the legislature was elected and gave itself broad powers.

53 Damien Kingsbury, 'The New Timor: A Xanana Republic?', *Jakarta Post*, 16 December 2000.

to the East Timorese, who are hungry for values: democracy (many of those who teach us never practised it in their own countries because they became UN staff members); human rights (many of those who remind us of them forget the situation in their own countries); gender (many of the women who attend the workshops know that in their countries this issue is no example for others); NGOs (numerous NGOs live off the aid 'business' to poor countries); youth (all those who remind us of this issue know that in their countries most of the youth are unemployed)...

It might sound as though I am speaking against these noble values of democratic participation. I do not mind if it happens in the democratic minds of people. What seems to be absurd is that we absorb standards just to pretend we look like a democratic society and please our masters of independence. What concerns me is the non-critical absorption of [universal] standards given the current stage of the historic process we are building.[54]

This bore interesting similarities to the 'Asian values' arguments of the 1990s, when south-east Asian leaders (and some Western commentators) defended authoritarian political systems on the basis of their alleged effectiveness in promoting economic success. Few UN staff felt comfortable even discussing the idea that good governance might not always be coterminous with multiparty democracy. For its part, of course, UNTAET could hardly lay claim to democratic legitimacy. Vieira de Mello held absolute power in East Timor at the pleasure of the UN Security Council, a body whose permanent members continued to reflect the balance of power at the end of the Second World War. Neither he nor his staff were accountable in any direct way to the Timorese population, an issue that is discussed in the second section of this chapter.

Criticism of the Timorese leadership's style was not limited to expatriates, however. Aderito de Jesus Soares, of the Timorese Jurists Association, spoke of the need to change the 'culture of command' in Timorese political life that developed within a clandestine resistance.[55] Other Timorese NGOs were also critical of the closed nature of Timorese political processes. The greatest point of leverage for international actors will be Timor's continued reliance on development assistance over the coming years, so it is highly unlikely that independent Timor-Leste will be overtly draconian. There is, however, a real danger that Timorese civil society will become regarded

[54] Jose 'Kay Rala Xanana' Gusmão, 'New Year's Message: The Right to Live in Peace and Harmony' (Dili, East Timor, 31 December 2000).

[55] Aderito de Jesus Soares, interview with the author, Dili, East Timor, 15 January 2001.

as simply a channel for aid rather than as a legitimate part of political life.[56]

1.3. Consultation and Responsibility

Transitional administrations are generally created to help a population achieve some form of political transformation—most obviously from conflict to peace, but also from informal to formal political structures. In order to oversee such a transformation effectively and to ensure its durability, it is essential that the local population have a stake in the creation of these structures and in the process by which power is transferred. Consultation is also important for the day-to-day governance of the territory. But final authority remains with the international presence and it is misleading to suggest otherwise. If the local population had the military and economic wherewithal to provide for their security and economic development then a transitional administration would not have been created. Where a transitional administration is created, its role is—or should be—precisely to undertake military, economic, and political tasks that are beyond existing local capacities.

These issues are quite distinct from the basic question of whether it is appropriate or possible to drive such a transformation from above. Nor is this intended to suggest that 'ownership' is unimportant. As the UN operation in Afghanistan suggests, it is possible (though difficult) to ground a post-conflict political transformation on local ownership and a light international presence.[57] It is disingenuous, however, to assert that a successful transitional administration requires both centralized control in the hands of a well-resourced special representative *and* ownership on the part of the local population. As Bosnia demonstrated, handing over power prematurely can be highly destabilizing—not least when it has to be taken back. In Kosovo, the ambiguity of the territory's final status prevented the transfer of meaningful power. Eastern Slavonia showed that consent of local parties may be less important than the clarity of the broader political settlement. In East Timor, by contrast, UNTAET was more clearly exercising power held on trust for the Timorese—once the threat to peace and security diminished, the primary obligation was to prepare the country for its independence.

What linked these otherwise disparate situations was the decision to create a temporary authority under international auspices with

[56] Cf. Jarat Chopra (2002) 'Building State Failure in East Timor', *Development and Change*, 33: 979.

[57] See Chapter Two, Section 3.1.

virtually unlimited powers. Such operations are not without historical precedent—most relevantly in the mandates and trusteeship systems of the League of Nations and the United Nations, as well as the military occupations following the First and Second World Wars.[58] Whereas these earlier examples were transparently premised on the military superiority of the colonial or occupying power, however, this reality is now sometimes seen as politically unpalatable, and therefore masked behind the language of ownership. This is a mistake: ownership may well be the end of the transitional administration, but by definition it is not the means. It does not follow, however, that meaningful power should not be transferred swiftly to local hands, or that local actors should not be engaged in meaningful consultative mechanisms. Rather, it suggests that such transfers should be seen as the incremental completion of the administration's mandate. This, in turn, suggests that power should generally be transferred first at the lower tiers of government, with careful attention paid to making clear what the relative capacities of local and international institutions are at each stage of the mission.[59] Kosovo fails on the latter aspect; Bosnia fails on both.

Premature discussion of ownership may also overshadow the capacity-building purpose of a transitional administration. In East Timor, for example, talk of 'Timorization' was sometimes conflated with ownership. Attention was therefore given to the appointment of local staff without focusing on the training that would enable them to do their jobs. The lack of skilled local workers was initially addressed by importing international staff (of varying quality and interest) who, it was assumed, would not only be able to fulfil civilian functions in the transitional administration but to train Timorese staff to do the same. Doing a job and training another person to do it are, however, quite distinct skills. The result, as UNTAET officials later acknowledged, was that Timorese staff spent less time receiving on-the-job training than standing around watching.

Such considerations are quite separate from administrative barriers to the transfer of power peculiar to the United Nations. East Timor's experiment with the ETTA structure, for example, ran into bureaucratic stonewalling when it was suggested that international staff should work directly under Timorese managers. There was great unwillingness on the part of international staff to submit to such oversight, which might have entailed Timorese officials completing field evaluation reports for mission staff, with consequences for subsequent mission placements and promotions. This reflected the reality that the

[58] See Chapter One. [59] See Chapter Seven, Section 1.

United Nations was not operating under the control of the nascent Timorese institutions, but also raised squarely the question of to whom these international staff are accountable for their performance in the governance of such territories.

2. *Accountability of International Actors*

The administrations in Eastern Slavonia, Kosovo, and East Timor derived their legal authority primarily from resolutions of the Security Council, which in turn finds its legitimacy in the UN Charter, a document that is the closest thing to a constitution for the current international order. In other situations, such as Bosnia, the High Representative's authority came from a treaty signed by interested parties that delegated power to the new institution. Still other situations, such as the post-war occupation of Germany and Japan, took place under conditions of unconditional surrender to victorious armies.

The latter two circumstances are *sui generis*, though international humanitarian law does prescribe some basic principles for belligerent occupation. For example, the 1907 Hague Regulations state that an occupying power must respect the laws in force in the country 'unless absolutely prevented'.[60] This was elaborated in the Geneva Conventions of 1949, which constrain the ability of an occupying power to alter laws or the status of public officials.[61] These principles are, of course, at odds with the cases being considered in this chapter, where the entire purpose of temporary occupation was to change the political structures in the occupied territory. The present section focuses on the first situation, where an administration receives a mandate from the Security Council, with particular reference to the more expansive operations in Kosovo and East Timor. In both territories, sweeping powers were delegated to the Special Representative who quite literally became 'the law'.

There are a number of reasons why checks should be established on the exercise of such power. First, decisions might be made that do not take local interests into account. The mechanisms that might address such concerns have been considered in the previous section on

[60] Convention (IV) Respecting the Laws and Customs of War on Land and Its Annex: Regulations Concerning the Laws and Customs of War on Land (1907 Hague Regulations), done at The Hague, 18 October 1907, available at www.icrc.org/ihl, art. 43.

[61] Convention Relative to the Protection of Civilian Persons in Time of War (Fourth Geneva Convention), done at Geneva, 12 August 1949, available at www.icrc.org/ihl, arts. 54, 64. See also the discussion in the Introduction.

consultation. As indicated, these have largely been seen as sources of input rather than genuine partnership. Even consultative mechanisms can use their minimal legitimacy as a form of leverage, however, in the manner that resignation was used by the Timorese.[62] A second reason for limiting the power of the international presence is that it might be abused in a criminal fashion. Manifestly dictatorial or corrupt acts on the part of the Special Representative would, presumably, lead to dismissal by the Secretary-General or action by the Security Council. In the case of individual criminal acts by those representing the United Nations (which have prominently included crimes of sexual violence), questions of personal immunity arise that are not considered here.[63] (Similarly, it will not be possible to examine the extent to which non-governmental organizations can and should be held accountable for their actions.[64])

Of particular interest in this section are two further aspects of accountability that are relevant to these operations. The first concerns the balance that a transitional administration strikes between responding to legitimate security threats and its obligation to protect and promote human rights. In Kosovo, active promulgation of human rights norms as the law of the land was accompanied by repeated refusals to apply those norms to UNMIK itself. This leads to a related concern: that the exercise of power by a transitional administration in a manner that contradicts principles intended to bind future local regimes—such as democratic principles, the rule of law, separation of powers, and respect for human rights—may actually harm the prospects of good governance in the longer term.[65]

2.1. Existing Mechanisms

The only mechanisms available in Kosovo or East Timor whereby a member of the local population could challenge decisions or actions

[62] See Section 1.2.1 in this chapter.

[63] See above, n. 6.

[64] See the brief discussion in Chapter Six, Section 4.

[65] A 'lessons learned' exercise in Somalia found that the lack of an accountability mechanism led some to perceive the United Nations to be 'above the law', which undercut its efforts to promote human rights. Including an ombudsperson within certain peacekeeping operations might mitigate this effect. See UN Department of Peacekeeping Operations, The Comprehensive Report on Lessons Learned from United Nations Operation in Somalia (UNOSOM) (New York: Lessons Learned Unit, December 1995), available at www.un.org/Depts/dpko/lessons, para. 57.

by UNMIK or UNTAET were those created by the administrations themselves. An ombudsperson was created in each territory, while East Timor had an additional check on the management of donor funds through the Office of the Inspector General. The ombudsperson concept had been floated more generally by the Secretary-General in September 1999 as part of his report on the protection of civilians in armed conflict. This called for the creation of ombudspersons in all peacekeeping operations to deal with complaints from the general public about the behaviour of peacekeepers, though it was clearly aimed at serious violations of international humanitarian and human rights law.[66]

2.1.1. Kosovo Kosovo's Ombudsperson, established by the OSCE on 21 November 2000, was intended to 'promote and protect the rights and freedoms of individuals and legal entities and ensure that all persons in Kosovo are able to exercise effectively the human rights and fundamental freedoms safeguarded by international human rights standards, in particular the European Convention on Human Rights and its Protocols and the International Covenant on Civil and Political Rights'. It was to act independently and without charge. The Ombudsperson had wide jurisdiction to receive and investigate complaints from any person in Kosovo concerning human rights violations and actions constituting an abuse of authority by UNMIK or any emerging central or local institution. This jurisdiction was limited to cases within Kosovo arising after 30 June 2000, and excluded cases involving the NATO-led Kosovo Force (KFOR) and disputes between UNMIK and its staff. During or following an investigation, the Ombudsperson's powers were essentially limited to making recommendations, including recommendations that disciplinary or criminal proceedings be instituted against a person. If the officials concerned did not take appropriate measures within a reasonable time, the Ombudsperson could draw the Special Representative's attention to the matter or make a public statement.[67]

By July 2002, approximately 3,500 people had contacted the Ombudsperson, with 590 formal applications being lodged. Most

[66] Report of the Secretary-General to the Security Council on the Protection of Civilians in Armed Conflict, UN Doc S/1999/957 (8 September 1999), recommendation 31.

[67] UNMIK Regulation 2000/38 (30 June 2000), On the Establishment of the Ombudsperson Institution in Kosovo. The Ombudsperson Institution was formally inaugurated on 21 November 2000.

concerned property issues (such as governmental takings of or damage to property, difficulties in gaining access to property), employment issues (such as discriminatory recruitment practices, unjust dismissals), fair trial issues, and impunity issues (governmental failures to investigate or prosecute crimes). Slightly more than half of these applications were rejected on formal grounds. The Ombudsperson also opened twenty-four investigations on his own initiative. Many complaints were received against KFOR; these were forwarded to KFOR for its 'consideration'. The Ombudsperson also released five 'Special Reports'. These reports addressed immunities of KFOR and UNMIK in their institutional capacities; the applicable law and primacy of human rights instruments; two aspects of deprivations of liberty under 'executive orders'; and the registration of contracts for the sale of real estate.[68]

The fact that UNMIK would continue to administer Kosovo for the foreseeable future raised particular questions about how it should govern. Within the UNMIK structure, there was an increasing tension between those who regarded respect for human rights and the rule of law as central to the institution-building aspect of UNMIK's mandate, and those who saw this as secondary to the overriding concerns of peace and security. This was epitomized in the different approaches taken to the detention of persons under executive orders.

The OSCE and the Ombudsperson in Kosovo both issued reports criticizing UNMIK's practice of holding arrested individuals in detention for extended periods of time before being brought before a judicial authority, and of extended detention prior to trial. Persons were also held in continued detention despite a lawful order by a judicial authority to release them, including orders by a panel of international judges. The OSCE reported, for example, that a judge ordered the release of Shaban Beqiri and Xhemal Sejdiu in November 1999, but that they were, nevertheless, held in detention by order of the Commander of KFOR until July 2000 and were brought to court in handcuffs.[69] KFOR argued that its power to detain derived from Security Council resolution 1244 (1999), which

[68] Ombudsperson Institution in Kosovo, First Annual Report 2000–2001 (18 July 2001), available at www.ombudspersonkosovo.org; Ombudsperson Institution in Kosovo, Second Annual Report.

[69] OSCE, Kosovo: Review of the Criminal Justice System (February–July 2000) (Pristina: OSCE, 2000), available at www.osce.org/kosovo; Ombudsperson Institution in Kosovo, Special Report No 3: On the Conformity of Deprivations of Liberty Under 'Executive Orders' with Recognized International Standards (29 July 2001), available at www.ombudspersonkosovo.org.

gave it the responsibility of 'ensuring public safety and order until the international civil presence can take responsibility for this task'.[70] Two years into the mission, UNMIK officials argued that Kosovo still ranked as an 'internationally-recognized emergency'. And, in such circumstances, 'international human rights standards accept the need for special measures that, in the wider interests of security, and under prescribed legal conditions, allow authorities to respond to the findings of intelligence that are not able to be presented to the court system'.[71] Human rights law does provide for derogation from particular norms including the right to a fair trial, although this is generally limited to a time of 'war or other public emergency threatening the life of the nation' and there must be some form of official notification of this situation.[72] No such notification was offered in Kosovo—due largely to political reservations against admitting that Kosovo even two years after UNMIK arrived remained a 'public emergency'. Rather, the view was taken that a chapter VII resolution adopted by the Security Council somehow absolved a UN operation from certain human rights obligations[73]—an odd conclusion to a war that was justified precisely on the grounds of its support for human rights.

One of the ironies of the current situation is that many of those who argue in favour of greater respect for human rights now argue implicitly that there should have been *less* respect for human rights at the start of the operation. Specifically, many international staff attribute some of the ongoing difficulties in establishing the rule of law in Kosovo to failures to assert such principles robustly in the first weeks and months of the operation.[74]

2.1.2. East Timor In East Timor, an Ombudsperson was appointed in September 2000, but only became operational around May 2001—even then without an UNTAET regulation establishing the institution's mandate. It engaged in some formal inquiries but was more limited in scope than Kosovo's Ombudsperson, lacking both the mandate to investigate human rights and the institutional support of

[70] SC Res 1244 (1999), para. 9(d).

[71] 'UNMIK Refutes Allegations of Judicial Bias and Lack of Strategy', *UNMIK News* (Pristina), 25 June 2001.

[72] See [European] Convention for the Protection of Human Rights and Fundamental Freedoms, done at Rome, 4 November 1950, 213 UNTS 222, art. 15; International Covenant on Civil and Political Rights, 16 December 1966, 999 UNTS 171, art. 4.

[73] See further Chapter Five, Section 2.2.

[74] See Chapter Three, Section 2.1.

being part of an organization like the OSCE. It was generally seen as ineffective.

A second body in East Timor, with no counterpart in Kosovo, was the Office of the Inspector General. Formally established in November 2000, this body emerged from a demand by CNRT to establish a Timorese body to verify the use of funds from the World Bank-administered Trust Fund for East Timor.[75] It operated under an interim mandate given by the Special Representative in January 2001 and released reports on issues such as misappropriation of fuel, the purchase of faulty computers, the purchase of school furniture, the rehabilitation of markets, the use of funds in the Department of Justice, and the employment of teachers at 'phantom schools'. Much of the Inspector General's time, however, was spent on more general dissemination activities—producing pamphlets on nepotism, bribery, and so on. The effectiveness of this position as a watchdog was, therefore, also limited.

2.2. *Do as I Say, Not as I Do*

From the rationales for accountability described earlier, it is clear that the mechanisms created in both Kosovo and East Timor regarded accountability as relevant in terms of the possibility of misuse of power. At the same time, it is also clear that misuse of power was regarded first and foremost as a political rather than legal problem. Thus the Ombudsperson in Kosovo had a broad mandate to address human rights violations, but no capacity to enforce its decisions. In the most egregious case of deprivation of liberty, change came as a result of political pressure from the Ombudsperson together with human rights organizations.

In East Timor, the active engagement of the Timorese population in political life, together with a secure environment and a clear political future, combined to mean that the lack of a fully functioning ombudsperson was never the subject of widespread criticism. In addition, UNTAET's Human Rights Unit provided an additional channel for complaints against the transitional administration. Local concern for good governance of the territory was reflected in the successful Timorese push to establish an Office of the Inspector General, though his mandate was limited to ETTA activities and later diverted onto uncontroversial activities such as dissemination rather than investigation.

[75] UNTAET Regulation 2000/34 (16 November 2000), On Appropriations (No 2); S/2001/42, para. 38.

In neither mission did international staff appear to see the inconsistency between what the transitional administration said and what it did as a significant problem. This was less of a concern in East Timor, where the high level of cooperation between Vieira de Mello and the Timorese leadership meant that no regulation proposed by the National Council was vetoed. In addition, East Timor was on track for independence, which it successfully attained in May 2002. In Kosovo, a combination of legitimate security concerns and the ambiguity of the territory's future appeared to lead senior UNMIK officials to view the rule of law as a barrier rather than a bedrock for their activities. The issue of executive detention was the most obvious example of this, with senior officials defending the policy on the basis that Kosovo continued to be in a state of emergency, while being unprepared to articulate this publicly for fear that it might reflect badly on the mission.

It is beyond the scope of this chapter to determine what impact this has had on the behaviour of local political actors. Certainly, it is Kosovo's ambiguous political future and ongoing security threats that provide the main hurdle to fully functioning government. But as a sustainable political arrangement is sought for the territory, more significant powers are going to have to be exercised by local actors. As that happens, the inconsistencies between what Kosovo's administrators say and what they do may become more important.

2.3. Other Forms of Accountability

In addition to the absence of formal accountability provisions available to local populations, any attempt to establish alternative routes for criticism must deal with the UN culture of generally trusting the perspective of those in the field. Each of the missions considered here has been under an obligation to submit reports to the Security Council: UNTAES was initially requested to report monthly to the Council;[76] UNMIK was to report 'at regular intervals', which tended to mean once every three months;[77] UNTAET had to report every six months, though it generally did so with higher frequency.[78] Reports to the Council are generally taken at face value, however, unless grand political issues or budgetary questions animate discussion. This may be contrasted with the manner in which reports were solicited from

[76] SC Res 1037 (1996), para. 4. The renewal of its mandate saw this reduced to requiring a report every three to four months: SC Res 1079 (1996), para. 6.

[77] SC Res 1244 (1999), para. 20.

[78] SC Res 1272 (1999), para. 18.

administering powers under the Trusteeship System, including provision for a questionnaire to be drafted by the Trusteeship Council and allowing it to accept petitions from inhabitants.[79]

Reactivation of the Trusteeship Council itself as an oversight body has been suggested in this context, though this seems improbable.[80] Nevertheless, there is no reason in principle why petitions might not be submitted directly to the Security Council or a committee constituted by it. The simplest mechanism to establish would be a transitional administration committee, modelled on the sanctions committees that oversee the Council's imposition of sanctions regimes. In 1999, the Council began to appoint independent investigative panels to provide the leverage of public exposure of sanctions busters while maintaining the distance necessary to continue quiet diplomacy on the ground.[81] It would not be necessary for such a committee to have any specific powers; its most important function would be to provide a forum in which grievances could be aired and the political trajectory of a transitional administration debated.[82]

Other alternatives, such as directly petitioning the Secretary-General or the General Assembly, would be unlikely to add much. The Secretary-General necessarily places considerable trust in a special representative and would be unlikely to second-guess him or her, while the Assembly is constrained from making recommendations on situations where the Council is playing an active part.[83]

3. Conclusion

The apparent inconsistency between the means and the ends of transitional administration stems in large part from a reluctance to accept that its legitimacy derives ultimately from military occupation. It is simply misleading to suggest that the international presence in Eastern Slavonia, Bosnia, Kosovo, or East Timor depended in any meaningful way on local consent or 'ownership'. Consent of the local population marks the most promising exit strategy for a transitional administration, mediated through some form of democratic process that establishes a sustainable political framework. But it is not the

[79] See Chapter One, Section 3.1. [80] See Chapter Two, Section 1.2.

[81] See David Cortright and George A. Lopez, *Sanctions and the Search for Security: Challenges to UN Action* (Boulder, CO: Lynne Rienner, 2002), 205–7.

[82] See further Chapter Eight, Section 1.1.

[83] UN Charter, art. 12(1). The Uniting for Peace procedure is, arguably, an exception to this principle. See Ian Brownlie, *International Law and the Use of Force by States* (Oxford: Clarendon Press, 1963), 334.

starting point. What becomes vital, therefore, is clarity as to how a temporary military occupation is to begin the process of transferring political control to local hands. This political trajectory will generally be laid out before the mission is established on the ground, however, which partly explains the paralysis of the operation in Kosovo and the ongoing difficulties in Bosnia. (The mission in Afghanistan, by contrast, lacked an occupation force and depended from the outset on maintaining at least the *appearance* of local consent.[84])

As a consequence, accountability of international actors will necessarily be limited during the opening phases of an operation. Nevertheless, once the political trajectory towards normalization of the political environment has begun, creating mechanisms by which the international presence may be held accountable can both encourage the emergence of an indigenous human rights and rule of law culture as well as improve the day-to-day governance of the territory. The failure to do so—or an actual or apprehended reversal of the political trajectory towards self-governance—will lead to frustration and suspicion on the part of local actors.

The resistance to comparisons of recent transitional administrations to the Trusteeship System or military occupation is suggestive of a broader uncertainty as to the appropriateness of imposing good governance by force of arms. And yet, most such operations are properly seen as the extension of a military intervention by outside powers precisely to replace malevolent or non-existent governance. Reconciling this tension is the most delicate political task of any such operation; how this takes place may also have the most lasting effect on the development of political culture in the territory under benevolent autocracy.

[84] See Chapter Two, Section 3.1.

5

Justice and Reconciliation: The Rule of Law in Post-Conflict Territories

> In hindsight, we should have put the establishment of the rule of law first, for everything else depends on it: a functioning economy, a free and fair political system, the development of civil society, public confidence in police and the courts.
>
> Paddy Ashdown[1]

One of the most important and difficult challenges confronting a post-conflict society is the re-establishment of faith in the institutions of the state. Respect for the rule of law in particular, implying subjugation to consistent and transparent principles under state institutions exercising a monopoly on the legitimate use of force, may face special obstacles. In territories where state institutions themselves have been used as a tool of oppression, building trust in the *idea* of the state requires a transformation in the way in which such institutions are seen. Informal mechanisms that emerge in times of conflict may also create economic and political incentives that militate against respect for the rule of law. These concerns are in addition to more immediate issues, such as the desire of some members of a population emerging from conflict to seize the opportunity of peace to exact immediate retribution for past injustices.

For most such societies, the choices extend from drawing an historical line and moving on, as Spain did after Franco, through lustration processes embraced in some Eastern European countries, truth and reconciliation processes along the lines of the Latin American or the

[1] Paddy Ashdown, 'What I Learned in Bosnia', *New York Times*, 28 October 2002.

South African models, to limited or more general criminal prosecutions before tribunals. In rare cases, international bodies may be established to try alleged offenders. This may be done without the cooperation of the state or states concerned, as in Nuremberg and Tokyo and the tribunals for the former Yugoslavia and Rwanda,[2] or through special agreement, as in the case of Sierra Leone and, eventually, Cambodia. The International Criminal Court may provide a more regular basis for such prosecutions in the future. A further possibility, also outside the control of the state concerned, is trial before a third state exercising universal jurisdiction.

These choices shift radically in the still rarer situation when the territory itself comes under international administration. Such circumstances, in which the institutions of the state are controlled on an interim basis by a benevolently autocratic power, are uncommon; practice in this area has, therefore, been improvisational rather than principled. What law should be enforced—and by whom? And, crucially, how should one resolve the potential dilemma between building capacity for sustainable local institutions and maintaining respect for international standards of justice?

This chapter sketches out the relationship between justice and reconciliation before examining these questions through the experiences of United Nations administrations in Kosovo (1999–) and East Timor (1999–2002) and the assistance mission in Afghanistan (2002–). Though the United Nations had exercised varying measures of executive power in previous missions, notably West New Guinea (1962–3), Cambodia (1992–3), and Eastern Slavonia (1996–8),[3] Kosovo and East Timor were the first occasions on which the United Nations exercised full judicial power within a territory.[4] These situations, therefore, merit

[2] Rwanda was on the Security Council in 1994 and voted against the Security Council resolution establishing the International Criminal Tribunal for Rwanda. Its cooperation with the Tribunal since then has varied.

[3] These missions are discussed in Chapter Two, Section 2. Bodies other than the United Nations have also exercised quasi-judicial power. In Somalia, for example, Australian peacekeepers attempted to re-establish a local police force and community courts in areas they entered: Martin R. Ganzglass, 'The Restoration of the Somali Justice System', in Walter Clarke and Jeffrey Herbst (eds.), *Learning from Somalia: The Lessons of Armed Humanitarian Intervention* (Boulder, CO: Westview, 1997), 20. See Chapter Two, Section 2.5.2; Chapter Three, Section 2.1.

[4] On Kosovo, see SC Res 1244 (1999), para. 11(a), (b)(i); UNMIK Regulation 1999/1 (25 July 1999), §1.1 ('All legislative and executive authority with respect to Kosovo, including the administration of the judiciary, is vested in UNMIK and is exercised by the Special Representative of the Secretary-General'). On East Timor, see SC Res 1272 (1999), para. 1; UNTAET Regulation 1999/1

some scrutiny and are considered in the second and third sections. The UN Assistance Mission in Afghanistan (UNAMA) represents a correction to the increasing aggregation of sovereign powers exercised in UN operations since the mid-1990s.[5] This operation will therefore be considered by way of counterpoint in the fourth section.

Transitional administration presents a hard case for many of the issues that run through the issue of externalized (or universalized) justice more generally.[6] Here, the issue is not so much *where* justice takes place as *who* administers it and according to what law. Many critics of the exercise of universal jurisdiction point to the disjunction between these 'ideal' proceedings and the cultural context within which the crimes actually took place, or to the unsustainability of international standards after the fleeting interest of international actors passes from a particular conflict situation. These concerns apply *a fortiori* to situations in which a primary purpose of engagement is to establish institutions that will outlast the international presence. Experience in the three states to be considered here has been, to say the least, mixed.

1. No Justice Without Peace?

The question of how an emerging regime should deal with past abuses has become a leitmotif in the literature on democratization.[7] In this section, the focus is on the role that international actors can and should play in 'transitional justice'. A central problem in this respect is that commentators with an international perspective often view such internal transitions through the lens of international criminal law: either the wrongdoers are held accountable, or they enjoy impunity.

(27 November 1999), §1.1 ('All legislative and executive authority with respect to East Timor, including the administration of the judiciary, is vested in UNTAET and is exercised by the Transitional Administrator').

[5] See Chapter Two, Section 3.1.

[6] See Chandra Lekha Sriram (2001) 'Externalizing Justice Through Universal Jurisdiction: Problems and Prospects', *Finnish Yearbook of International Law*, 12: 53.

[7] See generally Neil J. Kritz (ed.), *Transitional Justice: How Emerging Democracies Reckon with Former Regimes*, 3 vols. (Washington, DC: United States Institute of Peace Press, 1995); Geoffrey Robertson, *Crimes Against Humanity: The Struggle for Global Justice* (London: Allen Lane, 1999); Gary Jonathan Bass, *Stay the Hand of Vengeance: The Politics of War Crimes Tribunals* (Princeton, NJ: Princeton University Press, 2000); Priscilla B. Hayner, *Unspeakable Truths: Confronting State Terror and Atrocities* (New York: Routledge, 2001).

In fact the situation is more complex. First, a useful distinction may be made between *acknowledgement*—whether to remember or forget the abuses—and *accountability*—whether to impose sanctions on the individuals who were responsible for the abuses.[8] This helps to distinguish between four types of responses to past abuses. At either extreme of the spectrum are criminal prosecutions and unconditional amnesty. Criminal prosecution was the official policy toward collaborators in all Western European states occupied by Germany during the Second World War, a history that continues to inform current attitudes to war crimes.[9] This may be contrasted with the general position of post-communist Eastern and Central Europe and the post-authoritarian regimes of Latin America, which have tended to favour amnesties. Between the extremes lie policies such as lustration and conditional amnesties, typically in the form of a truth commission.

The word 'lustration' derives from the Latin term for the purifying sacrifice that followed a quinquennial census in Rome. In the present context, it denotes the disqualification of a former elite, of the secret police and their informers, or of civil servants from holding political office under the new regime. Such disqualification of political and civil rights may accompany a criminal conviction, as it did in post-war Belgium, France, and the Netherlands. In situations such as post-communist Eastern and Central Europe it has sometimes provided a way to sidestep prosecutions. The United States used it for similar purposes to exclude Iraqi Baath Party officials in 2003, but its bluntness as a tool led to criticisms that it unfairly imposed a form of collective guilt on party members—of whom there were approximately 30,000—and that it excluded capable Iraqis from the reconstruction process.[10]

Conditional amnesties linked to truth commissions serve a different agenda, putting a high priority on investigating the abuses of the former regime. The goal of such a commission is not to prosecute or punish but to disclose the facts of what took place. Truth commissions have been established with varying success across Latin America,[11]but

[8] Luc Huyse (1995) 'Justice After Transition: On the Choices Successor Elites Make in Dealing with the Past', *Law and Social Inquiry*, 20: 51.

[9] See Chapter One, Section 2.2.

[10] International Crisis Group, Baghdad: A Race Against the Clock (Baghdad/Amman/Brussels: ICG Middle East Briefing, 11 June 2003), available at www.crisisweb.org.

[11] See Priscilla B. Hayner (1994) 'Fifteen Truth Commissions, 1974–1993: A Comparative Study', *Human Rights Quarterly*, 16: 597; Hayner, *Unspeakable Truths*.

the linkage between truth and amnesty is epitomized by the South African Truth and Reconciliation Commission, which ran from 1995–2002. The goals that it embodied were expressed in the 1993 Interim Constitution: 'there is a need for understanding but not for vengeance, a need for reparation but not retaliation, a need for *ubuntu* but not for victimization.'[12] A person could apply to the Truth and Reconciliation Commission for amnesty for any act, omission, or offence that took place between 1 March 1960 and 11 May 1994. To be granted amnesty, the person had to satisfy the Committee on Amnesty that the act was associated with a political objective committed in the course of the conflicts of the past, and that full disclosure of all relevant facts had been made.[13] East Timor's Commission for Reception, Truth, and Reconciliation was an innovative variation on this theme, linking the need for reconciliation to the need for reconstruction. The Commission was empowered to establish non-prosecutorial 'Community Reconciliation Processes' (usually some form of community service) that barred future prosecution for criminal acts not amounting to serious crimes.[14]

Various peace agreements concluded in the 1990s incorporated provisions demanding individual accountability. The Paris Agreements on Cambodia that were adopted in 1991 included a requirement that Cambodia recognize its obligations under relevant human rights instruments, which included obligations under the Genocide Convention to prosecute those responsible for genocide.[15] The 1992 El Salvador peace agreements provided for the creation of a truth commission, along with a watered-down pledge to end impunity, but were followed by a broad amnesty law.[16] A 1994 agreement on human

[12] Constitution of the Republic of South Africa Act 200 of 1993 (South Africa), Epilogue. *Ubuntu* may be translated as the essence of being human, linked to an inclusive sense of community: see Desmond Tutu, 'The World Can Learn from South Africa's Restitution', *Independent* (London), 31 October 1999.

[13] Promotion of National Unity and Reconciliation Act 34 of 1995 (South Africa), §20. See generally Alex Boraine, *A Country Unmasked: Inside South Africa's Truth and Reconciliation Commission* (Oxford: Oxford University Press, 2000); Richard J. Goldstone, *For Humanity: Reflections of a War Crimes Investigator* (New Haven, CT: Yale University Press, 2000).

[14] UNTAET Regulation 2001/10 (13 July 2001). See Frederick Rawski (2001) 'Truth-Seeking and Local Histories in East Timor', *Asia-Pacific Journal on Human Rights and the Law*, 1: 77.

[15] Agreements on a Comprehensive Political Settlement of the Cambodia Conflict, done at Paris, 23 October 1991, 31 ILM 183, art. 15(2).

[16] Mexico Agreements, Commission on the Truth, in Steven R. Ratner (1999) 'New Democracies, Old Atrocities: An Inquiry in International Law',

rights in Guatemala committed the government to criminalizing disappearances and extra-judicial executions, though this was accompanied by an amnesty for past crimes.[17] The 1995 Dayton Peace Agreement included a pledge by the parties to the conflict in Bosnia and Herzegovina to cooperate with the International Criminal Tribunal for the Former Yugoslavia, as well as the exclusion of indicted fugitives from positions of authority in the new state.[18] Significantly, though each of these agreements obliged parties to establish particular regimes of accountability, none contained an explicit obligation to punish any offences.[19] In negotiations prior to the Paris Agreements, Hun Sen's Cambodian People's Party (CPP) was strongly dissuaded from insisting on punishment of Khmer Rouge officials on the grounds that this was more appropriately left to the new Cambodian government contemplated in the negotiations. This was political cover for the more practical reason for rejecting the demand—that any attempt to include such provisions, let alone to capture Khmer Rouge leaders, would have threatened the Agreements and provoked the resumption of war.[20]

A far more common feature of such peace agreements is provision for amnesty. Amnesty laws of varying breadths covering governmental atrocities have been passed or honoured throughout Latin America in the past decade in Chile, Brazil, Uruguay, Argentina, Nicaragua, Honduras, El Salvador, Haiti, Peru, and Guatemala. A similar practice now appears to be accompanying transitions to democracy in Africa, reflected in Côte d'Ivoire, South Africa, Algeria, Sierra Leone,

Georgetown Law Journal, 87: 707, 717. But see Law on General Amnesty for the Consolidation of Peace, Decree No 485, 20 March 1993 (El Salvador), reprinted in Kritz (ed.), *Transitional Justice*, vol. 3, 546.

[17] Comprehensive Agreement on Human Rights (Guatemala), UN Doc A/48/928–S/1994/448, Annex I (29 March 1994), art. III. But see Ley de Reconciliación Nacional, Decreto No 145–96, 18 December 1996 (Guatemala) in Ratner, 'New Democracies', 723. See further Susanne Jonas, *Of Centaurs and Doves: Guatemala's Peace Process* (Boulder, CO: Westview, 2000), 90–1.

[18] General Framework Agreement for Peace in Bosnia and Herzegovina (Dayton Agreement), Bosnia and Herzegovina–Croatia–Federal Republic of Yugoslavia, done at Dayton, 14 December 1995, UN Doc S/1995/999, available at www.yale.edu/lawweb/avalon/intdip/bosnia/daymenu.htm, art. IX; Annex 4 (Constitution), art. IX(1).

[19] Ratner, 'New Democracies', 717.

[20] International Crisis Group, Cambodia: The Elusive Peace Dividend (Phnom Penh/Brussels: ICG Asia Report No 8, 11 August 2000), available at www.crisisweb.org, 27. Australian Foreign Minister Bill Hayden's 1984 proposals for UN intervention were undermined by his calls for an international tribunal to try Khmer Rouge leaders—at the very least, this ensured the alienation of China from any such proposal.

and Liberia.[21] The international reaction to such amnesties has been ambiguous. With a few notable exceptions, the United Nations and its member states have been reluctant to condemn amnesties. Following the amnesty in Guatemala in 1996, for example, the General Assembly adopted a weak resolution in which it recognized 'the commitment of the Government and civil society of Guatemala to advance in the fight against impunity and towards the consolidation of the rule of law'.[22] In 1994, the United States actively encouraged the democratically elected government that it had helped to return to power in Haiti to grant amnesty to the prior junta.[23] Exceptions to this trend include the US criticism of Peru in 1997, and the UN Secretary-General's criticism of El Salvador the same year.[24] More robust criticism has come from the UN Human Rights Committee established under the International Covenant on Civil and Political Rights. The Committee first condemned amnesties by referring to their negative effect on respect for the prohibition of torture, but later extended its concern to blanket amnesties generally.[25]

In Sierra Leone, international actors were heavily involved in the peace process but backed away from criticizing an amnesty that granted impunity to participants in a conflict notorious for its viciousness. The Lomé Peace Agreement, signed on 7 July 1999, was brokered by the United Nations, the Organization of African Unity (OAU), and the Economic Community of West African States (ECOWAS). It nevertheless provided for the pardon of Corporal Foday Sankoh and a complete amnesty for any crimes committed by members of the fighting forces during the conflict from March 1991 up until the date of the signing of the agreement.[26] At the last minute, the UN Secretary-General's Special Representative, Francis Okelo, appended

[21] See Simon Chesterman, 'No Justice Without Peace? International Criminal Law and the Decision to Prosecute', in Simon Chesterman (ed.), *Civilians in War* (Boulder, CO: Lynne Rienner, 2001), 145, 154; Somini Sengupta, 'Leader of Liberia Surrenders Power and Enters Exile', *New York Times*, 12 August 2003.

[22] GA Res 51/197 (1997), para. 8.

[23] Michael P. Scharf (1996) 'Swapping Amnesties for Peace: Was There a Duty to Prosecute International Crimes in Haiti?', *Texas International Law Journal*, 31: 1, 6–8.

[24] Ratner, 'New Democracies', 724 n. 779.

[25] Human Rights Committee, General Comment 20(44), art. 7, para. 15, in Report of the Human Rights Committee, 47 GAOR (Supp No 40), UN Doc A/47/49, Annex VI (16 December 1992) ('Amnesties are generally incompatible with the duty of States to investigate such acts'); Human Rights Committee, Preliminary Observations on Peru, UN Doc CCPR/C/79/Add.67 (25 July 1996), para. 9.

[26] Peace Agreement between the Government of Sierra Leone and the Revolutionary United Front of Sierra Leone, done at Lomé, Togo, 7 July 1999, UN Doc S/1999/777.

a hand-written disclaimer to the agreement, stating that the United Nations would not recognize the amnesty provisions as applying to genocide, crimes against humanity, war crimes, and other serious violations of international humanitarian law. Secretary-General Kofi Annan acknowledged at the time that the sweeping amnesty had caused some discomfort:

As in other peace accords, many compromises were necessary in the Lomé Peace Agreement. As a result, some of the terms under which this peace has been obtained, in particular the provisions on amnesty, are difficult to reconcile with the goal of ending the culture of impunity, which inspired the creation of the United Nations Tribunals for Rwanda and the Former Yugoslavia, and the future International Criminal Court. Hence the instruction to my Special Representative to enter a reservation when he signed the peace agreement, explicitly stating that, for the United Nations, the amnesty cannot cover international crimes of genocide, crimes against humanity, war crimes and other serious violations of international humanitarian law. At the same time, the Government and people of Sierra Leone should be allowed this opportunity to realize their best and only hope of ending their long and brutal conflict.[27]

The Lomé Peace Agreement encapsulated the central policy dispute over whether to pursue prosecutions as opposed to amnesties, and their relative potential to end cycles of state violence and to consolidate democratic transitions.[28] The terms of this debate are usually limited to the question of criminal accountability for past abuses—there is general agreement that ongoing or future violations should not be the subject of amnesties—and opinions fall broadly into two camps. On the one hand, officials in states undergoing transitions frequently claim that criminal accountability undermines the transition to democracy, and must therefore be limited in whole or in part. On the other, human rights non-governmental organizations (NGOs), victims' groups, certain international bodies, and most commentators on the subject argue that criminal punishment is the most effective insurance against future repression.

The first view has been voiced by heads of state, legislatures, and courts, though different rationales have been advanced in support of it. In a minority of cases it has been justified in terms of simple

[27] Seventh Report of the Secretary-General on the United Nations Observer Mission in Sierra Leone, UN Doc S/1999/836 (30 July 1999), para. 54. See now Agreement Between the United Nations and the Government of Sierra Leone on the Establishment of a Special Court for Sierra Leone, done at Freetown, 16 January 2002, Annex, art. 10.

[28] Diane F. Orentlicher (1991) 'Settling Accounts: The Duty to Prosecute Human Rights Violations of a Prior Regime', *Yale Law Journal*, 100: 2537, 2541–2.

realpolitik: a regime promulgates a self-amnesty, or refuses to surrender power unless it is granted such an amnesty. More commonly, it is linked to the question of reconciliation and the argument that criminal prosecutions may be an obstacle to this goal. This may be due to fears about the power of the former regime and the prospect of instability if trials are carried out (e.g. Chile, Argentina, and Uruguay) or due to a political decision that persons who committed abuses should nevertheless remain part of the polity (e.g. South Africa, Mozambique, and East Timor). A related concern may be the practical impossibility of prosecuting large numbers of people.

The view that accountability supports democracy also has its variants. The UN Human Rights Committee has declared that impunity is 'a very serious impediment to efforts undertaken to consolidate democracy'.[29] Human rights NGOs often stress a link between accountability, reconciliation, peace, and democracy.[30] Others have argued the more modest point that trials serve to advance liberal government or the rule of law.[31] The specific concern that trials may also foster instability—in the form of entrenching divisions between communities and retaliatory violence—is frequently ignored, however, with the result that the debate often resolves to a simple opposition of idealists and realists.[32]

It seems clear that claims for a causal relationship between accountability and democracy are overstated. Carlos Nino, a human rights adviser to post-junta Argentine President Raúl Alfonsín, notes that trials can be destabilizing, but concludes that the link ultimately depends on what makes democracy self-sustainable: 'If one believes that self-interested motivations are enough, then the balance works heavily against retroactive justice. On the other hand, if one believes that impartial value judgments contribute to the consolidation of democracy, there is a compelling political case for retroactive justice.'[33]

It is also arguable that a distinction should be drawn between internal and international conflicts. The second Additional Protocol

[29] Human Rights Committee, Peru, para. 9.

[30] See, e.g. Somini Sengupta, 'Besieged Liberian', *New York Times*, 11 July 2003; Kenneth Roth, Letter to Secretary of Defence Donald Rumsfeld (New York: Human Rights Watch, 8 August 2003), available at www.hrw.org.

[31] Ratner, 'New Democracies', 735.

[32] Cf. Mark Osiel (2000) 'Why Prosecute? Critics of Punishment for Mass Atrocity', *Human Rights Quarterly*, 22: 118.

[33] Carlos Santiago Nino, *Radical Evil on Trial* (New Haven, CT: Yale University Press, 1996), 134.

to the Geneva Conventions, which concerns the law applicable to non-international armed conflicts, calls on states after the conclusion of civil wars to 'grant the broadest possible amnesty to persons who have participated in the armed conflict'.[34] It has been argued that this was not intended to include amnesties for those having violated international humanitarian law,[35] but in practice such amnesties have tended to be blanket ones. This provision may be contrasted with the Geneva Conventions themselves, which require that states parties undertake to enact legislation necessary to provide effective penal sanctions for persons committing grave breaches, such as wilful killing, torture, and inhuman treatment.[36] In a case examining the constitutional legitimacy of the Truth and Reconciliation Commission, the South African Constitutional Court explained the distinction as follows:

> It is one thing to allow the officers of a hostile power which has invaded a foreign state to remain unpunished for gross violations of human rights perpetrated against others during the course of such conflict. It is another thing to compel such punishment in circumstances where such violations have substantially occurred in consequence of conflict between different formations within the same state in respect of the permissible political direction which that state should take with regard to the structures of the state and the parameters of its political policies and where it becomes necessary after the cessation of such conflict for the society traumatised by such a conflict to reconstruct itself. The erstwhile adversaries of such a conflict inhabit the same sovereign territory. They have to live with each other and work with each other and the state concerned is best equipped to determine what measures may be most conducive for the facilitation of such reconciliation and reconstruction.[37]

These qualifications on the appropriateness of legal and political approaches to dealing with a post-conflict situation do not provide answers to simple questions, such as whether international actors should push for international tribunals as part of a peace deal. As the response to Indonesia's half-hearted trials of military officials accused

[34] Protocol Additional to the Geneva Conventions of 12 August 1949, and relating to the Protection of Victims of Non-International Armed Conflicts (Additional Protocol II), 8 June 1977, 1125 UNTS 609, available at www.icrc.org/ihl, art. 4.

[35] Naomi Roht-Arriaza (1996) 'Combating Impunity: Some Thoughts on the Way Forward', *Law and Contemporary Problems*, 59: 93, 97.

[36] See, e.g. Convention Relative to the Protection of Civilian Persons in Time of War (Fourth Geneva Convention), done at Geneva, 12 August 1949, available at www.icrc.org/ihl, art. 146.

[37] *Azanian Peoples Organization (AZAPO)* v *President of the Republic of South Africa* (1996) 4 SA 671, para. 31.

of abuses in East Timor shows, it may sometimes come down to a more subtle question of pressuring a state to make its legal investigations credible.[38] At the same time, it is clear that criminal prosecutions are no longer regarded as a categorical good—there seems to be a general acceptance of South Africa's decision to grant amnesties rather than prosecute, for example.

Nor does the Rome Statute of the International Criminal Court provide solutions. In the course of the drafting negotiations, the question of how the Court should deal with amnesties or pardons was dropped when it appeared unlikely that a compromise could be reached.[39] This presents two points of uncertainty in the Statute. In the case of amnesties, the Statute requires that a case is or has been the subject of a *criminal* investigation in order to be inadmissible before the Court.[40] A blanket amnesty would clearly not fall within this provision. Nor, however, would a truth commission of the nature of South Africa's Truth and Reconciliation Commission, where immunity from prosecution is drawn from the simple telling of truth to a non-judicial body. Unless the Security Council intervened, the decision of whether it would be appropriate to commence a prosecution before the Court after such proceedings would fall to the discretion of the Prosecutor. This discretion is considerable: the Statute permits the Prosecutor to decline to initiate an investigation or to continue with a prosecution where there are 'substantial reasons to believe that an investigation would not serve the interests of justice'. The reconciliation process in South African might fall within this provision; the amnesty granted in the Lomé Peace Agreement might not. The position is still less clear concerning pardons that follow a criminal prosecution. If it could be established that those proceedings were undertaken for the purpose of shielding the person from criminal responsibility, or if the proceedings were not otherwise conducted independently or impartially, the Court would not be precluded from hearing the case. This might be difficult, however, particularly if

[38] Human Rights Watch, Justice Denied for East Timor (December 2002).

[39] John T. Holmes, 'The Principle of Complementarity', in Roy S. K. Lee (ed.), *The International Criminal Court: The Making of the Rome Statute* (The Hague: Kluwer, 1999), 41, 60.

[40] Statute of the International Criminal Court (Rome Statute), UN Doc A/Conf.183/9 (17 July 1998), art. 17 refers to 'investigation', which might in isolation be interpreted as including the work of a truth commission. Nevertheless, the standard for determining that an investigation is not genuine is that the proceedings are 'inconsistent with an intent to bring the person concerned to justice', suggesting a criminal proceeding.

the prosecution and the pardon are undertaken by different political organs.[41]

Though commonly discussed in the abstract, these questions are far from hypothetical. The following three sections will examine how they have been resolved in Kosovo, East Timor, and Afghanistan.

2. *Kosovo: Justice in Limbo*

Kosovo's experience of justice reflects the intentional ambiguity of the resolution to the 1999 conflict between NATO and the Federal Republic of Yugoslavia (FRY) over Kosovo. Though the chances of it ever returning to direct control under Belgrade are negligible, Kosovo's final status remains indeterminate. This uncertainty has increased the challenges of post-conflict reconstruction as it is unclear what form of institutions should be built by the 'interim administration'. In particular, there was considerable reluctance to hand over power to the Kosovar Albanians in the form of quasi-independent institutions that might quickly assert actual independence; at the same time, the hostile environment led the United Nations to adopt security measures that in themselves arguably undermined respect for the rule of law. There was, therefore, no 'ownership' on the part of the local community and frequently little leadership on the part of the United Nations. Though hardly the largest of the many problems confronting Kosovo, these factors have not helped the prospects for the rule of law as the province slouches its way towards Europe.

The central contradiction of the UN Interim Admission Mission in Kosovo's (UNMIK) mandate was that it lacked a political resolution for the sovereignty question posed by the Serbian province. On the ground, it was soon recognized that returning Kosovo to direct control under Belgrade was inconceivable. Nevertheless, the authorizing resolutions and official statements emphasized continuing respect for the territorial integrity and political independence of the FRY. In itself, this contradiction presented a serious barrier to the re-establishment of the rule of law in Kosovo—a problem exacerbated still further by the security vacuum that was left after the departure of the Serb institutions of state, discussed in Chapter Three. Three aspects of this problem as it manifested in Kosovo are considered here: the choice of law to

[41] Ibid., arts. 20(3), 53. See also John Dugard (2000) 'Dealing with Crimes of a Past Regime: Is Amnesty Still an Option?', *Leiden Journal of International Law*, 12: 1001.

be applied in Kosovo; the appointment of local and later international judges; and the question of executive detention by UNMIK.[42]

2.1. Applicable Law

The failure to establish political credibility from the outset of the mission compounded the internal contradictions of UNMIK's mandate. At Russian insistence, and consistent with the terms of resolution 1244 (1999), the first UNMIK regulation established that the law in force prior to 24 March 1999 (the day on which NATO's air campaign commenced) would apply, provided that this law was consistent with internationally recognized human rights standards and Security Council resolution 1244.[43] The largely Albanian judiciary that was put in place by UNMIK rejected this, however, with some judges reportedly stating that they would not apply 'Serbian' law in Kosovo. Though they accepted some federal laws, such as the federal code of criminal procedure, the judges insisted on applying the Kosovo Criminal Code and other provincial laws that had been in effect in March 1989, asserting that these had been illegally revoked by Belgrade. (The judges, nevertheless, 'borrowed' from the 1999 law to deal with cases involving crimes not covered in the 1989 Code, such as drug-trafficking and war crimes.) In addition to lowering hopes that Serb judges would return to office, this dispute further undermined local respect for UNMIK—especially when it finally reversed its earlier decision in December 1999 and passed a regulation declaring that the laws in effect on 22 March 1989 would be the applicable law in Kosovo.[44]

UNMIK also had to reverse itself on the question of appointing international judges to oversee the legal system. Despite the resignation of Serb judges and concerns about ethnic bias and intimidation within the Albanian judiciary, UN officials were reluctant to introduce international judges.[45] A senior UN official reportedly responded to

[42] Other aspects of the Kosovo operation are discussed in greater detail elsewhere in the book. On background, see Chapter Two, Section 2.4.2. On consultation, see Chapter Four, Section 1.1.3. On elections and exit strategies, see Chapter Seven, Section 3.2.

[43] UNMIK Regulation 1999/1 (25 July 1999), §§2, 3.

[44] UNMIK Regulation 1999/24 (12 December 1999), §1.1.

[45] See, e.g. Report of the Secretary-General on the United Nations Interim Administration Mission in Kosovo, UN Doc S/1999/779 (12 July 1999), para. 66: 'There is an urgent need to build genuine rule of law in Kosovo, including through the immediate re-establishment of an independent, impartial and multi-ethnic judiciary.'

such a recommendation by stating: 'This is not the Congo, you know.' Instead, fifty-five local judges and prosecutors, operating under the Joint Advisory Council on Provisional Judicial Appointments, were proposed in the first months of the mission.[46] By February 2000, the rebellion of Albanian judges and a series of attacks against their few Serb counterparts led to a regulation allowing Special Representative of the Secretary-General Bernard Kouchner to appoint international judges to the district court in Mitrovica as an emergency measure. Within three months, this had been extended to every district court in Kosovo.[47]

2.2. *Executive Detentions*

One of the consequences of the diminished credibility of UNMIK and its own lack of faith in the local judiciary was recourse to detention on executive orders. On 28 May 2000, Afram Zeqiri, a Kosovar Albanian and former Kosovo Liberation Army (KLA) fighter, was arrested on suspicion of murdering three Serbs in the village of Cernica, including the shooting of a four-year-old boy. An Albanian prosecutor ordered him released for lack of evidence, raising suspicions of judicial bias. The decision was upheld by an international judge, but Kouchner nevertheless ordered that Zeqiri continue to be detained under an 'executive hold', claiming that the authority to issue such orders derived from 'security reasons' and Security Council resolution 1244 (1999).[48]

Similar orders were made by Kouchner's successor, Hans Haekkerup. In February 2001, a bus carrying Serbs from Nis into Kosovo was bombed, killing eleven. British KFOR troops arrested Florim Ejupi, Avdi Behluli, Çelë Gashi, and Jusuf Veliu in mid-March on suspicion of being involved, but on 27 March a panel of international judges of the District Court of Pristina ordered that Behluli, Gashi, and Veliu be released. The following day, Haekkerup issued an executive order extending their detention for thirty days, later extended by six

[46] UNMIK Emergency Decree No 1999/1 (28 June 1999) and UNMIK Emergency Decree No 1999/2 (28 June 1999) creating the legal basis for Joint Advisory Council and appointing its members (three internationals, four locals—two Albanian, one Serb, and one Bosniak). This was later succeeded by the Advisory Judicial Commission: UNMIK Regulation 1999/7 (7 September 1999).

[47] UNMIK Regulation 2000/6 (15 February 2000); UNMIK Regulation 2000/34 (27 May 2000).

[48] William G. O'Neill, *Kosovo: An Unfinished Peace* (Boulder, CO: Lynne Rienner, 2002), 86.

more such orders. (Ejupi was reported to have 'escaped' from the high-security detention facility at Camp Bondsteel.)[49]

Following criticism by the OSCE Ombudsperson, as well as international human rights organizations such as Human Rights Watch and Amnesty International, a Detention Review Commission of international experts was established by UNMIK in August 2001 to make final decisions on the legality of administrative detentions.[50] The Commission approved extension of the detentions of the alleged Nis bombers until 19 December 2001—a few weeks after Kosovo's first provincial elections—ruling that 'there are reasonable grounds to suspect that each of the detained persons has committed a criminal act'. At the end of that period, the three-month mandate of the Commission had not been renewed; in its absence, the Kosovo Supreme Court ordered the release of the three detainees.[51] The last person held under an Executive Order, Afrim Zeqiri, was released by a judge on bail in early February 2002 after approximately twenty months in detention.[52]

2.3. Kosovo in Limbo

Kosovo demonstrates the most difficult aspects of administering justice under international administration. Some of these difficulties arose from the security environment on the ground; others from the high politics surrounding every aspect of NATO's intervention and the subsequent role of the United Nations. Together, these factors encouraged inconsistent policies on the part of the international administration, in turn giving rise to its own contradictions as the body charged with instilling the values of human rights and the rule of law detained persons in apparent contempt of international judges. A clearer distinction between an initial period of martial law and subsequent judicial reconstruction might have ameliorated

[49] See Arben Qirezi, 'Kosovo: Court Overturns Haekkerup Detention Orders', *IWPR Balkan Crisis Report No 308*, 11 January 2002.

[50] See Ombudsperson Institution in Kosovo, Special Report No 3: On the Conformity of Deprivations of Liberty Under 'Executive Orders' with Recognized International Standards (29 July 2001), available at www.ombudspersonkosovo.org; Human Rights Watch, *World Report 2002* (New York: Human Rights Watch, 2002), 386; Amnesty International, Press Release (21 February 2001); UNMIK Regulation 2001/18 (25 August 2001), On the Establishment of a Detention Review Commission for Extra-Judicial Detentions Based on Executive Orders.

[51] Qirezi, 'Kosovo: Court Overturns Haekkerup Detention Orders'; UNMIK, Press Release (19 December 2001).

[52] See also Chapter Four, Section 2.1.1.

some (though not all) of these problems. Given the particular controversy concerning the choice of law in Kosovo, it might have been appropriate also for the United Nations to impose a generic penal code and code of criminal procedure for an interim period, along the lines recommended by the Brahimi Report on UN Peace Operations.[53] A deeper problem underlying UNMIK's difficulties is the lack of any serious interest in reconciliation on the part of the local actors. Virtually all parties remain ethnically 'pure', and until the final status question is resolved the prospects of dealing with the past locally remain slim.

3. *East Timor: Post-Colonial Justice*

In East Timor, the United Nations faced the task of building a judicial system literally from the ground up. As the United Nations prepared to establish a transitional administration, the Secretary-General observed that 'local institutions, including the court system, have for all practical purposes ceased to function, with... judges, prosecutors, and other members of the legal profession having left the territory'.[54] This apocalyptic view of the situation was borne out by early estimates that the number of lawyers remaining in the territory was fewer than ten.[55]

Unlike Kosovo, then, East Timor's experiences reflected a distinct set of concerns with internationally administered justice. Although there was an initial assumption that East Timor required quick law and order measures to maintain peace and security (learning, in part, from the experiences of Kosovo), it soon became clear that the main focus should be on developing institutions that would be sustainable. Greater

[53] Report of the Panel on United Nations Peace Operations (Brahimi Report), UN Doc A/55/305–S/2000/809 (21 August 2000), available at www.un.org/peace/reports/peace_operations, paras. 80–3 (calling for the Secretary-General to invite a panel of international legal experts to evaluate the feasibility and utility of developing an interim criminal code, including possible regional adaptations, for use in transitional administration operations pending the re-establishment of local rule of law and local law enforcement capacity).

[54] Report of the Secretary-General on the Situation in East Timor, UN Doc S/1999/1024 (4 October 1999), para. 33.

[55] See Hansjoerg Strohmeyer (2000) 'Building a New Judiciary for East Timor: Challenges of a Fledgling Nation', *Criminal Law Forum*, 11: 259, 263. The World Bank estimated that over 70 per cent of all administrative buildings were partially or completely destroyed, and almost all office equipment and consumable materials were totally destroyed: World Bank, Report of the Joint Assessment Mission to East Timor (8 December 1999), available at www.worldbank.org, para. 15.

efforts were made to 'Timorize' the judiciary than most other civil and political institutions, but this led to substantial trade-offs in terms of qualifications. Balancing the need to respect international human rights standards against the need for sustainability—and the reluctance of Indonesia to cooperate with any form of international tribunal[56]—led to the establishment of special panels for serious crimes. Plagued by various concerns irrelevant to the situation of the Timorese (such as internal UN management difficulties), this panel enjoyed less legitimacy than the Timorese-driven Commission for Reception, Truth, and Reconciliation.[57] Meanwhile, frustration with the pursuit of serious offenders and the questionable efforts by Indonesia to prosecute its own nationals led to renewed Timorese calls for a full international criminal tribunal to be convened.

3.1. 'Timorizing' the Judiciary

Though East Timor presented fewer security and political problems than Kosovo (choice of law, for example, was uncontroversial[58]), the lack of local capacity presented immense challenges. Under Indonesian rule, no East Timorese lawyers had been appointed as judge or prosecutor. A Transitional Judicial Service Commission was established, comprising three East Timorese and two international experts,[59] but the absence of a communications network meant that the search for qualified lawyers had to be conducted through leaflet drops by International Force in East Timor (INTERFET) planes. Within two months, sixty qualified East Timorese with law degrees had applied for positions and the first eight judges and two prosecutors were sworn in on 7 January 2000.[60]

As in Kosovo, the decision to rely on inexperienced local jurists came from a mix of politics and pragmatism. Politically, the

[56] Such a tribunal had been called for by, among others, the International Commission of Inquiry on East Timor: Report of the International Commission of Inquiry on East Timor to the Secretary-General, UN Doc A/54/726–S/2000/59, Annex (31 January 2000), para. 152.

[57] See Section 1 in this chapter.

[58] UNTAET Regulation 1999/1 (27 November 1999), §3.1 defined the applicable law as 'the laws applied in East Timor prior to 25 October 1999'. This language (referring to 'the laws applied', rather than 'the applicable laws') was chosen in order to avoid the retroactive legitimation of the Indonesian occupation of East Timor: Strohmeyer, 'Building a New Judiciary', 267 n. 218.

[59] UNTAET Regulation 1999/3 (3 December 1999), §2.

[60] Hansjoerg Strohmeyer (2001) 'Collapse and Reconstruction of a Judicial System: The United Nations Missions in Kosovo and East Timor', *American Journal of International Law*, 95: 46, 53–4.

appointment of the first Timorese legal officers was of enormous symbolic importance. At the same time, the emergency detentions under INTERFET required the early appointment of judges who understood the local civil law system and who would not require the same amount of translation services demanded by international judges. In addition, appointment of international judges would necessarily be an unsustainable temporary measure that would cause further dislocation when funds began to diminish.

The UN Transitional Administration in East Timor (UNTAET) was more aggressive in Timorizing the management of judicial systems than the institutions working in political and civil affairs.[61] The trade-off, of course, was in formal qualifications and practical experience. Some of the appointees had worked in law firms and legal aid organizations in Indonesia; others as paralegals with Timorese human rights organizations and resistance groups.[62] None had ever served as a judge or prosecutor. Timorization thus referred more to the identity of a particular official, rather than the establishment of support structures to ensure that individuals could fulfil their responsibilities. UNTAET developed a three-tier training approach, comprising a one-week 'quick impact' course prior to appointment, ongoing training, and a mentoring scheme. Limited resources and difficulties in recruiting experienced mentors with a background in civil law posed serious obstacles to the training programme, however, which UNTAET officials later acknowledged was grossly insufficient.

3.2. *Infrastructure and Support*

Even more so than Kosovo, the destruction wrought in East Timor presented substantial practical difficulties in the administration of justice. The first judges to be sworn in worked out of chambers and courtrooms that were still blackened by smoke. The judges lacked not merely furniture and computers, but virtually any legal texts. Some books were retrieved from the destroyed buildings, but most had to be sought in the form of donations from private law firms and law schools in Indonesia and Australia.[63]

61 See, e.g. Joel C. Beauvais (2001) 'Benevolent Despotism: A Critique of UN State-Building in East Timor', *New York University Journal of International Law and Politics*, 33: 1101, 1149.

62 Strohmeyer, 'Collapse and Reconstruction', 54.

63 Strohmeyer, 'Building a New Judiciary', 268–9.

A non-obvious priority in the first months of the operation was to construct correctional facilities. Virtually all detention facilities had been destroyed prior to the arrival of INTERFET, limiting the capacity to detain alleged criminals. This problem was inherited by UNTAET, with the result that UN civilian police were forced to release alleged criminals in order to detain returning militia implicated in the commission of grave violations of international humanitarian law during the post-referendum violence. One of the barriers to dealing with the shortage of space was the reluctance of donors to fund, either directly or indirectly, the building of prisons.[64]

Many of the gaps in the legal system, in particular the provision of legal assistance, were filled by enterprising NGOs, such as the civil rights organization Yayasan HAK.[65] Such initiatives deserve the support of international actors, particularly where bureaucratic or political obstacles delay UN initiatives in the same area. Nevertheless, by November 2000, the Security Council Mission to East Timor found that 'the judicial sector remains seriously under-resourced. Consequently, the current system cannot process those suspects already in detention, some of whom have been held for almost a year.'[66] These delays, combined with the lack of access to qualified defence lawyers, were blamed when over half the Timorese prison population escaped in August 2002.[67]

3.3. *Serious Crimes*

In Kosovo, the judicial system existed parallel to the ongoing jurisdiction of the International Criminal Tribunal for the Former Yugoslavia. In the course of NATO's 1999 bombing campaign, the Prosecutor issued an indictment for Yugoslav President Slobodan Milosevic and other Serbian leaders for alleged offences committed in Kosovo. Milosevic was transported to The Hague in unusual circumstances in

[64] Human Rights Watch, Unfinished Business: Justice for East Timor, Press Backgrounder (August 2000), available at www.hrw.org/backgrounder/asia/timor/etimor-back0829.htm; Strohmeyer, 'Collapse and Reconstruction', 58. See Chapter Six, Section 1.3.

[65] Yayasan HAK (Foundation for Law, Human Rights, and Justice) was established in 1997 by a group of young East Timorese intellectuals and NGO activists. See www.yayasanhak.minihub.org.

[66] Report of the Security Council Mission to East Timor and Indonesia, UN Doc S/2000/1105 (20 November 2000), para. 8.

[67] See Jill Jolliffe, 'Jail Breakout over Delays', *The Age* (Melbourne), 17 August 2002.

June 2001. The first indictments of Kosovar Albanians were issued in February 2003, concerning KLA leaders accused of war crimes. Given the politicization of the Kosovo judiciary described earlier, conducting any of these trials within Kosovo would have posed a substantial challenge to the judicial system.[68]

In East Timor, no such international tribunal existed. Prosecution of those accused of the most serious crimes was, therefore, handled as part of the East Timorese domestic process. In March 2000, UNTAET passed a regulation establishing the exclusive jurisdiction of the Dili District Court and the Court of Appeal in Dili in relation to serious crimes. These were defined as including genocide, crimes against humanity, war crimes, and torture, as well as murder and sexual offences committed between 1 January 1999 and 25 October 1999. The cases were to be heard by mixed panels of both international and East Timorese judges, and prosecuted by a new Serious Crimes Unit. The first hearings took place in January 2001.[69]

In addition to the constraints on resources, management problems contributed to the extremely slow functioning of the serious crimes panels. By early 2001 there were over 700 unprocessed cases in the serious crimes category alone and detention facilities were filled to capacity with pre-trial detainees, with the result that some alleged perpetrators had to be released.[70] These problems continued through 2001 with a number of resignations from the Serious Crimes Unit. Dissatisfaction with the progress in serious crimes was one factor that encouraged the East Timorese to look for alternative accountability mechanisms for the abuses of September 1999. More importantly, however, the inadequacy of Indonesia's efforts to deal with alleged perpetrators in its territory led many to believe that an international tribunal was the only way in which high-level perpetrators would ever face justice.[71] This might have been based on unrealistic expectations of what such a tribunal could achieve; in any case, such a proposal appeared unlikely to draw much support from governments.

68 Gary Jonathan Bass (2003) 'Milosevic in the Hague', *Foreign Affairs*, 82(3): 82; Alissa J. Rubin, 'Three Albanians to Face Kosovo War Crimes Charges; a Fourth Indictee Is in Custody', *Los Angeles Times*, 19 February 2003.

69 UNTAET Regulation 2000/11 (6 March 2000), §10; UNTAET Regulation 2000/15 (6 June 2000); Report of the Secretary-General on the United Nations Transitional Administration in East Timor (for the period 27 January to 26 July 2000), UN Doc S/2000/738 (26 July 2000), para. 42.

70 Beauvais, 'Benevolent Despotism', 1155.

71 Ian Martin, 'No Justice in Jakarta', *Washington Post*, 27 August 2002.

3.4. East Timor in Transition

In the panoply of UN peace operations, East Timor will almost certainly be regarded as a success. Its independence on 20 May 2002 was the culmination of over twenty-five years of struggle by the Timorese and billions of dollars in international assistance. And yet, upon independence, it became the poorest country in Asia.[72] Unemployment remains high, literacy remains low, and the foundations for a stable and democratic society are untested. The aggressive policies in promoting Timorese leadership in the law and order area were laudable, but the slow pace of the legal system that was created undermined faith in the rule of law as such.

A major test of this system will be on the question of land title. For essentially political reasons, UNTAET deferred consideration of the land title issue until after independence—and therefore beyond its mandate. This enormously complex problem includes claims arising from Indonesian and Portuguese colonial rule, and perhaps claims under customary norms pre-dating Portuguese colonization.[73] How Timor-Leste deals with this issue, and the incentives for corruption that go with it, will undoubtedly challenge this newest of countries' political and legal systems. Although the outcome is clearly up to the Timorese themselves, how the new regime responds to that challenge will be a measure of the success of the rule of law policies put in place by UNTAET.

4. Afghanistan: Justice and the 'Light Footprint'

In Afghanistan, the combination of restricting the international security presence to Kabul and the desire to encourage Afghan capacity-building—the 'light footprint' approach—led to a minimal international presence. In addition, Afghanistan's undisputed sovereignty substantially limited the role that the international presence played in the area of the rule of law. Nevertheless, key areas of the judicial system were still potentially 'externalized' and provide an interesting contrast with the approach adopted in the earlier missions. These areas included establishing the applicable law under the imprimatur of the United Nations, granting the United Nations the right to investigate human rights violations, and establishing

72 See Chapter Six.

73 See Dennis Schulz, 'East Timor's Land Rights Mess', *The Age* (Melbourne), 23 December 2000. Cf. Strohmeyer, 'Building a New Judiciary', 280–1 (arguing that it was 'indispensable to establish. . .a land and property commission').

a Judicial Commission to rebuild the domestic justice system 'with the assistance of the United Nations'.[74]

4.1. Applicable Law

The Bonn Agreement provided for the legal framework that applied in Afghanistan until the adoption of a new constitution by a Constitutional Loya Jirga, which was to be convened within eighteen months of the establishment of the Transitional Authority. The interim legal framework was based on the 1964 Constitution, 'with the exception of those provisions relating to the monarchy and to the executive and legislative bodies provided in the Constitution'. Existing laws and regulations would continue to apply, 'to the extent that they are not inconsistent with this agreement or with international legal obligations to which Afghanistan is a party'.[75]

As in Kosovo, the legal order established by previous regimes was itself controversial in Afghanistan. The Bonn Agreement, therefore, attempted to mediate these concerns by reverting to an earlier period.[76] Falling back on the 1964 Constitution in particular reflected an attempt to connect the peace process with memories of a more stable Afghanistan—though exclusion of provisions concerning the monarchy and the purely symbolic role for 'His Majesty Mohammed Zaher, the former King of Afghanistan'[77] suggested ambivalence about the historical analogy. At the same time, reference to 'existing laws and regulations' sought to provide for necessary amendments following thirty-seven years of legal development.

Precisely how such updating might occur was an open question. Similarly, although the Bonn Agreement explicitly incorporated only the international legal instruments to which Afghanistan was a party—rather than the entire corpus of 'internationally recognized human rights standards', as in Kosovo[78] and East Timor[79]—the nascent

[74] Agreement on Provisional Arrangements in Afghanistan Pending the Re-Establishment of Permanent Government Institutions (Bonn Agreement), done at Bonn, 5 December 2001, UN Doc S/2001/1154, art. II(2). See Chapter Two, Section 3.1.

[75] Bonn Agreement, arts. I(6), II(1)(i)–(ii).

[76] Afghanistan saw a series of constitutions adopted following successive coups in 1973 (leading to the constitution of February 1977), 1978, and 1979, the Soviet occupation from 1979–89 (with a new constitution in 1987, replaced by a constitution in 1990), the coup by mujahideen forces in 1992, and the disputed Taliban rule from 1996.

[77] Bonn Agreement, art. I(4), III(2).

[78] UNMIK Regulation 1999/1 (25 July 1999), §§2–3.

[79] UNTAET Regulation 1999/1 (27 November 1999), §3.1. These standards were requested in East Timor by the CNRT, which had endorsed them in its 'Magna Carta' in 1998, adopted at the East Timorese National Convention in the

Supreme Court of Afghanistan still enjoyed considerable latitude. (The major difference was that Afghanistan had not ratified the Convention on the Elimination of All Forms of Discrimination Against Women.) In the two earlier missions, the vagueness of the qualifying clauses and the lack of any attempt at training caused uncertainty as to the validity of certain laws, such as the maximum length of pre-trial detention.[80] Nevertheless, the paralysis of the Afghan legal system after Bonn left these questions unanswered.

4.2. Human Rights and Transitional Justice

Justice in Afghanistan under the Taliban was notoriously capricious and brutal; their overthrow was brutal in its own way. In addition to allegations that anti-Taliban forces summarily executed prisoners of war during the fighting, there were several reports that Rashid Dostum's troops killed hundreds of Taliban detainees while transporting them in sealed freight containers. There was little willingness to investigate these and other allegations against members of Hamid Karzai's new government.[81]

The Bonn Agreement provided that the Interim and later Transitional Authority should, 'with the assistance of the United Nations, establish an independent Human Rights Commission, whose responsibilities will include human rights monitoring, investigation of violations of human rights, and development of domestic human rights institutions'. At the same time, the United Nations was separately granted 'the right to investigate human rights violations and, where necessary, recommend corrective action', as well as developing and implementing a human rights education programme.[82]

In keeping with the 'light footprint' philosophy, senior UN staff were circumspect about taking the lead in human rights.[83] The first

Diaspora, Peniche, Portugal (25 April 1998). See also Outcomes of the CNRT National Congress (Dili, 21–30 August 2000).

80 See, e.g. Strohmeyer, 'Building a New Judiciary', 276.

81 Human Rights Watch, *World Report 2003* (New York: Human Rights Watch, 2003), 198. The detention of Afghan and alleged Al Qaeda forces on US military bases also raised serious questions of international humanitarian law.

82 Bonn Agreement, art. III.C(6), Annex II, para. 6.

83 Interesting human rights issues more general than those discussed here are raised by the UNAMA mission structure. Rather than concentrating human rights in a single component, UNAMA has a Human Rights Coordinator in the Office of the SRSG with two full-time human rights staff and works with relevant staff located in the mission's two operational pillars (Pillar I: 'political' and Pillar II: 'relief, recovery and reconstruction'). See Office of the SRSG

National Workshop on Human Rights was convened in Kabul on 9 March 2002, chaired by Interim Authority Vice-Chair Sema Samar. Although UN High Commissioner for Human Rights Mary Robinson and Special Representative of the Secretary-General Lakhdar Brahimi addressed the meeting, the participants were drawn from members of the Interim Authority, Afghan specialists, and representatives of national NGOs. The workshop established four national working groups to carry the process forward in accordance with twenty guiding principles. These principles concerned the role of the proposed Human Rights Commission, as well as the question of transitional justice. With respect to past violations, the principles called for decisions on appropriate mechanisms of transitional justice to be made by the Afghan people themselves, based on 'international human rights standards, Afghan cultural traditions, and Islam'.[84]

In his opening address to the workshop, Interim Authority Chairman Hamid Karzai had raised the possibility of an Afghan truth commission in a speech that departed from his prepared text:

> Yet another important matter to consider is the question of the violations of the past. I cannot say whether the current Interim Administration has full authority to address this. But it is my hope that the Loya Jirga government will have the authority to establish a truth commission and ensure that the people will have justice. The people of Afghanistan must know that there will be a body to hear their complaints.
>
> Indeed, we must hear what the people have to say. Mass graves have been found in which hundreds were buried, houses and shops burnt, so many cruel acts, and about which nothing had been heard or known before. So many of our people have been murdered, mothers killed as they embraced their children, people burnt, so much oppression, so many abuses. This is why a truth commission is needed here: to protect our human rights, and to heal the wounds of our people.[85]

for Afghanistan, Human Rights in the United Nations Assistance Mission for Afghanistan (UNAMA) (Kabul: UNAMA-OSRSG, 2002).

[84] Office of the SRSG for Afghanistan, Human Rights Advisory Note No 3: Implementing the Accountability Provisions of the Bonn Agreement: Toward an Afghan National Strategy for Human Rights Monitoring, Investigations and Transitional Justice (Kabul: UNAMA-OSRSG, March 2002). See also The Situation in Afghanistan and Its Implications for International Peace and Security (Report of the Secretary-General), UN Doc A/56/875–S/2002/278 (18 March 2002), para. 42.

[85] Hamid Karzai, 'A Vision of Human Rights in the New Afghanistan' (Kabul: Afghan National Workshop on Human Rights: Toward Implementation of the Human Rights Provisions of the Bonn Agreement, 9 March 2002), 3 (unofficial translation from the original Dari).

This desire to confront transitional justice questions directly was repeated in the working groups established out of the initial workshop. An all-Afghan working group on 'approaches to human rights monitoring, investigation and remedial action' recast its mandate to include transitional justice issues.[86]

The process of national reconciliation that this may herald is necessarily slow. Nevertheless, mission staff were keen to avoid scenes common in the past, with foreign consultants parachuting into a country like Afghanistan, lecturing the local population, and then departing. The consultations that took place were generally regarded as fruitful, though perhaps open to the criticism that the main interlocutors came from a very narrow cross section of Afghan civil society. Still less can be said about achievements in the justice sector.

4.3. Justice Sector

Under the Bonn Agreement, the Interim Authority was to establish, 'with the assistance of the United Nations, a Judicial Commission to rebuild the domestic justice system in accordance with Islamic principles, international standards, the rule of law and Afghan legal traditions'.[87]

The Secretary-General's 18 March 2002 report made brief reference to the Judicial Commission, noting that it would 'touch on issues central to the values and traditions of different segments of Afghan society. It is imperative, therefore, that the Afghan men and women chosen to serve on the Commission be highly respected, apolitical and suitably qualified to discharge their duties.' The lead role was attributed to the Interim Authority, which was to 'cooperate closely with lawyers and judges, other interested parties and individuals and the United Nations to identify potential candidates for the Commission, with a view to establishing it as soon as possible.'[88] On 26 March 2002, the Office of the Special Representative announced that it had 'prepared a paper on the Judicial Commission, outlining its proposed mission, composition, powers and operating procedures.'[89] Nevertheless, a Judicial Adviser was appointed only in the first week of May 2002.[90]

86 S/2002/278, para. 42.

87 Bonn Agreement, art. II(2).

88 S/2002/278, para. 44.

89 Press Release, UN Doc SC/7339 (26 March 2002).

90 In part, this was due to difficulties recruiting the right person. The current Judicial Adviser, Amin M. Medani, was previously Office of the High Commissioner for Human Rights Representative for the Arab Region.

A document from the Office of the Special Representative from the same month stated that

> all agree that global experience in justice reform and development has shown that non-strategic, piecemeal and 'interventionist' approaches can have dire consequences for the effective development of [the justice] sector. A strategic, comprehensive, Afghan led, integrated programme of justice sector reform and development can only begin with a comprehensive sectoral review and assessment of domestic needs, priorities, initiatives and capacities for reconstruction and development of this crucial sector. To date, none has been undertaken.[91]

Given the experiences of Kosovo and East Timor, these assumptions are highly debatable. UNMIK in particular found that failure to engage *immediately* with rule of law questions can lead to missing the opportunity for the maximum impact of international engagement. It is true that a strategic, comprehensive approach is desirable—but not if it means indefinite delays until the security environment allows for a thorough review. If necessary, skeletal legal reforms might be made on an emergency basis until a more strategic approach can be formulated.[92]

In Afghanistan, UNAMA's mandate was interpreted as requiring the United Nations to facilitate rather than lead. In areas such as the choice of laws, the structure of the legal system, and appointment of judges, this was entirely appropriate. Such arguments were less persuasive in relation to basic questions of rebuilding courthouses, procuring legal texts and office equipment, and training of judges. Instead, it appeared that rule of law was simply not a priority. In the forty-eight-page National Development Framework drafted by the Afghan Assistance Coordination Authority (AACA) in April 2002, the justice system warranted only a single substantive sentence.[93] Similarly, although Italy agreed to serve as 'lead donor' on the justice sector at the Tokyo pledging conference in January 2002, there was little evidence of activity in this area. The Afghan Interim Authority did appoint some new judges, including a number of women, but those courts that functioned at all continued to do so erratically. This was

[91] Office of the SRSG for Afghanistan, Proposal for a Multi-Agency Review of Justice Sector Development in Afghanistan (Kabul: UNAMA-OSRSG, May 2002), 2.

[92] See, e.g. A Review of Peace Operations: A Case for Change (London: King's College London, March 2003), 263.

[93] National Development Framework (Draft for Consultation) (Kabul: Afghan Assistance Coordination Authority, April 2002), 47: 'The judicial system will be revived through a sub-program that provides training, makes laws and precedents available, and rehabilitates the physical infrastructure of the judicial sector'.

not helped by Karzai's appointment of a septuagenarian Chief Justice who had never studied secular law.[94]

4.4. Tiptoeing Through Afghanistan

As indicated earlier, UNAMA served in some ways as a correction to the expanding mandates asserted by the United Nations through the 1990s, culminating in the missions in Kosovo and East Timor. At the same time, the light footprint approach adopted in Afghanistan led to little being achieved in the justice sector in the six-month Interim Authority period. This was, in part, due to the limited role given to the United Nations in these areas under the Bonn Agreement, and the need to consult closely with the Afghan Interim Authority and other actors on the appropriate nature of the assistance that might be offered.[95] But it seems also fair to say that rule of law was not seen as a priority by either the Interim Authority, UNAMA, or the donor community.

Afghanistan, of course, posed challenges distinct from those of Kosovo and East Timor. Rather than being in a position of government, the function of the United Nations was to provide assistance to the political structures created in Bonn. Also, despite the suffering of the previous twenty-three years, Afghanistan was not as riven with ethnic tension as Kosovo, nor was it establishing the first independent political institutions as in East Timor. Nevertheless, as the Afghan state is being rebuilt, respect for the consistency and transparency of that state's laws will become as important as respect for the leaders that emerge from the ongoing political process laid down by the Bonn Agreement.

5. Conclusion

In 1944, Judge Learned Hand spoke at a ceremony in Central Park, New York, to swear in 150,000 naturalized citizens. 'Liberty lies in the hearts of men and women', he observed: '[W]hen it dies there, no

[94] Hafizullah Gardish, 'Chief Justice Under Scrutiny', *IWPR Afghan Recovery Report No 54*, 1 April 2003.

[95] In his report of 18 March 2002, the Secretary-General stated that the UN's approach to human rights 'will be guided by Afghan human rights organizations and activists, who are best placed to advise on how international human rights law and standards can be implemented in Afghanistan's particular social, political and cultural context': S/2002/278, para. 43.

constitution, no law, no court can save it; no constitution, no law, no court can even do much to help it.'[96]

Building or rebuilding faith in the idea of the rule of law requires a similar transformation in mentality as much as it does in politics. An important test of the success of such a transformation is whom people turn to for solutions to problems that would normally be considered 'legal'. In each of the three territories considered here, the results of that test would be uncertain. It is possible, however, to draw some broad principles from these experiments in judicial reconstruction, principles that may be relevant the next time the United Nations or another international body has effective legal control over a territory. The principles fall into three broad themes.

First, the administration of justice should rank among the higher priorities of a post-conflict peace operation.[97] There is a tendency on the part of international actors to conflate armed conflict and criminal activity more generally. Drawing a clearer distinction and being firm on violations of the law increases both the credibility of the international presence and the chances of a peace agreement holding. This encompasses both the lawlessness that flourishes in conflict and post-conflict environments and vigilantism to settle scores. Swift efforts to re-establish respect for law may also help to lay a foundation for subsequent reconciliation processes. Failure to prioritize law enforcement and justice issues undermined the credibility of the international presence in Kosovo and led to missed opportunities in East Timor. In Afghanistan, rule of law simply did not feature on the agenda.

Second, as argued in Chapter Three, in an immediate post-conflict environment lacking a functioning law enforcement and judicial system, rule of law functions may have to be entrusted to military personnel on a temporary basis. Recourse to the military for such functions is a last resort, but may be the only alternative to a legal vacuum. Measures to create a standby network of international jurists who could be deployed at short notice to post-conflict areas would facilitate the establishment of a judicial system (primarily as trainers and mentors), but are unlikely to be able to deploy in sufficient time

96 Learned Hand, *The Spirit of Liberty*, 3rd edn. (Chicago: University of Chicago Press, 1960), 190.

97 See, e.g. Brahimi Report, para. 47(b): 'The Panel recommends a doctrinal shift in the use of civilian police, other rule of law elements and human rights experts in complex peace operations to reflect an increased focus on strengthening rule of law institutions and improving respect for human rights in post-conflict environments'.

and numbers to establish even an ad hoc system on their own. This role for the military may also include the emergency construction of detention facilities. The law imposed in such circumstances should be simple and consistent. If it is not feasible to enforce the law of the land, martial law should be declared as a temporary measure, with military lawyers (especially if they come from different national contingents) agreeing upon a basic legal framework. Persons detained under such an ad hoc system should be transferred to civilian authorities as quickly as possible.[98]

Third, once the security environment allows the process of civil reconstruction to begin, sustainability should generally take precedence over temporary standards in the administration of basic law and order. Whether internationalized processes are appropriate for the most serious crimes should be determined through broad consultation with local actors. In some situations, such as those in which conflict is ongoing, this consultation will not be possible. In circumstances where there are concerns about bias undermining the impartiality of the judicial process, some form of mentoring or oversight may be required. In all cases, justice sector development must be undertaken with an eye to its coordination with policing and the penal system.

These themes are necessarily general. Indeed, the idea that one could construct a rigid template for reconstructing the judicial system in a post-conflict environment is wrongheaded. As Judge Hand recognized, the major transformation required is in the hearts of the general population; any foreign involvement must, therefore, be sensitive to the particularities of that population. This is not to say that 'ownership' requires that locals must drive this process in all circumstances. On the contrary, international engagement will sometimes abrogate the most basic rights to self-governance on a temporary basis. But although the levels of foreign intervention may vary from the light footprint in Afghanistan, through the ambiguous sovereignty in Kosovo, to benevolent autocracy in East Timor, the guiding principle must be an appropriate balance of short-term measures to assert the (re-)establishment of the rule of law, and longer-term institution-building that will last beyond the life of the mission and the fickle interest of international actors.

[98] See Aspen Institute, *Honoring Human Rights Under International Mandates: Lessons from Bosnia, Kosovo, and East Timor* (Washington, DC: Aspen Institute, 2003), 18–19.

6

Relief and Reconstruction: The Politics of Humanitarian and Development Assistance

> We are not interested in a legacy of cars and laws, nor are we interested in a legacy of development plans for the future designed by [people] other than East Timorese. We are not interested in inheriting an economic rationale which leaves out the social and political complexity of East Timorese reality. Nor do we wish to inherit the heavy decision-making and project implementation mechanisms in which the role of the East Timorese is to give their consent as observers rather than the active players we should start to be.
>
> Xanana Gusmão[1]

East Timor presents two contradictory stories in the history of UN peace operations. On the one hand, it is presented as an outstanding success. In two and a half years, a territory that had been reduced to ashes after the 1999 referendum on independence held peaceful elections and celebrated independence. On the other hand, however, East Timor can be seen as a series of missed opportunities and wastage. Of the UN Transitional Administration's annual budget of over $500 million, around one-tenth actually reached the East Timorese. At one point, $27 million was spent annually on bottled water for the international staff—approximately half the budget of the embryonic Timorese government, and money that might have paid for water purification plants to serve both international staff and locals well beyond the

[1] Xanana Gusmão, quoted in Mark Dodd, 'Give Us a Say, Urges Gusmao', *The Age* (Melbourne), 10 October 2000.

life of the mission. More could have been done, or done earlier, to reconstruct public facilities. This did not happen in part because of budgetary restrictions on UN peacekeeping operations that, to the Timorese, were not simply absurd but insulting. Such problems were compounded by coordination failures, the displacement of local initiatives by bilateral donor activities, and the lack of any significant private sector investment. When East Timor (now Timor-Leste) became independent, it did so with the dubious honour of becoming the poorest country in Asia.[2]

The political economy of humanitarian and development assistance in post-conflict territories is the subject of an entire literature in its own right.[3] Here, the focus is on the immediate needs of a territory under United Nations or other international administration. The chapter first considers the political context within which relief and reconstruction is delivered. Assistance is notoriously supply- rather than demand-driven, with the result that it is more influenced by donor politics than those of the recipient communities. The second section then examines claims to ownership in the delivery of assistance. As indicated in earlier chapters, this claim is often made disingenuously; nevertheless, the assistance mission to Afghanistan from 2002 suggests a different model whereby 'ownership' on the part of local actors may begin to mean something. The final section turns to the perverse economic effects of the large foreign presence that typically accompanies a transitional administration—in particular, the destabilizing effect of the bubble economy for providing services to expatriates and the distortions it causes in the labour market. In different ways, each of these three areas demonstrates the impact of donor policies on political and economic capacity in a post-conflict environment.

The chapter addresses both humanitarian and development assistance. While often conflated in a post-conflict environment (sometimes termed recovery or reconstruction aid), it is important to acknowledge the distinction between the two. Humanitarian assistance is intended to relieve immediate suffering; development aims to support the emergence of a self-sustaining economy. Where assistance takes the

[2] 'Getting Ready for Statehood', *Economist*, 13 April 2002.

[3] See Mats R. Berdal and David M. Malone (eds.), *Greed and Grievance: Economic Agendas in Civil Wars* (Boulder, CO: Lynne Rienner, 2000); Hernando de Soto, *The Mystery of Capital: Why Capitalism Triumphs in the West and Fails Everywhere Else* (New York: Basic Books, 2000); Paul Collier, *Breaking the Conflict Trap: Civil War and Development Policy* (New York: Oxford University Press, 2003); Michael Pugh and Neil Cooper, *War Economies in a Regional Context: The Challenge of Transformation* (Boulder, CO: Lynne Rienner, 2004).

form of providing basic public goods, such as medical care, or when famine relief blends into agricultural reform, the two may overlap. However, as with the distinction between development assistance and peacekeeping—which determines how different parts of a complex peace operation are funded—the dichotomy between humanitarian and development assistance is generally of more interest to donors than it is to the people they are seeking to help.

1. *Charity with Interest*

The Marshall Plan, described in Chapter One, is regularly invoked as the paradigm of economic assistance.[4] The scale of the commitment, its regional focus, and the channelling of funds through local institutions certainly bear some lessons for contemporary efforts. These factors were, however, linked to the political context within which the Marshall Plan was formulated and implemented. The very different circumstances in which aid is delivered today suggest the limits of this analogy.

Four themes stand out. First, the resolution of the Second World War provided a clear military and political context for reconstruction. Strategic concerns dominated, ensuring greater resources and a sustained commitment; the clarity of the outcome of the war and the recognition of most borders in Europe also ensured that the legitimacy of recipient governments was, for the most part, uncontested. More recent conflicts have tended to be localized, frequently involving irregular forces and leading to an inconclusive peace. The absence of a common threat and the prominence of actors other than the United States have meant that multiple donors pursue independent objectives, at times inconsistently. Domestic considerations may thus complicate coordination between different governments, with each seeking to finance 'pet' projects.

Second, post-war Europe was very different from recipient countries today. The Marshall Plan targeted relatively wealthy democracies with advanced capitalist economies and highly educated populations; the approach was regional in character and built upon political and military alliances. Recipients now tend to be fragile democracies at best, usually of limited long-term interest to donors. The economies in question are constrained in their capacity to absorb a sudden influx of aid, which tends to be concentrated over a relatively short period. Where state

[4] The plan's official title was the 'European Recovery Program'. See Chapter One, Section 2.3.

institutions are weak or non-existent, this aid may be largely in the form of emergency humanitarian relief at the expense of development-oriented assistance.[5]

Third, the number of actors has greatly increased, most obviously with the rise of non-governmental organizations (NGOs). This proliferation has fostered niche assistance that contributes targeted assistance in some sectors, but further complicates coordination. Many NGOs now function more as service providers for donor agencies rather than as programming agencies in their own right. This encourages some to become 'ambulance chasers', deploying to a crisis situation with little or no funding. Though they may bring skills and commitment to the emergency, considerable initial effort is spent raising funds from local donor missions and UN agencies. One Afghan analyst in Kabul wryly observed that 'NGOs are cows that drink the milk themselves'. Reliance upon multiple sources of funding has also increased the influence of the media, encouraging a focus on crises that are the subject of public attention and sometimes limiting assistance to the duration of that attention. A further consequence is the rise of 'flag-waving' activities on the part of donors and NGOs, which seek to gain maximum credit for their activities. This may, in turn, lead to competition for telegenic projects and a reluctance to engage in mundane or unattractive projects.

Finally, the Marshall Plan took place in an era when the benefits of government intervention were generally uncontested. Donor scepticism today about the appropriate role of government in economic activity at home has, at times, challenged approaches to foreign assistance abroad. The prevailing view in the industrialized world now is that the function of government is to do little more than facilitate a market economy and provide a very few public goods. This is at odds with the widespread view that a strong government often lies at the heart of post-conflict economic and political reconstruction.[6]

The context within which assistance is delivered to post-conflict territories is, therefore, quite different from the aftermath of the Second World War. Political considerations continue to play a major part in the decision to provide assistance, but the purposes that assistance is

[5] See Susan L. Woodward, 'Economic Priorities for Successful Peace Implementation', in Stephen John Stedman, Donald Rothchild, and Elizabeth M. Cousens (eds.), *Ending Civil Wars: The Implementation of Peace Agreements* (Boulder, CO: Lynne Rienner, 2002), 183; Joanna Macrae, *Aiding Recovery? The Crisis of Aid in Chronic Political Emergencies* (New York: Zed Books, 2001).

[6] See Shepard Forman and Stewart Patrick, 'Introduction', in Shepard Forman and Stewart Patrick (eds.), *Good Intentions: Pledges of Aid for Postconflict Recovery* (Boulder, CO: Lynne Rienner, 2000), 1, 2–4.

intended to serve are less coherent than the grand strategy envisioned in the Marshall Plan. This is, of course, if it arrives at all. When President George W. Bush compared the US reconstruction effort in Afghanistan to the Marshall Plan, he was rebuked for not providing the funds to match his rhetoric.[7] Funds for post-conflict relief may not arrive, or arrive only very slowly. Actors implementing programmes on the ground must take this into account when they construct budgets, often requiring them to engage in fictional accounting for targets that they know will not be met. This makes responsible financial planning still more difficult.

1.1. The Purposes of Assistance

As indicated earlier, humanitarian and development assistance are discrete forms of aid. Humanitarian assistance is, in theory, driven by need and intended to relieve suffering. Development assistance in the aftermath of conflict aims more generally at helping an economy to recover and, in theory, become self-sustaining. It may target human welfare (health, education, children's welfare, de-mining), institution-building (new structures of governance, rebuilding of ministries), or addressing rule of law issues (police salaries, construction of prisons). In reality, humanitarian and development assistance are both supply- rather than demand-driven, and donors may fail to distinguish between the two. Donors commit funds largely on the basis of their domestic priorities and capacity, with international agencies balancing the need to seek equity in human suffering against the need to capitalize on telegenic crises that correspond to donor priorities. For this reason, the crises in the Balkans typically received far more assistance per capita assistance than comparable or worse crises in Africa.[8]

In addition to determining which crises receive funds, these considerations also determine how those funds are allocated and with what political conditions attached. Here, the distinction between humanitarian and development assistance becomes more important, as the attachment of political conditions to humanitarian assistance arguably removes its 'humanitarian' character. The Commentary on the Fourth Geneva Convention, for example, defines humanitarian as

[7] See Chapter One, Section 2.3.

[8] In 1999, for example, the annual per capita assistance received in the Democratic Republic of the Congo was $8; in Sierra Leone it was $16; in Angola it was $48; for the former Yugoslavia the figure was $207: Oxfam, An End to Forgotten Emergencies? (Oxford: Oxfam GB Briefing Paper 5/00, May 2000), available at www.oxfam.org.uk.

'being concerned with the condition of man considered solely as a human being, regardless of his value as a military, political, professional or other unit', and 'not affected by any political or military consideration'.[9] Similarly, the International Court of Justice has held that an 'essential feature of truly humanitarian aid is that it is given "without discrimination" of any kind'.[10] Nevertheless, political conditions are frequently attached to nominally humanitarian assistance, as in the European Union's 'Energy for Democracy' programme (1999–2000), which allowed the delivery of heating oil to 'democratic' Serbian municipalities, meaning those that had voted for opponents of President Slobodan Milosevic.[11]

The attachment of such conditions is typically intended to influence a peace process within which assistance is being delivered, but this may embrace a variety of distinct purposes, each dependent in turn on a specific dynamic within the post-conflict environment. Assistance may be expected to provide incentives and rewards to peacebuilders, or to punish spoilers. It may be intended to demonstrate the benefits of peace to ordinary people, in the hope that a popular constituency for the peace process can be cultivated. Or it may seek to address the underlying causes of grievance in a society and dampen potential triggers for violence. Assistance rarely lives up to these aspirations, but carrots may often be a useful supplement to a peace process—especially when, as in Afghanistan, sticks are few and far between.[12]

Other forms of conditions may be less attuned to local political circumstances. Macroeconomic conditions imposed by the Bretton Woods Institutions (the International Monetary Fund (IMF) and the World Bank), for example, have given rise to disputes when applied to a peace process. In Cambodia, the IMF and the Bank pressed the coalition government that succeeded the UN Transitional Authority in Cambodia (UNTAC) to reduce the civil service by 20 per cent. This was never politically viable and ignored the devastation that

[9] Convention Relative to the Protection of Civilian Persons in Time of War (Fourth Geneva Convention), done at Geneva, 12 August 1949, available at www.icrc.org/ihl, Commentary, art. 10.

[10] *Military and Paramilitary Activities in and Against Nicaragua (Nicaragua* v *United States of America)* [1986] ICJ Rep 243.

[11] See UN Office for the Coordination of Humanitarian Assistance, Humanitarian Risk Analysis No. 12 Federal Republic of Yugoslavia (Belgrade: OCHA, 9 August 2000), available at www.reliefweb.int.

[12] See Alvaro de Soto and Graciana del Castillo, 'Obstacles to Peacebuilding in El Salvador', *Foreign Policy* 94, Spring 1994, 69; James K. Boyce, *Investing in Peace: Aid and Conditionality After Civil Wars* (Oxford: Oxford University Press, 2002). See also Section 2.2 in this chapter.

the previous decades had wrought on Cambodia's civil service and its intelligentsia.[13] From the mid-1990s, the Bank began a process of reassessing its role in rebuilding post-conflict territories and in 1997 created an internal Post-Conflict Unit (renamed in 2001 the Conflict Prevention and Reconstruction Unit). The IMF was slower to adapt its procedures to post-conflict needs, continuing to impose conditions tied to macroeconomic stability and structural adjustment. This ignored the fact that, in an immediate post-conflict environment, equity is generally of greater concern than efficiency, but reflected a tendency among many donors to view complex emergencies as a 'blip' on an otherwise steady development path. It also underestimated the effect that conflict can have on a society and the range of transitions that are required in the move from war to peace, from a controlled to a market economy, and from autocratic to democratic governance.[14]

These institutional changes were part of a broader transformation as development actors began establishing small units and budget lines dedicated to more traditionally humanitarian forms of assistance. Two years before the Bank established its Post-Conflict Unit, the UN Development Programme (UNDP) created an Emergency Response Division (later the Bureau for Crisis Prevention and Recovery), setting aside 5 per cent of its core budget for assistance to 'countries in special development situations'. Other UN agencies followed suit: the UN Children's Fund (UNICEF) set up an Office of Emergency Operations and the World Food Programme (WFP) generated Protracted Relief and Recovery Operations. Some now argue that demand and resource flows have transformed WFP and UNICEF from development to humanitarian actors.[15]

1.2. Disbursement of Funds

Whatever conditions are attached to assistance, these may be less disruptive to economic reconstruction than the fact that a significant proportion of pledged resources either does not materialize or does

[13] James K. Boyce, 'Beyond Good Intentions: External Assistance and Peace Building', in Forman and Patrick (eds.), *Good Intentions*, 367, 375–6.

[14] Stewart Patrick, 'The Donor Community and the Challenge of Postconflict Recovery', in Forman and Patrick (eds.), *Good Intentions*, 35, 45.

[15] Michèle Griffin (2003) 'The Helmet and the Hoe: Linkages Between United Nations Development Assistance and Conflict Management', *Global Governance*, 9(2): 199, 203.

so very slowly.[16] As the World Bank itself has observed, 'pledges are made, but commitment takes longer, and there is a considerable lag before actual disbursement takes place. Sustainable transitions out of conflict take several years, yet there is a tendency for donors to disengage once the conflict has receded from public attention.'[17] For example, $880 million was pledged at the Conference on Rehabilitation and Reconstruction of Cambodia in June 1992. By the time the new government was formed in September 1993, only $200 million had been disbursed, rising to only $460 million by the end of 1995.[18]

The reasons for unfulfilled and delayed pledges are attributable both to donors and recipients. On the 'supply' side, ostensibly generous pledges at multilateral conferences may in fact simply repackage previously committed funds. Lengthy bureaucratic formalities, legislative reviews, and inefficient procurement procedures add to these delays. Donors tend to focus on their own political interests—including the interests of their national service providers, who may be tasked with implementing reconstruction contracts. And poor coordination among donors and recipients may result in duplicated or contradictory efforts. On the 'demand' side, states recovering from war may lack the capacity to absorb large sums of money and in-kind assistance. Administrative structures may be inadequate to receive funds from diverse sources and for multiple purposes. Inadequate legal structures may encourage inefficiency and corruption.[19]

This has improved slightly. In Afghanistan, for example, three-quarters of the $2 billion pledged for 2002 had been disbursed by the end of the calendar year, though much of it was on emergency relief and revealed that donors had underestimated need in the first years of recovery.[20] This highlights a different bottleneck for international assistance: the lag between disbursement and the financing of effective projects. By May 2003, completed reconstruction

[16] Forman and Patrick, 'Introduction', 1.

[17] World Bank, Post-Conflict Reconstruction: The Role of the World Bank (Washington, DC: World Bank, 1998), 21.

[18] Shepard Forman, Stewart Patrick, and Dirk Salomons, Recovering from Conflict: Strategy for an International Response (New York: Center on International Cooperation, 2000), available at www.cic.nyu.edu, 51.

[19] Forman and Patrick, 'Introduction', 9. Cf. Graham Hancock, *Lords of Poverty: The Free-Wheeling Lifestyles, Power, Prestige, and Corruption of the International Aid Business* (London: Macmillan, 1989).

[20] Mukesh Kapila and Karin Wermester, 'The Afghan Job Is Bigger Than Expected', *International Herald Tribune*, 14 January 2003.

projects in Afghanistan had a total expenditure of less than $200 million.[21]

Effective early assistance is vital in order to establish the foundations for peace, but also to capitalize on the brief period of international goodwill that accompanies a crisis. In fact, needs in post-conflict situations generally rise over the first few years of recovery, as the absorptive capacity of the economy increases. Given the political nature of assistance, however, most donor money is likely to be committed in the first six months to a year of a crisis, when it is splashed across newspapers and donors and agencies can get maximum recognition for their funds and activities.

1.3. Donor Policies

The fact that donor countries wish to retain control over how their money is spent is not, in itself, controversial. In most cases, this money comes from taxes paid by constituents who hold their respective governments accountable for how tax revenue is spent. Although donor behaviour may be rational from the donor government's perspective, however, the sum total of donor policies rarely presents a rational whole.[22]

In considering the ways in which donor policies affect the overall assistance effort, it is useful to separate three discrete factors: national interest, domestic politics, and local bureaucratic procedures. Geopolitics, though less significant than during the cold war, continues to influence the delivery of assistance. European and North American support for Bosnia and Herzegovina and Kosovo through the 1990s, Japanese and Australian support for East Timor at the end of the decade, and the sudden rise in assistance to Afghanistan in late 2001 after years of neglect were all attributable to strategic interests. Interest, of course, is not necessarily a bad thing in the formulation of aid policies. The engagement of high-level policymakers in a post-conflict environment can ensure a more sustained commitment, but raising the political stakes complicates donor policies by binding them to a domestic political agenda rather than a humanitarian one. Peace and prosperity in Afghanistan, for example, was less important to the United States than ensuring that the territory was not used as a haven for terrorists; this

21 Barnett R. Rubin, Humayun Hamidzada, and Abby Stoddard, Through the Fog of Peacebuilding: Evaluating the Reconstruction of Afghanistan (New York: Center on International Cooperation, June 2003), available at www.cic.nyu.edu.

22 This subsection draws upon work in progress at the Humanitarianism and War Project at Tufts University. See hwproject.tufts.edu.

military agenda at times ran against the broader aims of peacebuilding. Similarly, the concentration of limited aid resources on situations of political importance may lower the standards to which other operations are held—thus order and stability in Somalia was less important than order and stability in Kosovo.

As most assistance from donor governments is derived from taxation, it is natural that donors are driven in part by domestic political considerations. These may take the form of historical or personal connections, favouring assistance to former colonies or the homeland from which a diaspora community derives. Physical proximity may also be important, especially when it raises the spectre of large refugee flows. Implementation may also be affected by domestic concerns, with some donors insisting on the use of their nationals in humanitarian programmes or on aid being delivered in the form of nationally-produced goods or through 'their' NGOs. The importance of domestic politics is frequently linked to the role of the media. Though the media is certainly important in determining aid priorities, this is sometimes overstated. North Korea, Sudan, and Angola, for example, each received considerable support for several years in the absence of ongoing media reporting. Nevertheless, well-reported events that capture public attention do create a spike in the flow of aid, with some evidence that this may correspond to reduction in aid to other crises. The mobilization of public support for Kosovo in 1999, for example, effectively diverted funds that might otherwise have gone to Angola.[23] By contrast, the role of political leadership in generating public support for assistance to a crisis is generally underestimated.[24]

The procedures for allocating and disbursing assistance vary considerably between countries, ranging from those that articulate clear guidelines for assistance to those that are framed more generally. Swiss law, for example, provides clear objectives for the activities of the Swiss Agency for Development and Cooperation and specifies

23 Vivienne Walt, 'Focus on Kosovo's Refugees Comes at a Price', *Washington Post*, 16 May 1999.

24 Ian Smillie and Larry Minear, 'Humanitarian Financing: Donor Behavior' (Montreux: Paper presented at Humanitarianism and War Project, 26–8 February 2003). When such assistance is offered, it may often be largely misunderstood by all but specialists. In his 2003 State of the Union address, Bush proposed a 50 per cent increase in foreign assistance. Opinion polls show, however, that Americans generally think that up to 20 per cent of government spending goes abroad, when the actual figure is less than one per cent. See, e.g. Adam Zagorin, 'Spreading the Wealth', *Hoover Digest*, Spring 2003.

that resources will be divided between the International Committee of the Red Cross, UN agencies, and NGOs. US legislation, by contrast, grants far greater discretion to officials—at times encouraging turf disputes between those branches of the executive that favour UN agencies (such as the State Department's Bureau for Population, Migration, and Refugees) and those that fund NGOs (such as the US Agency for International Development). The Office of Management and Budget, which oversees the US national budget, is largely uninterested in humanitarian policy.[25] These turf disputes may be dismissed as petty politics, but they can cause significant problems in areas such as security sector reform. If assistance to the security sector is not classed as official development assistance (ODA), the funding base may be uncertain, reducing the stabilizing effect that such assistance is intended to have. At the same time, if all military assistance were to fall within ODA, this could lead to a reduction in real humanitarian assistance. Some governments have, therefore, established pooled funds for activities that straddle this functional divide.[26]

The outcome of these various influences on policy is that each donor drafts its own assistance strategy. Britain produces a 'Country Strategy Paper', Japan develops 'Country Aid Implementation Guidelines', the United States has a 'Strategic Plan', UNDP uses a 'Country Cooperation Framework', and so on. This is replicated in the International Financial Institutions, which follow a 'Policy Framework Paper' (IMF), a 'Country Assistance Strategy' (World Bank), and so forth. Attempts to coordinate these disparate activities are, needless to say, complicated. There has been some progress, including greater cooperation between donors with semi-annual meetings of functional bureaus to share information and resources, establish common standards, and collect 'lessons learned'.[27] But there remains great resistance to the coordination of activities at a strategic level.

One of the most important forms of coordination for donors is the pledging conference. In the absence of funds that can be disbursed

[25] Smillie and Minear, 'Donor Behaviour'.

[26] For example, the British Department for International Development, Ministry of Defence, and Foreign and Commonwealth Office have begun pooling funds and developing joint strategies in their response to conflict areas: [British] Centre for Management and Policy Studies, Nine Key Characteristics of Modern Policy-Making (London: Cabinet Office, January 2002), available at www.cmps.co.uk.

[27] See, e.g. OECD, Helping Prevent Violent Conflict, Development Assistance Committee Guidelines (Paris: OECD, 2001), available at www.oecd.org.

quickly to a recovery process, significant external resources typically arrive only after such a conference, which brings donor states, UN agencies, and the international financial institutions together with local representatives to evaluate proposed reconstruction plans. The relative transparency of these meetings reduces the temptation of donors to 'free-ride' on the efforts of others. More subtly, by involving disparate actors in providing support for post-conflict recovery as a form of public good, the pledging conference encourages the notion of a 'donor community', bound by certain ethical obligations towards the recovering state. Pledging conferences also enable donors to shape and publicize recovery plans jointly, which may increase domestic support for foreign assistance as part of an international effort. For recipients, pledging conferences offer the opportunity to focus the minds of donors on a crisis and to gain public assurances that some of their needs will be met. While these aspects are positive, pledging conferences often bear the trappings of political theatre. As indicated earlier, donors may make grand gestures that in reality double-count resources previously committed to a country, or which cannot be delivered promptly. In addition, mediating different donor interests through a conference does not remove the problems caused by the inconsistency of those interests. Donors continue to avoid controversial areas like security sector reform, preferring to fund items that will gain recognition and prestige. Finally, despite the public nature of the pledges made, there is no consistent monitoring process to ensure that pledges are realistic and transparent.[28]

Within the UN framework, the consolidated inter-agency appeal process (CAP) is nominally the vehicle for coordinating humanitarian assistance.[29] It is far from clear, however, whether a CAP is primarily intended to set priorities, to coordinate efforts, or simply to raise funds. Different donors appear to view the process differently, but it cannot function effectively as all three. The variable funding also lends a certain artificiality to the process. In 2001, the CAP realized only 55 per cent of its overall requests; provisional figures for 2002 showed 68 per cent of total requests being met, varying by country or region from 20 per cent to 95 per cent.[30] This creates a vicious circle where agencies artificially

[28] Stewart Patrick, 'The Donor Community and the Challenge of Postconflict Recovery', in Forman and Patrick (eds.), *Good Intentions*, 35, 40–1.

[29] See GA Res 46/182 (1991).

[30] UN Office for the Coordination of Humanitarian Assistance, Consolidated Inter-Agency Humanitarian Assistance Appeals: Summary of Requirements and Contributions by Affected Country/Region, available at www.reliefweb.int/fts.

inflate requests, leading in turn to donor scepticism about the merits of supporting a CAP in its entirety.[31]

In post-conflict situations administered by the United Nations, a further layer of complication is the bureaucratic framework within which funds supporting a transitional administration must be spent. Funding for such operations typically comes from two sources: assessed and voluntary contributions. Assessed contributions for peacekeeping operations are calculated on the basis of gross national product (GNP) and range from 0.001 per cent of the budget to 25 per cent. The 2003–4 budget for peacekeeping was $2.2 billion.[32] Voluntary contributions from member states support specialized agencies and subsidiary organizations of the UN family, including UNDP, the UN High Commissioner for Refugees (UNHCR), and so on.

In East Timor, despite the repeated assertions that this was a unique operation, the mission was subject to the same budgetary procedures as other peacekeeping operations—meaning a strict division between funds that could be used to support the peacekeeping mission and funds that could be used for humanitarian and development assistance. This might be reasonable in a country where the UN operation sits parallel to an existing government, but when the United Nations *was* the government it led to absurdity. Speaking in June 2000, Special Representative of the Secretary-General Sergio Vieira de Mello noted Timorese frustration with the slow pace of reconstruction. In part, this was due to the slow rate of disbursement into the World Bank Trust Fund, but on a more basic level he acknowledged that criticism was certain to continue while UN engineers were prohibited from fixing buildings used by Timorese officials.[33]

Coordinating the many interests, policies, and practices of donors and agencies outlined in this section can be an overwhelming task. The obvious solution would appear to be to allow recipients a measure of control in how funds are allocated and spent. Local 'ownership', however, is more frequently invoked in word than in deed.

[31] Patrick, 'Donor Community', 43.

[32] Press Release, UN Doc GA/AB/3570 (4 June 2003). Assessed contributions for peacekeeping vary slightly from those to the regular budget of the United Nations, taking into account the 'special status' of the permanent members of the Security Council.

[33] Press Release, UN Doc SC/6882 (27 June 2000). See also Michael G. Smith, *Peacekeeping in East Timor* (Boulder, CO: Lynne Rienner, 2003), 136–7. In practice, these funding distinctions are often blurred—de-mining, for example, is sometimes funded through assessed contributions when it coincides with a peacekeeping operation.

2. *Ownership*

Ownership is frequently asserted in both the political and economic processes of transition, though its meaning is often unclear. It certainly does not mean control and often does not even imply a direct input. Sometimes qualified by 'a sense of', ownership appears to bear more psychological than political import. This meaning in English, however, does not always translate well into local languages—in the languages of the Balkans, for example, 'ownership' only makes sense in the way that one might own a car.

As discussed in Chapter Four, political ownership may well be the end of a transitional administration, but it is not the means of achieving it.[34] Local leadership may be desirable in development projects in general, but in a post-conflict situation this must be tempered by those concerns that brought international administration to the country concerned in the first place. Nevertheless, structuring assistance around local needs as articulated by local actors may help to mitigate the supply-driven nature of aid. In addition, the transfer of funds directly to local hands is more likely to stimulate sustainable economic activity and reduce dependence on handouts.

Managing expectations, as in every other aspect of post-conflict transition, is vital. Recipients may have inflated expectations of what donors can and should do—expectations that are sometimes fostered by political leaders in both recipient and donor countries. This section considers two ways in which local ownership can and should be taken seriously in the immediate post-conflict environment. If it is not possible to allow local actors to control how assistance is distributed, this power may be exercised on their behalf by a trustee. Trust funds have been a common feature of post-conflict recovery, but donors have often been reluctant to embrace them; such funds have, therefore, tended to be relatively marginal players. The alternative, of course, is actually to empower local officials to manage assistance for themselves.

2.1. *Trust Funds*

The obvious solution to the problem of coordination assistance is to pool resources and centralize the processes of assessing needs and disbursing funds. This runs up against another form of ownership, however, which is the desire of donors to retain control over the manner in which scarce resources are spent. Centralization in the form of

[34] See Chapter Four, Section 1.3.

a trust fund has clear benefits. It enables a more strategic approach to recovery, encouraging earlier local planning and sustaining multi-year projects. This is important in economies where the capacity to absorb a sudden influx of aid may be low—in such situations, supply may initially exceed demand. A trust fund should also encourage a division of labour among implementing partners and facilitate coordination. Providing a basket of resources also reduces the likelihood of redundant or duplicated projects and simplifies reporting requirements for the recipients.[35]

Donors—especially larger contributors—have generally refused to commit significant resources to trust funds, however. This has been for good reasons and bad. The good reasons concern the high overheads and at times glacial pace of the World Bank and UNDP, which are typically nominated to oversee trust funds. The bad reasons are that countries often want their names up in lights next to pet programmes, often being implemented by their own national NGOs. Everyone wants to be seen sending children back to school; no one wants to pay military salaries.

The result is that many donors insist on doing their own feasibility studies—sometimes on the same sector, sometimes even using the same consultant. This leads to a proliferation of local NGOs (and, in Afghanistan, government agencies) spending an increasing proportion of their time working out how to get foreign money and keep donors happy than actually running their programmes. Chairman of the Afghan Interim Authority Hamid Karzai railed against this at an April 2002 donors conference, attacking criticism of Afghan bureaucracy when donor procedures were at least as obtuse: 'We will not remove our red-tapeism unless you remove yours… Don't expect us to give you a report every month: we will give you a report when we like to give you a report. There are too many groups of donors, reconstruction groups, assistance groups. I don't know the names of all of them.'[36] Other recipient states would have been quietly cheering him on.

A radical approach to dealing with this problem in Afghanistan was proposed in early 2002 but not pursued. This was to retain a private consulting firm to set up a trust fund that could be drawn upon directly by the Interim Authority, overseen by a board that would include

[35] See World Bank, Financing and Aid Management Arrangements in Post-Conflict Settings (Washington, DC: Conflict Prevention and Reconstruction Unit, CPR Note 12, June 2003), available at www.worldbank.org/conflict.

[36] 'Karzai Urges Donors to Fulfil Pledges', *Financial Times* (London), 11 April 2002.

both Afghan and UN members. Such a mechanism might allay the concerns of donors about giving funds directly to the United Nations or the World Bank, while at the same time directing money where it is most needed and encouraging fiscal responsibility on the part of the new regime. This would only be possible where local partners were in a position to absorb the money, which seemed to be the case in Afghanistan. It remains an interesting hypothesis.

In the short term, a realistic innovation would be to ensure that the special representative of the Secretary-General is given a discretionary budget to finance political goals as they arise. In Mozambique, for example, the smooth transition to peace was lubricated by the creation of a $17.5 million fund under the control of Special Representative Aldo Ajello to support the transformation of the Mozambique National Resistance (Renamo) from a fighting force into a political party.[37] Lakhdar Brahimi fought to secure the use of a similar fund in Afghanistan.

2.2. Local Control in Afghanistan

Although 'ownership' has long been a mantra of the development community, consistency has generally been limited to the lip service that is paid to this concept. 'Afghan solutions for Afghan problems', for example, was a catchphrase of the preparations for Afghanistan's reconstruction late in 2001. But this was one of the first such missions where some of the local population themselves truly attempted to take charge.

If the 'light footprint' approach complicated the high-level diplomacy of the UN Assistance Mission in Afghanistan's (UNAMA) political pillar, it turned the development components of the UN mission on their head.[38] During the chaotic Taliban period, humanitarian and development agencies frequently ran their programmes in Afghanistan without any formal relations with the government (with the notable exception of the health sector). In the absence of government capacity, UN agencies sometimes functioned as a surrogate ministry of planning. Under UNAMA, with a recognized Afghan administration and a UN commitment to respect its authority, agencies and NGOs had to undergo a mental revolution.

In part this unusual dynamic was the work of one man. Ashraf Ghani, formerly employed at the senior levels of the World Bank, returned to Afghanistan and established an organization called the Afghan Assistance Coordination Authority (AACA). Chaired by

[37] Woodward, 'Economic Priorities', 205.

[38] See Chapter Two, Section 3.1.

Karzai, AACA functioned like a cabinet office on development issues. This combination of experience and relative legitimacy ruffled feathers, particularly when the AACA refused to let development agencies and NGOs unroll their pre-packaged programmes and lay them out over Afghanistan.

Ghani, who was later appointed Finance Minister, stated in the most explicit terms that he was determined not to allow Afghanistan to become a beggar state, dependent on international aid. The draft National Development Framework issued by AACA in April 2002 at times read like a manifesto to which many developing countries might subscribe: 'donor-funded investment projects, unless they are anchored in coherent programs of government, are not sustainable. Structural adjustment programs, unless they are translated into feasible projects, do not result in reform.'[39] Agencies and NGOs complained that their programmes were being held up at the whim of a single person. AACA responded that aid packages with recurrent expenditures either had to fit into a national framework or they would undermine it. Together with the Interim and later Transitional Authority, AACA generated a National Development Budget to guide donors and agencies.

This served a political function also. The legitimacy of the Afghan Interim Authority depended on being seen to deliver a peace dividend. Agencies were, therefore, encouraged to do less of their own flag-waving (at least within Afghanistan) and to present their projects as action taken in support of the Karzai administration. As a senior UN development official in Kabul described it, 'we are supporting the creation of the *appearance* of authority in the hope that it leads to the creation of *actual* authority'.

Afghanistan is unusual but not unique in the level of support given directly to local institutions. Mozambique in the period 1992–4 benefited from donors that were prepared to criticize the IMF and strengthen the capacity of the Ministry of Finance and Planning.[40] Assistance to Ethiopia after 1994 drew upon a largely intact bureaucracy through which much assistance could be channelled.[41] What is unusual about Afghanistan is the extent to which this was locally driven. This raises questions about whether lessons learned from this experience can be generalized—for every Ashraf Ghani there may be

[39] National Development Framework (Draft for Consultation) (Kabul: Afghan Assistance Coordination Authority, April 2002), 6.

[40] Nicole Ball and Sam Barnes, 'Mozambique', in Forman and Patrick (eds.), *Good Intentions*, 159, 195–8.

[41] Macrae, *Aiding Recovery*, 89.

a dozen kleptocrats who will waste, squander, or steal aid money. At the very least, the benefits of coordinating assistance through locally generated budgets (whether they are in fact generated by locals or expatriates) appear uncontroversial. Tailoring assistance programmes to local needs is an obvious point, but one that is often understood in isolation from the broader political transformations that accompany humanitarian and development assistance. Constructing a budget and explicitly linking oversight of assistance activities to the institutions of the state—regardless of who actually implements programmes—is a useful way of laying the groundwork for true ownership of an economy.

3. Perverse Effects

The road to Hell, as the sixteenth-century proverb has it, is paved with good intentions. One of the least studied aspects of humanitarian and development assistance is the perverse effect that a large international presence can have on the economy of a post-conflict territory. This is particularly acute in transitional administration operations, where an unusually large influx of expatriate personnel dominates the local economy for a period of years—precisely the period in which international assistance should be making its greatest contribution to the establishment of a self-sustaining economy.

Afghanistan's economy under Taliban rule through the late 1990s was based on agriculture and narcotics. By 2003 it was based on agriculture, narcotics, and the international presence. These three sectors sometimes intersected in unusual ways. For example, WFP guidelines prevented it from purchasing grain from the relatively fertile south of the country in order to address food shortages in the north. Meanwhile, efforts to reduce opium production led to Afghan farmers being offered cash if they switched from poppies to crops like grain. Enterprising grain farmers thus switched from grain to poppies in order to be paid to switch back again.

Every significant UN mission creates a parasitic and unsustainable economy to serve the needs of the transient internationals. As in cities from Dili to Freetown, the rental market in Kabul exploded, accompanied by dubious evictions of existing tenants to make way for more lucrative foreign occupants. This can be a benefit to the economy if, as sometimes happened in East Timor, families move into a back room and rent out the rest of the house, using some of the income to renovate their property. In Kabul, however, many houses were of questionable ownership, or were claimed by absentee landlords. Much foreign money that entered the country thus left almost as quickly, while occupants formerly in cheaper accommodation become homeless. In some cases, UN agencies rented property from organized criminal networks—exactly the groups that the UN presence should be attempting to remove. In addition to diversion of other resources to sustain a temporary service economy focused on restaurants and bars, prostitution and illegal drug use tend to rise, with predictable effects on local health and, some argue, morals.[42]

When disputes have arisen over the microeconomic impact of the UN presence, they have tended to focus on the question of salaries. The average monthly salary of an Afghan civil servant working for the government in early 2002 was about $28, a figure that rose to $40 for some ministers, or $80 for a Supreme Court judge. An Afghan national doing the same work for the United Nations or an international NGO earned between 15 and 400 times that amount, according to salary scales established by the International Civil Services Commission (ICSC). In May 2002, this figure was increased. Such differences foster and deepen the bubble economy, with staff leaving government positions to take the short-term international jobs on offer— even if it means that a judge is working as a driver, or an electrical engineer as a security guard. This causes predictable problems as staff are poached from one place to the next, with organizations losing their institutional memories and such local capacity as actually exists being distorted into servicing the needs of the internationals.

The problem is unfairly blamed on the United Nations alone, when it is the ICSC that independently establishes the pay scales for national staff. A creature of the UN General Assembly, modification of its procedures requires the initiative of a member state. Moves to lower the pay of national staff are unpopular in New York, however. The problems in Kabul were exacerbated by the low and relatively flat pay-scales of the Afghan administration.

[42] See UN Development Fund for Women, Women, War, and Peace: The Independent Experts' Assessment on the Impact of Armed Conflict on Women and Women's Role in Peacebuilding (New York: UNIFEM, October 2002), 61–74. UNTAC suffered fifty-eight deaths from hostile fire, accidents, and disease during the eighteen-month operation. The impact of sexually transmitted diseases was probably far more lethal, with one estimate suggesting that nearly three times as many former UNTAC workers were likely to die of AIDS: Elisabeth Uphoff Kato, 'Quick Impacts, Slow Rehabilitation in Cambodia', in Michael W. Doyle, Ian Johnstone, and Robert C. Orr (eds.), *Keeping the Peace: Multidimensional Peacekeeping in Cambodia and El Salvador* (Cambridge: Cambridge University Press, 1997), 186, 202.

Raising basic pay and increasing the differential on the basis of responsibility might help reduce the incentive for skilled local staff to leave their positions, but a post-conflict government will never be able to compete with the United Nations and international NGOs. Innovative solutions have been mooted, such as a proactive policy to recruit UN staff from diaspora communities, and establishing two-way secondments between UN agencies and the government. In the short-term, basic respect for notice requirements in contracts would help minimize the disruption of sudden staff changes in the various programmes. This could be enforced through a code of conduct—if such things were routinely adopted. Ultimately, such problems solve themselves. As the international presence peaks and begins to decline, the job and property balloon bursts.

4. Conclusion

The introduction of the euro to Kosovo in January 2002 was intended to have at least as much impact on the political system as on Kosovo's economy. The change of currency was explicitly used to cultivate aspirations to membership of the European Union, and thereby the political values that go with membership. This reflected a curious by-product of a decade of international engagement in the Balkans—after four years of inter-ethnic war and ongoing tensions, the only inter-ethnic cooperation across the region was in the single black market. Peacemakers often speak of getting combatants to 'buy into' a peace process. This is generally meant metaphorically, but it should also be understood literally.

And yet, the dominant factors affecting how assistance is allocated and spent are the politics of donor countries themselves. This means that donors typically fail to engage meaningfully with local 'partners' or to see the opportunity that aid can present. None of this is intended to malign the charitable impulses that contribute to the provision of aid, but it often appears that the giving is more important than the receiving. Assistance flows most freely to humanitarian relief, but this rarely addresses the underlying causes of poverty and conflict. In fact, it may undermine medium-term recovery by establishing relationships of dependency and distorting the economy with unsustainable allocations of resources. There is, however, astonishingly little interest in assessing whether aid actually achieves what it is intended to do. Within donor agencies, incentives are generally aimed at 'moving money' rather than ensuring that it is employed productively.

Codes of conduct to regulate the behaviour of donors are a minimum requirement for reducing the distortion caused by a sudden influx of assistance. There have been some efforts at formulating guidelines at a fairly general level within the United Nations,[43] the World Bank,[44] the OECD,[45] and NGOs.[46] Further layers of coordination have also been generated within the UN system, including the Executive Committees on Peace and Security (ECPS) and Humanitarian Assistance (ECHA), the UN Development Group (UNDG), the Inter-Agency Standing Committee (IASC) Reference Group on Post-Conflict Reintegration, and the Humanitarian Segment of the Economic and Social Council (ECOSOC). The problem with these initiatives is that placing the United Nations at the centre of several concentric rings of actors presumes that other players, such as major bilateral donors and NGOs, are of secondary importance. In reality, it is often the United Nations that plays a peripheral role.[47]

Humanitarian and development assistance remains, therefore, a voluntary and essentially ad hoc enterprise. Coordination at the level of donors is less of a problem, however, than the impact that such inconstant charity can have on the ground. The most realistic assertion of ownership might be simply to establish a mechanism that monitors aid flows. This could ensure that pledged money actually arrives and is spent efficiently. More ambitiously, Afghanistan shows that even if it is not possible to create coordination structures from above, it may sometimes be possible to do so from below.

[43] See, e.g. Draft Generic Guidelines for a Strategic Framework Approach for Response to and Recovery from Crisis (New York: United Nations, Office of the Deputy Secretary-General, 27 October 1997). The related move towards 'principled common programming' led in part to the institutionalization of the CAP. See Penny Harrison, *The Strategic Framework and Principled Common Programming: A Challenge to Humanitarian Assistance* (London: Overseas Development Institute, 10 September 2001), available at www.odihpn.org.

[44] World Bank, Post-Conflict Reconstruction: The Role of the World Bank.

[45] OECD, DAC Guidelines on Conflict, Peace, and Development Cooperation (Paris: OECD, 1997), available at www.oecd.org; OECD, Helping Prevent Violent Conflict.

[46] See, e.g. Sphere Project, *The Humanitarian Charter and Minimum Standards in Disaster Response* (Oxford: Oxfam Publishing, 2000), available at www.sphereproject.org.

[47] Forman, Patrick, and Salomons, *Recovering from Conflict*, 31.

7

Elections and Exit Strategies: No Exit Without a Strategy, or No Strategy Without an Exit?

> It is more difficult to pass over from totalitarianism to democracy than from democracy to totalitarianism. Democracy calls for deep-going, value-oriented changes in the public mentality—it calls for time.
>
> Karl Popper[1]

In his April 2001 report on the closure or transition of complex peacekeeping operations, UN Secretary-General Kofi Annan warned that the embarrassing withdrawal of peacekeepers from Somalia should not be repeated in future operations. 'No Exit Without a Strategy', the report was called.[2] Such warnings apply all the more strongly to those situations in which an international presence does not merely provide a measure of security but in effect constitutes the government of the territory in question. For the UN Transitional Administration in East Timor (UNTAET), elections provided the basis for transfer of power to local authorities; they also set in place political processes that would last well beyond the mission and the development assistance that followed. In Kosovo, where the UN operation was determinedly called an 'interim' administration, the absence of an agreed end-state

[1] 'Interview with K. R. Popper', *Moscow News*, 25 November to 2 December 1990.

[2] No Exit Without Strategy: Security Council Decision-Making and the Closure or Transition of United Nations Peacekeeping Operations (Report of the Secretary-General), UN Doc S/2001/394 (20 April 2001). On the withdrawal from Somalia, see Chapter Three, Section 1.2.

left the territory in political limbo. Elections were, nonetheless, held in Kosovo, though their political significance was ambiguous. The municipal elections in 2000, for example, were a rare example of local elections in which the primary campaign issue was foreign policy, with virtually all parties that participated calling for independence. These elections were intended less to determine the legitimate representatives of the population than they were to engage the Kosovars—especially the Kosovar Albanians—in non-violent political activity. Reflection on the absence of an exit strategy from Kosovo, following on the apparently endless operation in Bosnia and Herzegovina, led some ambassadors to the Security Council to turn the Secretary-General's phrase on its head: 'No strategy', the rallying cry went, 'without an exit'.

This chapter examines the use of elections in transitional administrations and their relation to the transfer of power from international to local hands. Though elections staged by the United Nations are now commonly associated with the complex peace operations of the 1990s and beyond, the Trusteeship Council sent eight missions to observe elections or plebiscites under the Trusteeship System beginning in 1956.[3] Since the end of the cold war, electoral assistance has become an accepted feature of the international political landscape, with the Electoral Assistance Division of the UN Department of Political Affairs receiving over 200 requests for assistance from member states. The United Nations and other bodies, notably the Organization for Security and Cooperation in Europe (OSCE), have developed an outstanding capacity to hold and monitor elections under the most challenging circumstances. Elections in conflict zones such as Cambodia and Bosnia, or impoverished countries such as East Timor, are rightly regarded as technical triumphs.[4]

Technical triumph, however, has only rarely been matched by political success. In general, the emphasis has been on form at the expense of substance. Elections are the preferred mechanism for handing over power from an undemocratic but internationally legitimate transitional administration to a democratic and (ideally) locally legitimate government. But the question of what elections are meant to achieve in themselves is often left unasked.[5] As a medium-term peacebuilding

[3] See Chapter One, Section 3.1.

[4] See, e.g. An Agenda for Democratization, UN Doc A/51/761 (20 December 1996), para. 13: 'Democratization is predominantly a new area for technical assistance.'

[5] A primary argument could be that democratic elections are the only legitimate basis for government. But for territory under transitional administration, power continues to be exercised largely by international officials.

strategy, there is implicit deference to the 'democratic peace' thesis, which holds that democracies are statistically less likely to go to war than states that are undemocratic.[6] Over-emphasis on this empirical argument (which has itself been contested) obscures a secondary finding in the democratic peace literature that an autocratic state in the process of democratization may in fact be *more* likely to descend into conflict, especially internal conflict.[7] More often, however, elections may simply be a short-term tactic that is used to encourage actors to buy into a peace process—or they are staged because they are part of an accepted template of what typically happens towards the end of a peace operation.

Two strategic questions should underlie the decision to hold post-conflict elections: when they should be held and what form they should take. The first two sections of this chapter examine these issues with particular reference to Bosnia, which has served as a kind of election laboratory since 1996, and Afghanistan, where the United Nations embraced an atypical type of popular consultation in the Loya Jirga of June 2002. The chapter then considers how elections have figured in the exit strategies embraced by the United Nations in Cambodia, Kosovo, and East Timor.

Elections and the political system that they introduce define the legacy left by a transitional administration. Too often, however, this legacy is viewed by international actors within a time frame of months, rather than years. Staging an election while a territory is in the political spotlight, with a significant peacekeeping presence and thousands of international observers, is relatively easy. Ushering in a legitimate and sustainable political system that lasts beyond the life of the mission is far harder.

1. *Timing of Elections*

By the mid-1990s, a nostrum of post-conflict reconstruction was that elections were an integral part of such operations. Theoretical and

[6] See generally Michael E. Brown, Sean M. Lynn Jones, and Steven E. Miller, *Debating the Democratic Peace* (Cambridge, MA: MIT Press, 1996); Joanne S. Gowa, *Ballots and Bullets: The Elusive Democratic Peace* (Princeton, NJ: Princeton University Press, 1999); Tarak Barkawi and Mark Laffey (eds.), *Democracy, Liberalism, and War: Rethinking the Democratic Peace Debate* (Boulder, CO: Lynne Rienner, 2001). Cf. Agenda for Democratization, paras. 15–25.

[7] Edward D. Mansfield and Jack Snyder, 'Democratization and the Danger of War', in Brown, Lynn Jones, and Miller (eds.), *Democratic Peace*, 301.

normative support came from the democratic peace thesis and the growing literature on a right to democratic governance;[8] anecdotal support was found in the apparent success of the operations in Namibia and Cambodia. At the conclusion of the Bosnian wars of 1992–5, this view coincided with the desire of President Bill Clinton to limit the commitment of US troops in the region: the Dayton Peace Agreement thus provided that elections would be held between six and nine months after conclusion of the peace, and that troops would be home in a year.[9]

This was a mistake. As elections soon demonstrated, in the immediate aftermath of a conflict the issues on which it is easiest to mobilize political support are precisely those same issues that were used to mobilize support for war—politics becomes the continuation of war by other means. The speed of elections and the unrealistic expectation that troops could be withdrawn within twelve months (not unconnected with Clinton's own election timetable) reified political divisions within Bosnia and missed opportunities for action in other areas. As Paddy Ashdown, by then the fourth person to hold the position of High Representative, admitted in 2002:

> We thought that democracy was the highest priority, and we measured it by the number of elections we could organize. The result seven years later is that the people of Bosnia have grown weary of voting. In addition, the focus on elections slowed our efforts to tackle organized crime and corruption, which have jeopardized quality of life and scared off foreign investment.[10]

Since 1996, elections have been held in Bosnia on an almost annual basis, in each case amounting to little more than a census on ethnicity. In October 2002, Bosnians re-elected many of the same nationalist leaders who had drawn them into war in the first place.[11]

[8] See Thomas M. Franck (1992) 'The Emerging Right to Democratic Governance', *American Journal of International Law*, 86: 46; Gregory H. Fox and Brad R. Roth (eds.), *Democratic Governance and International Law* (Cambridge: Cambridge University Press, 2000).

[9] General Framework Agreement for Peace in Bosnia and Herzegovina (Dayton Agreement), Bosnia and Herzegovina–Croatia–Federal Republic of Yugoslavia, done at Dayton, 14 December 1995, UN Doc S/1995/999, available at www.yale.edu/lawweb/avalon/intdip/bosnia/daymenu.htm, Annex 3, art. II(4) (elections); SC Res 1031 (1995), para. 21 (troops). For early expressions of doubt about the timing, see John Pomfret, 'Success of Bosnia Pact Hangs on Timing, Tests; Peace Pact Faces Series of Hurdles', *Washington Post*, 20 December 1995.

[10] Paddy Ashdown, 'What I Learned in Bosnia', *New York Times*, 28 October 2002.

[11] John Phillips, 'Nationalist Vote Could Set Back Bosnia Peace', *The Times* (London), 4 October 2002.

The question of when to hold elections balances competing tensions that depend separately on the local population and the level of international interest. The first tension concerns the impact elections will have on emerging political structures and personalities. In some circumstances, as in Bosnia, early elections may have the effect of turning generals into politicians, formalizing ethnic divisions into political fault lines. In less developed states lacking adequate bureaucratic institutions, elections held before those institutions can be created may hinder long-term democratic practices and stability.[12] In other situations, however, early elections may lock in a peace process and provide tangible political gains to stakeholders in the peace. Kosovo's elections were delayed, in part because of concerns about the impact that they had had in Bosnia. With the benefit of hindsight, it might have made more sense to stage early elections in order to capitalize on the popularity of the moderates among the Kosovar Albanian community and involve them more directly in the peace process.[13] The second tension concerns the ephemeral nature of international interest in a crisis, and whether it is preferable—whatever the political situation on the ground—to run elections on a timetable agreed with donors so that the vote takes place while international attention is concentrated on the territory.

Elections held after inadequate political groundwork can, on occasion, actually contribute to the resumption of conflict. This was arguably the case in Angola's 1992 presidential election—the first ever in Angola—held under the May 1991 Bicesse Agreement, which was part of a peace process aimed at ending a civil war that had been running since the country's independence from Portugal in 1975.[14] The dominant parties in the election were the political wings of two liberation movements, the governing People's Liberation Movement of Angola, led by President Eduardo dos Santos, and Jonas Savimbi's National

[12] See, e.g. Samuel P. Huntington, *The Third Wave: Democratization in the Late Twentieth Century* (Norman: University of Oklahoma Press, 1991); Goran Hyden, 'Governance and the Reconstitution of Political Order', in Richard Joseph (ed.), *State, Conflict and Democracy in Africa* (Boulder, CO: Lynne Rienner, 1999), 179, 192.

[13] For an early argument along these lines, see Giuseppe Di Palma, *To Craft Democracies: An Essay on Democratic Transitions* (Berkeley: University of California Press, 1990), 85.

[14] See Margaret Joan Anstee, *Orphan of the Cold War: The Inside Story of the Angolan Peace Process, 1992–1993* (New York: St Martin's Press, 1996); James Ciment, *Angola and Mozambique: Postcolonial Wars in Southern Africa* (New York: Facts on File, 1997).

Union for the Total Independence of Angola (UNITA). A hastily drafted electoral law provided for a run-off between the top two candidates in the event that no one gained a majority in the first round of voting. As Ben Reilly notes, the impact of this formula was two-fold. First, it removed any possibility of power-sharing between the two main combatants. Second, however, it also provided a strategic opportunity for parties weakly committed to the process to gauge their support base after the first round. When Savimbi saw that he was unlikely to win the election, he rejected the process and went back to war. Such an outcome might have been inevitable, but the incentives to withdraw from the contest could have been lowered under a different process that enabled some period of power-sharing.[15]

These aspects of peace agreements may be better understood by the local population than international observers. In 1997, Liberians elected Charles Taylor president in a landslide victory, the very man who had drawn the country into civil war and fomented instability across West Africa since 1989. Many Liberians appeared to believe that a vote for Taylor was a vote for peace—or at least that a vote against Taylor would be interpreted by him as a vote for war.[16] Most post-conflict elections now try to avoid a winner-takes-all scenario.[17]

A separate question is how to coordinate national and regional or municipal elections. It is sometimes argued that new democracies should hold national before regional elections, in order to encourage the creation of national rather than regional political parties.[18] Others call for the simultaneous staging of both, as this may facilitate the mutual dependence of regional and national leaders, creating incentives for an integrated party system.[19] Over the course of the various state-building operations in the 1990s, however, the received wisdom came to be that a 'bottom-up' approach, beginning with municipal elections, was most suited to encouraging the development of party politics and introducing voters to the routines of electoral politics.[20]

[15] Benjamin Reilly (2002) 'Post-Conflict Elections: Constraints and Dangers', *International Peacekeeping*, 9(2): 118, 120.

[16] Adekeye Adebajo, *Liberia's Civil War Nigeria, ECOMOG, and Regional Security in West Africa* (Boulder, CO: Lynne Rienner, 2002), 223.

[17] See Section 2.2 in this chapter.

[18] Juan J. Linz and Alfred C. Stepan, *Problems of Democratic Transition and Consolidation: Southern Europe, South America, and Post-Communist Europe* (Baltimore: Johns Hopkins University Press, 1996), 98–107.

[19] Larry Jay Diamond, *Developing Democracy: Toward Consolidation* (Baltimore: Johns Hopkins University Press, 1999), 158.

[20] Reilly, 'Post-Conflict Elections', 122.

How this question is answered should, of course, depend on the local context. In Kosovo, where the institutions of government were themselves controversial, municipal elections were seen as a useful way in which to satisfy popular demand for political engagement without opening the grand political question of Kosovo's final status. The stakes are lower in local elections and the responsibilities of the officials to be chosen should be focused on service delivery rather than national politics. In East Timor, the territory's small size and the concentration of political actors in Dili meant that municipal or regional elections were never seriously contemplated, though Jarat Chopra has argued forcefully that the failure to decentralize Timorese political authority missed an opportunity to introduce genuine democracy rather than a simulacra that disguised a one-party state.[21]

Afghanistan suggests another model again, with a quasi-democratic process (the Loya Jirga) ushering in a quasi-legitimate authority to hold power for two years until national elections. Even so, elections in mid-2004 were still seen by some observers (Afghan and international) as premature—not least because a census was unlikely to be completed before the vote.[22] Donors, notably the United States, made it clear, however, that even questioning the timetable for elections was inadvisable. Raising questions might undermine some of the urgency that was required to complete the necessary preparations for elections. In addition, donors privately made clear that there was no possibility of an extension of financial assistance anyway.

2. *Institutions and Processes*

Drafting constitutions and organizing elections have become niche markets in international assistance, accompanied by a proliferation of specialized non-governmental organizations (NGOs) and a broad literature.[23] This section focuses on the impact of constitutional

[21] See Jarat Chopra (2002) 'Building State Failure in East Timor', *Development and Change*, 33: 979. See also Section 3.3 in this chapter.

[22] Carlotta Gall, 'Armed with Pencils, Army of Census Workers Fans out into Afghan Outback', *New York Times*, 13 July 2003. See also Section 2.2.3 in this chapter.

[23] See, e.g. Adam Przeworski (ed.), *Sustainable Democracy* (Cambridge: Cambridge University Press, 1995); Timothy D. Sisk, *Power Sharing and International Mediation in Ethnic Conflicts* (Washington, DC: United States Institute of Peace/Carnegie Commission on Preventing Deadly Conflict, 1996); Krishna Kumar (ed.), *Postconflict Elections, Democratization, and International Assistance* (Boulder, CO: Lynne Rienner, 1998); Benjamin Reilly, *Democracy in*

structures and electoral systems on efforts to establish a sustainable peace. It then turns to the related question of how political parties should be viewed.

2.1. Constitutional Structures

A constitution is neither a suicide pact nor a panacea. In the literature on post-conflict constitution-building, much emphasis is placed on the questions of whether a state should be federal or unitary, and whether it should have a strong executive president. These questions are important, but the precise constitutional structures put in place may be of less importance than the legitimacy that they hold in the eyes of the population. Though Japan and, to a lesser extent, Germany are examples of successful states where there was little domestic involvement in the drafting of their constitutions, for the most part 'ownership'—understood here to mean actual control—of this political process has been vital to the stability of the structures that it puts into place.

States with regionally based ethnic divisions are, as a rule, more stable under federal rather than unitary structures. A curious sub-literature exists on the precise number of subunits that are desirable—systems with two are notoriously unstable (as in Pakistan until 1971 and Czechoslovakia until 1992), and systems with four also appear to struggle. Five units and above is believed to be about right, with another band of stability around 20–25. The foundation of this esoteric calculus is the ability of federal structures to diffuse decision-making power through different layers of government, increasing the number of arenas for peaceful resolution of political differences.[24] The effectiveness of such power-sharing arrangements, however, relies less on the structures themselves than on the willingness of parties to operate within them. Where elite groups have relatively clear and loyal constituencies organized as political parties, labour unions, or other institutions, structured political life will be more stable. These institutions rarely exist in a post-conflict environment, however, and the strategic question of whether to opt into the peace process may be revisited by belligerent groups periodically through the transition. This was the case in Bosnia: despite powerful international pressure to

Divided Societies: Electoral Engineering for Conflict Management (Cambridge: Cambridge University Press, 2001).

[24] See, e.g. Alfred C. Stepan (1999) 'Federalism and Democracy: Beyond the US Model', *Journal of Democracy*, 10(4): 19; Nancy Bermeo (2002) 'The Import of Institutions', *Journal of Democracy*, 13(2): 96.

coerce parties into power-sharing arrangements, parties to the conflict simply refused to cooperate with the new multi-ethnic and inter-entity institutions.[25]

A separate problem with federal models is that the construction of dispersed institutions of government can undermine the development of strong central institutions that are needed to build trust in the post-conflict state. For example, various international experts recommended a federal structure for Afghanistan, where much power had been effectively devolved to—or seized by—local commanders or warlords. Strongly held popular opinion opposed even discussing the possibility of a federal Afghanistan, however, due to fears that this would confirm the position of the local commanders and open the possibility of a federal subunit seceding from the whole. It also failed to capitalize on the greatest strength of Afghan civil society: that despite a quarter of a century of violent conflict, no major group had contemplated secession. Amin Saikal rightly refers to this as Afghanistan exhibiting a weak state, but a strong society.[26]

Similar issues arise with the question of whether a post-conflict state should have a strong executive president. If a popular figure is elected with a large majority and given the powers to lead, he or she may serve as a driving force in the recovery process. Unless the outcome is very clear, however, a strong presidential system can be a divisive contest between leaders of opposing groups, as it was in Angola.[27] Few international actors would admit to building constitutional structures around the personalities of prominent individuals, but the fact that Xanana Gusmão would become president in East Timor was assumed by many involved in the drafting of the constitution.[28] In the Balkans, the need to accommodate different ethnic constituencies and the egos of various leaders gave rise to the eight-month rotating presidency

[25] Terrence Lyons, 'The Role of Postsettlement Elections', in Stephen John Stedman, Donald Rothchild, and Elizabeth M. Cousens (eds.), *Ending Civil Wars: The Implementation of Peace Agreements* (Boulder, CO: Lynne Rienner, 2002), 215, 220–1; Elizabeth M. Cousens, 'From Missed Opportunities to Overcompensation: Implementing the Dayton Agreement on Bosnia', in Stedman, Rothchild, and Cousens (eds.), *Ending Civil Wars*, 531.

[26] Amin Saikal, 'Afghanistan: Weak State, Strong Society', in Simon Chesterman, Michael Ignatieff, and Ramesh Thakur (eds.), *Making States Work: State Failure and the Crisis of Governance* (Tokyo: United Nations University Press, forthcoming).

[27] See above n. 14–15.

[28] This included Fretilin representatives, who ensured that his powers were curtailed: See Section 3.3 in this chapter.

in Bosnia, and no less than two presidents and a prime minister in Kosovo's Provisional Institutions of Self-Government.[29]

Writing a constitution is not difficult in itself. With access to the Internet, the constitution of virtually every country that has one can be accessed; cutting and pasting from these constitutions is something of a hobby for lawyers and consultants involved in post-conflict reconstruction.[30] The adoption of the basic law for a territory, however, is one area in which genuine 'ownership' is essential, understood here to mean actual control of both process and substance by a representative group of local officials, who themselves engage in consultations with a wide cross-section of the community. This is not to suggest that a constitution cannot be imposed, as it was in Japan and Germany after the Second World War. But these territories were exceptional in the comprehensiveness of their defeat, the utter discrediting of the ideology of the former regime, the level of development of the society concerned, and the length and depth of foreign engagement.[31] Bosnia and Kosovo are modern examples of post-conflict constitutional structures being imposed on a population—and of the level of sustained commitment that is required to keep them in place. Though Bosnia remains a work in progress, every federation that has broken apart since the Second World War had a political structure imposed by foreign actors. Some dissolutions were peaceful, such as the British West Indies in 1962 and Czechoslovakia in 1992, but most were violent.[32]

Fiji provides a case study in the best intentions of constitutional engineers arguably contributing to the breakdown of democratic order. The constitutional rewrite was precipitated by a demographic shift, as Indo-Fijians descended from Indian plantation workers transported to Fiji in the nineteenth century surpassed the indigenous Polynesian and Melanesian communities in absolute numbers. Two coups in 1987 led to the adoption of a 1990 constitution that guaranteed majorities for ethnic Fijians in both houses of the legislature, but also provided for a review of the constitution in 1997. A three-person commission (two Fijians and a New Zealander) travelled the world seeking advice from leading constitutional design specialists on the best practice approach to solving the problems of their divided state. The report was a magisterial overview of constitutional engineering and the options available to Fiji. It concluded that Fiji should adopt

29 See Section 3.3 in this chapter.

30 See, e.g. www.constitution.org.

31 See Chapter One, Section 4.

32 Alfred C. Stepan, *Arguing Comparative Politics* (Oxford: Oxford University Press, 2001), 323–4; Bermeo, 'Import of Institutions', 107.

an open seat system with the alternate preferential vote and a grand coalition executive, with all parties winning over 10 per cent of the vote guaranteed seats in the cabinet. These were all reasonable proposals. When adopted by parliament in 1997, however, compromises in the text undermined those mechanisms intended to foster interethnic bargaining. The grand coalition cabinet was retained but never functioned as it was intended: majority decisions within the cabinet structure meant that there was little incentive to do more than select pliable minorities and co-opt them into coalition.[33] More worryingly, the constitution came to be viewed—rightly or wrongly—as imposed by foreign technocrats. When the 1999 elections brought to power an Indian-led party, which held a majority through partnership with a moderate indigenous party, it was overthrown by a coup in the following year.[34]

As the Timorese engaged in public consultations on their own constitutional process in January 2001, the experience of Fiji was cited as a warning of the dangers of transplanting foreign solutions onto local problems. These consultations followed soon after the US presidential elections that had seen George W. Bush defeat Al Gore in contentious circumstances, which included an apparently partisan vote by the Supreme Court. A senior US official then working for the United Nations advised the Timorese to learn from the United States also: in some people's eyes the wrong person had been appointed president in a flawed process, but the population accepted the result because they believed that, however flawed, that process—the Electoral College system, the role of the Supreme Court as final arbiter in disputes about election laws—was itself legitimate. Cultivating legitimacy, therefore, was at least as important as achieving a good text.[35]

[33] Brij V. Lal and Tomasi R. Vakatora (eds.), *Fiji Constitutional Review Commission Research Papers* (Suva: School of Social and Economic Development, University of the South Pacific, 1997); Andrew Reynolds, 'First, Do No Harm: Applying the Science of Medicine to the Art of Constitutional Design' (Liechtenstein: Paper presented at Building a Viable and Effective Afghan State, 13–16 March 2003).

[34] See Jonathan Fraenkel (2001) 'The Alternative Vote System in Fiji: Electoral Engineering or Ballot-Rigging?', *Journal of Commonwealth and Comparative Politics*, 39(2): 1; Andrew Robertson (2001) 'Island of Intolerance?', *Harvard International Review*, 23(1): 11.

[35] Zimbabwe, among others, offered to send electoral observers to oversee a recount in the United States: 'Election 2000: Foreigners Chide and Poke Fun at US After Years of Lectures on Fair Elections', *Wall Street Journal*, 10 November 2000.

2.2. Electoral Systems

Closely related to the constitutional structure that allocates power is the electoral system that determines who gets to wield it. The design of an electoral system can also have a significant influence on political behaviour. Writing in 1991, Donald Horowitz argued that the electoral system 'is by far the most powerful lever of constitutional engineering for accommodation and harmony in severely divided societies'.[36] Though there is consensus on the importance of electoral systems, however, there is profound disagreement about how this lever should be used.

2.2.1. Proportional Representation and Preference Swapping The orthodox position has long been that some form of proportional representation is the surest way to ensure the survival of democracy in a deeply divided society.[37] This is now referred to as the 'consociational' approach to managing ethnic cleavages, which seeks to share power between elites by encouraging the formation of ethnically based political parties that are assured some measure of representation in elected bodies. The use of large, multimember electoral districts maximizes proportionality, and thus the prospect of multiple parties in parliaments, encouraging the formation of a cross-ethnic governing coalition. This is the method that has been used in virtually all of the major transitional elections since the end of the cold war, including those held under UN auspices. Party-list proportional representation has become the norm for parliamentary elections in such situations, with the presidency decided through a run-off election.[38]

Critics of consociationalism argue that its structures do not allow for the formation of a viable institutionalized opposition, and that structuring government around segmented competing interests hardens the divisions between those interests. Moreover, the driving principle is to make leadership difficult by requiring consensus among disparate groups—arguably the last thing that a fragile post-conflict democracy needs. An alternative approach, sometimes referred to as 'integrative'

36 Donald L. Horowitz, *A Democratic South Africa? Constitutional Engineering in a Divided Society* (Berkeley: University of California Press, 1991), 163.

37 See, e.g. W. Arthur Lewis, *Politics in West Africa* (New York: Oxford University Press, 1965).

38 Arend Lijphart (1969) 'Consociational Democracy', *World Politics*, 21: 207; Sisk, *Power Sharing*, 34–40; Reilly, 'Post-Conflict Elections', 127–30. Haiti's 1995 parliamentary elections, which used a run-off system, were the main deviation from this trend.

or 'centripetal', holds that political processes should undermine rather than reinforce the divisive effects of ethnicity. These processes might include rules that encourage vote pooling and preference swapping in order to encourage inter-ethnic bargaining and promote accommodation between ethnic groups. The basic aim is to make political leaders dependent on the support of members of groups other than their own. Instead of proportional representation, preferential systems such as the alternative vote and single transferable vote permit or require voters to indicate not merely their first but also their second, third, and subsequent choices. This may encourage preference-trading agreements between disparate political actors and negotiation on broader policy issues.[39] There is no guarantee that such agreements will actually be concluded, however, or that they will be respected when a party gets into power.

In addition to the relative political merits of the two systems, national proportional representation systems have been favoured for administrative reasons. Removing the need to demarcate electoral districts greatly simplifies voter registration, and a single ballot paper can be used throughout the territory. If the concern is to hold elections quickly—often a time constraint imposed by external actors—national proportional representation may be the only feasible method. The downside of this absolutist version of proportional representation is that it removes any 'geographic accountability' that links elected officials to a particular constituency. This has led to the recent popularity of 'mixed' electoral systems, such as that used in East Timor in 2001, where the eighty-eight-member constituent assembly consisted of seventy-five seats elected on a nationwide basis by proportional representation and thirteen seats elected by a first-past-the-post method from each of thirteen electoral districts.[40]

2.2.2. Quotas Proportional representation should remove the need for quotas to ensure ethnic representation,[41] but quotas have on occasion been used to ensure the participation of women in the

[39] Donald L. Horowitz, *Ethnic Groups in Conflict* (Berkeley: University of California Press, 1985); Sisk, *Power Sharing*, 40–5; Reilly, 'Post-Conflict Elections', 128–9. The 1998 Northern Ireland elections are seen as an example of this, with centrist parties supported by the single transferable vote system.

[40] Reilly, 'Post-Conflict Elections', 130–1. The large majority of seats elected by proportional representation was intended to reduce the likelihood of Fretilin winning a clean sweep of seats. See Section 3.3 in this chapter.

[41] Quotas were, however, used in Kosovo to compensate for low participation by the Serb community. See Section 3.2 in this chapter.

political process. The importance of involving women in areas such as peacebuilding and security sector reform is now widely accepted. In October 2000, the Security Council adopted resolution 1325 (2000) that, among other things, urged member states to increase the representation of women in conflict-resolution mechanisms and invited the Secretary-General to study the impact of armed conflict on women and girls, the role of women in peacebuilding, and the gender dimensions of peace processes and conflict resolution. When he reported back two years later, the Secretary-General outlined the disproportionate suffering of women and children in contemporary armed conflict:

> But if women suffer the impact of conflict disproportionately, they are also the key to the solution of conflict. Women's groups and networks at grassroots level have provided many examples of the imaginative strategies and flexible approaches required for effective conflict prevention. They have worked tirelessly and courageously in preserving social order in the midst of chaos, and promoting reconciliation through informal processes that receive very little support. However, with few exceptions, women are not present at the formal negotiating tables and at formal peace negotiations.[42]

In Kosovo, for example, the Kosovo Police Service (KPS) made recruitment of women a high priority and classes were soon averaging 18 per cent female cadets. In addition to lowering the 'testosterone level', women were often the first to reach out to other ethnic groups.[43] Elections for the Provisional Institutions of Self-Government included a requirement that at least every third candidate in the top two-thirds of any party's list had to be female, which led to thirty-four women being elected out of the 120 seats.[44] In Kosovo, this was an OSCE initiative; East Timor's National Council rejected a similar proposal for Timor's elections, in part because it was not pressed very hard by international staff.[45] Sergio Vieira de Mello later delivered a *mea culpa* for this and other omissions:

> I was against the creation of a Gender Affairs Unit for the UN's Transitional Authority in East Timor. I did not think a Gender Unit would help rebuild institutions from the ashes of what the militia left. I was wrong. The first

[42] SC Res 1325 (2000), paras. 1, 16. Press Release, UN Doc SC/7551 (28 October 2002). See also Report of the Secretary-General on Women, Peace and Security, UN Doc S/2002/1154 (16 October 2002).

[43] William G. O'Neill, *Kosovo: An Unfinished Peace* (Boulder, CO: Lynne Rienner, 2002), 112–13.

[44] OSCE Central Election Commission, Electoral Rule No 8/2001 (16 August 2001), §3.

[45] See International IDEA and Stockholm University, Global Database of Quotas for Women, available at www.idea.int/quota.

regulation I passed guaranteed human rights standards, including [the Convention on the Elimination of All Forms of Discrimination Against Women] as a foundation of all new government institutions we created. The Unit brought this to life reaching out to East Timorese women, and, together with [the UN Development Fund for Women (UNIFEM)], provided support that resulted in a higher percentage of women in the Constituent Assembly than in many other countries. The Unit worked with East Timorese women to create what is now the East Timorese Government Office for the Advancement of Women.[46]

These are all regarded as positive steps in how the United Nations approaches conflict, but 'gender-mainstreaming' in peace operations still means little more than the appointment of a gender adviser and the insertion of a standard paragraph or two solicited from UNIFEM into the Secretary-General's reports to the Security Council. It is also far from clear that inclusion of women on the basis that they are more caring and community-oriented than men does more than reinforce gender stereotypes about the respective roles of each in society.[47]

2.2.3. Form and Substance Almost as important as the way in which a population votes is the manner in which those votes are counted. Holding a perfect election is comparatively simple when international attention is drawn to the ballot: in Kosovo's 2001 provincial elections, for example, around 2000 international and almost 13,000 domestic observers were registered to oversee an election in which 800,000 people voted. Such levels of oversight—nearly one observer for every fifty voters—are unsustainable. Some energy in East Timor went into the creation of an Independent Electoral Commission, though for the first election Timorese leaders made it clear that they wanted only international staff actually to count the votes. In Bosnia and Kosovo, the OSCE developed a recognized capacity to organize elections; acknowledging the importance of developing local institutions, direct

[46] Sergio Vieira de Mello, statement on the first anniversary of SC Res 1325 (2000), quoted in UN Development Fund for Women, Women, War, and Peace: The Independent Experts' Assessment on the Impact of Armed Conflict on Women and Women's Role in Peacebuilding (New York: UNIFEM, October 2002).

[47] See further Cynthia H. Enloe, *Bananas, Beaches, and Bases: Making Feminist Sense of International Politics* (London: Pandora, 1989); Dyan E. Mazurana and Susan R. McKay, *Women and Peacebuilding* (Montreal: International Centre for Human Rights and Democratic Development, 1999); Barnett R. Rubin, *Blood on the Doorstep: The Politics of Preventive Action* (New York: Century Foundation Press, 2002), 180.

administration of the election process in Bosnia was handed over to national authorities in November 2001. As in many other areas, the danger is that international engagement will set in place systems and standards that cannot be maintained. This means balancing the benefits of one-off international election observation missions (sometimes derided by locals as 'electoral tourism') against the benefits of directly supporting domestic institutions and local observer groups.[48]

Underlying the discussion of electoral systems is an assumption that democracy is a necessary and desirable end for a territory in transition, and that the means of achieving it is swift establishment of a universal and secret franchise directly electing senior government representatives. This need not be the case. In Afghanistan, the practical and political difficulties of staging elections in a post-conflict environment led to some creativity on the part of Afghan and international actors. The statement adopted on 12 November 2001 by the 'Six Plus Two' group of Afghanistan's six neighbours, Russia, and the United States called for a 'broad based, multi-ethnic, politically balanced, freely-chosen Afghan administration representative of their aspirations and at peace with its neighbours'.[49] This was close to, but not identical with democracy. Declarations by the European Union similarly called for 'responsible and representative government' rather than democracy as such.[50] The December 2001 Bonn Agreement acknowledged 'the right of the people of Afghanistan to freely determine their own political future in accordance with the principles of Islam, democracy, pluralism and social justice'. It provided for elections to be held by June 2004, with an Interim Authority holding power until it could convene an Emergency Loya Jirga (National Assembly) in six months. This forum, which traditionally brought Afghan tribal elders together to settle affairs of the nation or rally behind a cause, was to determine the composition of the Transitional Authority that would lead Afghanistan until elections.[51]

48 Reilly, 'Post-Conflict Elections', 126.

49 Statement on the Situation in Afghanistan Adopted by the Ministers for Foreign Affairs and Other Senior Representatives of the Six Plus Two, UN Doc A/56/681–S/2001/1157, Annex (12 November 2001).

50 See, e.g. General Affairs and External Relations Council of the EU, Afghanistan: Council Conclusions (15 April 2002), available at http://europa.eu.int.

51 Agreement on Provisional Arrangements in Afghanistan Pending the Re-Establishment of Permanent Government Institutions (Bonn Agreement), done at Bonn, 5 December 2001, UN Doc S/2001/1154, preamble, art. I(4). See also

As indicated in Chapter Two, few regarded the Loya Jirga as a meaningful popular consultation. When Special Representative of the Secretary-General Lakhdar Brahimi briefed the UN Security Council on the Loya Jirga, he was candid about its dubious democratic credentials:

> The Loya Jirga is a traditional institution which, historically, has not been very representative. This Loya Jirga, which took place only six months after the end of a long and bitter conflict, was not designed to be, nor could it realistically have been, a perfectly democratic or representative process. It did, nevertheless, incorporate significant and innovative democratic elements. As a result, two-thirds of the 1,600 delegates who took part were actually selected by the people themselves, the members spanned every ethnic and political group, and 200 of them were women. There was no precedent for any of this in Afghanistan. For more than a week, these delegates gathered together, in the absence of guns and bullets, to begin debating some of the most difficult and controversial issues facing the country, providing great hope for national reconciliation. In all of these senses, the Loya Jirga, even if it was not perfect, represents a significant step forward in the peace process.[52]

The aim, then, was to encourage those who wielded power in Afghanistan to exercise it through politics rather than through the barrel of a gun. The Loya Jirga took place peacefully on 11–19 June 2002 and did produce a somewhat more representative administration than that established in the Bonn process. In addition to 1,051 elected delegates, a further 450 were appointed by refugee groups, universities, and other civil society bodies, with a final hundred or so added under pressure at the last minute. Hamid Karzai, Chairman of the Interim Authority, was elected President of the Transitional Authority by an overwhelming majority, though his main opponents withdrew their candidacy not long before the Loya Jirga took place, apparently under intense pressure from the United States. In particular, the former King, Mohammed Zaher, stated that he would not seek election as head of state—an announcement that embarrassingly came some hours after US envoy Zalmay Khalilzad had announced that the King would have no position in the transitional government.[53]

Barnett R. Rubin (1998) 'Lineages of the State in Afghanistan', *Asian Survey*, 28(11): 1191, 1199.

[52] Briefing to the Security Council by the Special Representative of the Secretary-General for Afghanistan (New York: United Nations, 19 July 2002).

[53] See Ahmed Rashid, 'Afghan Assembly Is Delayed a Day by Dispute over Role of Monarch—US-Brokered Deal Taking Him Out of Politics Angers Deputies at Historic Council', *Wall Street Journal*, 11 June 2002; International Crisis Group, The Afghan Transitional Administration: Prospects and

The most perilous aspect of any exit strategy from Afghanistan is the similarity between the current domestic political constellation and the situation in 1992, when the Soviet-backed Najibullah regime collapsed and international interest began to wander from Afghanistan. Then, as now, a weak central government sought to hold the country together, while Rashid Dostum wielded power in the north, Ismael Khan held the west, and Gulbuddin Hekmatyar lurked in the wings. The disorder to which this gave rise—and, importantly, the disruption it caused to trade routes—was an important factor in the emergence of the Taliban in 1994. If international attention wanders from Afghanistan again this downward spiral could be repeated.[54]

2.3. Political Parties

In addition to constitutional structures and electoral systems, a third aspect of post-conflict political development that is frequently overlooked is the question of political parties. Should the formation of parties be encouraged? Parties are an important tool for recruiting candidates, organizing constituencies, and aggregating public preferences for expression in political forums. Nevertheless, post-conflict elections can serve as a catalyst for the creation of political parties that are primarily—and sometimes solely—vehicles to provide local elites with access to governing power. Such parties may be little more than a repackaging of the armed groups that fought the original conflict. As indicated in the first section, the generals-to-politicians transformation has been a particular problem in Bosnia, epitomized by the dominance of the Bosniak Party of Democratic Action (SDA), the Croatian Democratic Community (HDZ), and the Serbian Democratic Party (SDS), which are exclusively Bosniak, Croat, and Serb respectively.[55]

In some circumstances, international actors may collude in efforts to repackage armed groups as political parties. The decision by the UN Transitional Authority in Cambodia (UNTAC) to treat the Khmer Rouge as a recalcitrant political party rather than an enemy

Perils (Kabul/Brussels: Afghanistan Briefing Paper, 30 July 2002), available at www.crisisweb.org, 4.

54 See Barnett R. Rubin, *The Fragmentation of Afghanistan* (New Haven, CT: Yale University Press, 1995); Ahmed Rashid, *Taliban: Militant Islam, Oil, and Fundamentalism in Central Asia* (New Haven, CT: Yale University Press, 2000). See also Chapter Two, Section 3.1.

55 Reilly, 'Post-Conflict Elections', 121–2.

of the peace process was deeply controversial at the time. Including it within the process and then isolating it when it withdrew from the elections—while tactically ignoring violence carried out by Hun Sen's State of Cambodia (SOC)—contributed to the collapse of the Khmer Rouge after the elections, at which point most of its soldiers sought amnesties and abandoned Pol Pot.[56] This might have been an exceptional situation, however. When UNITA withdrew from elections in Angola and the Revolutionary United Front (RUF) from the peace process in Sierra Leone, they were ultimately defeated—but only after military confrontations.

Different problems arise when parties coalesce around former liberation movements, such as East Timor's Revolutionary Front of Independent East Timor (Fretilin). Support for the party may be cultivated as identical to nationalism or a national identity, an unhealthy basis for multiparty democracy.[57] This may be contrasted with the National Council of Timorese Resistance (CNRT), presided over by Gusmão, which was dissolved in June 2001.[58] The temptation to transform an independence movement into the natural party of government is natural, but the danger is that such a party comes to view itself as the 'natural' party of government—and the leader may come to regard himself as indispensable. In India, for example, M. K. Gandhi urged that the Indian National Congress, which had served as a vehicle for the independence struggle against British colonial rule, should be disbanded upon achieving its aim in order to avoid 'unhealthy competition with political parties and communal bodies'.[59] Instead, Congress entered government and remained there for most of the following five decades under Jawaharlal Nehru, his daughter, and his grandson. Strong leadership may be essential to the success of an independence movement or seeing a country through the instability that independence can bring, but for every Julius Nyerere (Tanzania) and Lee Kuan Yew (Singapore), there is a General Ne Win (Burma/Myanmar), Idi Amin (Uganda), Mobutu Sese Seko (Congo/Zaïre), Robert Mugabe (Zimbabwe), and many others.

One way of avoiding these problems is to remove political parties from the process. Democracy is commonly assumed to require a party

[56] Sorpong Peou, 'Implementing Cambodia's Peace Agreement', in Stedman, Rothchild, and Cousens (eds.), *Ending Civil Wars*, 499.

[57] Tanja Hohe (2002) 'Totem Polls: Indigenous Concepts and "Free and Fair" Elections in East Timor', *International Peacekeeping*, 9(4): 69, 73–4.

[58] See Chapter Four, Section 1.2.1.

[59] M. K. Gandhi, *Hind Swaraj and Other Writings* (Cambridge: Cambridge University Press, 1997), 191–2.

system, though the United States itself did not develop functioning political parties until well into the nineteenth century. Without parties, however, political life is dominated exclusively by the elite personalities involved: this is the danger of a 'no-party democracy' such as that embraced in Yoweri Museveni's Uganda.[60] Such a system may be attractive to a population in a country with a history of political violence, where party divisions are seen less as divergent opinions on how the state should be governed than as fault-lines that threaten a return to civil war. This was the case in East Timor, where many Timorese questioned the need for parties, an uncertainty borne of the belief that divisions between Timorese independence parties had been exploited by Indonesia in 1974–5.[61] If it is not possible to mobilize political activity around structured arguments for how the state should be governed, however, the issues on which political argument will turn are likely to be the inherently unstable factors of personality, or ethnic or religious affiliation.

3. *Elections, Exits, and Strategies*

The Secretary-General's report cited at the beginning of this chapter considered three circumstances that might prompt discussion of an 'exit' or significant alteration of a peace operation: successful completion of the mandate, partial success, and failure. But how should one evaluate the success or failure of a transitional administration? The UN Operation in the Congo (ONUC) (1960–4) is regarded by some commentators as having successfully implemented its mandate. Given that what followed was over three decades of President Mobutu Sese Seko's kleptocratic rule, the operation might well have been a success, but the patient died anyway.[62]

In a transitional administration, the transfer of power to local hands is the exit strategy, with the international presence shifting into a more traditional relationship of development assistance. How that transfer is managed and what foundations are laid for the future stability and prosperity of the territory should be central to the evaluation of such an operation. Elections, which are held up as the benchmark of success, are only one part of this process. This section examines the changing way in which the Cambodian elections came to be viewed, before considering how elections in Kosovo have become a substitute for strategy. East Timor, by contrast, suggests

60 'You Like Parties? We Don't', *Economist*, 22 July 1995.

61 See Chapter Four, Section 1.2.1.

62 See Chapter Two, Section 2.5.1.

the limits of democratization through encouraging a post-conflict territory to take on the form of democracy without necessarily establishing the foundations for such a political system to be embraced in substance.

3.1. Evaluating the Cambodian Elections

Evaluations of UNTAC varied considerably in the course of the mission and have continued to do so with the benefit of hindsight. Prior to the 1993 election, prophecies of doom were widespread, with questions raised about the capacity of the United Nations to complete a large military and administrative operation.[63] Immediately after the election was held with minimal violence, Cambodia was embraced as a success and a model for future such tasks.[64] Subsequent events suggested that these initially positive evaluations were premature. Many commentators outside the United Nations now regard UNTAC as a partial failure, pointing to the departure from democratic norms in the 1997 coup. Within the United Nations, UNTAC continues to be regarded as a partial success.[65]

The important variable is how one views the political context within which UNTAC operated. If the purpose of the mission was to transform Cambodia into a multiparty liberal democracy in eighteen months, it clearly did not succeed. If, however, one takes the view that Hun Sen—who had led Cambodia from 1979 and later seized power from his coalition partners in a coup four years after the 1993 elections—was always going to be the dominant political force in Cambodia, and that the purpose of the mission was to mollify the exercise of that power through introducing the language of human rights to Cambodian civil society, fostering the establishment of a relatively free press, and taking steps in the direction of a democratic basis for legitimate government, the mission was indeed a partial success.

Two lessons were (or should have been) learned in Cambodia. The first was to underscore the fragility of complex peace operations. Even though UNTAC was, at the time, the largest and most expensive operation in UN history, it still faced enormous difficulties in

[63] See, e.g. William Branigin, 'UN Performance at Issue as Cambodian Vote Nears', *Washington Post*, 20 May 1993.

[64] 'A UN Success in Cambodia', *Washington Post*, 18 June 1993.

[65] See Chapter Two, Section 2.3.1. On Cambodia's July 2003 election, see 'Counting on the Young: Cambodia's General Election', *Economist*, 2 August 2003.

bringing about a fundamental change in the psyche of the country. Without peace and security, and without the rule of law, democratic processes may in themselves be unsustainable. Providing these foundations, if it was possible at all, would have required a more sustained commitment to remaining in Cambodia after the elections. The counterfactual is hypothetical as there was no willingness before or after the vote for UNTAC to remain beyond the completion of its mandate.

Second, the aftermath of the UN engagement in Cambodia—the 1997 coup, the flawed elections in 1998—began to raise questions about the relative importance of democracy. Though it may not be directly traceable to Cambodia, a shift began to occur in the rhetoric that saw 'good governance' sometimes replace democracy in the peacebuilding and development jargon. 'Good governance' was an intentionally vague term that spoke less to the formal structures of government than how a state is governed. A typical statement from the UN Development Programme (UNDP) is the following:

> Good governance is, among other things, participatory, transparent and accountable. It is also effective and equitable. And it promotes the rule of law. Good governance ensures that political, social and economic priorities are based on broad consensus in society and that the voices of the poorest and the most vulnerable are heard in decision-making over the allocation of development resources.[66]

The term 'governance' itself emerged within the development discourse in the 1990s as a means of expanding the prescriptions of donors to embrace not merely projects and structural adjustment but government policies. Though intergovernmental organizations like the World Bank and the International Monetary Fund are technically constrained from referring to political processes as such, 'governance' provides a convenient euphemism for precisely that.[67]

Elections mark an important stage in the political evolution of a state, but it is now recognized that they may achieve little in isolation from broader and more far-ranging transformations in the political environment. Wariness of a rush to democracy has inspired some creativity in Afghanistan, as indicated earlier.[68] In Kosovo and East Timor, commitment to 'immaculate' elections has occasionally obscured the larger aims of political and economic development.

[66] UN Development Programme, Governance for Sustainable Human Development (New York: UNDP, January 1997), available at http://magnet.undp.org/policy.

[67] Hyden, 'Governance'.

[68] See Section 2.2.3 in this chapter.

3.2. Politics As Process: Kosovo

Kosovo was stillborn as a political entity. As long as its final status remains undecided, its political development will continue to be undermined by uncertainty. Given this political ambiguity, and the fact that all political parties in Kosovo remain divided along ethnic lines, it bears asking why the United Nations and the OSCE have been so enthusiastic about staging elections in 2000, 2001, 2002, and beyond.

When questioned as to the purpose of elections, officials from the UN Interim Administration Mission in Kosovo (UNMIK) presented a raft of different and sometimes inconsistent answers. Notably, traditional democratic principles of legitimacy and accountability in government were not first among their responses—in part because UNMIK itself was neither democratically legitimate nor accountable in any way to the local population.[69] Instead, the attitude towards elections reflected the competing concerns of peace and security on the one hand, and the promotion of human rights and the rule of law on the other. For the most part, however, officials used the language of democracy to justify ends based on a concern for peace and security.

First and foremost, UNMIK officials stressed that elections provided a focus for non-violent political activity in Kosovo. With independence off the table, it was hoped that election campaigns and the transfer of limited civilian powers in Kosovo would keep the majority Albanian community engaged in a political process that was consistent with but not committed to independence. Periodic elections should be seen, then, as part of broader attempts to end the cycle of violence in both the short and the medium term. As a senior OSCE representative put it prior to the November 2001 elections, 'Elections will buy us three years of stability.'

Second, it was hoped that the structures being filled would encourage the emergence of politically moderate parties and credible leaders.[70] The municipal elections held in October 2000 were rightly cited as an example of a successful election being held in Kosovo (albeit with negligible Serb participation), but hardly supported the view that compromises and power sharing would take place once representatives assumed office. As the Secretary-General reported to the

[69] See Chapter Four, Section 1.1.3.

[70] Report of the Security Council Mission on the Implementation of Security Council Resolution 1244 (1999), UN Doc S/2001/600 (19 June 2001), para. 31: 'The current political process is crucial to combating extremism and encouraging moderates on all sides.'

Security Council in June 2001, coherent planning at the municipal level remained 'hampered by a general lack of ability on the part of all political parties to organize their activities and engage in a constructive manner'.[71] The three main Albanian parties (Ibrahim Rugova's Democratic League of Kosovo (LDK), Ramush Haradinaj's Alliance for the Future of Kosovo (AAK), and, more reluctantly, Hashim Thaçi's Democratic Party of Kosovo (PDK)) agreed to take part in the November 2001 elections, as did most of the non-Serb minorities, and there is some evidence of change in the way they approach their roles.[72]

A third purpose for elections concerned the Kosovar Serb community. Virtually no one believed that Serbs would participate in the 2001 elections in significant numbers—an OSCE democratization officer in one majority Serb area confessed that he would be shocked if they decided to vote at all. In fact, the decision was seen as one that would be made in Belgrade, from where most of the Kosovar Serbs continued to take their lead. The best hope of senior UN staff was that Belgrade would accept the inevitability of some form of partition and 'gently turn its back' on the remaining Kosovar Serbs. The Constitutional Framework for Provisional Self-Government, adopted in 2001, may serve as a wedge in that relationship. In addition to the allocation of positions in the presidency and ministries to non-Albanians, the framework provided for guaranteed levels of community representation in the assembly.[73] As the assembly treated all of Kosovo as a single electoral district and representatives were to be elected on the basis of proportional representation, guaranteed representation should not have been necessary. That is, if Serbs made up 7 per cent of the population of Kosovo, they should win about 7 per cent of seats in a free and fair election. Instead, the framework provided for an additional ten seats to go to Serb representatives, and a further ten to be divided among the other communities. Abedin Ferovic, a Bosniak law professor who was the 'other communities' representative on the working group that drafted the framework, says that he raised this question with the UN

[71] Report of the Secretary-General on the United Nations Interim Administration Mission in Kosovo (for the period 13 March 2001 to 7 June 2001), UN Doc S/2001/565 (7 June 2001), para. 36.

[72] International Crisis Group, Kosovo's Ethnic Dilemma: The Need for a Civic Contract (Pristina/Brussels: ICG Balkans Report No 143, 28 May 2003), available at www.crisisweb.org, 6.

[73] A Constitutional Framework for Provisional Self-Government in Kosovo, UNMIK Regulation 2001/9 (15 May 2001), available at www.unmikonline.org/constframework.htm, chapter nine.

staff who had proposed the formula. The provisions were included because the Serbs were not expected to vote in the 2001 elections, but that this would guarantee them a minimum number of seats in order to encourage some sort of participation in the new structures.[74]

In addition, however, it is significant that the framework specified that these seats would be distributed in proportion to the number of valid votes received by Serb parties in the election to the assembly. If only one party broke ranks with the Kosovar Serb line and decided to encourage its constituents to vote, it would be virtually guaranteed ten seats in the assembly, as well as a position on the presidency. This arrangement, presumably intentionally, put the Kosovar Serbs into a prisoner's dilemma. The most likely intra-Serb division is between the Serbs living in enclaves such as Gracanica and those living in Northern Mitrovica (which borders Serbia proper). Such a split would increase the chances of an eventual partition of Kosovo itself, with the enclaves in the south remaining as cantons.[75]

Ferovic and the Kosovar Albanian representatives on the working group agreed to the over-representation provisions, but pushed for an elected president of Kosovo and explicit reference to the 'will of the people' in the text of the document that they proposed calling the 'Provisional Constitution of Kosovo'. The framework as adopted did provide for a President of Kosovo appointed by the assembly (in addition to the President of the Assembly and a Prime Minister). But UNMIK could not accept text that stated that the purpose of the Provisional Institutions of Self-Government was to facilitate 'the determination of Kosovo's future status in conformity with the express will of the people'.[76] Even a guarded reference to the possibility of a referendum was regarded as unacceptable; the preamble as adopted states that Kosovo's future status will be determined 'through a process at an appropriate future stage which shall, in accordance with [Security Council resolution] 1244 (1999), take full account of relevant factors including the will of the people'.[77]

[74] Abedin Ferovic, interview with the author, Pristina, 26 June 2001.

[75] Serbs did vote in significant numbers for Koalition Povrotak (Coalition Return), which received over 89,000 votes, or more than 11 per cent of votes cast in the 2001 Kosovo Assembly Elections. More than 53,000 of these votes were cast outside Kosovo, however—mostly in Serbia proper. See OSCE, Detailed Certified Results (Pristina: OSCE Mission in Kosovo, Central Election Commission, 24 November 2001), available at www.osce.org/kosovo/elections.

[76] Legal Framework for the Provisional Institutions of Self-Government in Kosovo/Provisional Constitution of Kosovo (provisional draft of 17 April 2001), preamble.

[77] Constitutional Framework, preamble.

These are not quite truths that one would hold to be self-evident. But the refusal to link Kosovo's future status to the will of the people reflected a more general reluctance to involve Kosovar Albanians and other communities in the political process. In part, this stemmed from concerns about the delays that wider consultations would cause, as well as the issues of 'political maturity' that elections were intended to address. It bears asking, however, whether in the absence of such compromises on the structure of representation it is worth going through the substance of elections either.

This raises the fourth reason for elections in Kosovo: the absence of alternatives. In the words of one OSCE official, 'Elections are what we do.' Elections provide a quantifiable measure of international activity in Kosovo—as they continue to in Bosnia. In a place where significant progress seems unlikely in the short term, elections provide 'instant gratification'. A senior US official in UNMIK noted that elections were 'about the only thing Washington gets excited about'. Transferring authority at the operational levels of government also made it possible to scale down the mission, satisfying domestic calls for an 'exit strategy'.

Thus the United Nations and its partners remain committed to elections in territories under their control, even if they are destined to criticize the results after the fact. Bosnia marks the extreme case in this spectrum, where the High Representative has repeatedly intervened to remove elected officials.[78] In Kosovo, UNMIK seems likely to continue criticizing Kosovar Albanian political parties for continuing to fight for independence—a fight that NATO effectively joined in 1999 but from which it later resiled—and criticizing the Serb communities for continuing to regard Belgrade rather than Pristina as their capital—a position supported in all relevant official documents.

For the time being, then, there is no exit strategy from Kosovo. Michael Steiner, Special Representative until July 2003, undertook a rhetorical move that sought to place 'standards before status'. The intention was to focus energy on certain standards for Kosovo's institutions to meet before status negotiations could begin, but as the consequences of meeting those standards remained studiedly unclear this merely deferred the final status question.[79] Richard Goldstone's Kosovo Commission was initially convened to examine NATO's actions during the 1999 conflict. The Commission revisited

[78] See Chapter Four, Section 1.1.1.

[79] International Crisis Group, Kosovo's Ethnic Dilemma, 1.

the province in 2001 and released a supplementary report calling for 'conditional independence', meaning self-government outside of the Federal Republic of Yugoslavia, but 'within a specific international framework in which the international community retains responsibility for the security of borders and for overseeing the protection of minorities'.[80] This appears to be the direction in which the province is going, but until a decision is made Kosovo's political and economic development will continue to be retarded by uncertainty, undermining serious political reforms and deterring foreign investment.

Thoughts of partitioning Kosovo, allowing the Serb-populated areas north of Mitrovica (where Serbian is spoken and the dinar is the dominant currency) to join Serbia proper and perhaps trading it for the Presevo Valley, should be considered only as a last resort. Quite apart from legitimizing ethnic-cleansing, this would almost certainly undermine the stability of neighbouring Macedonia. Idle speculation that partition of Kosovo could be combined with carving up Bosnia (giving the Republika Srpska to Serbia and Croatian parts of the Federation to Croatia) could lead to reopening the Pandora's Box of Balkan conflicts all over again.[81] Kosovar Albanians might not accept such an arrangement anyway, if it meant giving up the Trepca Mine complex in northern Kosovo—even though rumours of the riches to be found there are wildly exaggerated.

Within the United Nations, Bosnia is sometimes seen as a model for how UNMIK might depart Kosovo. The closure of the UN Mission in Bosnia and Herzegovina (UNMIBH) in December 2002 was, however, only an exit for the United Nations itself, transferring its responsibilities to the European Union. A similar 'conditional independence' may be the best option for Kosovo over the coming decade or so, though it provides few lessons for other regions.[82]

[80] Independent International Commission on Kosovo, The Follow-up of the Kosovo Report: Why Conditional Independence? (Sweden: Kosovo Commission, September 2001).

[81] See, e.g. Richard K. Betts (2001) 'The Lesser Evil: The Best Way Out of the Balkans', *The National Interest*, 64: 53; Anna Matveeva and Wolf-Christian Paes, 'Trapped in Its Own Maze', *World Today*, July 2002, 19.

[82] Kosovo was not unusual for being held hostage to high politics irrelevant to the actual circumstances on the ground, of course. In February 1999, China vetoed extension of the UN Preventive Deployment Force (UNPREDEP) in the Former Yugoslav Republic of Macedonia, a month after Skopje switched its diplomatic recognition from Beijing to Taipei. Recognition of Taiwan was believed to be in exchange for over $130 million in loans and aid (reports ranged

3.3. Democracy in East Timor

Unlike the first elections in post-apartheid South Africa, where people celebrated in the long queues to vote, East Timor's first elections on 30 August 2001 were so calm as to be almost boring. This was unfortunate for the journalists who had journeyed to East Timor—a few left even before the election—but it was the best possible news for the Timorese people. They queued up peacefully to cast their ballots and then went home. Such boredom is a thing worth fighting for. Fretilin, the dominant party of national liberation, won a clear majority—fifty-five of eighty-eight seats—but fell short of the two-thirds majority it needed to be able to impose a constitution unilaterally. Presidential elections followed, and on 14 April 2002 Gusmão was elected with an overwhelming majority of the vote, though his powers were limited by the constitution adopted a month earlier. East Timor was declared independent (as Timor-Leste) on 20 May 2002 and UNTAET was replaced by the UN Mission of Support in East Timor (UNMISET), which remained with a scaled-down peacekeeping presence until a projected departure in June 2004.

East Timor's elections were formal successes, enjoying large turnouts and swift certification as 'free and fair' by, among other organizations, the Carter Center and the European Union. But the translation of institutions into local terms sometimes effaced elements of their meaning. 'Democracy', for example, was translated into Tetum as *biti boot* [big mat], referring to the woven grass mats on which elders sat when they discussed communal problems.[83] Like 'good governance', this is close to, but not identical with democracy. Chapter Four discussed some of the problems associated with the institutions of consultation and government established during the UNTAET period; here the emphasis is on the elections themselves.[84]

The actual voting in the 30 August 2001 elections went off with only a few minor hitches, contested by sixteen political parties and five independent candidates. There was a clear commitment to a peaceful vote, helped by Gusmão's statement a week earlier that he would run for president only if not a drop of blood was spilt. The turnout was high and calm. Voter education seemed to have been broadly successful, and most people seemed to understand the voting process. In

up to $1 billion); the withdrawal of UNPREDEP contributed to the outbreak of fighting in Macedonia in early 2001: see Jane's Sentinel Security Assessments, Macedonia (3 April 2001), available at www.janes.com.

[83] Hohe, 'Totem Polls', 78.

[84] See Chapter Four, Section 1.2.

particular, there was evidence of strategic voting. This was clearest in Aileu district, where the new Timorese Social Democratic Association (ASDT) was a popular party. In each district, voters could vote for a national and a district candidate; the national ballot was chosen by proportional representation, the district candidate by simple plurality. In Aileu, however, ASDT did not field a district candidate. The result was that in the national ballot from Aileu ASDT won 52 per cent of the vote. In the district vote, Fretilin won, but 40 per cent of the votes were spoiled (compared with 4–5 per cent of votes spoiled in other districts).

People appeared to know, then, how to vote, but not necessarily why. Civic education left a great deal to be desired: by January 2001 the United Nations had not run a single program of significance. Confusion about the vote was not simply a matter of education, however. A country of around 800,000 people was electing an eighty-eight-member constituent assembly, with the dual functions of coming up with a constitution and serving as a provisional legislature. These two functions are not necessarily compatible. Most obviously, while one might want a strong government to implement policy and push through legislation, a dominant party may be the last thing one wants when drafting a constitution.[85]

A senior Timorese official acknowledged that the population voted for party symbols in the constituent assembly. There was, naturally, strong support for the Fretilin flag, which many associated with the independence struggle. Others equated support for Fretilin with a kind of neutrality, not wishing to hear about other parties because they felt it was up to educated people to deal with politics.[86] Once constituent assembly representatives were chosen, however, it became apparent that many people did not know the individuals for whom they had voted—in particular, they did not realize that they were electing a sub-group of the diaspora (the 'Mozambique clique') to executive power.

Independence on 20 May 2002 concluded the most expansive assertion of sovereignty by the United Nations in its history—in addition to administering East Timor, passing laws, and overseeing the judiciary, UNTAET had negotiated treaties for the territory.[87] Even so, as discussed in Chapter Six, East Timor celebrated independence as the poorest country in the region. It faced a period of great economic instability at least until tax revenues from oil taken from the Timor Gap begin to accrue—estimated at up to $3 billion over seventeen

[85] See also Chapter Four, Section 1.2.2.

[86] See Hohe, 'Totem Polls', 74.

[87] See Chapter Two, Section 2.1.2.

years beginning in around 2006. There was also evidence of political instability. On 4 December 2002, riots in Dili left two dead and Prime Minister Marí Alkatiri's house burned to the ground. A month later, twenty or thirty men armed with automatic weapons attacked villages in the Ermera district, killing five. With UNMISET's consent, the Timorese Defence Force (Falintil-FDTL) was given temporary responsibility for the defence of the area, where they detained ninety people.[88]

The disturbances led to discussion about the possibility of delaying the drawdown of UN peacekeepers, though there was little enthusiasm for this on the part of the states contributing troops. Instead of an extension of the projected mandate, the speed of the drawdown was paused for 2003, keeping troop strength at just under 4,000. This would then be followed by an accelerated withdrawal in 2004 handing over defence responsibility to Falintil-FDTL on 20 May 2004.[89] In the absence of a riot control capacity within the Timor Leste Police Service (TLPS), it is expected that Falintil-FDTL will continue to be active in internal as well as external security. Some UNMISET officials worry that East Timor may now follow a path not dissimilar to Indonesia, where the military operates largely independent of civilian political control while on occasion playing a capricious role itself in government.

Through embracing formal processes that led to Fretilin's domination of the political landscape while endorsing the charismatic legitimacy of Gusmão, UNTAET sowed the seeds of a possible confrontation between Fretilin, which consolidated power in the institutions of government, and a president who commands the affection of the population and the loyalty of the military. It is not clear that this will force a choice between one-party rule and violent political confrontation,[90] but it is far from ideal as an exit strategy. After investing so much in East Timor, the United Nations and its member states have a considerable interest in remaining engaged to ensure that this was not an investment in a failed state.

4. *Conclusion*

Post-conflict elections carry a heavy burden. At a time of national crisis, they are called in order to settle issues of internal and external legitimacy—in many cases the very issues that took a country into

[88] Special Report of the Secretary-General on the UN Mission of Support in East Timor, UN Doc S/2003/243 (3 March 2003), paras. 6–8.

[89] Ibid., paras. 24–9.

[90] Cf. Hohe, 'Totem Polls', 85.

war—against a backdrop of insecurity, institutional breakdown, and economic uncertainty. These are not conditions that favour the introduction of democracy.[91] But democracy should not *be* the focus. Rather, the focus should be precisely on peace and security, sustainable institutions, and economic stability. Elections, then, may be part of an exit strategy, but they should not be the focal point of international involvement.[92]

Technical perfection is desirable but not essential—the turnout at Namibia's celebrated 1989 elections was 102.3 per cent.[93] If substantial numbers of people are unable to vote, or if there are significant irregularities, trouble may ensue. The problems that have accompanied internationally supervised elections, however, have derived from underlying political differences rather than disputes over the ballot as such. Greater attention needs to be paid to the strategic purposes that an election is intended to serve and how it relates to the other facets of the transition process. A central aim must be the demilitarization of politics. Perversely, elections held too early may in fact have the opposite effect, if democratic legitimacy is conferred on non-democratic actors.

In the Security Council debate on the 'No Exit Without a Strategy' report, US Ambassador Richard Holbrooke emphasized that exit strategies should not be confused with exit deadlines.[94] This points to the need for acting states to manage public opinion effectively. The US occupation of Iraq began in 2003 with claims that it would be limited in size and duration. These claims rested on assumptions that a small occupation force could co-opt most of the Iraqi bureaucracy and a significant amount of its security sector in order to ensure that the day-to-day running of Iraq could be handled by Iraqis, with the senior leadership 'decapitated' and replaced with Americans until agreeable Iraqis were found. When General Eric K. Shinseki, Chief of Staff of the US Army, testified to the Senate Armed Services Committee three weeks before the war commenced that 200,000 soldiers might be required for the post-war operation, he was criticized by the civilian leadership of the Defence Department as 'way off the mark' and saw

[91] See Lyons, 'Postsettlement Elections'.

[92] As Richard Caplan has argued, there should be a phased exit strategy that incorporates ongoing assistance to the territory and incentives for future 'good behaviour' (such as membership of regional organizations such as the European Union): Richard Caplan, *A New Trusteeship? The International Administration of War-Torn Territories* (Oxford: Oxford University Press, 2002), 61–4.

[93] Andrew Reynolds, *Electoral Systems and Democratization in Southern Africa* (Oxford: Oxford University Press, 1999), 38.

[94] Press Release, UN Doc SC/6951 (15 November 2000).

out the final months before his retirement under a cloud. Following the swift victory in Iraq, initial plans to begin withdrawing US troops had to be reversed in the face of lawlessness and violence. Shinseki's estimate began to look more credible and renewed calls were made to allies to support the peacebuilding process.[95]

State-building after a war will always take years, perhaps decades, and it is disingenuous to suggest otherwise to domestic publics. Elections and limited devolution notwithstanding, international actors will remain in Kosovo and Bosnia for the foreseeable future, certainly with a strong military presence and with at least a supervisory civilian authority. As Karl Popper recognized, the transition to democracy requires a transformation in public mentality similar to that which underpins respect for the rule of law.[96] Elections may provide evidence of this transformation, but they are only a small part of what is required to realize it.

[95] Vernon Loeb, 'Cost of War Remains Unanswered Question', *Washington Post*, 1 March 2003; Peter J. Boyer, 'The New War Machine', *New Yorker*, 30 June 2003, 55. See Chapter Two, Section 3.2.

[96] See above n. 1. On transformation and the rule of law, see Chapter Five, Section 5. Cf. Agenda for Democratization, para. 10: 'It is not for the United Nations to offer a model of democratization or democracy or to promote democracy in a specific case. Indeed, to do so could be counter-productive to the process of democratization which, in order to take root and to flourish, must derive from the society itself.'

8

'You, the People': The Future of State-Building

> The apparent ease of colonial administration generated in the inheritors of the post-colonial nation the illusion that control of the state would allow them to pursue as easily their much more ambitious objectives. 'Seek ye first the political kingdom,' Nkrumah famously urged. But that kingdom was designed to manage limited goals. Once it was turned to the tasks of massive developments in infrastructure... it proved unequal to the task. When the post-colonial rulers inherited the apparatus of the colonial state, they inherited the reins of power; few noticed, at first, that they were not attached to a bit.
>
> Kwame Anthony Appiah[1]

A measure of the speed with which the UN Interim Administration Mission in Kosovo was established is the name itself. UN operations typically operate under an acronym, but 'UNIAMIK' was dismissed as too much of a mouthful. 'UNIAK' sounded like a cross between 'eunuch' and 'maniac'—associations judged unlikely to help the mission. 'UNMIK' was the final choice, having the benefits of being short, punchy, and clear: only in English, however. Once the operation was on the ground, it was discovered that *anmik*, in the dialect of Albanian spoken in Kosovo, means 'enemy'. No one within the United Nations was aware of the confusion until it was too late, at which point instructions went out to pronounce the acronym 'oon-mik'.

The disjunction between politics as it happens in the minds of international administrators and politics as it happens on the ground has

[1] Kwame Anthony Appiah, *In My Father's House: Africa in the Philosophy of Culture* (New York: Oxford University Press, 1992), 266.

been a recurrent theme in this book, running from the varied ways in which 'ownership' is invoked to the very names of the operations.[2] Underlying discussion in the preceding chapters of the history of transitional administration and the issues of security, governance, justice, reconstruction, and exit strategies is a more fundamental question: whether the limited means available to the United Nations can and should be used to attempt such ambitious ends at all. This question raises a second one, concerning the uncertain status and limited capacities of the United Nations at a time when the United States has assumed a position of unchallenged dominance but is profoundly ambivalent about institutions of global order. Many operations have not only stood or fallen on the willingness of the United States to support them, but were established only after military engagements in which the United States played a decisive role. Since the participation of the United States is vital to the means and often determines the ends, how should its relationship to the United Nations be managed?

As Appiah suggests, the problems of decolonization prefigured many of the dilemmas that arise in the context of transitional administration. Political structures created for foreign control (benevolent or not) tend to be unsuited to local rule. The reason for this, in part, is that the 'limited goals' of foreign control (benevolent or not) are generally determined with limited regard to local circumstances. Nevertheless, although transitional administration is an inherently flawed enterprise that has, on occasion, been subverted to the foreign policy interests of Great Powers, there will be future situations in which there is demand to establish such operations. This final chapter examines the contradictions of transitional administration, the challenges and opportunities

[2] Local plays on the odd names chosen by international actors are common in the operations considered here, often with uncanny similarities to subversive forms of resistance to colonial occupation in earlier times. In Bosnia and Herzegovina, the peacekeeping operation was derided as UNSPROFOR—the UN *Self*-Protection Force—and President Clinton's desire to demonstrate progress on the eve of a US presidential election led to the OSCE becoming known locally as the Organization to Save Clinton's Election: Richard Caplan, *A New Trusteeship? The International Administration of War-Torn Territories* (Oxford: Oxford University Press, 2002), 40. President George W. Bush referred repeatedly to the war on terror as a 'crusade'; this language resonated in both Afghanistan and Iraq, where European Crusaders were known as 'Franks'—coincidentally the surname of the US General who commanded both battles. And in Iraq, the dysfunctional Office of Reconstruction and Humanitarian Assistance (ORHA) soon became known as 'HAHA': Michael Hirsh, 'Our New Civil War', *Newsweek*, 12 May 2003.

presented by US power, and the prospects for such operations in the future.

1. Contradictions of Transitional Administration

The UN missions sometimes referred to as complex peace operations bear a curious heritage. In the heady days of the early 1990s, traditional or 'first generation' peacekeeping, which was non-threatening and impartial, governed by the principles of consent and minimum force, was swiftly succeeded by two further generations. Second generation or 'multidimensional' peacekeeping was used to describe post-cold war operations in Cambodia, El Salvador, Mozambique, and Angola, but, retrospectively, might also have included the Congo operation in 1960–4. Third generation peacekeeping, sometimes called 'peace enforcement', operating under a chapter VII mandate, began with the Somalia operation. The genealogy was curious—the third generation appearing a mere six months after the second—but the terminology also misleadingly suggested a linear development in peacekeeping doctrine.[3] As Chapters Two and Three argued, evolution is a more appropriate metaphor than selective breeding, with essentially unpredictable events demanding new forms of missions and practice running well ahead of theory.

If military doctrine developed through natural selection, civil administration was a random mutation. The fact that such operations continue to be managed by the UN Department of Peacekeeping Operations is suggestive of the ad hoc approach that has characterized transitional administration, an historical accident perpetuated by the reluctance to embrace temporary governance of post-conflict territory as an appropriate and necessary task for the United Nations. This was evident in the Brahimi Report on UN Peace Operations, which noted the likely demand for such operations as well as the 'evident ambivalence' within governments and the UN Secretariat itself concerning the development of an institutional capacity to undertake them. Because of this ambivalence it was impossible to achieve any

[3] See, e.g. Marrack Goulding (1993) 'The Evolution of United Nations Peacekeeping', *International Affairs*, 69: 451; Michael W. Doyle, 'War-Making and Peace-Making: The United Nations' Post-Cold War Record', in Chester A. Crocker, Fen Osler Hampson, and Pamela Aall (eds.), *Turbulent Peace: The Challenges of Managing International Conflict* (Washington, DC: United States Institute of Peace Press, 2001), 529, 532–3.

consensus on recommendations, so the Department of Peacekeeping Operations continues to play the dominant supporting role.[4]

These doctrinal and operational concerns are valid, but have frequently overshadowed the more basic political problems confronting transitional administration. This section, therefore, returns to the three sets of contradictions raised in the Introduction. In different ways, each challenges the very idea of creating a legitimate and sustainable state through a period of benevolent autocracy: the means are inconsistent with the ends, they are frequently inadequate for those ends, and in many situations the means are irrelevant to the ends.

1.1. Inconsistent

UNMIK in Kosovo and the High Representative in Bosnia and Herzegovina govern through military occupation. In East Timor, the United Nations completed the task of decolonization that was abandoned by Portugal and interrupted by Indonesia. The fact that these powers have been exercised benevolently does not deprive them of their authoritarian character. More important than the benevolence of intention is the acceptance of the subject population that power is being exercised for ends that are both clear and achievable. The post-war experiences of Germany and Japan suggest that it is not impossible to create democracies through military occupation, but those operations were very different from more recent instances of transitional administration, with the possible exception of Iraq.[5] Decolonization may be a more fitting model, but there are valid concerns about embracing such language only half a century after one-third of the world's population lived under colonial rule.[6] Whatever euphemism is used, however, it is both inaccurate and counter-productive to assert that transitional administration depends upon the consent or 'ownership' of local populations. It is inaccurate because if genuine local control were possible then a transitional administration would not be necessary. It is counter-productive because insincere claims of local ownership lead to frustration and suspicion on the part of local actors.[7]

Clarity is central to the effective management of post-conflict reconstruction. Instead of institutional transformations, such as rejuvenating the Trusteeship Council or creating a new body to administer territories under the auspices of the United Nations,[8] a modest but important

[4] See Chapter Two, Section 1.2.
[5] See Chapter Two, Section 3.2.
[6] See Chapter One, Section 3.
[7] See Chapter Four.
[8] See Chapter Two, Section 1.2.

area of reform would be to require clarity in three key areas: as to the strategic objectives; as to the relationship between international and local actors and how this will change over time; and as to the commitment required of international actors in order to achieve objectives that warrant the temporary assumption of autocratic powers under a benevolent international administration. Structured discussion within the UN Security Council would be one way to achieve this, in the form of transitional administration committees, modelled on the sanctions committees that now routinely monitor the implementation, effects, and humanitarian impact of economic sanctions.[9]

In a case like East Timor, the strategic objective—independence—was both clear and uncontroversial. Frustration with the slow pace of reconstruction or the inefficiencies of the UN presence could generally be tempered by reference to the uncontested aim of independence and a timetable within which this was to be achieved. In Kosovo, failure to articulate a position on its final status inhibits the development of a mature political elite and deters foreign investment. The present ambiguity derives from a compromise that was brokered between the United States and Russia at the end of the NATO campaign against the Federal Republic of Yugoslavia in 1999, formalized in Security Council resolution 1244 (1999). Nevertheless, it is the United Nations itself that is now blamed for frustrating the aspirations of Kosovars for self-determination.[10]

Obfuscation of the political objective leads to ambiguity in the mandate. In a speech at the tenth anniversary of the Department of Peacekeeping Operations in 2002, Jacques Paul Klein, former Special Representative of the Secretary-General for the UN Transitional Administration for Eastern Slavonia (UNTAES), contrasted his own mandate with that governing international efforts to bring peace to Bosnia. The UN Protection Force (UNPROFOR) was governed by no less than seventy Security Council resolutions and dozens of Presidential statements. Political negotiating authority was divided between the United Nations, the European Union, and the Contact Group. The Dayton Peace Agreement had 150 pages, eleven Annexes, forty pages of Peace Implementation Council declarations, ninety-two post-accession criteria for membership of the Council of Europe, and a host of further agreements—most of which were never fulfilled.

> In contrast, the mandate of UNTAES contained just thirteen sentences that could be distilled into six quantifiable objectives... My point here is twofold: if you start out and don't know where you want to go, you will probably

[9] See Chapter Four, Section 2.3.

[10] See Chapter Seven, Section 3.2.

end up somewhere else. And secondly, the mandate is the floor (but not the ceiling) for everything the Mission does. If the mandate is vague for whatever reason—including the inability of Security Council members to agree on a political end state—dysfunction will plague the lifespan of the Mission.[11]

This echoed sentiments in the Brahimi Report applicable to peace operations generally.[12]

Niche mandate implementation by a proliferation of post-conflict actors further complicates the transition. More than five years after the Dayton Peace Agreement, a 'recalibration' exercise required the various international agencies present in Bosnia to perform an institutional audit to determine what, exactly, each of them did.[13] Subsidiary bodies and specialized agencies of the United Nations should in principle place their material and human resources at the direct disposal of the transitional administration: all activities should be oriented towards an agreed political goal, which should normally be legitimate and sustainable government.[14] Ideally, the unity of civilian authority should embrace command of the military also. In reality, the reluctance of the United States and other industrialized countries to put their troops under UN command makes this highly improbable. Coordination thus becomes more important, to avoid some of the difficulties encountered in civil–military relations in Afghanistan.[15]

Clarity in the relationship between international and local actors raises the question of ownership. As argued in Chapters Four and Six, this term is often used disingenuously—either to mask the assertion of potentially dictatorial powers by international actors or to carry a psychological rather than political meaning in the area of

[11] Jacques Paul Klein, 'What Does It Take to Make UN Peacekeeping Operations Succeed? Reflections from the Field' (New York: Paper presented at 10th Anniversary of the Department of Peacekeeping Operations, 29 October 2002).

[12] Report of the Panel on United Nations Peace Operations (Brahimi Report), UN Doc A/55/305–S/2000/809 (21 August 2000), available at www.un.org/peace/reports/peace_operations, para. 56: 'Rather than send an operation into danger with unclear instructions, the Panel urges that the Council refrain from mandating such a mission.' For an earlier argument along the same lines, see Marrack Goulding, 'Current Rapid Expansion Unsustainable Without Major Changes', in John Roper (ed.), *Keeping the Peace in the Post-Cold War Era: Strengthening Multilateral Peacekeeping* (New York: Trilateral Commission, 1993), 93, 101.

[13] International Crisis Group, Bosnia: Reshaping the International Machinery (Sarajevo/Brussels: ICG Balkans Report No 121, 29 November 2001), available at www.crisisweb.org, 13.

[14] See Chapter Seven.

[15] See Chapter Two, Section 3.1.

reconstruction.[16] Ownership in this context is usually not intended to mean control and often does not even imply a direct input into political questions. This is not to suggest that local control is a substitute for international administration. As the operation in Afghanistan demonstrates, a light footprint makes the success of an operation more than usually dependent on the political dynamic of local actors. Since the malevolence or collapse of that political dynamic is precisely the reason that power is arrogated to an international presence, the light footprint is unsustainable as a model for general application. How much power should be transferred and for how long depends upon the political transition that is required; this, in turn, is a function of the root causes of the conflict, the local capacity for change, and the degree of international commitment available to assist in bringing about that change.[17]

Local ownership, then, must be the end of a transitional administration, but it is not the means. Openness about the trustee-like relationship between international and local actors would help locals by ensuring transparency about the powers that they will exercise at various stages of the transition. But openness would also help the states that mandate and fund such operations by forcing acknowledgement of their true nature and the level of commitment that is needed in order to effect the transition that is required.

Clarifying the commitment necessary to bring about fundamental change in a conflict-prone territory is, however, a double-edged sword. It would ensure that political will exists prior to authorizing a transitional administration, but perhaps at the expense of other operations that would not be authorized at all. The mission in Bosnia was always expected to last beyond its nominal twelve-month deadline, but might not have been established if it had been envisaged that troops would remain on the ground for a full decade or more. Donors contemplating Afghanistan in November 2001 baulked at early estimates that called for a ten-year, $25 billion commitment to the country.[18] In the lead-up to the war with Iraq, the Chief of Staff of the US Army was similarly pooh-poohed by the leadership of the Defence Department when he testified to the Senate that 200,000 soldiers would be required for post-war duties.[19] Lack of political will already limits the choice of

[16] See Chapter Four, Section 1.3; Chapter Six, Section 2.

[17] Doyle, 'War-Making and Peace-Making', 546. See generally Chapter Two, Section 2.

[18] Bronwen Maddox, 'Trust Funds on Offer for the Other "Ground Zero"', *The Times* (London), 30 November 2001.

[19] See Chapter Seven, Section 4.

missions, however: not for lack of opportunity, no major transitional administration has been established in Africa, where the demands are probably greatest.[20]

Resolving the inconsistency between the means and the ends of transitional administration requires a clear-eyed recognition of the role of power. As argued in Chapters Four and Five, the collapse of formal state structures does not necessarily create a power vacuum; political life does not simply cease. Rather, power comes to be exercised through informal political and legal structures, complicating efforts to construct political institutions and to instantiate the rule of law. Constructive engagement with power on this local level requires both an understanding of culture and history as well as respect for the political aspirations of the population. Clarity will help here also: either the international presence exercises quasi-sovereign powers on a temporary basis or it does not. This clarity must exist at the formal level, but leaves much room for nuance in implementation. Most obviously, assertion of executive authority should be on a diminishing basis, with power devolved as appropriate to local institutions. This is not, therefore, an argument for unilateralism in the administration of post-conflict territories, but an argument for the transfer of power to be of more than symbolic value: once power is transferred to local hands, whether at the municipal or national level, local actors should be able to exercise that power meaningfully, constrained only by the rule of law. Unless and until genuine transfer is possible, consultation is appropriate but without the pretence that this is the same as control. In such situations, additional efforts should be made to cultivate civil society organizations such as local non-governmental organizations (NGOs), which can provide a legitimate focus for the political activities of the local population and lobby international actors. Where international actors do not exercise sovereign power—because of the size of the territory, the complexity of the conflict, or a simple lack of political will—this is not the same as exercising no power at all. Certain functions may be delegated to the international presence, as they were in Cambodia and Afghanistan, and international actors will continue to exercise considerable behind-the-scenes influence either because of ongoing responsibilities in a peace process or as a gatekeeper to international development assistance. In either case, the abiding need is for clarity as to who is in charge and, equally important, who is *going* to be in charge.

[20] See Chapter Two, Section 2.5.

1.2. Inadequate

Speaking in Cincinnati, Ohio, on 7 October 2002, US President George W. Bush made one of his strongest early statements concerning the threat that Iraq posed to the United States. In the course of his speech, he also alluded to the aftermath of war, stating that the lives of Iraqi citizens would 'improve dramatically if Saddam Hussein were no longer in power, just as the lives of Afghanistan's citizens improved after the Taliban'.[21] Ten months after the Bonn Agreement, Afghanistan was hardly a success story—Bush's remarks could equally have been intended as an optimistic assessment of that troubled mission, or a pessimistic downplaying of expectations for what might follow the impending war with Iraq.

The ephemeral nature of international interest in post-conflict operations is a cliché, exacerbating the inefficiencies described in Chapter Six. When the United States overthrew the Taliban regime in Afghanistan, Bush likened the commitment to rebuild the devastated country to the Marshall Plan.[22] Just over twelve months later, in February 2003, the White House apparently forgot to include *any* money for reconstruction in the 2004 budget that it submitted to Congress. Legislators reallocated $300 million in aid to cover the oversight.[23] Such oversights are disturbingly common: much of the aid that is pledged either arrives late or not at all. This demands a measure of artificiality in drafting budgets for reconstruction, which in turn leads to suspicion on the part of donors—sometimes further delaying the disbursement of funds.[24] The problem is not simply one of volume: Bosnia has received more per capita assistance than Europe did under the Marshall Plan, but the incoherence of funding programmes, the lack of a regional approach, and the inadequacy of state and entity institutions have contributed to it remaining in financial crisis.[25]

[21] George W. Bush, 'President Bush Outlines Iraqi Threat' (Cincinnati, Ohio, 7 October 2002), available at www.whitehouse.gov.

[22] See Chapter One, Section 2.3.

[23] Paul Krugman, 'The Martial Plan', *New York Times*, 21 February 2003; James G. Lakely, 'Levin Criticizes Budget for Afghanistan; Says White House Isn't Devoting Enough to Rebuilding', *Washington Times*, 26 February 2003. Aid was later increased further: David Rohde, 'US Said to Plan Bigger Afghan Effort, Stepping Up Aid', *New York Times*, 25 August 2003.

[24] See Chapter Six, Section 1.2.

[25] See, e.g. International Crisis Group, Bosnia's Precarious Economy: Still Not Open for Business (Sarajevo/Brussels: ICG Balkans Report No 115, 7 August 2001), available at www.crisisweb.org.

Many of these problems would be reduced if donors replaced the system of voluntary funding for relief and reconstruction for transitional administrations with assessed contributions, which presently fund peacekeeping operations. The distinction between funds supporting a peacekeeping operation and those providing assistance to a government makes sense when there is some form of indigenous government, but is arbitrary in situations where the peacekeeping operation *is* the government.[26] Given existing strains on the peacekeeping budget, however, such a change is unlikely. A more realistic proposal would be to pool voluntary contributions through a trust fund, ideally coordinated by local actors or a mixed body of local and international personnel, perhaps also drawing upon private sector expertise. Even more modest proposals along these lines have faced stiff resistance from the larger donors—in part due to concerns about accountability and additional red tape, in part due to fears that this would remove the discretion to direct funds to projects that are more popular at home than they are necessary abroad. At the very least, a monitoring mechanism to track aid flows would help to ensure that money that is promised at the highpoint of international attention to a crisis is, in fact, delivered and spent.[27]

Parsimony of treasure is surpassed by the reluctance to expend blood in policing post-conflict territories. In the absence of security, however, meaningful political change in a post-conflict territory is next to impossible. Unless and until the United Nations develops a rapidly deployable civilian police capacity, either military tasks in a post-conflict environment will include basic law and order functions or these functions will not be performed at all. The military—especially the US military—is understandably reluctant to embrace duties that are outside its field of expertise, but as Chapter Three showed this is symptomatic of an anachronistic view of UN peace operations. The dichotomy between peacekeeping and enforcement actions was always artificial, but in the context of internal armed conflict where large numbers of civilians are at risk it becomes untenable.[28] Moreover, as most transitional administrations have followed conflicts initiated under the auspices or in the name of the United Nations, inaction is not the same as non-interference—once military operations commence, external actors have already begun a process of political transformation on

[26] See Chapter Six, Section 1.3.

[27] See Chapter Six, Section 4. For a discussion of the proposal that Iraqi oil revenues fund the US military occupation, see Chapter Two, Section 3.2.

[28] See Chapter Three, Section 1.

the ground. And, as the Independent Inquiry on Rwanda concluded, whether or not a peace operation has a mandate or the will to protect civilians, its very presence creates an expectation that it will do so.[29]

A key argument in the Brahimi Report was that missions with uncertain mandates or inadequate resources should not be created at all:

> Although presenting and justifying planning estimates according to high operational standards might reduce the likelihood of an operation going forward, Member States must not be led to believe that they are doing something useful for countries in trouble when—by under-resourcing missions—they are more likely agreeing to a waste of human resources, time and money.[30]

Applied to transitional administration, this view finds some support in the report of the International Commission on Intervention and State Sovereignty, *The Responsibility to Protect*, which calls for the 'responsibility to rebuild' to be seen as an integral part of any intervention. When an intervention is contemplated, a post-intervention strategy is both an operational necessity and an ethical imperative.[31] There is some evidence of this principle now achieving at least rhetorical acceptance—despite his aversion to 'nation-building', Bush stressed before and during operations in Afghanistan and Iraq that the United States would help in reconstructing the territories in which it had intervened.[32]

More than rhetoric is required. Success in state-building, in addition to clarity of purpose, requires time and money. A lengthy international presence will not ensure success, but an early departure guarantees failure. Similarly, an abundance of resources will not make up for the lack of a coherent strategy—but the fact that Kosovo has been the recipient of twenty-five times more money and fifty times more troops, on a per capita basis, than Afghanistan goes some way towards explaining the modest achievements in developing democratic institutions and the economy.[33]

[29] See Chapter Three, Section 3.

[30] Brahimi Report, para. 59.

[31] International Commission on Intervention and State Sovereignty, The Responsibility to Protect (Ottawa: International Development Research Centre, December 2001), available at www.iciss.gc.ca, paras. 2.32, 5.1–5.6.

[32] See Section 2.1 in this chapter.

[33] See James Dobbins et al., *America's Role in Nation-Building: From Germany to Iraq* (Santa Monica, CA: RAND, 2003), 160–6.

1.3. Irrelevant

The irrelevance of available means to desired ends presents the opposite problem to that of the inadequacy of resources. While the question of limited resources—money, personnel, and international attention—depresses the standards against which a post-conflict operation can be judged, artificially high international expectations may nevertheless be imposed in certain areas of governance. Particularly when the United Nations itself assumes a governing role, there is a temptation to demand the highest standards of democracy, human rights, the rule of law, and the provision of services.

Balancing these against the need for locally sustainable goals presents difficult problems. A computerized electoral registration system may be manifestly ill-suited to a county with a low level of literacy and intermittent electricity, but should an international NGO refrain from opening a world-class clinic if such levels of care are unsustainable? An abrupt drop from high levels of care once the crisis and international interest passes would be disruptive, but lowering standards early implies acceptance that people who might otherwise have been treated will suffer. This was the dilemma faced by the International Committee of the Red Cross, which transferred control of the Dili National Hospital to national authorities in East Timor almost a year before independence.[34]

Although most acute in areas such as health, the issue arises in many aspects of transitional administration. In the best tradition of autocracies, Bosnia and Kosovo subscribed to the vast majority of human rights treaties and then discovered *raisons d'Etat* that required these to be abrogated.[35] Efforts to promote the rule of law tend to focus more on the prosecution of the highest profile crimes of the recent past than on developing institutions to manage criminal law in the near future.[36] Humanitarian and development assistance is notorious for being driven more by supply than demand, with the result that those projects that are funded tend to represent the interests—and, frequently, the products and personnel—of donors rather than recipients.[37] Finally, staging elections in conflict zones has become

[34] Lise Boudreault, 'Official Handover Speech Given by ICRC East Timor Head of Delegation' (Dili, East Timor, 29 June 2001); Report of the Secretary-General on the United Nations Transitional Administration in East Timor (for the period from 25 July to 15 October 2001), UN Doc S/2001/983 (18 October 2001), paras. 53–4.

[35] See Chapter Four.

[36] See Chapter Five.

[37] See Chapter Six.

something of an art-form, though East Timor's elections ushered in a one-party state and more than half a dozen elections in Bosnia have yet to produce a workable government.[38]

Different issues arise in the area of human resources. Staffing such operations always takes place in an atmosphere of crisis, but personnel tend to be selected from a limited pool of applicants (most of them internal) whose skills may be irrelevant to the tasks at hand. In East Timor, for example, it would have made sense to approach Portuguese-speaking governments to request that staff with experience in public administration be seconded to the UN mission. Instead, it was not even possible to require Portuguese (or Tetum or Bahasa Indonesia) as a language. Positions are often awarded for political reasons or simply to ensure that staff lists are full—once in place, there is no effective mechanism to assess an individual's suitability or to remove him or her quickly if this proves warranted. A separate problem is the assumption that international staff who do possess relevant skills are also able to train others in the same field. This is an entirely different skill, however, and simply pairing international and local staff tends to provide less on-the-job training than extended opportunities to stand around and watch—a problem exacerbated by the fact that English tends to be used as the working language.[39] One element of the 'light footprint' approach that is certainly of general application is the need to justify every post occupied by international staff rather than a local. Cultivating relations with diaspora communities may help address this problem, serving the dual function of recruiting culturally aware staff and encouraging the return of skilled expatriates more generally.[40]

The 'can-do' attitude of many people within the UN system is one of the most positive qualities that staff bring to a mission. If the problem is getting a hundred tonnes of rice to ten thousand starving refugees, niceties of procedure are less important than getting the job done. When the problem is governing a territory, however, procedure is more important. In such circumstances, the 'can-do' attitude may become a cavalier disregard for local sensibilities. Moreover, many staff in such situations are not used to criticism from the population that they are 'helping', with some regarding it as a form of ingratitude. Where the United Nations assumes the role of government, it should expect and welcome criticism appropriate to that of the sort of political environment it hopes to foster. Security issues may require limits on this,

38 See Chapter Seven.

39 See Chapter Four, Section 1.3.

40 See generally Charles King and Neil J. Melvin (1999) 'Diaspora Politics', *International Security*, 24(3): 108.

but a central element in the development of local political capacity is encouraging discussion among local actors about what sort of country theirs is going to be.

2. State-Building and Empire

The primary barrier to establishing transitional administration-type operations in areas such as Somalia, Western Sahara, and the Democratic Republic of the Congo has less to do with the difficulty of such operations than with the absence of political will to commit resources to undertake them. The 'war on terror' has transformed this agenda, though triage is performed less according to need than to the strategic priorities of the dominant actors, most prominently the United States. Though the operations in Afghanistan and Iraq are not transitional administrations as understood in this book, they are suggestive of how the state-building agenda has changed.

In the course of the US-led intervention in Afghanistan in late 2001—in particular, as the likelihood of capturing Osama bin Laden 'dead or alive' diminished—a rhetorical shift became evident in the Bush administration's war aims. 'Nation-building',[41] something that Bush had previously derided as inappropriate for the US military, came back onto the US agenda. And, with increasing frequency, the Taliban regime and its mistreatment of the Afghan civilian population were presented as the real evil, rather than being ancillary to the man and the organization that attacked the United States on 11 September 2001. These developments highlighted the changing strategic and political environment within which state-building takes place. The proximate cause was the adoption of state-building as a tool in the 'war on terror', but underlying this was an emerging view that the United States should be more ready to use its power in the world.

2.1. Nation-Building and the National Interest

During the 2000 US presidential campaign, candidate Bush was openly critical of the use of US military resources for nation-building purposes. He affirmed this position once in office, including statements in July 2001 stressing that the United States military 'should be used to fight and win war'.[42] Bush made similar comments in the weeks

[41] The term 'state-building' is preferred in this book. On the distinction between the two concepts, see the Introduction, text accompanying n. 8–9.

[42] George W. Bush, 'Remarks by the President in Roundtable Interview with Foreign Press' (Washington, DC, 17 July 2001), available at www.whitehouse.gov.

after the 11 September 2001 attacks, when he stated that 'we're not into nation-building, we're focused on justice'.[43] Days before the United States commenced military operations in Afghanistan, however, the President's spokesman marked a slight shift in position as it became apparent that international support for the impending conflict might depend on the broader consequences for the Afghan people: the United States had no intention of engaging in nation-building, but it would 'help those who seek a peaceful, economically-developing Afghanistan that's free from terrorism'.[44] This was elaborated by the President himself in a news conference after the military action had begun, including a more substantial role for the United Nations in rebuilding Afghanistan:

> I believe that the *United Nations* would—could provide the framework necessary to help meet those conditions. It would be a useful function for the United Nations to take over the so-called 'nation-building'—I would call it the stabilization of a future government—after our military mission is complete. We'll participate; other countries will participate... I've talked to many countries that are interested in making sure that the post-operations Afghanistan is one that is stable, and one that doesn't become yet again a haven for terrorist criminals.[45]

The US war aims thus evolved from a retributive strike, to a defensive response, and finally to embrace the broader goals of ensuring the stability of post-conflict Afghanistan. As the war aims changed, so, with the benefit of hindsight, did the asserted motivation for US military operations in the first place. This appeared to be a carefully scripted shift, as shown in two important speeches by Bush. Speaking to the United Nations in November 2001, he equated the Taliban regime with the terrorists who had attacked the United States: the regime and the terrorists were 'virtually indistinguishable. Together they promote terror abroad and impose a reign of terror on the Afghan people. Women are executed in Kabal's [*sic*] soccer stadium. They can be beaten for wearing socks that are too thin. Men are jailed for missing prayer meetings. The United States, supported by many nations, is bringing justice to the terrorists in Afghanistan.'[46] Then, in his 2002 State

[43] George W. Bush, 'Remarks by President Bush and Prime Minister Koizumi of Japan in Photo Opportunity' (Washington, DC, 25 September 2001), available at www.whitehouse.gov.

[44] Ari Fleischer, 'Press Briefing' (Washington, DC, 4 October 2001), available at www.whitehouse.gov.

[45] George W. Bush, 'President Holds Prime Time News Conference' (Washington, DC, 11 October 2001), available at www.whitehouse.gov.

[46] George W. Bush, 'Remarks by the President to United Nations General Assembly' (New York, 10 November 2001), available at www.whitehouse.gov.

of the Union Address, Bush sought to expand this into a more general doctrine intimating that the US action stemmed from goals loftier than self-defence:

> We have no intention of imposing our culture. But America will always stand firm for the non-negotiable demands of human dignity: the rule of law; limits on the power of the state; respect for women; private property; free speech; equal justice; and religious tolerance. America will take the side of brave men and women who advocate these values around the world, including the Islamic world, because we have a greater objective than eliminating threats and containing resentment. We seek a just and peaceful world beyond the war on terror.[47]

One year after the 11 September 2001 attacks, nation-building was implicitly included in the National Security Strategy issued by the White House. Much of the document elaborated and justified the concept of pre-emptive intervention; together with the stated policy of dissuading potential adversaries from hoping to equal the power of the United States, it implicitly asserted a unique status for the United States as existing outside of international law as it applies to other states.[48] At the same time, however, the National Security Strategy noted that threats to the United States now came not from fleets and armies but from 'catastrophic technologies in the hands of the embittered few'. In such a world, failing states pose a greater menace to US interests than conquering ones.[49]

The transformed strategic environment presents both opportunities and dangers for state-building. Recognition that weak states can create threats that reach beyond their borders may increase the level of international interest in supporting those states, indirectly providing benefits to the populations. This argument has been made, for example, to encourage intervention for human protection purposes in Liberia

Cf. Thomas M. Franck (2001) 'Terrorism and the Rights of Self-Defense', *American Journal of International Law*, 95: 839.

[47] George W. Bush, 'State of the Union Address' (Washington, DC, 29 January 2002), available at www.whitehouse.gov.

[48] The National Security Strategy of the United States of America (Washington, DC: President of the United States, September 2002), available at www.whitehouse.gov/nsc/nss.html. Cf. the draft Defense Planning Guidance leaked in 1992: 'Excerpts from Pentagon's Plan: "Prevent the Re-Emergence of a New Rival"', *New York Times*, 8 March 1992. The 1992 document was drafted by Paul D. Wolfowitz, then Under-Secretary of Defense for Policy and later Deputy Secretary of Defense under President George W. Bush, for approval by Dick Cheney, Secretary of Defense in 1992 and later Vice-President. Criticism of its unilateralist message led to a substantial redrafting.

[49] National Security Strategy, 1.

by the United States and in the South Pacific by Australia, although in both cases the link with terrorism was tenuous.[50] The connection was also made in the National Security Strategy, which stressed that when violence erupts and states falter, the United States will 'work with friends and partners to alleviate suffering and restore stability'.[51] When interventions are justified by the national interest, however, this may lower the standards against which post-conflict reconstruction is held. The level of physical and economic security required in Afghanistan to prevent it becoming a terrorist haven, for example, is not the same as that required for the basic peace and prosperity of the general population. This was reflected in the methods used by the United States to pursue its objectives in Afghanistan: by minimizing the use of its own troops in favour of using Afghan proxies, more weapons were introduced into a country that was already heavily armed, empowering groups that fought on the side of the United States—whether or not they supported the embryonic regime of Hamid Karzai. Many Afghans saw these power relations as reinforced by the Emergency Loya Jirga in June 2002, which appeared to show that the position of warlords and other local commanders would not be challenged by international actors.[52]

None of this, of course, is new. Coercive diplomacy, the use of force, and military occupation have long been used by powerful states to further their interests; claims that occupation serves noble motives have an equally long pedigree.[53] As Chapter One noted, what is relatively new is the rejection of colonization as an element of foreign policy

[50] See, e.g. Augustine Toure, 'Liberia: Why Doing Too Little May Hurt US Long-term Interest', *New Democrat* (Heerlen), 16 July 2003; Elsina Wainwright, Our Failing Neighbour: Australia and the Future of Solomon Islands (Canberra: Australian Strategic Policy Institute, June 2003), available at www.aspi.org.au, 14.

[51] National Security Strategy, 9.

[52] Chris Johnson et al., Afghanistan's Political and Constitutional Development (London: Overseas Development Institute, January 2003), available at www.odi.org.uk/hpg. See Chapter Two, Section 3.1.

[53] See, e.g. Jean Pictet (ed.), *Convention Relative to the Protection of Civilian Persons in Time of War (Fourth Geneva Convention): Commentary* (Geneva: International Committee of the Red Cross, 1958), available at www.icrc.org/ihl, art. 47: 'During the Second World War Occupying Powers intervened in the occupied countries on numerous occasions and in a great variety of ways, depending on the political aim pursued... Of course the Occupying Power usually tried to give some colour of legality and independence to the new organizations, which were formed in the majority of cases with the co-operation of certain elements among the population of the occupied country, but it was obvious that they were in fact always subservient to the will of the Occupying Power.'

from around the middle of the twentieth century. Modern sensibilities therefore prevent explicit reference to occupation or colonization as a model for transitional administration, a constraint that at times prevents the learning of valuable lessons from decolonization in particular.[54] There is a danger, however, that strategic interests may now begin to erode this prohibition in favour of a greater preparedness not merely to intervene, but to occupy and transform other states along the models of Afghanistan and Iraq. Such a development would be undesirable in principle, as it forms part of a broader attack on international law that proposes to order the world not around norms and institutions but the benevolent goodwill of the United States.[55] And yet it would also be undesirable in practice, as it is far from clear that the United States is either willing or able to fulfil such a role.

2.2. *The Indispensable Nation*

In debates within the United Nations and elsewhere, much attention has been focused on the unwillingness of the United States to engage in state-building. But there is also some evidence that the United States is not well-suited to such activities. The importance of domestic politics in the exercise of US power means that it has an exceptionally short attention span—far shorter than is needed to complete the long and complicated task of rebuilding countries that have seen years or decades of war, economic ostracism, and oppression under brutal leaders. More importantly, when the United States has assumed state-building responsibilities in Afghanistan and Iraq, it was justified at home as an element of the war on terror. This was reflected in the strategies adopted in each case, with military priorities ranking well above political goals for either country.

The United States is not alone in suffering from foreign policy 'attention deficit disorder', but its hegemonic position and global footprint increase the significance of this condition. The United States spends more on its defence budget than the next fifteen countries combined, it is the only country with five military commands spanning the entire planet, and it is unrivalled in its capacity to move troops and hardware.[56] A blessing and a curse of the present age is that the United States is an imperial power but gives the appearance of being unaware of this.

[54] See Chapter One, Section 4.

[55] See, e.g. Richard Perle, 'Thank God for the Death of the UN', *Guardian* (London), 21 March 2003.

[56] See James Fallows, 'The Military-Industrial Complex', *Foreign Policy*, November–December 2002, 34.

It is a blessing because, despite fierce opposition to any constraints on US power, the United States remains a relatively benevolent power that generally refrains from arbitrary interference in the affairs of other states. But it is a curse because, by holding others in its thrall yet refraining from acting itself, its wariness of foreign entanglements leads to absent-minded engagement with an empire that it does not tend.[57] If a major lesson for the United Nations is to accept the contradictions between the means and the ends of transitional administration, the greatest danger concerning the United States is that it will focus only on the means: where the United Nations cannot see transitional administration as military occupation, the United States sometimes appears unable to see them as anything else.

Should this be the beginning of an American empire, then, it promises to be different from those that came before it. The English historian Simon Schama illustrates this by contrasting the imperial grandiloquence of George Nathaniel Curzon, Viceroy of India from 1898–1905, with that of retired US General Jay Garner, pro-consul of Iraq for four weeks in 2003. In a speech in London 1904, Curzon exhorted the British public not to imagine that either their presence or their legacy in India would have an end: 'To me the message is carved in granite, it is hewn out of the rock of doom—that our work is righteous and that it shall endure.'[58] Here is Garner a century later on the prospects for US imperium in Iraq: 'If we make headway on a lot of major things, we will put ourselves in a marvellous up-ramp where things can begin happening. If we don't do that, we're on a negative ramp.'[59] The dress code of empire has also gone downhill. Meeting with the Emir of Afghanistan in 1894, Curzon hired his uniform from a theatrical costumier, replete with gold epaulettes and various foreign decorations; to this he added a pair of patent leather boots and a gigantic curved sword borrowed from the Commander-in-Chief in India.[60] Garner, by contrast, wandered about the ruins of Baghdad in something closer to a scoutmaster's uniform. Garner's replacement, L. Paul Bremer III, replaced dress-down-Friday casuals with the battledress of the CEO—'crisply pressed suit, high-end haircut, peekaboo breast-pocket handkerchief—to project an air of mildly corporate persuasiveness, just the right note for an empire that

[57] Cf. Richard Haass, *The Reluctant Sheriff: The United States After the Cold War* (New York: Council on Foreign Relations, 1997).

[58] David Gilmour, *Curzon* (London: J. Murray, 1994), 285.

[59] Eric Schmitt and David E. Sanger, 'Looting Disrupts Detailed US Plan to Restore Iraq', *New York Times*, 19 May 2003.

[60] Gilmour, *Curzon*, 97–9.

fancies it can be run like a business opportunity'.[61] The differences go beyond style, of course: few empires have overseen subjects begging for the supply of basic law and order, as was the case in both Iraq and Afghanistan.

Reference to US imperialism, which increased exponentially with the invasions of Afghanistan and Iraq, was common during the years of the Vietnam War. What is different in its contemporary manifestation is that the discussion is often neither hostile nor apologetic—indeed, a common criticism of the perceived US Empire is that it does not exercise its power sufficiently. Michael Ignatieff has termed this phenomenon 'Empire Lite', though it bears similarities to the British policies of indirect rule.[62] Whereas indirect rule was developed in part out of weakness, however (notably the practical impossibility of administering Nigeria[63]), US imperial ambivalence derives in equal part from its democratic traditions, its isolationist tendencies, and its adherence to anti-colonial norms that it helped to establish.[64] The potential for a US imperium is also constrained by the changed nature of how power is exercised: US military power may be unrivalled, but its economic strength is not. Both economically and culturally, the United States has greater influence than any other state, but that influence depends upon a free flow of capital and ideas that would be undermined by extensive reliance upon military might.[65]

This may change. How the United States manages its de facto empire and the choices that it makes between unilateral and multilateral responses to problems that are increasingly global will determine much of twenty-first-century history. Machiavelli advised his Prince that it was better to be feared than loved, but this was only because it was difficult to unite both qualities in one person.[66] It is perhaps a uniquely American notion that countries inferior in power to the United States should not resent their subordinate status—that, if it is nice enough,

61 Simon Schama, 'Curzon in India', *New Yorker*, 9 June 2003, 98.

62 Michael Ignatieff, *Empire Lite: Nation Building in Bosnia, Kosovo, Afghanistan* (London: Minerva, 2003). See generally Niall Ferguson, *Empire: The Rise and Demise of the British World Order and the Lessons for Global Power* (New York: Basic Books, 2003).

63 See, e.g. F. D. Lugard, *The Dual Mandate in British Tropical Africa*, 3rd edn. (Edinburgh and London: W. Blackwood & Sons, 1926); Ntieyong U. Akpan, *Epitaph to Indirect Rule: A Discourse on Local Government in Africa* (London: Cassell, 1956).

64 See Chapter One, Section 3.

65 See generally Joseph S. Nye, *The Paradox of American Power: Why the World's Only Superpower Can't Go It Alone* (Oxford: Oxford University Press, 2002).

66 Niccolò Machiavelli, *The Prince and the Discourses* [1531], translated by Christian E. Detmold (New York: Modern Library, 1950), ch. xvii.

Washington might construct a benevolent empire in which all love it.[67] Afghanistan and Iraq may serve as proving grounds for this vision.

3. Conclusion

> Above all we must remember that the ways of Orientals are not our ways, nor their thoughts our thoughts. Often when we think them backward and stupid, they think us meddlesome and absurd. The loom of time moves slowly with them, and they care not for high pressure and the roaring of the wheels. Our system may be good for us; but it is neither equally, nor altogether good for them. Satan found it better to reign in hell than to serve in heaven; and the normal Asiatic would sooner be misgoverned by Asiatics than well governed by Europeans. (George Nathaniel Curzon)[68]

Just as generals are sometimes accused of planning to refight their last war, so the United Nations experiments in transitional administration have reflected only gradual learning. Senior UN officials now acknowledge that, to varying degrees, Kosovo got the operation that should have been planned for Bosnia four years earlier, and East Timor got that which should have been sent to Kosovo. Afghanistan's very different 'light footprint' approach draws, in turn, upon the outlines of what Lakhdar Brahimi argued would have been appropriate for East Timor in 1999.

The United Nations may never again be called upon to repeat operations comparable to Kosovo and East Timor, where it exercised sovereign powers on a temporary basis. Even so, it is certain that the circumstances that demanded such interventions will recur. Lessons derived from past experiences of transitional administration will be applicable whenever the United Nations or other international actors engage in complex peace operations that include a policing function, civilian administration, development of the rule of law, establishment of a national economy, the staging of elections, or all of the above. Learning from such lessons has not, however, been one of the strengths of the United Nations. A senior Secretariat official describes this as an unwritten rule that 'no wheel shall go un-reinvented'.[69]

67 Stephen Peter Rosen (2003) 'An Empire, If You Can Keep It', *The National Interest*, 71: 51.

68 George N. Curzon, *Persia and the Persian Question*, vol. 2 (London: Frank Cass, 1966), 630.

69 Alvaro de Soto, interview with the author, New York, 12 August 2003. Alvaro de Soto is Special Representative of the Secretary-General for Western Sahara at the rank of Under-Secretary-General.

Even more important than learning from past mistakes, however, is learning about future circumstances. Curzon's observations from his 1889 trip to Persia on 'the ways of Orientals' were insightful but uncharacteristic. As Viceroy of India, he did not appoint a single Indian to his advisory council; when asked why, he replied, absurdly, that in the entire country there was not an Indian fit for the post.[70] Modern trusteeships demand, above all, trust on the part of local actors. Earning and keeping that trust requires a level of understanding, sensitivity, and respect for local traditions and political aspirations that has often been lacking in transitional administration. How that trust is managed will, in large part, determine its legacy.

The title of this book, *You, the People*, points to the tension between the ends of liberal democracy and the means of benevolent autocracy. As the autocratic New York builder Robert Moses was fond of saying, however, 'If the ends don't justify the means, what does?'[71] Transitional administration will remain an exceptional activity, performed on an ad hoc basis in a climate of institutional and political uncertainty. But in those rare situations in which the United Nations and other international actors are called upon to exercise state-like functions, they must not lose sight of their limited mandate to hold that sovereign power in trust for the population that will ultimately claim it.

[70] Gilmour, *Curzon*, 168.

[71] Robert A. Caro, *The Power Broker: Robert Moses and the Fall of New York* (New York: Knopf, 1974).

Appendix

Table A.1. Peace Operations with Civilian Administration Functions

Territory	Mission	Date	Head of mission	Primary responsibility for police?	Primary responsibility for referendum?	Primary responsibility for elections?	Executive power?	Legislative power?	Judicial power?	Treaty power?
Congo	ONUC	1960–1964	Special representative of the Secretary-General (SRSG)	De facto in limited areas			De facto in limited areas			
West Papua	UNTEA	1962–1963	Secretary-General's Representative and Temporary Administrator	Yes		Regional elections only	Yes	Limited		
Namibia	UNTAG	1989–1990	SRSG			Yes				De facto (Council for Namibia)
Western Sahara	MINURSO	1991–	SRSG		Yes					
Cambodia	UNTAC	1992–1993	SRSG	Yes		Yes	As necessary			
Somalia	UNOSOM II	1993–1995	SRSG					Disputed		
Bosnia and Herzegovina (a)	Office of the High Representative (before Bonn powers)[a]	1995–1997	High Representative			Yes (OSCE)				

Bosnia and Herzegov-ina (b)	Office of the High Representative (after Bonn powers)[a]	1997–	High Representative			Yes (OSCE)	De facto			
Bosnia and Herzegovina (c)	UNMIBH	1995–2002	SRSG	De facto						
Eastern Slavonia (Croatia)	UNTAES	1996–1998	SRSG and Transitional Administrator	Yes		Yes	Yes			
East Timor (a)	UNAMET	1999	SRSG and Transitional Administrator		Yes					
Sierra Leone	UNAMSIL	1999–	SRSG	De facto					Limited (Special Court)	
Kosovo (Federal Republic of Yugoslavia/ Serbia and Montenegro)	UNMIK	1999–	SRSG	Yes		Yes (OSCE)	Yes	Yes	Yes	
East Timor (b)	UNTAET	1999–	SRSG and Transitional Administrator	Yes		Yes	Yes	Yes	Yes	De facto
Afghanistan	UNAMA	2002–	SRSG							
Iraq (a)	Coalition Provisional Authority[a]	2003–	US Presidential Envoy to Iraq	As occupying power		Unclear	As occupying power	Limited	Limited	
Iraq (b)	UNAMI	2003–	SRSG							

[a]Not a UN operation.

Bibliography

1. *Treaties*

Convention (IV) Respecting the Laws and Customs of War on Land and Its Annex: Regulations Concerning the Laws and Customs of War on Land (1907 Hague Regulations), done at The Hague, 18 October 1907, available at www.icrc.org/ihl.

Treaty of Peace, done at Versailles, 28 June 1919, 2 Bevans 43, available at www.yale.edu/lawweb/avalon/imt/menu.htm.

Treaty of Rapallo, Kingdom of the Serbs, Croats, and Slovenes–Italy, done at Rapallo, 12 November 1920, 18 LNTS 388.

Treaty Between Colombia and Peru Regarding Frontiers and Free Inland Navigation, done at Lima, 24 March 1922, 74 LNTS 13.

Convention Concerning Upper Silesia, Germany–Poland, done at Geneva, 15 May 1922, 9 LNTS 466.

Convention Concerning the Territory of Memel, France–Italy–Japan–Lithuania–United Kingdom, done at Paris, 8 May 1924, 29 LNTS 87.

Agreement Relating to the Procedure for Putting into Effect the Recommendations Proposed by the Council of the League of Nations, Peru–Colombia, done at Geneva, 25 May 1933, 138 LNTS 253.

Protocol of Friendship and Co-operation, Colombia–Peru, done at Rio de Janeiro, 24 May 1934, 164 LNTS 21.

Atlantic Charter, United Kingdom–United States, 14 August 1941, available at www.yale.edu/lawweb/avalon/wwii/atlantic.htm.

Declaration by United Nations, done at Washington, DC, 1 January 1942, available at www.yale.edu/lawweb/avalon/decade/decade03.htm.

Moscow Declaration, Republic of China–Soviet Union–United Kingdom–United States, done at Moscow, October 1943, available at www.yale.edu/lawweb/avalon/wwii/moscow.htm.

Protocol on Zones of Occupation in Germany and the Administration of 'Greater Berlin', Soviet Union–United Kingdom–United States, done at London, 12 September 1944.

Agreement on Control Machinery in Germany, Soviet Union–United Kingdom–United States, done at London, 14 November 1944.

Protocol of Proceedings of the Crimea Conference (Declaration of Liberated Europe), Soviet Union–United Kingdom–United States, done at Yalta, 11 February 1945, available at www.yale.edu/lawweb/avalon/wwii/yalta.htm.

Declaration Regarding the Defeat of Germany and the Assumption of Supreme Authority by Allied Powers, Soviet Union–United Kingdom–United States–Provisional Government of the French Republic, done at Berlin, 5 June 1945, available at www.yale.edu/lawweb/avalon/wwii/ger01.htm.

Agreement for the Provisional Administration of Venezia Giulia, Yugoslavia–United Kingdom–United States, done at Belgrade, 9 June 1945, 59 Stat 1855, available at www.yale.edu/lawweb/avalon/wwii/venezia.htm.

Potsdam Declaration, Soviet Union–United Kingdom–United States, done at Berlin, 2 August 1945, available at www.yale.edu/lawweb/avalon/decade/decade17.htm.

Convention on the Privileges and Immunities of the United Nations, 13 February 1946, 1 UNTS 15.

Treaty of Peace with Italy, done at Paris, 10 February 1947, 49 UNTS 126.

Convention on the Prevention and Punishment of the Crime of Genocide, 9 December 1948, 78 UNTS 277.

North Atlantic Treaty, done at Washington, DC, 4 April 1949, 34 UNTS 243, available at www.yale.edu/lawweb/avalon/nato.htm.

Occupation Statute Promulgated by Military Governors and Commanders-in-Chief of the Western Zones of Germany, 12 May 1949.

Convention Relative to the Protection of Civilian Persons in Time of War (Fourth Geneva Convention), done at Geneva, 12 August 1949, available at www.icrc.org/ihl.

[European] Convention for the Protection of Human Rights and Fundamental Freedoms, done at Rome, 4 November 1950, 213 UNTS 222.

Convention on the Rights and Obligations of Foreign Forces and Their Members in the Federal Republic of Germany, France–United Kingdom–United States–Federal Republic of Germany, done at Bonn, 26 May 1952, 332 UNTS 3.

Memorandum of Understanding Regarding the Free Territory of Trieste, Italy–United Kingdom–United States–Yugoslavia, done at London, 5 October 1954.

Protocol on the Termination of the Occupation Regime in the Federal Republic of Germany, France–United Kingdom–United States–Federal Republic of Germany, done at Paris, 23 October 1954.

Agreement Concerning West New Guinea (West Irian), Indonesia–Netherlands, 15 August 1962, 437 UNTS 274.

International Covenant on Civil and Political Rights, 16 December 1966, 999 UNTS 171.

Treaty Between the Socialist Federal Republic of Yugoslavia and Italy, done at Osimo, 10 November 1975.

Protocol Additional to the Geneva Conventions of 12 August 1949, and relating to the Protection of Victims of Non-International Armed Conflicts (Additional Protocol II), 8 June 1977, 1125 UNTS 609, available at www.icrc.org/ihl.

Agreement Among the People's Republic of Angola, the Republic of Cuba, and the Republic of South Africa, 22 December 1988, 28 ILM 957.

Treaty on the Final Settlement with Respect to Germany, done at Moscow, 12 September 1990, 1992 UNTS 124.

Agreements on a Comprehensive Political Settlement of the Cambodia Conflict, done at Paris, 23 October 1991, 31 ILM 183.

Memorandum of Understanding on Mostar, Member States of the European Union–Member States of the Western European Union–Republic of Bosnia and Herzegovina–Federation of Bosnia and Herzegovina–Local Administration of Mostar East–Local Administration of Mostar West–Bosnian Croats, 5 July 1994.

Basic Agreement on the Region of Eastern Slavonia, Baranja, and Western Sirmium (Erdut Agreement), Government of the Republic of Croatia–local Croatian Serb authorities, done at Erdut, 12 November 1995, UN Doc S/19995/951, Annex, reprinted in 35 ILM 189.

General Framework Agreement for Peace in Bosnia and Herzegovina (Dayton Agreement), Bosnia and Herzegovina–Croatia–Federal Republic of Yugoslavia, done at Dayton, 14 December 1995, UN Doc S/1995/999, available at www.yale.edu/lawweb/avalon/intdip/bosnia/daymenu.htm.

Agreement on the Question of East Timor, Indonesia–Portugal, done at New York, 5 May 1999, UN Doc S/1999/513, Annex I.

Agreement Regarding the Modalities for the Popular Consultation of the East Timorese Through a Direct Ballot, Indonesia–Portugal–Secretary-General of the United Nations, done at New York, 5 May 1999, UN Doc S/1999/513, Annex II.

East Timor Popular Consultation (Security Provisions), Indonesia–Portugal–Secretary-General of the United Nations, done at New York, 5 May 1999, UN Doc S/1999/513, Annex III.

Peace Agreement between the Government of Sierra Leone and the Revolutionary United Front of Sierra Leone, done at Lomé, Togo, 7 July 1999, UN Doc S/1999/777.

A Constitutional Framework for Provisional Self-Government in Kosovo, UNMIK Regulation 2001/9, 15 May 2001, available at www.unmikonline.org/constframework.htm.

Agreement on Provisional Arrangements in Afghanistan Pending the Re-Establishment of Permanent Government Institutions (Bonn Agreement), done at Bonn, 5 December 2001, UN Doc S/2001/1154.

Agreement Between the United Nations and the Government of Sierra Leone on the Establishment of a Special Court for Sierra Leone, done at Freetown, 16 January 2002.

2. *Selected UN Documents*

UN Special Committee on Palestine Report to the General Assembly, UN Doc A/364 (31 August 1947).

[Draft] Statute of Jerusalem, UN Doc T/118 Rev. 2 (21 April 1948).

Principles of International Law Recognized in the Charter of the Nuremberg Tribunal and in the Judgment of the Tribunal, 5 GAOR (Suppl. No 12), UN Doc A/1316 (29 July 1950).

Report of the Secretary-General on Basic Points for the Presence and Functioning in Egypt of the United Nations Emergency Force, UN Doc A/3302 (6 November 1956).

Second Progress Report to the Secretary General from his Special Representative in the Congo, Mr Rajeshwar Dayal, UN Doc S/4557 (2 November 1960).

Report of the Secretary-General Regarding the Act of Self-Determination in West Irian, 24 GAOR, Annex, Agenda Item 98, p. 2, UN Doc A/7723 (6 November 1969).

Report of the Secretary General on the Implementation of Security Council Resolution 340 (1973), UN Doc S/11052/Rev. 1 (27 October 1973).

Letter dated 10 April 1978 from the representatives of Canada, Germany, France, the United Kingdom, and the United States to the President of the Security Council, 33 SCOR (Suppl. for April, May, and June), UN Doc S/12636 (10 April 1978).

Report of the Secretary-General submitted pursuant to paragraph 2 of Security Council resolution 431 (1978) concerning the situation in Namibia (UNTAG Plan), 33 SCOR (Suppl. for July, August, and September), UN Doc S/12827 (29 August 1978).

Security Council Summit Statement Concerning the Council's Responsibility in the Maintenance of International Peace and Security, UN Doc S/23500 (31 January 1992).

An Agenda for Peace: Preventive Diplomacy, Peacemaking and Peacekeeping (Report of the Secretary-General pursuant to the statement adopted by the Summit Meeting of the Security Council on 31 January 1992), UN Doc A/47/277–S/24111 (17 June 1992).

Second Progress Report of the Secretary-General on the United Nations Transitional Authority in Cambodia, UN Doc S/24578 (21 September 1992).

Report of the Human Rights Committee, 47 GAOR (Suppl. No 40), UN Doc A/47/49 (16 December 1992).

Report of the Secretary-General Pursuant to Security Council Resolution 836 (1993), UN Doc S/25939 (14 June 1993).

Comprehensive Agreement on Human Rights (Guatemala), UN Doc A/48/928–S/1994/448, Annex I (29 March 1994).

Report of the Commission of Inquiry Established Pursuant to Security Council Resolution 885 (1993) to Investigate Armed Attacks on UNOSOM II Personnel Which Led to Casualties Among Them, UN Doc S/1994/653 (1 June 1994).

Report of the Secretary-General on the Work of the Organization, UN Doc A/49/1 (2 September 1994).

Supplement to An Agenda for Peace: Position Paper of the Secretary-General on the Occasion of the Fiftieth Anniversary of the United Nations, UN Doc A/50/60–S/1995/1 (3 January 1995).

Human Rights Committee, Preliminary Observations on Peru, UN Doc CCPR/C/79/Add.67 (25 July 1996).

Report of the Secretary-General on the United Nations Transitional Administration for Eastern Slavonia, Baranja, and Western Sirmium, UN Doc S/1996/705 (28 August 1996).

An Agenda for Democratization, UN Doc A/51/761 (20 December 1996).

Report of the Secretary-General on the United Nations Transitional Administration for Eastern Slavonia, Baranja, and Western Sirmium, UN Doc S/1997/953 (4 December 1997).

Update on Regional Developments in the Former Yugoslavia, UN High Commissioner for Refugees, 48th Session, EC/48/SC/CRP.10 (2 April 1998).

Statute of the International Criminal Court (Rome Statute), UN Doc A/Conf.183/9 (17 July 1998).

Report of the Secretary-General on the United Nations Interim Administration Mission in Kosovo, UN Doc S/1999/779 (12 July 1999).

Seventh Report of the Secretary-General on the United Nations Observer Mission in Sierra Leone, UN Doc S/1999/836 (30 July 1999).

Question of East Timor: Report of the Secretary-General, UN Doc S/1999/862 (9 August 1999).

Report of the Secretary-General to the Security Council on the Protection of Civilians in Armed Conflict, UN Doc S/1999/957 (8 September 1999).

Report of the Secretary-General on the Situation in East Timor, UN Doc S/1999/1024 (4 October 1999).

First Periodic Report on the Operations of the Multinational Force in East Timor, UN Doc S/1999/1025, Annex (4 October 1999).

Report of the Independent Inquiry into the Actions of the United Nations During the 1994 Genocide in Rwanda, UN Doc S/1999/1257 (15 December 1999).

Second Report of the Secretary-General Pursuant to Security Council Resolution 1270 (1999) on the United Nations Mission in Sierra Leone, UN Doc S/2000/13 (11 January 2000).

Report of the Secretary-General on the United Nations Transitional Administration in East Timor, UN Doc S/2000/53 (26 January 2000).

Report of the International Commission of Inquiry on East Timor to the Secretary-General, UN Doc A/54/726–S/2000/59, Annex (31 January 2000).

Fourth Report of the Secretary-General Pursuant to Security Council Resolution 1270 (1999) on the United Nations Mission in Sierra Leone, UN Doc S/2000/455 (19 May 2000).

Security Council Briefed by Sergio Vieira de Mello, Special Representative for East Timor, UN Doc SC/6882 (27 June 2000).

Report of the Secretary-General on the United Nations Transitional Administration in East Timor (for the period 27 January to 26 July 2000), UN Doc S/2000/738 (26 July 2000).

Report of the Panel on United Nations Peace Operations (Brahimi Report), UN Doc A/55/305–S/2000/809 (21 August 2000), available at www.un.org/peace/reports/peace_operations.

Report of the Secretary-General on the Establishment of a Special Court for Sierra Leone, UN Doc S/2000/915 (4 October 2000).

Report of the Secretary-General on the Implementation of the Report of the Panel on United Nations Peace Operations, UN Doc A/55/502 (20 October 2000).

Report of the Security Council Mission to East Timor and Indonesia, UN Doc S/2000/1105 (20 November 2000).

Report of the Secretary-General on the United Nations Transitional Administration in East Timor (for the period 27 July 2000 to 16 January 2001), UN Doc S/2001/42 (16 January 2001).

No Exit Without Strategy: Security Council Decision-Making and the Closure or Transition of United Nations Peacekeeping Operations (Report of the Secretary-General), UN Doc S/2001/394 (20 April 2001).

Report of the Secretary-General on the United Nations Interim Administration Mission in Kosovo (for the period 13 March 2001 to 7 June 2001), UN Doc S/2001/565 (7 June 2001).

Report of the Security Council Mission on the Implementation of Security Council Resolution 1244 (1999), UN Doc S/2001/600 (19 June 2001).

Report of the Secretary-General on the Situation Concerning Western Sahara, UN Doc S/2001/613 (20 June 2001).

Draft Framework Agreement on the Status of Western Sahara, UN Doc S/2001/613, Annex I (20 June 2001).

Report of the Secretary-General on the United Nations Transitional Administration in East Timor (for the period from 25 July to 15 October 2001), UN Doc S/2001/983 (18 October 2001).

Statement on the Situation in Afghanistan Adopted by the Ministers for Foreign Affairs and Other Senior Representatives of the Six Plus Two, UN Doc A/56/681–S/2001/1157, Annex (12 November 2001).

Report of the Secretary-General on the United Nations Mission in Bosnia and Herzegovina, UN Doc S/2001/1132 (29 November 2001).

Implementation of the Recommendations of the Special Committee on Peacekeeping Operations and the Panel on United Nations Peace Operations (Report of the Secretary-General), UN Doc A/56/732 (21 December 2001), available at www.un.org/peace/reports/peace_operations.

The Situation in Afghanistan and Its Implications for International Peace and Security (Report of the Secretary-General), UN Doc A/56/875–S/2002/278 (18 March 2002).

Report of the Secretary-General on Women, Peace and Security, UN Doc S/2002/1154 (16 October 2002).

Special Report of the Secretary-General on the UN Mission of Support in East Timor, UN Doc S/2003/243 (3 March 2003).

Report of the Secretary-General on the Situation Concerning Western Sahara, UN Doc S/2003/565 (23 May 2003).

Report of the Secretary-General Pursuant to Paragraph 24 of Security Council Resolution 1483 (2003), UN Doc S/2003/715 (17 July 2003).

3. Selected Reports

Draft Generic Guidelines for a Strategic Framework Approach for Response to and Recovery from Crisis (New York: United Nations, Office of the Deputy Secretary-General, 27 October 1997).

Conclusions of the Peace Implementation Conference (Bonn: Peace Implementation Council, 9–10 December 1997), available at www.oscebih.org.

Helsinki European Council, Presidency Conclusions (10–11 December 1999), available at http://ue.eu.int/en/info/eurocouncil.

Role of UNDP in Crisis and Post-Conflict Situations (Policy Paper Distributed to the Executive Board of the United Nations Development Programme and of the United Nations Population Fund), DP/2001/4 (New York: UNDP, 27 November 2000), available at www.undp.org.

National Development Framework (Draft for Consultation) (Kabul: Afghan Assistance Coordination Authority, April 2002).

The National Security Strategy of the United States of America (Washington, DC: President of the United States, September 2002), available at www.whitehouse.gov/nsc/nss.html.

A Review of Peace Operations: A Case for Change (London: King's College London, March 2003).

Aspen Institute, *Honoring Human Rights Under International Mandates: Lessons from Bosnia, Kosovo, and East Timor* (Washington, DC: Aspen Institute, 2003).

[Australian] Department of Foreign Affairs and Trade (Australia), *East Timor in Transition 1998–2000: An Australian Policy Challenge* (Canberra: Brown and Wilton, 2000).

[British] Centre for Management and Policy Studies, Nine Key Characteristics of Modern Policy-Making (London: Cabinet Office, January 2002), available at www.cmps.co.uk.

Forman, Shepard, Patrick, Stewart, and Salomons, Dirk. Recovering from Conflict: Strategy for an International Response (New York: Center on International Cooperation, 2000), available at www.cic.nyu.edu.

Gardiner, Nile and Rivkin, David B. Blueprint for Freedom: Limiting the Role of the United Nations in Post-War Iraq (Washington, DC: Heritage Foundation, Backgrounder No 1646, 2003).

General Affairs and External Relations Council of the EU, Afghanistan: Council Conclusions (15 April 2002), available at http://europa.eu.int.

Harrison, Penny, The Strategic Framework and Principled Common Programming: A Challenge to Humanitarian Assistance (London: Overseas Development Institute, 10 September 2001), available at www.odihpn.org.

Human Rights Watch, Unfinished Business: Justice for East Timor, Press Backgrounder (August 2000), available at www.hrw.org/backgrounder/asia/timor/etimor-back0829.htm.

——, Justice Denied for East Timor (December 2002).

——, *World Report 2002* (New York: Human Rights Watch, 2002).

Human Rights Watch, *World Report 2003* (New York: Human Rights Watch, 2003).

Independent International Commission on Kosovo, *The Kosovo Report* (Oxford: Oxford University Press, 2000).

—— The Follow-up of the Kosovo Report: Why Conditional Independence? (Sweden: Kosovo Commission, September 2001).

International Commission on Intervention and State Sovereignty, The Responsibility to Protect (Ottawa: International Development Research Centre, December 2001), available at www.iciss. gc.ca.

International Crisis Group, Back from the Brink: Cambodian Democracy Gets a Second Chance (Phnom Penh/Brussels: ICG Cambodia Report No 4, 26 January 1999), available at www.crisisweb.org.

——, Reunifying Mostar: Opportunities for Progress (Sarajevo/Washington/ Brussels: ICG Balkans Report No 90, 19 April 2000), available at www.crisisweb.org.

——, Cambodia: The Elusive Peace Dividend (Phnom Penh/Brussels: ICG Asia Report No 8, 11 August 2000), available at www.crisisweb.org.

——, Bosnia's November Elections: Dayton Stumbles (Sarajevo/Brussels: ICG Balkans Report No 104, 18 December 2000), available at www.crisisweb.org.

——, Bosnia's Precarious Economy: Still Not Open for Business (Sarajevo/Brussels: ICG Balkans Report No 115, 7 August 2001), available at www.crisisweb.org.

——, Bosnia: Reshaping the International Machinery (Sarajevo/Brussels: ICG Balkans Report No 121, 29 November 2001), available at www.crisisweb.org.

——, Courting Disaster: The Misrule of Law in Bosnia and Herzegovina (Sarajevo/Brussels: ICG Balkans Report No 127, 25 March 2002), available at www.crisisweb.org.

——, The Afghan Transitional Administration: Prospects and Perils (Kabul/Brussels: Afghanistan Briefing Paper, 30 July 2002), available at www.crisisweb.org.

——, Kosovo's Ethnic Dilemma: The Need for a Civic Contract (Pristina/Brussels: ICG Balkans Report No 143, 28 May 2003), available at www.crisisweb.org.

——, Bosnia's Brcko: Getting In, Getting On, and Getting Out (Sarajevo/Brussels: ICG Balkans Report No 144, 2 June 2003), available at www.crisisweb.org.

——, Baghdad: A Race Against the Clock (Baghdad/Amman/Brussels: ICG Middle East Briefing, 11 June 2003), available at www.crisisweb.org.

——, Bosnia's Nationalist Governments: Paddy Ashdown and the Paradoxes of State-Building (Sarajevo/Brussels: ICG Balkans Report No 146, 22 July 2003), available at www.crisisweb.org.

International Peace Academy, *Peacekeeper's Handbook* (New York: Pergamon Press, 1984).

Jane's Sentinel Security Assessments, Macedonia (3 April 2001), available at www.janes.com.

Johnson, Chris, Maley, William, Thier, Alexander, and Wardak, Ali. Afghanistan's Political and Constitutional Development (London: Overseas Development Institute, January 2003), available at www.odi.org.uk/hpg.

Lewis, William Hubert, and Marks, Edward. Strengthening International Civilian Police Operations (Washington, DC: Center for Strategic and International Studies, 2000).

National Democratic Institute and the Faculty of Social and Political Science of the University of East Timor, Carrying the People's Aspirations: A Report on Focus Group Discussions in East Timor (Dili: NDI, February 2002).

OECD, DAC Guidelines on Conflict, Peace, and Development Cooperation (Paris: OECD, 1997), available at www.oecd.org.

——, Helping Prevent Violent Conflict, Development Assistance Committee Guidelines (Paris: OECD, 2001), available at www.oecd.org.

Office of the SRSG for Afghanistan, Human Rights in the United Nations Assistance Mission for Afghanistan (UNAMA) (Kabul: UNAMA-OSRSG, 2002).

——, Human Rights Advisory Note No. 3: Implementing the Accountability Provisions of the Bonn Agreement: Toward an Afghan National Strategy for Human Rights Monitoring, Investigations and Transitional Justice (Kabul: UNAMA-OSRSG, March 2002).

——, Proposal for a Multi-Agency Review of Justice Sector Development in Afghanistan (Kabul: UNAMA-OSRSG, May 2002).

Ombudsperson Institution in Kosovo, First Annual Report 2000–2001 (18 July 2001), available at www.ombudspersonkosovo.org.

——, Special Report No 3: On the Conformity of Deprivations of Liberty Under 'Executive Orders' with Recognized International Standards (29 July 2001), available at www.ombudspersonkosovo.org.

——, Second Annual Report 2001–2002 (10 July 2002), available at www.ombudspersonkosovo.org.

OSCE, Kosovo: Review of the Criminal Justice System (February-July 2000) (Pristina: OSCE, 2000), available at www.osce.org/kosovo.

——, Detailed Certified Results (Pristina: OSCE Mission in Kosovo, Central Election Commission, 24 November 2001), available at www.osce.org/kosovo/elections.

Oxfam, An End to Forgotten Emergencies? (Oxford: Oxfam GB Briefing Paper 5/00, May 2000), available at www.oxfam.org.uk.

Roth, Kenneth. Letter to Secretary of Defense Donald Rumsfeld (New York: Human Rights Watch, 8 August 2003), available at www.hrw.org.

Rubin, Barnett R., Hamidzada, Humayun, and Stoddard, Abby. Through the Fog of Peacebuilding: Evaluating the Reconstruction of Afghanistan

(New York: Center on International Cooperation, June 2003), available at www.cic.nyu.edu.

Sphere Project, The Humanitarian Charter and Minimum Standards in Disaster Response (Oxford: Oxfam Publishing, 2000), available at www.sphereproject.org.

United Nations, *The Blue Helmets: A Review of United Nations Peacekeeping*, 1st edn. (New York: UN Department of Public Information, 1985).

——, *The United Nations and East Timor: Self-Determination Through Popular Consultation* (New York: UN Department of Public Information, 2000).

UN Department of Peacekeeping Operations, The Comprehensive Report on Lessons Learned from United Nations Operation in Somalia (UNOSOM) (New York: Lessons Learned Unit, December 1995), available at www.un.org/Depts/dpko/lessons.

——, General Guidelines for Peacekeeping Operations, UN Doc UN/210/TC/GG95 (October 1995), available at www.un.org/Depts/dpko/training.

——, Comprehensive Report on Lessons Learned from the United Nations Transitional Administration for Eastern Slavonia (New York: Lessons Learned Unit, June 1998), available at www.un.org/Depts/dpko/lessons.

——, Disarmament, Demobilization and Reintegration of Ex-Combatants in a Peacekeeping Environment: Principles and Guidelines (New York: Lessons Learned Unit, December 1999), available at www.un.org/Depts/dpko/lessons.

——, Guidelines for the Development of Rules of Engagement for UN Peacekeeping Operations (Provisional), UN Doc MD/FHS/0220.0001 (May 2002).

UN Development Fund for Women, Women, War, and Peace: The Independent Experts' Assessment on the Impact of Armed Conflict on Women and Women's Role in Peacebuilding (New York: UNIFEM, October 2002).

UN Development Programme, Governance for Sustainable Human Development (New York: UNDP, January 1997), available at http://magnet.undp.org/policy.

UN Office for the Coordination of Humanitarian Assistance, Humanitarian Risk Analysis No 12 Federal Republic of Yugoslavia (Belgrade: OCHA, 9 August 2000), available at www.reliefweb.int.

UN War Crimes Commission, *History of the United Nations War Crime Commission and the Development of the Laws of War* (London: H. M. Stationery Office, 1948).

US Army, Field Manual 100–23 Peace Operations (Headquarters, Department of the Army, December 1994), available at www.dtic.mil/doctrine/jel/service_pubs/fm100_23.pdf.

Wainwright, Elsina, Our Failing Neighbour: Australia and the Future of Solomon Islands (Canberra: Australian Strategic Policy Institute, June 2003), available at www.aspi.org.au.

World Bank, Post-Conflict Reconstruction: The Role of the World Bank (Washington, DC: World Bank, 1998).
——, Report of the Joint Assessment Mission to East Timor (8 December 1999), available at www.worldbank.org.
——, Financing and Aid Management Arrangements in Post-Conflict Settings (Washington, DC: Conflict Prevention and Reconstruction Unit, CPR Note 12, June 2003), available at www.worldbank.org/conflict.

4. *Books and Periodicals*

The Cambridge History of the British Empire, 2nd edn. (Cambridge: Cambridge University Press, 1963).
Abi-Saab, Georges. *The United Nations Operation in the Congo 1960–1964* (Oxford: Oxford University Press, 1978).
Adebajo, Adekeye. 'Sheikhs, Soldiers and Sand', *World Today*, January 2000, 19.
——. *Liberia's Civil War Nigeria, ECOMOG, and Regional Security in West Africa* (Boulder, CO: Lynne Rienner, 2002).
Akpan, Ntieyong U. *Epitaph to Indirect Rule: A Discourse on Local Government in Africa* (London: Cassell, 1956).
Allin, Dana H. 'Unintended Consequences: Managing Kosovo Independence', in Dimitrios Triantaphyllou (ed.), *What Status for Kosovo?* (Paris: Institute for Security Studies, Western European Union, 2001).
Anderson, Benedict. *Imagined Communities: Reflections on the Origin and Spread of Nationalism* (London: Verso, 1983).
Anstee, Margaret Joan. *Orphan of the Cold War: The Inside Story of the Angolan Peace Process, 1992–1993* (New York: St Martin's Press, 1996).
Appiah, Kwame Anthony. *In My Father's House: Africa in the Philosophy of Culture* (New York: Oxford University Press, 1992).
Baker, Ray Stannard. *Woodrow Wilson and World Settlement* (Garden City, NY: Doubleday, Page & Co, 1922).
Ball, Nicole and Barnes, Sam. 'Mozambique', in Shepard Forman and Stewart Patrick (eds.), *Good Intentions: Pledges of Aid for Postconflict Recovery* (Boulder, CO: Lynne Rienner, 2000), 159.
Barkawi, Tarak and Laffey, Mark (eds.). *Democracy, Liberalism, and War: Rethinking the Democratic Peace Debate* (Boulder, CO: Lynne Rienner, 2001).
Bass, Gary Jonathan. *Stay the Hand of Vengeance: The Politics of War Crimes Tribunals* (Princeton, NJ: Princeton University Press, 2000).
—— (2003) 'Milosevic in the Hague', *Foreign Affairs*, 82(3): 82.
Bassiouni, M. Cherif. *The Statute of the International Criminal Court: A Documentary History* (Ardsley-on-Hudson, NY: Transnational, 1998).

Beauvais, Joel C. (2001) 'Benevolent Despotism: A Critique of UN State-Building in East Timor', *New York University Journal of International Law and Politics*, 33: 1101.

Bell, Sydney Smith. *Colonial Administration of Great Britain* [1859] (New York: Augustus M. Kelley, 1970).

Berdal, Mats R. *Whither UN Peacekeeping?* (London: International Institute for Strategic Studies, 1993).

—— and Malone, David M. (eds.). *Greed and Grievance: Economic Agendas in Civil Wars, A Project of the International Peace Academy* (Boulder, CO: Lynne Rienner, 2000).

Berman, Nathaniel (1993). "'But the Alternative Is Despair": Nationalism and the Modernist Revival of International Law', *Harvard Law Review*, 106: 1792.

Bermeo, Nancy (2002) 'The Import of Institutions', *Journal of Democracy*, 13(2): 96.

Betts, Richard K. (2001) 'The Lesser Evil: The Best Way Out of the Balkans', *The National Interest*, 64: 53.

Bisschop, W. R. *The Saar Controversy* (London: Sweet & Maxwell, 1924).

Bleimaier, John Kuhn (1989) 'The Legal Status of the Free City of Danzig 1920–1939: Lessons to be Derived from the Experience of a Non-State Entity in the International Community', *Hague Yearbook of International Law*, 69.

Boraine, Alex. *A Country Unmasked: Inside South Africa's Truth and Reconciliation Commission* (Oxford: Oxford University Press, 2000).

Bowden, Mark. *Black Hawk Down: A Story of Modern War* (New York: Atlantic Monthly Press, 1999).

Boyce, James K. 'Beyond Good Intentions: External Assistance and Peace Building', in Shepard Forman and Stewart Patrick (eds.), *Good Intentions: Pledges of Aid for Postconflict Recovery* (Boulder, CO: Lynne Rienner, 2000), 367.

——. *Investing in Peace: Aid and Conditionality After Civil Wars* (Oxford: Oxford University Press, 2002).

Boyer, Peter J. 'The New War Machine', *New Yorker*, 30 June 2003, 55.

Brown, Michael E., Jones, Sean M. Lynn, and Miller, Steven E. *Debating the Democratic Peace* (Cambridge, MA: MIT Press, 1996).

Brownlie, Ian. *International Law and the Use of Force by States* (Oxford: Clarendon Press, 1963).

——. *Principles of Public International Law*, 5th edn. (Oxford: Clarendon Press, 1998).

Burkholder, Mark A. (ed.). *Administrators of Empire* (Aldershot: Ashgate, 1998).

Burns, Arthur Lee and Heathcote, Nina. *Peacekeeping by UN Forces: From Suez to the Congo* (New York: Praeger for the Center for International Studies, Princeton, 1963).

Callahan, Michael D. *Mandates and Empire: The League of Nations and Africa, 1914–1931* (Brighton: Sussex Academic Press, 1999).

Caplan, Richard. *A New Trusteeship? The International Administration of War-Torn Territories* (Oxford: Oxford University Press, 2002).

Carnegie, A. (1963) 'Jurisdiction over Violations of the Laws and Customs of War', *British Yearbook of International Law*, 39: 421.

Caro, Robert A. *The Power Broker: Robert Moses and the Fall of New York* (New York: Knopf, 1974).

Cassese, Antonio. *Self-Determination of Peoples: A Legal Reappraisal* (Cambridge: Cambridge University Press, 1995).

Chandler, David. *Bosnia: Faking Democracy After Dayton* (London: Pluto Press, 1999).

Chesterman, Simon. (1997) 'Never Again... and Again: Law, Order and the Gender of War Crimes in Bosnia and Beyond', *Yale Journal of International Law*, 22: 299.

——. *Just War or Just Peace? Humanitarian Intervention and International Law* (Oxford: Oxford University Press, 2001).

——— (ed.). *Civilians in War* (Boulder, CO: Lynne Rienner, 2001).

———. 'No Justice Without Peace? International Criminal Law and the Decision to Prosecute', in Simon Chesterman (ed.), *Civilians in War* (Boulder, CO: Lynne Rienner, 2001), 145.

—— (2002) 'East Timor in Transition: Self-Determination, State-Building and the United Nations', *International Peacekeeping*, 9(1): 45.

—— (2002) 'Walking Softly in Afghanistan: The Future of UN State-Building', *Survival*, 44(3): 37.

—— (2003) 'Blue Helmet Blues', *Security Dialogue*, 34: 365.

——, Ignatieff, Michael, and Thakur, Ramesh (eds.). *Making States Work: State Failure and the Crisis of Governance* (Tokyo: United Nations University Press, forthcoming).

Chopra, Jarat (ed.). *The Politics of Peace-Maintenance* (Boulder, CO: Lynne Rienner, 1998).

—— (2000) 'The UN's Kingdom of East Timor', *Survival*, 42(3): 27.

—— (2002) 'Building State Failure in East Timor', *Development and Change*, 33: 979.

Ciment, James. *Angola and Mozambique: Postcolonial Wars in Southern Africa* (New York: Facts on File, 1997).

Clark, Wesley K. *Waging Modern War: Bosnia, Kosovo, and the Future of Combat* (New York: Public Affairs, 2001).

Clarke, Walter and Herbst, Jeffrey. (1996) 'Somalia and the Future of Humanitarian Intervention', *Foreign Affairs*, 75(2): 70.

——— (eds.). *Learning from Somalia: The Lessons of Armed Humanitarian Intervention* (Boulder, CO: Westview, 1997).

Clemens, Diane Shaver. *Yalta* (New York: Oxford University Press, 1970).

Cliffe, Lionel. *The Transition to Independence in Namibia* (Boulder, CO: Lynne Rienner, 1994).

Cobban, Alfred. *The Nation State and National Self-Determination*, rev. edn. (London: Collins, 1969).

Cohen, Theodore. *Remaking Japan: The American Occupation as New Deal* (New York: Free Press, 1987).

Collier, Paul. *Breaking the Conflict Trap: Civil War and Development Policy* (New York: Oxford University Press, 2003).

Cortright, David and Lopez, George A. *Sanctions and the Search for Security: Challenges to UN Action* (Boulder, CO: Lynne Rienner, 2002).

Cousens, Elizabeth M. 'Introduction', in Elizabeth M. Cousens and Chetan Kumar (eds.), *Peacebuilding as Politics* (Boulder, CO: Lynne Rienner, 2001), 1.

——. 'From Missed Opportunities to Overcompensation: Implementing the Dayton Agreement on Bosnia', in Stephen John Stedman, Donald Rothchild, and Elizabeth M. Cousens (eds.), *Ending Civil Wars: The Implementation of Peace Agreements* (Boulder, CO: Lynne Rienner, 2002), 531.

—— and Cater, Charles K. *Toward Peace in Bosnia: Implementing the Dayton Accords* (Boulder, CO: Lynne Rienner, 2001).

—— and Kumar, Chetan (eds.). *Peacebuilding as Politics* (Boulder, CO: Lynne Rienner, 2001).

Crawford, James. *The Creation of States in International Law* (Oxford: Clarendon Press, 1979).

——. 'The Charter of the United Nations as a Constitution', in Hazel Fox (ed.), *The Changing Constitution of the United Nations* (London: British Institute of International and Comparative Law, 1997), 1.

Crawford, Neta C. *Argument and Change in World Politics: Ethics, Decolonization, and Humanitarian Intervention* (Cambridge: Cambridge University Press, 2002).

Crocker, Chester A., Hampson, Fen Osler, and Aall, Pamela (eds.). *Turbulent Peace: The Challenges of Managing International Conflict* (Washington, DC: United States Institute of Peace Press, 2001).

Curzon, George N. *Persia and the Persian Question* (London: Frank Cass, 1966).

Di Palma, Giuseppe. *To Craft Democracies: An Essay on Democratic Transitions* (Berkeley: University of California Press, 1990).

Diamond, Larry Jay. *Developing Democracy: Toward Consolidation* (Baltimore: Johns Hopkins University Press, 1999).

Djilas, Milovan. *Conversations with Stalin*, translated by Michael B. Petrovich (New York: Harcourt, Brace, and World, 1962).

Dobbins, James, McGinn, John G., Crane, Keith, Jones, Seth G., Lal, Rollie, Rathmell, Andrew, Swanger, Rachel, and Timilsina, Anga. *America's Role in Nation-Building: From Germany to Iraq* (Santa Monica, CA: RAND, 2003).

Donnison, F. S. V. *Civil Affairs and Military Government North-West Europe, 1944–1946* (London: H. M. Stationery Office, 1961).

Douglas, Lawrence. (1995) 'Film as Witness: Screening Nazi Concentration Camps Before the Nuremberg Tribunal', *Yale Law Journal*, 105: 449.

Dower, John W. *Embracing Defeat: Japan in the Wake of World War II* (New York: W. W. Norton, 1999).

Doyle, Michael W. *UN Peacekeeping in Cambodia: UNTAC's Civil Mandate* (Boulder, CO: Lynne Rienner, 1995).

——. 'War-Making and Peace-Making: The United Nations' Post-Cold War Record', in Chester A. Crocker, Fen Osler Hampson, and Pamela Aall (eds.), *Turbulent Peace: The Challenges of Managing International Conflict* (Washington, DC: United States Institute of Peace Press, 2001), 529.

——, Johnstone, Ian, and Orr, Robert C. (eds.). *Keeping the Peace: Multidimensional Peacekeeping in Cambodia and El Salvador* (Cambridge: Cambridge University Press, 1997).

Drysdale, John, *Whatever Happened to Somalia?* (London: Haan Associates, 1994).

Dugard, John. (2000) 'Dealing with Crimes of a Past Regime: Is Amnesty Still an Option?', *Leiden Journal of International Law*, 12: 1001.

Dumbuya, Peter A. *Tanganyika Under International Mandate, 1919–1946* (Lanham, MD: University Press of America, 1995).

Durch, William J. (ed.). *The Evolution of UN Peacekeeping: Case Studies and Comparative Analysis* (New York: St Martin's Press, 1993).

——. 'The UN Operation in the Congo: 1960–1964', in William J. Durch (ed.), *The Evolution of UN Peacekeeping: Case Studies and Comparative Analysis* (New York: St Martin's Press, 1993), 315.

—— (ed.). *UN Peacekeeping, American Policy, and the Uncivil Wars of the 1990s* (New York: St Martin's Press, 1996).

——. 'Introduction to Anarchy: Humanitarian Intervention and "State-Building" in Somalia', in William J. Durch (ed.), *UN Peacekeeping, American Policy, and the Uncivil Wars of the 1990s* (New York: St Martin's Press, 1996), 311.

Enloe, Cynthia H. *Bananas, Beaches, and Bases: Making Feminist Sense of International Politics* (London: Pandora, 1989).

Falk, Richard A. (1994) 'The United Nations and the Rule of Law', *Transnational Law and Contemporary Problems*, 4: 611.

Fallows, James. 'The Military-Industrial Complex', *Foreign Policy*, November–December 2002, 34.

Ferguson, Niall. *Empire: The Rise and Demise of the British World Order and the Lessons for Global Power* (New York: Basic Books, 2003).

Fieldhouse, David Kenneth. *The Colonial Empires: A Comparative Survey from the Eighteenth Century* (London: Weidenfeld and Nicolson, 1966).

Findlay, Trevor. *Cambodia: The Legacy and Lessons of UNTAC* (Oxford: Oxford University Press, 1995).

——. *The Use of Force in UN Peace Operations* (Oxford: SIPRI & Oxford University Press, 2002).

Forman, Shepard and Patrick, Stewart (eds.). *Good Intentions: Pledges of Aid for Postconflict Recovery* (Boulder, CO: Lynne Rienner, 2000).

Fox, Gregory H. 'The Right to Political Participation in International Law', in Gregory H. Fox and Brad R. Roth (eds.), *Democratic Governance and International Law* (Cambridge: Cambridge University Press, 2000), 48.

—— and Roth, Brad R. (eds.). *Democratic Governance and International Law* (Cambridge: Cambridge University Press, 2000).

Fox, Hazel (ed.). *The Changing Constitution of the United Nations* (London: British Institute of International and Comparative Law, 1997).

Fraenkel, Jonathan. (2001) 'The Alternative Vote System in Fiji: Electoral Engineering or Ballot-Rigging?', *Journal of Commonwealth and Comparative Politics*, 39(2): 1.

Franck, Thomas M. (1992) 'The Emerging Right to Democratic Governance', *American Journal of International Law*, 86: 46.

—— (2001) 'Terrorism and the Rights of Self-Defense', *American Journal of International Law*, 95: 839.

Frankel, Marvin E. *Out of the Shadows of Night: The Struggle for International Human Rights* (New York: Delacorte Press, 1989).

Friedmann, Wolfgang Gaston. *The Allied Military Government of Germany* (London: Stevens, 1947).

Gandhi, M. K. *Hind Swaraj and Other Writings* (Cambridge: Cambridge University Press, 1997).

Ganzglass, Martin R. 'The Restoration of the Somali Justice System', in Walter Clarke and Jeffrey Herbst (eds.), *Learning from Somalia: The Lessons of Armed Humanitarian Intervention* (Boulder, CO: Westview, 1997).

Garton Ash, Timothy. 'Anarchy and Madness', *New York Review*, 10 February 2000, 48.

Gilbert, Martin. *Winston S. Churchill, Volume 7: Road to Victory, 1941–1945* (Boston: Houghton Mifflin, 1986).

Gilmour, David. *Curzon* (London: J. Murray, 1994).

Goldstone, Richard J. *For Humanity: Reflections of a War Crimes Investigator* (New Haven, CT: Yale University Press, 2000).

Goulding, Marrack. 'Current Rapid Expansion Unsustainable Without Major Changes', in John Roper (ed.), *Keeping the Peace in the Post-Cold War Era: Strengthening Multilateral Peacekeeping* (New York: Trilateral Commission, 1993), 93.

—— (1993) 'The Evolution of United Nations Peacekeeping', *International Affairs*, 69: 451.

—— (1996) 'The Use of Force by the United Nations', *International Peacekeeping* 3(1): 1.

——. *Peacemonger* (London: John Murray, 2002).

Gowa, Joanne S. *Ballots and Bullets: The Elusive Democratic Peace* (Princeton, NJ: Princeton University Press, 1999).

Greenwood, Christopher. 'The Administration of Occupied Territory in International Law', in Emma Playfair (ed.), *International Law and the Administration of Occupied Territories* (Oxford: Clarendon Press, 1992), 241.

Griffin, Michèle. (2003) 'The Helmet and the Hoe: Linkages Between United Nations Development Assistance and Conflict Management', *Global Governance*, 9(2): 199.

Grose, Peter. (1997) 'The Marshall Plan—Then and Now', *Foreign Affairs*, 76(3): 159.

Guha, Ranajit (ed.). *A Subaltern Studies Reader, 1986–1995* (Minneapolis: University of Minnesota Press, 1997).

Haass, Richard. *The Reluctant Sheriff: The United States After the Cold War* (New York: Council on Foreign Relations, 1997).

Hainsworth, Paul and McCloskey, Stephen (eds.). *The East Timor Question: The Struggle for Independence from Indonesia* (London: I. B. Tauris, 2000).

Hammer, Joshua and Soloway, Colin. 'Who's in Charge Here?' *Newsweek*, 26 May 2003.

Hancock, Graham. *Lords of Poverty: The Free-Wheeling Lifestyles, Power, Prestige, and Corruption of the International Aid Business* (London: Macmillan, 1989).

Hand, Learned. *The Spirit of Liberty*, 3rd edn. (Chicago: University of Chicago Press, 1960).

Hannum, Hurst. (1993) 'Rethinking Self-Determination', *Virginia Journal of International Law*, 34: 1.

Hansen, Annika S. *From Congo to Kosovo: Civilian Police in Peace Operations* (Oxford: Oxford University Press for the International Institute for Strategic Studies, 2002).

Hayner, Priscilla B. (1994) 'Fifteen Truth Commissions, 1974–1993: A Comparative Study', *Human Rights Quarterly*, 16: 597.

——. *Unspeakable Truths: Confronting State Terror and Atrocities* (New York: Routledge, 2001).

Hearn, Roger. *UN Peacekeeping in Action: The Namibian Experience* (Commack, NY: Nova Science, 1999).

Heater, Derek. *National Self-Determination: Woodrow Wilson and his Legacy* (London: St Martin's Press, 1994).

Helman, Gerald B. and Ratner, Steven R. 'Saving Failed States', *Foreign Policy* 89, Winter 1992, 3.

Hersh, Seymour M. 'Selective Intelligence', *New Yorker*, 12 May 2003, 44.

Higgins, Rosalyn. *United Nations Peacekeeping 1946–1967: Documents and Commentary: Vol 2, Asia* (London: Oxford University Press, 1970).

——. *United Nations Peacekeeping 1946–1967: Documents and Commentary: Vol 3, Africa* (London: Oxford University Press, 1980).

Hillen, John. *Blue Helmets: The Strategy of UN Military Operations*, 2nd edn. (Washington, DC: Brassey's, 2000).

Hirsch, John L. *Sierra Leone: Diamonds and the Struggle for Democracy* (Boulder, CO: Lynne Rienner, 2001).

—— and Oakley, Robert. *Somalia and Operation Restore Hope: Reflections on Peacemaking and Peacekeeping* (Washington, DC: United States Institute of Peace Press, 1995).

Hirsh, Michael. 'Our New Civil War', *Newsweek*, 12 May 2003.

Hobbes, Thomas. *Leviathan* [1651] (London: Dent, 1914).

Hogan, Michael J. *The Marshall Plan: America, Britain, and the Reconstruction of Western Europe, 1947–1952* (Cambridge: Cambridge University Press, 1987).

Hohe, Tanja. (2002) 'Totem Polls: Indigenous Concepts and "Free and Fair" Elections in East Timor', *International Peacekeeping*, 9(4): 69.

Holborn, Hajo. *American Military Government: Its Organization and Policies* (Washington, DC: Infantry Journal Press, 1947).

Holbrooke, Richard. *To End a War* (New York: Random House, 1998).

Holmes, John T. 'The Principle of Complementarity', in Roy S. K. Lee (ed.), *The International Criminal Court: The Making of the Rome Statute* (The Hague: Kluwer, 1999), 41.

Honig, Jan Willem and Both, Norbert. *Srebrenica: Record of a War Crime* (London: Penguin, 1996).

Horowitz, Donald L. *Ethnic Groups in Conflict* (Berkeley: University of California Press, 1985).

——. *A Democratic South Africa? Constitutional Engineering in a Divided Society* (Berkeley: University of California Press, 1991).

Hoskyns, Catherine. *The Congo Since Independence: January 1960 to December 1961* (Oxford: Oxford University Press, 1965).

Huntington, Samuel P. *The Third Wave: Democratization in the Late Twentieth Century* (Norman: University of Oklahoma Press, 1991).

Huyse, Luc. (1995) 'Justice After Transition: On the Choices Successor Elites Make in Dealing with the Past', *Law and Social Inquiry*, 20: 51.

Hyden, Goran. 'Governance and the Reconstitution of Political Order', in Richard Joseph (ed.), *State, Conflict and Democracy in Africa* (Boulder, CO: Lynne Rienner, 1999), 179.

Ignatieff, Michael. *Virtual War: Kosovo and Beyond* (New York: Metropolitan, 2000).

——. 'Intervention and State Failure', *Dissent*, Winter 2002, 114.

——. *Empire Lite: Nation Building in Bosnia, Kosovo, Afghanistan* (London: Minerva, 2003).

Jackson, Robert H. *The Nürnberg Case* (New York: Knopf, 1947).

Jackson, Scott. (1979) 'Prologue to the Marshall Plan: The Origins of the American Commitment for a European Recovery Program', *Journal of American History*, 65: 1043.

Jonas, Susanne. *Of Centaurs and Doves: Guatemala's Peace Process* (Boulder, CO: Westview, 2000).

Joseph, Richard (ed.). *State, Conflict and Democracy in Africa* (Boulder, CO: Lynne Rienner, 1999).

Judah, Tim. *Kosovo: War and Revenge* (New Haven, CT: Yale University Press, 2000).

Kaela, Laurent C. W. *The Question of Namibia* (London: Macmillan, 1996).

Kelsen, Hans. *The Law of the United Nations* (London: Stevens & Sons, 1950).

Kindleberger, Charles P. (1997) 'In the Halls of the Capitol', *Foreign Affairs*, 76(3): 185.

King, Charles and Melvin, Neil J. (1999) 'Diaspora Politics', *International Security*, 24(3): 108.

Kingsbury, Damien (ed.). *Guns and Ballot Boxes: East Timor's Vote for Independence* (Clayton: Monash Asia Institute, 2000).

Knappen, Marshall. *And Call It Peace* (Chicago: University of Chicago Press, 1947).

Kritz, Neil J. (ed.). *Transitional Justice: How Emerging Democracies Reckon with Former Regimes*, 3 vols. (Washington, DC: United States Institute of Peace Press, 1995).

Kumar, Krishna (ed.). *Postconflict Elections, Democratization, and International Assistance* (Boulder, CO: Lynne Rienner, 1998).

Kunz, Diane B. (1997) 'The Marshall Plan Reconsidered: A Complex of Motives', *Foreign Affairs*, 76(3): 162.

Lal, Brij V. and Vakatora, Tomasi R. (eds.). *Fiji Constitutional Review Commission Research Papers* (Suva: School of Social and Economic Development, University of the South Pacific, 1997).

Lee, Roy S. K. (ed.). *The International Criminal Court: The Making of the Rome Statute* (The Hague: Kluwer, 1999).

LeMarquand, David G. *International Rivers: The Politics of Cooperation* (Vancouver: Westwater Research Centre, University of British Columbia, 1977).

Leurdijk, Dick A. *The United Nations and NATO in Former Yugoslavia: Partners in International Cooperation* (The Hague: Netherlands Atlantic Commission, 1994).

Lewis, W. Arthur. *Politics in West Africa* (New York: Oxford University Press, 1965).

Lijphart, Arend. (1969) 'Consociational Democracy', *World Politics*, 21: 207.

Linz, Juan J. and Stepan, Alfred C. *Problems of Democratic Transition and Consolidation: Southern Europe, South America, and Post-Communist Europe* (Baltimore: Johns Hopkins University Press, 1996).

Lorenz, F. M. (1993) 'Law and Anarchy in Somalia', *Parameters: US Army War College Quarterly*, 23(4): 27.

Lugard, F. D. *The Dual Mandate in British Tropical Africa*, 3rd edn. (Edinburgh and London: W. Blackwood & Sons, 1926).

Lush, David. *Last Steps to Uhuru: An Eye-Witness Account of Namibia's Transition to Independence* (Windhoek: New Namibia, 1993).

Lyon, Peter. (1993) 'The Rise and Fall and Possible Revival of International Trusteeship', *Journal of Commonwealth and Comparative Politics*, 31(1): 96.

Lyons, Terrence. 'The Role of Postsettlement Elections', in Stephen John Stedman, Donald Rothchild, and Elizabeth M. Cousens (eds.), *Ending*

Civil Wars: The Implementation of Peace Agreements (Boulder, CO: Lynne Rienner, 2002), 215.

Machiavelli, Niccolò. *The Prince and the Discourses* [1531], translated by Christian E. Detmold (New York: Modern Library, 1950).

MacLaughlin, Jim. *Reimagining the Nation-State: The Contested Terrains of Nation-Building* (London: Pluto Press, 2001).

MacMillan, Margaret. *Paris 1919: Six Months That Changed the World* (New York: Random House, 2002).

Macrae, Joanna. *Aiding Recovery? The Crisis of Aid in Chronic Political Emergencies* (New York: Zed, 2001).

Malone, David M. *Decision-Making in the UN Security Council: The Case of Haiti, 1990–1997* (Oxford: Clarendon Press, 1998).

—— and Thakur, Ramesh. (2001) 'UN Peacekeeping: Lessons Learned?', *Global Governance*, 7(1): 11.

Mansfield, Edward D. and Snyder, Jack. 'Democratization and the Danger of War', in Michael E. Brown, Sean M. Lynn Jones, and Steven E. Miller (eds.), *Debating the Democratic Peace* (Cambridge, MA: MIT Press, 1996), 301.

Marshall, George C. (1947) 'Speech delivered by General George Marshall at Harvard University on 5 June 1947', *Department of State Bulletin*, XVI(415): 1159.

Martin, Ian. *Self-Determination in East Timor: The United Nations, the Ballot, and International Intervention* (Boulder, CO: Lynne Rienner, 2001).

Matveeva, Anna and Paes, Wolf-Christian. 'Trapped in Its Own Maze', *World Today*, July 2002, 19.

Mayall, James (ed.). *The New Interventionism 1991–1994: United Nations Experience in Cambodia, Former Yugoslavia and Somalia* (Cambridge: Cambridge University Press, 1996).

Mazurana, Dyan E. and McKay, Susan R. *Women and Peacebuilding* (Montreal: International Centre for Human Rights and Democratic Development, 1999).

McCormack, Timothy, L. H., and Simpson, Gerry J. (eds.). *The Law of War Crimes: National and International Approaches* (The Hague: Kluwer, 1997).

Miller, David Hunter (ed.). *The Drafting of the Covenant* (New York: G. P. Putnam's Sons, 1928).

Morrow, Ian F. D. *The Peace Settlement in the German-Polish Borderlands: A Study of Conditions Today in the Pre-War Prussian Provinces of East and West Prussia* (London: Oxford University Press, 1936).

Murphy, Sean D. (2002) 'Contemporary Practice of the United States Relating to International Law', *American Journal of International Law*, 96: 237.

Murray, James N., Jr. *The United Nations Trusteeship System* (Urbana, IL: University of Illinois Press, 1957).

Nino, Carlos Santiago. *Radical Evil on Trial* (New Haven, CT: Yale University Press, 1996).

Northedge, F. S. *The League of Nations: Its Life and Times, 1920–1946* (Leicester: Leicester University Press, 1986).

Novosseloff, Alexandra. *Le Conseil de sécurité des Nations Unies et la maîtrise de la force armée: Dialectique du politique et du militaire en matière de paix et de sécurité internationale* (Brussels: Bruylant, 2003).

Nye, Joseph S. *The Paradox of American Power: Why the World's Only Superpower Can't Go It Alone* (Oxford: Oxford University Press, 2002).

O'Neill, William G. *Kosovo: An Unfinished Peace* (Boulder, CO: Lynne Rienner, 2002).

Orentlicher, Diane F. (1991) 'Settling Accounts: The Duty to Prosecute Human Rights Violations of a Prior Regime', *Yale Law Journal*, 100: 2537.

Osiel, Mark. (2000) 'Why Prosecute? Critics of Punishment for Mass Atrocity', *Human Rights Quarterly*, 22: 118.

Patnam, Robert G. (1997) 'Disarming Somalia: The Contrasting Fortunes of US and Australian Peacekeepers During UN Intervention, 1992–93', *African Affairs*, 96: 509.

Patrick, Stewart. 'The Donor Community and the Challenge of Postconflict Recovery', in Shepard Forman and Stewart Patrick (eds.), *Good Intentions: Pledges of Aid for Postconflict Recovery* (Boulder, CO: Lynne Rienner, 2000), 35.

Pauwels, Natalie (ed.). *War Force to Work Force: Global Perspectives on Demobilization and Reintegration, BICC Disarmament and Conversion Studies No 2* (Baden-Baden: Nomos, 2000).

Pelt, Adrian. *Libyan Independence and the United Nations: A Case of Planned Decolonization* (New Haven, CT: Yale University Press for the Carnegie Endowment for International Peace, 1970).

Peou, Sorpong. *Conflict Neutralization in the Cambodian War: From Battlefield to Ballot-Box* (Oxford: Oxford University Press, 1997).

——. *Intervention and Change in Cambodia: Towards Democracy?* (New York: St Martin's Press, 2000).

——. 'Implementing Cambodia's Peace Agreement', in Stephen John Stedman, Donald Rothchild, and Elizabeth M. Cousens (eds.), *Ending Civil Wars: The Implementation of Peace Agreements* (Boulder, CO: Lynne Rienner, 2002), 499.

Peterson, Edward N. *The American Occupation of Germany: Retreat to Victory* (Detroit: Wayne State University Press, 1977).

Pictet, Jean (ed.). *Convention Relative to the Protection of Civilian Persons in Time of War (Fourth Geneva Convention): Commentary* (Geneva: International Committee of the Red Cross, 1958), available at www.icrc.org/ihl.

Playfair, Emma (ed.). *International Law and the Administration of Occupied Territories* (Oxford: Clarendon Press, 1992).

Prunier, Gérard. 'The Experience of European Armies in Operation Restore Hope', in Walter Clarke and Jeffrey Herbst (eds.), *Learning from*

Somalia: The Lessons of Armed Humanitarian Intervention (Boulder, CO: Westview, 1997), 135.

Przeworski, Adam (ed.). *Sustainable Democracy* (Cambridge: Cambridge University Press, 1995).

Pugh, Michael and Cooper, Neil. *War Economies in a Regional Context: The Challenge of Transformation* (Boulder, CO: Lynne Rienner, 2004).

Raghavan, Chakravarthi. *Recolonization: GATT, the Uruguay Round, and the Third World* (London: Zed, 1990).

Rashid, Ahmed. *Taliban: Militant Islam, Oil, and Fundamentalism in Central Asia* (New Haven, CT: Yale University Press, 2000).

Ratner, Steven R. *The New UN Peacekeeping: Building Peace in Lands of Conflict After the Cold War* (New York: St Martin's Press, 1996).

—— (1999) 'New Democracies, Old Atrocities: An Inquiry in International Law', *Georgetown Law Journal*, 87: 707.

Rawski, Frederick. (2002) 'To Waive or Not to Waive: Immunity and Accountability in UN Peacekeeping Operations', *Connecticut Journal of International Law*, 18: 103.

—— (2002) 'Truth-Seeking and Local Histories in East Timor', *Asia-Pacific Journal on Human Rights and the Law*, 1: 77.

Reilly, Benjamin. *Democracy in Divided Societies: Electoral Engineering for Conflict Management* (Cambridge: Cambridge University Press, 2001).

—— (2002) 'Post-Conflict Elections: Constraints and Dangers', *International Peacekeeping*, 9(2): 118.

Reychler, Luc and Paffenholz, Thania (eds.). *Peacebuilding: A Field Guide* (Boulder, CO: Lynne Rienner, 2001).

Reynolds, Andrew. *Electoral Systems and Democratization in Southern Africa* (Oxford: Oxford University Press, 1999).

Reynolds, David. (1997) 'The European Response: Primacy of Politics', *Foreign Affairs*, 76(3): 171.

Roberts, Adam. (1995) 'The Laws of War: Problems of Implementation', *Duke Journal of Comparative and International Law*, 6: 11.

Robertson, Andrew. (2001) 'Island of Intolerance?', *Harvard International Review*, 23(1): 11.

Robertson, Geoffrey. *Crimes Against Humanity: The Struggle for Global Justice* (London: Allen Lane, 1999).

Roht-Arriaza, Naomi. (1996) 'Combating Impunity: Some Thoughts on the Way Forward', *Law and Contemporary Problems*, 59: 93.

Roosevelt, Elliott. *As He Saw It* (New York: Duell, Sloan, and Pearce, 1946).

Roper, John (ed.). *Keeping the Peace in the Post-Cold War Era: Strengthening Multilateral Peacekeeping* (New York: Trilateral Commission, 1993).

Rose, Michael. *Fighting for Peace: Lessons from Bosnia* (London: Warner, 1999).

Rosen, Stephen Peter. (2003) 'An Empire, If You Can Keep it', *The National Interest*, 71: 51.

Rostow, Walt W. (1997) 'Lessons of the Plan: Looking Forward to the Next Century', *Foreign Affairs*, 76(3): 205.

Rotberg, Robert I. (ed.). *When States Fail: Causes and Consequences* (Princeton, NJ: Princeton University Press, 2004).

Roth, Brad R. *Governmental Illegitimacy in International Law* (Oxford: Clarendon Press, 1999).

Rubin, Barnett R. *The Fragmentation of Afghanistan* (New Haven, CT: Yale University Press, 1995).

—— (1998) 'Lineages of the State in Afghanistan', *Asian Survey*, 28(11): 1191.

——. *Blood on the Doorstep: The Politics of Preventive Action* (New York: Century Foundation Press, 2002).

Russell, Frank M. *The International Government of the Saar* (Berkeley: University of California Press, 1926).

Russell-Wood, A. J. R. (ed.). *Government and Governance of European Empires: 1450–1800* (Aldershot: Ashgate, 2000).

Saikal, Amin. 'Afghanistan: Weak State, Strong Society', in Simon Chesterman, Michael Ignatieff, and Ramesh Thakur (eds.), *Making States Work: State Failure and the Crisis of Governance* (Tokyo: United Nations University Press, forthcoming).

Saltford, John. *The United Nations and the Indonesian Takeover of West Papua, 1962–1969: The Anatomy of Betrayal* (London: RoutledgeCurzon, 2002).

Sarooshi, Danesh. *The United Nations and the Development of Collective Security: The Delegation by the UN Security Council of its Chapter VII Powers* (Oxford: Clarendon Press, 1999).

Schaller, Michael. *The American Occupation of Japan* (Oxford: Oxford University Press, 1985).

Schama, Simon. 'Curzon in India', *New Yorker*, 9 June 2003, 98.

Scharf, Michael P. (1996) 'Swapping Amnesties for Peace: Was There a Duty to Prosecute International Crimes in Haiti?', *Texas International Law Journal*, 31: 1.

Schear, James A. 'Riding the Tiger: The UN and Cambodia', in William J. Durch (ed.), *UN Peacekeeping, American Policy, and the Uncivil Wars of the 1990s* (New York: St Martin's Press, 1996), 135.

Schofield, Richard. *Kuwait and Iraq: Historical Claims and Territorial Disputes* (London: Royal Institute of International Affairs, 1991).

Schoups, Johan. 'Peacekeeping and Transitional Administration in Eastern Slavonia', in Luc Reychler and Thania Paffenholz (eds.), *Peacebuilding: A Field Guide* (Boulder, CO: Lynne Rienner, 2001), 389.

Scott, George. *The Rise and Fall of the League of Nations* (London: Hutchinson, 1973).

Seyersted, Finn. *United Nations Forces in the Law of Peace and War* (Leyden: A. W. Sijthoff, 1966).

Shain, Yossi and Linz, Juan J. *Between States: Interim Governments and Democratic Transitions* (Cambridge: Cambridge University Press, 1995).

Sisk, Timothy D. *Power Sharing and International Mediation in Ethnic Conflicts* (Washington, DC: United States Institute of Peace/Carnegie Commission on Preventing Deadly Conflict, 1996).

Smith, Michael G. *Peacekeeping in East Timor* (Boulder, CO: Lynne Rienner, 2003).

Smuts, Jan. 'The League of Nations: A Practical Suggestion', in David Hunter Miller (ed.), *The Drafting of the Covenant* vol. 2 (New York: G. P. Putnam's Sons, 1928), 23.

de Soto, Alvaro and del Castillo, Graciana. 'Obstacles to Peacebuilding in El Salvador', *Foreign Policy* 94, Spring 1994, 69.

de Soto, Hernando. *The Mystery of Capital: Why Capitalism Triumphs in the West and Fails Everywhere Else* (New York: Basic Books, 2000).

Sriram, Chandra Lekha. (2001) 'Externalizing Justice Through Universal Jurisdiction: Problems and Prospects', *Finnish Yearbook of International Law*, 12: 53.

Stedman, Stephen John. (1997) 'Spoiler Problems in Peace Processes', *International Security*, 22(2): 5.

Stedman, Stephen John, Rothchild, Donald, and Cousens, Elizabeth M. (eds.). *Ending Civil Wars: The Implementation of Peace Agreements* (Boulder, CO: Lynne Rienner, 2002).

Stepan, Alfred C. (1999) 'Federalism and Democracy: Beyond the US Model', *Journal of Democracy*, 10(4): 19.

——. *Arguing Comparative Politics* (Oxford: Oxford University Press, 2001).

Strohmeyer, Hansjoerg. (2000) 'Building a New Judiciary for East Timor: Challenges of a Fledgling Nation', *Criminal Law Forum*, 11: 259.

——. (2001) 'Collapse and Reconstruction of a Judicial System: The United Nations Missions in Kosovo and East Timor', *American Journal of International Law*, 95: 46.

Tan, Patricia Shu Ming. 'Idea Factories: American Policies for German Higher Education and Reorientation, 1944–1949' (D.Phil thesis, Modern History, University of Oxford, 2000).

Taylor, Telford. *The Anatomy of the Nuremberg Trials: A Personal Memoir* (New York: Knopf, 1992).

Temperley, Harold William Vazeille (ed.). *A History of the Peace Conference of Paris*, 6 vols. (London: Oxford University Press, 1920).

Tessler, Mark. *A History of the Israeli-Palestinian Conflict* (Bloomington, IN: Indiana University Press, 1994).

Tharoor, Shashi. (1995) 'The Changing Face of Peace-Keeping and Peace-Enforcement', *Fordham International Law Journal*, 19: 408.

Triantaphyllou, Dimitrios (ed.). *What Status for Kosovo?* (Paris: Institute for Security Studies, Western European Union, 2001).

Uphoff Kato, Elisabeth. 'Quick Impacts, Slow Rehabilitation in Cambodia', in Michael W. Doyle, Ian Johnstone, and Robert C. Orr (eds.), *Keeping the Peace: Multidimensional Peacekeeping in Cambodia and El Salvador* (Cambridge: Cambridge University Press, 1997), 186.

Urquhart, Brian. *A Life in Peace and War* (New York: W. W. Norton, 1987).

——. *Ralph Bunche: An American Life* (New York: W. W. Norton, 1993).

van der Veur, Paul W. (1964) 'The United Nations in West New Guinea: A Critique', *International Organization*, 18: 53.

Walters, F. P. *A History of the League of Nations* (New York: Oxford University Press, 1952).

Wambaugh, Sarah. *The Saar Plebiscite* (Westport, CT: Greenwood Press, 1971).

Ward, Robert E. and Toshikuzu, Sakamoto. *Democratizing Japan: The Allied Occupation* (Honolulu: University of Hawaii Press, 1987).

Weber, Max. *The Theory of Social and Economic Organization* [1922], translated by A. M. Henderson and Talcott Parsons (Oxford: Oxford University Press, 1947).

Wellens, Karel. *Remedies Against International Organisations* (Cambridge: Cambridge University Press, 2002).

Wexler, Imanuel. *The Marshall Plan Revisited* (Westport, CT: Greenwood Press, 1983).

White, N. D. *The United Nations and the Maintenance of International Peace and Security* (Manchester: Manchester University Press, 1990).

Whomersley, C. A. (1993) 'The International Legal Status of Gdansk, Klaipeda and the Former East Prussia', *International and Comparative Law Quarterly*, 42: 919.

Wilde, Ralph. (2001) 'From Danzig to East Timor and Beyond: The Role of International Territorial Administration', *American Journal of International Law*, 95: 583.

Wiseman, Henry (ed.). *Peacekeeping: Appraisals and Proposals* (New York: Pergamon Press, 1983).

——. 'United Nations Peacekeeping: An Historical Overview', in Henry Wiseman (ed.), *Peacekeeping: Appraisals and Proposals* (New York: Pergamon Press, 1983), 19.

Woodward, Susan L. *Balkan Tragedy: Chaos and Dissolution After the Cold War* (Washington, DC: Brookings Institution, 1995).

——. 'Economic Priorities for Successful Peace Implementation', in Stephen John Stedman, Donald Rothchild, and Elizabeth M. Cousens (eds.). *Ending Civil Wars: The Implementation of Peace Agreements* (Boulder, CO: Lynne Rienner, 2002), 183.

Woolsey, L. H. (1933) 'The Leticia Dispute Between Colombia and Peru', *American Journal of International Law*, 27: 317.

——. (1935) 'The Leticia Dispute Between Colombia and Peru', *American Journal of International Law*, 29: 94.

Wright, Quincy. *Mandates Under the League of Nations* (Chicago: University of Chicago Press, 1930).

X [George Kennan]. (1947) 'The Sources of Soviet Conduct', *Foreign Affairs*, 25(4): 566.

Yanaihara, Tadao. *Pacific Islands Under Japanese Mandate* (London: Oxford University Press, 1940).

Ydit, Méir. *Internationalised Territories: From the 'Free City of Cracow' to the 'Free City of Berlin'* (Leyden: A. W. Sythoff, 1961).

Zagorin, Adam. 'Spreading the Wealth', *Hoover Digest*, Spring 2003.

Zahar, Marie-Joëlle. 'Protégés, Clients, Cannon Fodder: Civil-Militia Relations in Internal Conflicts', in Simon Chesterman (ed.), *Civilians in War* (Boulder, CO: Lynne Rienner, 2001), 43.

Ziemke, Earl F. *The US Army in the Occupation of Germany, 1944–1946* (Washington, DC: Center of Military History, 1975).

Zink, Harold. *The United States in Germany, 1944–1955*, 2nd edn. (Westport, CT: Greenwood Press, 1974).

Zinni, Anthony. (1995) 'It's Not Nice and Neat', *Proceedings, US Naval Institute*, 121(8): 26.

Index